A Short History of Asia

Third Edition

Colin Mason

First edition published 2000
Second edition published 2005
Third edition published 2014 by
PALGRAVE MACMILLAN

Palgrave Macmillan in the UK is an imprint of Macmillan Publishers Limited, registered in England, company number 785998, of Houndmills, Basingstoke, Hampshire RG21 6XS.

Palgrave Macmillan in the US is a division of St Martin's Press LLC, 175 Fifth Avenue, New York, NY 10010.

Palgrave Macmillan is the global academic imprint of the above companies and has companies and representatives throughout the world.

Palgrave® and Macmillan® are registered trademarks in the United States, the United Kingdom, Europe and other countries.

ISBN 978–1–137–34059–7   hardback
ISBN 978–1–137–34060–3   paperback

This book is printed on paper suitable for recycling and made from fully managed and sustained forest sources. Logging, pulping and manufacturing processes are expected to conform to the environmental regulations of the country of origin.

A catalogue record for this book is available from the British Library.

A catalog record for this book is available from the Library of Congress.

Typeset by MPS Limited, Chennai, India.

Printed in China

Contents

Part III   The Modern Nations

List of Maps

1 *Introduction*

Six out of every ten people who exist today are Asian. Most are Chinese or Indian – these two Asian giants make up two and a half billion of the world population, contrasting with the third runner, the United States, at 312 million, and around 700 million in the whole of Europe. China is rapidly becoming the wealthiest nation on earth, she has the largest and fastest growth of new infrastructure in history, her middle class is growing in size and affluence so fast that Chinese tourists spent more on foreign travel in 2012 than any other nation, while Asian central banks held more than half of world reserves of foreign exchange and gold in that year.

This represents a huge global change from the economic and political dominance of the West, yet in spite of this, and its portents for the future, many people, especially Westerners, seem largely uninformed about Asia's history, especially that before the colonial era, and sometimes have vague perceptions even at the most fundamental level, views still coloured by the opinions of the years of 'empire', with assumptions of white supremacy, and vague, shocking concepts like the well at Cawnpore and 'the black hole of Calcutta'. To them, Asian people sometimes say and do things that seem not to make sense. Just what are the influences on them of religion, so often categorized as violent and fundamentalist? Many Asians seem 'Westernized', but are they really? Are the Chinese, Islamists, refugees intent on taking over the world? Why don't Asians embrace 'democracy'? All these, like anything else not properly understood, prompt disquiet and, unhappily, often ill-judged action.

Most inappropriate of all is to visualize Asia as a homogeneous entity, when it is in fact a region of many different cultures and peoples speaking hundreds of languages and with widely differing traditions and ideas. However, that said, this diversity is increasingly being overlaid by a commonality of actions and objectives so significant it cannot be ignored. The sheer size of these influences is already having huge effects on the region, and they will be even more momentous in the future. Such things as major population movements from the countryside into fast-growing cities, industrialization, the impact of climate change, pollution and its

1

attendant damage to the environment and public health, increasing competition for arable land, population growth and a drift to authoritarian politics shaped around influential families or military 'elites, are now common to much of the region. They will transform Asia, and beyond it the world, for good or ill.

A mindset still lingers that sees Asia as a region of 'under-development', in which huge and growing populations work hard on the land to eke out a tenuous existence, largely uneducated and without access to the basic services the 'developed' nations take for granted. Poor, living in primitive conditions, and ignorant, they are frequently considered 'basket cases', in need of constant aid from an affluent West, and offering it little competition. While in some places much of this is still valid, it is rapidly becoming less so. Even in the poorest countries key indicators like child mortality are improving, many people have access to a mobile phone, more new and modern cities are being built – faster and at times larger than the world has seen before – and in these live not only a fast-growing middle class of hundreds of millions with much the same aspirations as their Western counterparts, but also a steady stream of hard-working migrants from the land who hope to become part of that middle class. And the numbers of these moderately affluent are indeed growing remarkably – on some estimates Asia will by 2030 be home to the majority of the world's middle class, made up of more than two billion people who will be the world's main producers and consumers of goods and services.

China is building new modern cities and upgrading old ones at an extraordinary rate – it has been said they are building Rome every week. The results are unlike anything previously achieved – the new cities look like something from a science fiction movie of the future, as the picture of Qingdao, a Chinese 'new city', on the cover of this book indicates. Consider Chengdu, the capital of the Chinese province of Sichuan, which with 14 million people is currently building 30 skyscrapers higher than 60 storeys and already has a futuristic glass pagoda-like structure that is the world's largest building. Almost a quarter of the world's computers are made in Chengdu – your iPad probably came from there – and it has a world-leading aerospace industry that makes parts for Boeing and Airbus, and produces China's formidable Black Eagle stealth fighter. Not far away Changsha, in an impressive *tour de force,* was building the world's tallest building – the 2749-foot Sky City – in just seven months in 2013. The second largest, the Burj Khalifa in Dubai, took six years to build.

Late in 2012 China opened the world's largest and fastest high-speed train service, running for 1500 miles between the major metropolises in the north and south, Beijing and Guangzhou. At an average speed of 186 mph, the trains cover the distance in eight hours, compared with 21 hours for conventional trains. More such fast train lines are planned, criss-crossing the country from north to south and east to west. A network of motorways has expanded from 2000 miles to 55 000 in less than 20 years, to accommodate middle-class drivers in a country that now has the fastest growth of car ownership in the world.

To do these things China has year after year used more than half of global cement production and more than a third of the world's steel. Over the last two decades its energy use doubled, and it accounted for 40 per cent of global consumption of copper and aluminium, becoming a major producer of almost every conceivable type of goods for the world. Millions of people flocking to the cities from the country provided an almost inexhaustible source of cheap labour, land for factories was cheap, capital and expertise flowed in – all these things combining to create industries that could make things dramatically cheaper, undercutting competitors in the West. Taiwan, South Korea and Singapore have made similar huge changes in their lifestyle and economies. The reconstruction of Japan's industry with modern methods and tools after the Second World War made her a major industrial power in a matter of years. India is industrializing rapidly, and nations like Bangladesh, Vietnam and Malaysia are moving along the same path.

However, dream cities and massive industries have their downside. More than 80 per cent of Asia's energy comes from burning polluting fossil fuels, so the region in 2013 emitted around 40 per cent of the world's greenhouse gases – that figure was 30 per cent in 2000. China, which is now the world's largest emitter, accounts for around half of the world's coal use. Thick, persistent clouds of smog and grey skies are now the norm in Asia's largest cities. In the first month of 2013 motor traffic had to be restricted and factories closed down in Beijing, which has more than 20 million people, because of extreme pollution even by that city's standards. Hospitals reported a doubling of heart attacks and were inundated with people suffering from respiratory illnesses, fine airborne particulates – PM2.5 – which can cause those conditions as well as lung cancer, rose to a catastrophic record figure of 886 micrograms per cubic metre. The World Health Organisation regards anything over 25 micrograms as undesirable. These fine particulates – in effect soot – are said to have contributed to almost 10 000 premature deaths in 2012 in Beijing, Shanghai, Guangzhou and Xi'an. A Beijing entrepreneur began selling canned fresh air from Tibet, and manufacturers could not keep up with the demand for air-freshening machines and masks.

According to the World Health Organisation, for the first time in 2012 air pollution ranked among the world's worst ten killer diseases, causing almost two million deaths in east and south Asia. In Kabul air and water pollution is killing more people than the ongoing Afghanistan war. Acute air pollution incidents occurred in 2012 in Bangladesh, Nepal and Pakistan.

Can Asia continue to grow as rapidly into the future as many economists are predicting, granted the alarming extent of these events? George Monbiot, writing in the *Guardian Weekly* late in 2012, asserts: 'The thousand-year legacy of current carbon emissions is long enough to smash anything resembling human civilisation into splinters. Complex societies have sometimes survived the rise and fall of empires, plagues, wars and famines. They won't survive six degrees of climate change, sustained for a millennium. In return for 150 years of explosive consumption, much of which does nothing to advance human welfare, we are atomizing the natural world and the human systems that depend on it.'

The six degrees mentioned refer to an increase in the world's average temperature of 6 °C, a catastrophe climatologists believe is possible this century *if greenhouse emissions continue to grow unchecked*. This, according to Mark Lynas in 2008 (*Six Degrees: Our Future on a Hotter Planet*), 'would cause a mass extinction of almost all life, and probably reduce humanity to a few struggling groups of survivors clinging to life near the poles', a view few climatologists are disagreeing with – according to the University of Adelaide's Professor Barry Brook, a six-degree rise would see 'most of life exterminated, near-worldwide deserts'. If there is a concerted effort around the world to bring down those emissions – particularly by ending the burning of coal to generate electricity – that temperature rise could be reduced to a still uncomfortable but tolerable level. This, then, is the dilemma the industrializing Asian nations face: they need enough power to continue to lift their people out of poverty and ill health, and they have concluded that for the foreseeable future they can get this only by burning more and more coal. How will they balance this against the dire consequences predicted from climate change?

It is difficult to overstate the importance of this issue for the world – it may well turn out that nothing is more important. And, regrettably, the most reliable forecasters are saying the use of coal will increase, not decrease, into the future, growing from the present seven billion tons a year by more than a billion tons a year over the next five years. Ninety per cent of this disastrous increase will come from China and India. Given the evident risks to individual health and the earth, can this be justified, and is the need real and urgent? In one of its regular special reports (13 October 2012) *The Economist* looks at economic and social disproportion in Asia: ' In little more than a generation Mao's egalitarian dystopia has become a country with an income distribution more skewed than America's. Asia's other two giants, India and Indonesia, have also seen disparities rise sharply, although less dramatically than China.'

By way of illustration, the report compared conditions on both side of the border between Beijing municipality and its neighbouring state, Hebei.

In almost every way the disparity is large. People in Hebei earn less, no one has a car, the roads are worse, schools are few and far between, and in the words of one Hebei villager, 'We live in a different country.' This inequality obtains almost generally in rural Asia, and is the reason why so many villagers flock to the cities to find work. So there is indeed an evident need to extend the prosperity of the cities to the countryside, and this can only be done if more electric power is generated. This has particular force in India, where even in the cities power supplies are limited and unreliable and children can be seen standing under street lamps to do their homework. Almost half the population have no power connection at all. Worse still, most people live in acute poverty and ill health. In Kolkata more than half of the population literally live on the streets. Almost half of the children are stunted and malnourished, and millions die before they reach the age of 5.

So if coal use increases indefinitely in the world's two largest countries, what might be the consequences? It is well over a hundred years since Queen Victoria's consort, Prince Albert, chaired the meeting of the Royal Institution in London at which the heat-blocking qualities of carbon dioxide and methane were first demonstrated by Irish scientist John Tyndall. Since then thousands of scientists have confirmed that increasing the amount of these 'greenhouse gases' contributes to global warming, a steady rise in the planet's overall temperature. It has already increased almost 1 °C in the last 50 years, much more than this on some of the continents, while the proportion of greenhouse gases has risen to over 400 parts per million, the highest level for millions of years. Any temperature rise beyond 2 °C is regarded as dangerous. By way of comparison, the world temperature difference between now and the height of the last ice age is only around 5 °C.

Global warming is predicted to cause more erratic and violent weather – flood rains alternating with long droughts, which substantially reduce the production of food crops – and storms of unprecedented severity, the first of which we have already experienced in the last decade. Throughout all of recorded human history until quite recently, the Arctic has had trillions of tons of massive and impenetrable ice. That is no longer the case. Temperatures there have risen by three degrees, and by the summer of 2012 the ice had dwindled to one and a third million square miles, 49 per cent below the average for 1979–2000, with predictions that the North Pole may be completely ice-free by 2050. This has already caused a small but significant rise in global sea-levels, with the likelihood of an increase of as much as three feet this century.

In Asia more than a billion people live on deltas of the great rivers and other densely populated and fertile lowlands in many places barely a metre above mean high-tide levels. Not only would predicted sea-level rises drive them from their homes, it would destroy land on which as much as a third of the world's food is grown. This would happen well before complete inundation, as salt water seeping in with flood tides poisoned the land. Most of the world's great deltas are in Asia, and often enough they are also the location of major cities, like Bangkok in Thailand, which is already experiencing regular abnormal flooding. Most of China's industry, and many of its major cities, are located in the delta regions and on the coastal plain. While sea-level rise is a slow-moving threat, its ultimate consequences are dire. Because heat acquired by the oceans will be retained for thousands of years, overall warming and the slow but steady melting of the icecaps must continue for as long. Melting of all the Greenland ice would raise sea levels by twenty feet, loss of the ice on the fragile West Antarctic sheet at least another ten feet. This is compounded by a steady subsidence of delta land – Shanghai, Guangzhou, Bangkok and Djakarta have all sunk more than two feet since the mid-1960s, because of distortion of the natural systems in the deltas on which they are built, mainly due to damming for hydro-electricity and excessive water use for irrigation from their rivers.

Asia's great rivers like the Yangzi, the Ganges, the Mekong and the Irrawaddy, on which millions of people depend to grow food, all have their source in the hundreds of Himalayan glaciers. For thousands of years a natural balance between glacial melting and snowfall has allowed these rivers generally to flow steadily. Now that balance has been disturbed as the glaciers recede, and the future is likely to see a destructive alternation between heavy flooding and drought. There is already evidence that climate change is affecting the life-giving annual Asian monsoon. Food security for millions more depends on its regularity.

And this is a critical effect because food shortages typically affect the very poor first, quickly and often fatally. The movement of Asia away from vestigial 'colonial' economies has reduced but not eliminated the economic gulf between the educated and modestly affluent and the millions of the poor, disease-afflicted and uneducated. If one considers the region as a whole, as many as three-quarters of its people are disadvantaged in at least one of these ways. Japan and Singapore are the only Asian countries with standards of living and affluence at high levels. China, South Korea, Taiwan and Thailand have made considerable progress, but in the nations of South Asia – India, Pakistan, Bangladesh, Sri Lanka, Afghanistan, and in much of south-east Asia, poverty and ignorance are, if anything, increasing.

There are, of course, reasons for the continuance of poverty in the world. A billion dollars a day given as subsidies to agriculture in the developed world is effectively money taken from farmers in the undeveloped world.

Unsubsidized agriculture cannot compete in the export market nor, often even more disastrously, in its own. And Asian governments since independence have persistently favoured urban elites. Typically, the average income in an Asian capital is as much as three times that in the surrounding countryside. Smallholdings are compounded into large agribusinesses as peasants are driven off their land by compulsion or by debt. Natural resources like forests are exploited without regard for the people living in them. The Philippines, Java and Thailand lost more than half their forests in the first two decades after the end of the Second World War and with a few exceptions, that depredation continues today. In Borneo and Sumatra, two of the most biodiverse regions of the world, huge areas of forest are destroyed every year so 50 million tons of palm oil can be produced.

In the past hereditary monarchs ruled most of Asia, backed by an elite of nobles. Another emerging commonality in the region is political leadership persisting generation after generation in the same families, each with their supporting elite. Three generations of the Kim family have ruled in North Korea, the Lee family maintains control of Singapore, the influence of the Gandhi family persists in India, daughters of previous leaders rule in Thailand and South Korea. The father of Japan's prime minister Shinzo Abe was foreign minister, his grandfather prime minister. The increasingly autocratic president of Sri Lanka, Mahinda Rajapaksa, has distributed senior ministerial positions to his brothers. And in many places a new pattern of government, controlled democracy, is emerging. While retaining the forms of parliamentary democracy – general elections, houses of parliament – a central oligarchy restricts their powers, as well as the political and human rights of the population, so government is not only imposed by the elite, but its actions and right to rule are asserted as beyond question. Behind controlled democracy is the cult of 'Asian values', which has it that limiting individual rights results in a more efficient society.

Chris Patten, the last governor of British Hong Kong, doesn't like many manifestations of what he has called 'Asian values ballyhoo' (*East and West*, 1999) but does accurately summarize its proponents' view that some people in the West 'are trying to foist Western standards and Western notions of governance on societies where they would be inappropriate or damaging. Asians benefit from a different culture with deep roots in Confucianism. They put more emphasis on order, stability, hierarchy, family and self-discipline than Westerners do. The individual has to recognise that there are broader interests to which he or she must be subordinate.' The architect of 'Asian values' and, indeed, controlled democracy, is Singapore elder statesman Lee Kuan Yew. That is the way Singapore is governed, and its undoubted prosperity and order, as well as Mr Lee himself, are greatly admired in China. There are those in high positions in China who see Singapore as a possible model for China's future. If this is so, the enshrining of 'Asian values' in east and south-east Asia could become very important, and the concept a major player in world politics.

Possibly because of the persisting blatant elitism of the wealthy, which might be regarded as an extreme form of controlled democracy, and in spite of the abject poverty of millions, Asia has built and is building an extraordinary array of multi-storey urban skyscrapers, presenting a bizarre contrast to the impoverished villages and urban slums. Expensive to build and requiring huge amounts of energy to maintain, this proliferation of more than 20 000 commercial towers often seems more the result of a desire to compete in 'face' terms than any intrinsic value to the communities in which they are built. These manifestations of elitism inevitably attract dissent, sometimes violent, which is usually put down forcibly. Long-drawn-out protest demonstrations in Thailand, the ugly succession of suicide bombings and assassinations in Pakistan and Afghanistan and the suppressed fury of the people of Burma are typical. The availability of cheap television and radios means the middle class outside the elite and the underprivileged are not unaware of the way they are being exploited by their leaders – this leads to a general mistrust of the machinery of government.

These consequences must exacerbate the tensions already evident as Asian nations compete for land and resources. Five nations – China, Japan, the Philippines, Vietnam and Malaysia – are disputing the ownership of some rocky islets in the South China Sea, and this has prompted noisy and at times violent demonstrations in all these countries. Some of these islands are so small they are not inhabited, nor do they produce any kind of resource. However, because they are seen as strategic, and possibly have reserves of oil and gas around them, they have provoked disputes which seem out of proportion to the size of the assets. There has been a good deal of military posturing, including naval ship movements, and mass demonstrations in both China and Japan over ownership of what the Japanese call the Senkaku and the Chinese the Diaoyu islands. China and Vietnam dispute possession of the Paracel and Spratly islands, on which only a few hundred people live. Both nations have invited international bids to explore the area for oil and gas, but because of the nature of the dispute the oil majors seem less than enthusiastic. A naval engagement in the Spratlys in 1988 killed 70 Vietnamese. The Philippines disputes ownership of the Scarborough Shoal with China.

Good arable land in Asia is overstressed already, with little potential to absorb future climate refugees. Considering this, the move by several of the world's wealthiest nations to acquire food-producing land in poorer countries to feed their own people is significant. Since in most of these places productive soil is already over-taxed, will these foreign-owned enclaves in the end be watched by hungry thousands outside the wire?

China's move towards world supremacy – and that without doubt is her intention – is, however, unlikely to be military, although military strength will be there to back it. It will be economic and social, and its front-line forces will be the influential network of Chinese businessmen and women in most Asian countries, and the emerging Chinese multinational corporations. This is not to forecast a vast Chinese territorial empire in Asia. The world's other powers would be unlikely to permit such a thing, in the first place. In the second place, China has had opportunities for that before, as far back as the 15th century, and rejected them. Her traditional attitude has been to attempt a loose authority among peripheral states, not unlike the US position in the Americas.

Chinese influence is increasing steadily in mainland south-east Asia, especially among her neighbours like Burma and Laos. In the mountainous northern regions of the south-east Asian mainland states roads have frequently been little more than muddy tracks, and in many cases foot-tracks negotiable only by mule caravans. Because of this in 1992 a United Nations (UN) authority, the Economic and Social Commission for Asia and the Pacific, proposed an Asian super highway, an 87 000-mile network of roads, bridges and ferries that would link most countries of the region with Europe. While 32 nations have endorsed the idea, 30 years later progress has been patchy, to say the least, with many segments of the project delayed by lack of finance or excessive red tape. However the North–South Corridor road, which connects China with Thailand through Laos, is largely complete, with a fourth Friendship Bridge over the Mekong River due to be opened in December 2013, at a cost of $45 million.*

Route AH1, the modern equivalent of the Silk Road, proposes to link Tokyo with Istanbul, passing 13 000 miles through China, both Koreas, central Asia and India. Although some sealed sections do exist, mostly in China, many of the links are still unpaved, deeply rutted and difficult to negotiate. An English car actually made this journey in 2007, but it took 49 days, crossing 18 countries. The Association of East Asian Nations meeting in 2010 sought to get this project back on track over the next five years, promising easier tourist visas and reforms to over-bureaucratic trade and customs regulations in many countries. However, if it is ever to reach fruition a great deal of money, co-operation, and work on the ground will be needed.

---

* Throughout the book all figures given in dollars are US dollars.

Central Asia consists of deserts and a series of ranges, rocky escarpments and bleak uplands from which rise the Himalayas, the highest mountains on earth. Among this wild and lightly populated mountain country the big rivers find their source in the perpetual snow and hundreds of glaciers. As they flow south, east and west these rivers broaden, meander and slow down into great, turbid, discoloured streams. Most of them, like the Ganges and the Yangzi, reach the sea in the midst of delta regions with miles of backwaters, low marshes and mangrove forests. Above the swamps are flat fertile plains which are regularly flooded and enriched with fresh deposits of alluvial silt. These plains have been for thousands of years the regions best suited for growing food. They have become both the centres of successive civilizations and a temptation to less well-endowed marauders from the hills.

As one proceeds north from the Indian plain, progressively higher mountain ranges block the way, giving the few possible roads, like the Khyber Pass, great strategic and political importance. Once across Afghanistan, Nepal and the southern valleys of Tibet, civilization peters out into a region of desolate, high plateaux. These plateaux, the Pamir Mountains and northern Tibet, give place in the east to the shifting sands and parched soils of Xinjiang in China. Thence, across Mongolia through the Gobi, the terrain changes to the fertile loess soils of north-west China and the Manchurian grasslands. This is East Asia, a second major concentration of population and culture. Once again, in China it is the fertile river valleys and deltas that make up the heartland. The valley of the Yangzi downstream from its celebrated gorges, now flooded, is the most fertile and populous.

The high, arid deserts of central Asia, with their cold, thin air and perpetual need for constant struggle simply to exist, have bred a group of toughened races who, for thousands of years, invaded and conquered the plains below. Good horsemen, bred from childhood to the saddle and the sword, they were typical nomads, who moved constantly from one grassy valley to the next, living in felt tents, driving their herds with them. The names of these nomad peoples and their leaders ring through history, the very epitome of battle and conquest – the Huns, the Mongols, Genghiz Khan.

To the south the picture is very different. Tropical Asia consists of two big promontories and thousands of islands. India projects nearly a thousand miles into the ocean that bears her name. On the other side of the Bay of Bengal is another peninsula shared by the mainland south-east Asian states, Burma, Thailand, Malaysia and the three Indo-Chinese nations, Vietnam, Cambodia and Laos.

Finally, in a great arc swinging from west to east and then northwards, lies an almost continuous chain of islands. Some, like Borneo and Sumatra, are among the major islands of the world, but the rest range down to tiny specks of land with only enough soil to support a few palm trees a few feet above the heave of the sea. One of the smaller of these islands, linked to the Malayan mainland by a causeway, contains a dynamic, mostly Chinese, city-state, Singapore. Seventeen thousand more, running across 3000 miles of equatorial sea to the south of Malaysia, make up Indonesia, with almost 250 million people the region's largest state and the world's fourth most populous. To the north, across the atoll-studded Sulu Sea, the archipelago merges with the islands of the Philippines. Less than 200 miles north from the principal Filipino island of Luzon is the southern promontory of Taiwan; once again to the north the Ryukyus lead to Japan.

The traveller has passed from the tropics to the temperate zone, then through the Japanese islands to the northernmost, Hokkaido, into a region of ice, snow, and fiery volcanoes. The craggy and inhospitable Kuriles lead to the last peninsula, Kamchatka, pointing out into the Pacific, south-west from the Arctic Circle.

In the year 1407, 2000 Chinese scholars compiled an encyclopaedia of the thought and writing of their nation's past. When completed it occupied over 11 000 volumes and so was too large to print. Any single volume of reasonable proportions that tries to encompass the history of the Asian nations requires ruthless selection and special care in priority of material. This has led to the omission of many interesting and important facts from this book, and more general statements than the writer would have liked.

The reader needs to know the basis on which selection has been made. The first objective has been to follow broad trends – constants, as it were – especially when these still have effect today. A common quality of Asian societies is this importance of the past, of tradition. Why did the Tamil Tigers pursue their rebellion against the central government in Sri Lanka with such dedication and ferocity? Why was it seen by modern Indonesians as natural that their first president ceremonially contacted the earth with his bare feet, exposed himself to electrical storms, hugged trees? Why has Western-style representative government generally not succeeded in Asia? Why might Indonesian schoolchildren believe their nation has a historic right to all of New Guinea, part of the Philippines, possibly even some of northern Australia? The answers to these questions and many others emerge from a knowledge of Asian history, especially that before the colonial era. Links to the past become all the more important because the new nations of Asia look back beyond the colonial era to their own often legendary and shadowy past for a sense of national identity. And sometimes they identify something that was probably not real, exaggerate something quite minor, in theories that have more to do with present-day politics than the facts of history.

A second priority is to sketch the enormous variety of peoples and cultures in Asia, and give due credit to the achievements and greatness of its societies, which are by no means properly appreciated or understood. It is, for instance, extraordinary that some Western children are still taught that Gutenberg invented printing with movable type in Germany around 1450, when movable type had been developed in China 300 years earlier; and that European seafarers 'discovered' Asia, when Arab commercial shipping traded with China 700 years before Columbus 'crossed the ocean blue'. A sunken 9th-century Arab shipwreck, the *Belitung*, discovered in Indonesian waters in 1998, contained 60 000 pieces of Chinese pottery, the product of a huge manufacturing industry that exported worldwide.

Most people would know that fireworks and the wheelbarrow were invented in China, but it may come as news to them that the 12th-century Song society had large libraries of printed books, used credit banking and cheques, and could inoculate against smallpox, and that there were Indian cities with mass-produced standard housing and efficient urban sewerage systems as early as 2500 BCE. Too often Asian histories by Europeans have been unduly preoccupied with the activities of European colonizers. This book tries, among other things, to redress that balance.

PART I
Before Imperialism

2 *Prehistory and the First Indian Civilizations*

The Asia of remote prehistory was very different from the teeming continent and islands of today. Its population was tiny and dispersed, living mostly on the seacoasts and the plains of the big rivers, each small group of humanity separated from the others by virgin forest, full of wild animals. Families stayed together, developed into clans for mutual protection. Life was precarious, death came early and was often sudden and violent.

This time of prehistory can be traced back at least a million years, when the humanoid species *homo erectus* is presumed to have moved out of east Africa into Europe, China and parts of south-east Asia. In 1891 the skull of a *homo erectus* individual, now thought to date back 1.8 million years, was found in central Java, and stone tools dated to 1.36 million years ago have been found in Hebei Province of China. Stone implements dating as far back as half a million years indicate a proto-human presence in India, while the remains of 'Peking man' found in China are estimated at half a million years ago. The bones of perhaps 50 people, including five almost complete skulls, were found at Dragon Bone Hill, 25 miles from the Chinese capital. Earlier conclusions that this ancient community used fire, made crude stone tools, and may have been capable of speech seem unlikely following the reports in 2004 of a Chinese/American research team at the site. These hominids were primitive creatures, and probably survived, as did other *homo erectus*, on what they could scavenge from the kills of large predators.

The most recent glacial of the quaternary ice age had major effects on the development and distribution of humans. Rigorous conditions caused by the extension of the ice shifted the areas of population. People, still in insignificant numbers, were forced towards the central belt of the planet, or were trapped behind barriers of ice, to adapt as best they could to the centuries of bitter cold.

These glacials lowered the level of the seas by as much as 300 feet, so that much of what was water became dry land. Australia was linked through Indonesia, except for two straits, to the Asian mainland. People could cross

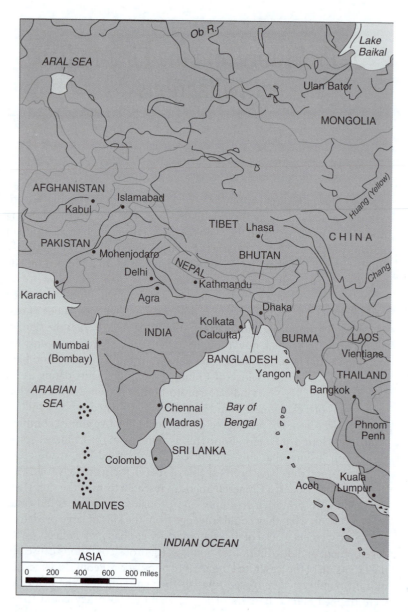

Map 1 Asia

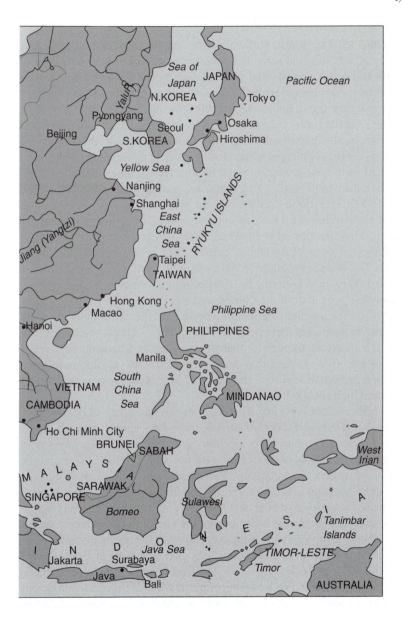

land bridges over much of what is now sea, and there is abundant evidence they did so. The Sunda Shelf, now the shallow seas of Indonesia and Malaysia, was dry land some 18,000 years ago. While much of the world, north and south, was covered with ice, the tropical zone was not, despite lower temperatures and rainfall. Temperatures on the huge Sunda Shelf – a region of almost two million square miles – would have been four to eight degrees Celsius cooler than now. Many of the racial patterns of the region were set by this pattern of rising and falling sea levels. In the interglacial periods the sea submerged what must have been huge areas of fertile plainland. An east Asian mountain range became the islands of Japan.

The nature of the earliest proto-humans is conjectural at best. However, to modern eyes these creatures would seem ape-like. Skulls recovered show them to have had low, slanting brows and small though developing brains. They are classed as hominids mainly because they stood upright and showed signs of significant development of the frontal lobe of the brain. This human evolution in Asia was not very different from that elsewhere in the world. Differing racial types began to emerge. It is believed the Mongolian type, that of the Chinese and other east Asian peoples, had its origins on the northern steppes of Siberia. One theory considers that the distinctive features of these people are due to the effects of the extreme cold on their ancestors, trapped for many generations in Siberia during the last glacial age. It is claimed that under these extreme conditions humans evolved protective features – the flat brow to protect the sinuses, deep-set eyes and high cheekbones.

Whether or not *homo erectus* evolved into later populations of *homo sapiens* is controversial. Modern man appears to have spread through southeast Asia about 40,000 years ago, during an interglacial. Sea levels were high, and the islands of the region were not joined to each other and the mainland as they would later be. This granted, the movement of humans by island-hopping is both interesting and important. These people must have used some kind of boat, so this could well have been the very beginning of human maritime history. From the end of the most recent glaciation about 12,000 years ago human evolution in the region becomes more coherent, with evidence of toolmaking, domestication of livestock and agricultural societies leading on to the village communities of the immediate past and present. Precise dating of pottery shards from many locations in Japan in 2013 indicated that pots were in use there in 15000 BCE, and that they were used to cook fish. These remarkable findings suggest a human movement away from the hunter-gatherer phase to agricultural village life much earlier than had been supposed. There is evidence of the growing of millet in China dated to 7000 BCE, and of village communities that buried their dead, made pottery, and built permanent housing by 5500 BCE. These developments are consistent with improving climates as the last ice age receded.

Early Chinese mainland societies also seem to have been the origin of many of the peoples of south-east Asia, Mongoloid types who appear to have migrated from southern China, displacing earlier Australoid peoples from about 7000 years ago onwards. From that time a relatively advanced agricultural society evolved in the fertile Yangzi valley of China and along much of the southern coast. These were probably the first people in the world to grow rice and to make woven matting and ropes. When migrants from this area moved into mainland south-east Asia they settled first in low-lying swampy areas where the soil proved fertile. Even at that time malaria was probably a great killer, due to the prevalence of its vector, the *Anopheles* mosquito – one reason why populations remained low.

About 4000 BCE small, primitive mud-brick villages developed in what is now India and Pakistan. In some, in the valleys and foothills of Baluchistan, their inhabitants may have domesticated cattle, sheep and goats. Some Indian scholars have speculated that a rather more developed society existed in western Rajasthan along the Sarasvati River, mentioned in ancient Indian texts, but now long since dry, as early as 6000 BCE. Villages like Amri, close to the Indus River in Sind, developed perhaps 3000 years later. Copper implements and decorated pottery, apparently made on a potter's wheel, have been found in this region, and some houses had stone walls or stone foundations.

The past of Egypt and Mesopotamia is fairly generally known, but a more extensive and developed civilization than either of these existed in Asia almost 5000 years ago, with the biggest cities and the most sophisticated society the world had yet seen. This society, still largely enigmatic, was utterly forgotten for more than 3000 years from the time of its demise until its ruins were investigated from 1922 onwards. It is called Harappa, from the name of one of its major cities, although there was also a second and similar city, Mohenjodaro.

More recent exploration has revealed a third major site, Rakhigarhi, in the Indian state of Haryana, which is situated on what is believed to be the dry bed of the Sarasvati River. Its location about 100 miles from Delhi indicates that the Harappa civilization extended further south into present-day India than had been believed. Penetration-radar surveys from 2006 show that Rakhigarhi was the largest Harrapan city, bigger than Harrapa itself, and that it was surrounded with scores of other towns and villages in Haryana. Some of these are said to date back as far as 6000 BCE, which would make them among the first known settled agricultural communities in the world. Excavations in the area recommenced in 2013.

Over almost 1000 miles along the Indus River and its tributaries are the remains of hundreds of other towns and villages with common characteristics. Their grid pattern of streets and lanes would have given them a strikingly modern, planned appearance. Their use of standardized materials and efficient sewerage and drainage systems was paralleled in Europe only in quite recent times. Inscriptions on fragments of pottery found in Harappa in 1999, and carbon dated to 3200 BCE, are considered by some archaeologists to be the world's first writing.

The Harappa site alone covered almost 400 acres and probably housed 30,000 people. The location of this culture on the floodplain of a big river is no accident, since the world's earliest cities were generally so situated. In most regions the soil became exhausted quickly from cropping and people had to move on to new fields. Only on the river plains, where annual floods deposited rich, new layers of silt on the land, were they able to stay long in one place. The city civilizations of Mesopotamia depended in this way on the Tigris and Euphrates rivers, and those of Egypt on the Nile.

The ruins of Mohenjodaro are in Sind, in what is now hot, forbidding desert. Those of Harappa are 350 miles north-east in the Punjab. However, distinctive Harappan artefacts have been found over an area larger than present-day Pakistan, indicating that at its height this society was considerably larger than either Egypt or the Sumerian empire at that time. The Harappa civilization had a flair for standardization unusual in the ancient world. Its kiln-baked salmon-coloured mud bricks were of uniform size everywhere and this has made it possible to identify Harappa remains with relative ease. These were the world's first planned urban centres, with grid-planned, straight streets and lanes orientated north and south, east and west, dividing the cities into 12 blocks. Corners were rounded off to allow carts and other traffic to turn easily.

This society was innovative and versatile, engaging in a wide range of art and manufacture and trading with other parts of the civilized world. These were probably the first people to grow cotton, spin it and weave it into cloth, which became a major export. Harappa traded with Sumer in Mesopotamia, probably as early as 2600 BCE. Its soapstone seals have been found in excavations at the ancient city of Ur. Lapis lazuli, tin, turquoise and silver were imported from Afghanistan and jadeite from Tibet, and made into ornaments. Trading was by sea, from the Arabian Sea port of Lothal.

Most Harappan architecture is strikingly similar. The buildings were plain and in the same style, the layout of streets and lanes geometrical.

Individual houses were built with the rooms facing on to a central court-yard, with few openings to the street frontages. These houses were well adapted to the hot, probably humid, climate of the time. They were provided with efficient covered drainage from the bathrooms to main sewers in the street outside, which carried waste water well away from the city. Every house had a bathing platform and a latrine. Some of the tiled bath-room floors still show signs of polish from the repeated contact of the bare feet of their users. The largest buildings seem to have been public ones – in Mohenjodaro a granary and a large pool.

The cities had internal fortifications – the postulated 'citadels' – but lacked any apparent defences against outside enemies, which suggests a small privileged class in control of the mass of the people rather than any need for protection against an outside invader. There is other evidence to support this: the ruins include long monotonous rows of small barrack-like structures which were probably workers' tenements.

It was once thought that the Harappa civilization emerged fully fledged about 2800 BCE, existed for 1000 years, and was then destroyed just as mysteriously. However, later archaeology indicates a continuous agrarian society from 7000 years ago, which was probably its forerunner and thus, arguably, the authentic beginning of Indian civilization. Excavations at a number of sites indicate a farming society that grew wheat and barley and had domesticated sheep and goats and the typical Indian hump-backed cow. There is evidence of a considerable pottery manufacture, using the wheel, by 3500 BCE.

Although the Harappa cities are presumed to have developed from this earlier society, they had distinctive and unusual features that still pose unanswered questions. Harappa had a written language, found on some 2000 soapstone seals recovered throughout the cities and villages, but this has not been deciphered. The Harappa showed considerable artistry in small objects. Among the ruins small figures in soapstone, alabaster and marble have been found depicting people, often in a sophisticated and lively style. There was a well-developed, distinctive system of weights and measures. Copper and bronze were used for tools and ornaments.

The nature of the religion is unclear, but there are strong indications of a connection with gods of the later, Hindu, period, with evidence particularly of worship of a mother-goddess concerned with the fertility of the earth and the creation of life. This is interesting because it is traditional Indian belief that a light-skinned people, who much later infiltrated into India from the north-west, were the first to evolve an ordered civilization there. The early Indian epics assert that when these people came they found only a simple village culture in north India. This was indeed the commonly held historical view until the Harappa ruins were investigated, but major Harappan contributions to early Indian society are now considered to be very likely.

A mysterious catastrophe severely damaged Harappa civilization about 1750 BCE. It must have been huge in its scope, because Mohenjodaro had been damaged many times before, probably by floods, and had been rebuilt regularly. There is evidence that the final blow was very sudden and very damaging. It might have been a combination of major earthquakes and flooding. Remnants of the society continued in some villages, but at a much reduced level. This was presumably what the pastoral people who are thought to have come into India from the north about 200 years later would have found.

This second influx of people, who, according to the epics, began to enter India from about 1500 BCE, had leaders who called themselves *aryas*, which means noble. The modern name of Persia, Iran, is significantly derived from it, and so is the term 'Aryan', applied to the language group to which these people belonged. This language group is now more commonly called Indo-European because of close links between the north Indian written language, Sanskrit, and some early European languages, including Greek, Celtic and High German. Hence a single ethnic group has been postulated, which spilled over into Europe as well as the north Indian plain.

At one stage, notably in Nazi Germany, it was romanticized into ideas of a super-race with almost divine rights to ascendancy over other humans, and a duty to maintain its genetic purity. However, India's new settlers appear to have been a simple people, much less sophisticated than the Harappa – herdsmen and hunters who worshipped deities that were manifestations of the elemental forces of nature. Their art was unspectacular and their architecture, in particular, suffers in comparison with Harappa. Since they used only wood, none of their buildings survive, but accounts in the Sanskrit classic, the *Rigveda*, describe small hut-like houses, grouped together inside earth and wooden palisades.

The *Rigveda* makes it clear than the newcomers disliked and despised the people they found already in north India. While there was, no doubt, much more intermarriage and cultural exchange with the existing population than the classics admit, the people from the north seem to have been much concerned with their racial purity. They were light-skinned, and placed much store on colour. It was regarded as good to be light-skinned and shameful to be dark – a prejudice still strong in India, and elsewhere, today. When my family lived in a north-east Thai market town people asked if they might simply touch my children, who were fair-haired with blue eyes, to bring good fortune.

By the 8th century BCE the former nomads, almost certainly mingled with the residual population from Harappa after its decline, had spread eastward across north India to the banks of the Ganges River. By 600 BCE they were using iron and planting rice, strengthening their agricultural society and expanding over the Ganges plain. Since the only verbal information we have about this stage is a bewildering assortment of myths, these must be approached with caution. A major point of interest was the gradual accumulation of this vast mass of religious strictures and legends which were committed to memory and carried on by word of mouth, and which are a basis of several major religions, and especially of Hinduism.

The extent to which these reflect the times in which they originated is doubtful. They must have been added to and modified extensively over the period – perhaps 1000 years – before they were written down. Out of the obscurity of this early period one can still make some deductions. The nomadic herdsmen who had come in from the north learned to be farmers and town-dwellers. A need for established law and order led to the selection of kings, who benefited from taxation – this much is evident from the myth describing how Manu, an early king, laid down quite specific percentages of produce and livestock as his own stipend.

The extensive co-operative work involved in developing agriculture led on to ordered villages and eventually to towns and cities, with hints of some communities that governed themselves by consensus consultation. There can be no question of an Indian 'nation' at this time. But there did evolve on the north Indian plain tribal groups and eventually states who fought each other ceaselessly in a struggle for land and power, but who nevertheless shared a common cultural heritage.

3 The Development of Indian Culture: Hinduism and Buddhism

A distinctive quality of this expansion of Indian culture was a class system of such vigour that it still exists today, although it is now infinitely more complex. This culture and religion – for it is both – is generally called Hinduism by Europeans, by Indians *sanatan dharma*.

Ancient India had four major classes. The highest, the priest-teachers, or *brahmins*, soon came to hold authority, even over nobles, by virtue of the roles they assumed as interpreters of religion. The old gods changed, and worship became more complex. Rituals and formality clouded what must once have been fundamentally a simple faith.

The second important class were the *kshatriyas*, the soldier-nobles, whose duty it was to fight for the state. Some historians believe that the many successful invasions of India, often by quite small armies, were effective because it was believed that only *kshatriyas* could or should fight back – in contrast with Korea, for instance, where peasant and even slave guerrilla forces made ferocious attacks on invaders from Manchuria and Japan. A third Indian caste of less importance were the *vaishyas*, the merchants. These three main classes, of lighter skin colour, had important privileges. They were described as 'twice-born' for, during late childhood, they were initiated into the rites of their high position. This was regarded as a mystic second birth.

The fourth main caste, the *shudras*, living on the fringes of society, were servants, forbidden to read, or even hear, the sacred scriptures. Even in the centuries before the Christian era, there existed a fifth caste, corresponding to the present *dalits*, formerly known as 'untouchables'. Most of these were the dark-skinned descendants of slaves and aborigines and were restricted to filthy and menial tasks. Once born into their class, death was the only escape. Generation after generation were compelled to carry out lowly and unpleasant work, and they were forbidden to marry outside their caste.

At the very bottom of the social heap are the *chandals*, the caste who carry out the actual work of cremations – cremation over a wood fire is the usual way of disposing of the bodies of adult Indians. Children's bodies are simply placed in rivers. The *chandals* use long iron rods to stir the ashes and remains, and to smash the skull and other larger bones so they will be totally consumed – this might take seven or eight hours. Although they no longer have to shout or ring bells to announce their presence, to avoid the ritual contamination of any other Indian, they are effectively cut off from the rest of society. Higher-caste persons would be contaminated even if the shadow of a *chandal* should fall on them. There are caste divisions even among the *dalits*, a present-day minority of more than 200 million people. In ascending order on the social scale are leatherworkers, lavatory cleaners and sweepers, and laundrymen.

This set pattern of privilege inevitably resulted in discrimination, oppression and harsh laws. The mass of the people, living in villages similar to those of today, were heavily taxed to support their masters. A complex legal code provided sweeping discriminatory provisions covering virtually every aspect of life for the lower orders. Often taxation reached such ruinous levels as to leave the peasants destitute, and even minor weather fluctuations resulted in major famines. The death penalty was imposed for a multitude of offences.

However, social inequality and art often flourish together, and such was the case in ancient India. This era produced the great Indian classics – the *Mahabharata* and the *Ramayana*. These writings stress the basic lesson that everyone must maintain his or her due place in society, that 'it is better to do one's own duty badly than another's well' – thus guaranteeing the privileged position of the twice-born. The *Mahabharata*, which is a collection of poems rather than a single story, is largely based on the fortunes of two rival ruling families, but its major significance is its statement of the duty of the religious, law-abiding man.

The other great epic is the story of Rama, a legendary prince who, although he is the legal heir, accepts banishment for 12 years. While in exile his wife Sita is kidnapped by Ravana, the devil king of Lanka, sometimes identified as Ceylon, now Sri Lanka. Rama, going to her rescue, enlists the aid of the monkey king, who provides an army of monkeys to tear up rocks, earth and trees to build a bridge between the Indian mainland and the island. Rama crosses the causeway, kills Ravana, and rescues his wife. He is then said to have created a virtually utopian society, of unprecedented peace and prosperity, based on his capital city of Ayudhya.

These epics must not be thought of as antiques without any present or future significance. Rama's Ayudhya, granted attributes far beyond what the historic record seems to justify, is regarded as an ideal to emulate in today's Hindu politics. The epics also play a much greater part in the lives of ordinary people in at least six Asian countries than their equivalents do among Westerners. Few people in most of mainland south-east Asia and in many parts of Indonesia, as well as the Indian continent itself, would fail to hear stories from these epics from early childhood. Ceremonies and carnivals, which often involve whole communities, annually celebrate the victory of Rama over Ravana. Art, especially painting, sculpture and the shadow theatre, uses themes from the epics extensively, as also do much of literature and drama. Although Indonesia is predominantly a Muslim country, Islam is the top layer of a succession of faiths, and Ardjuna, one of the heroes of the *Mahabharata*, is a widely revered and loved figure.

The growing complexity of Hinduism resulted in a huge variety of schools and shades of thought. The present state of the Christian religion is comparable. Basic to all systems, however, was the feeling that life is evil, that material things are deceptive if not downright illusory, and that man's objective is a purification of the spirit achieved by renouncing carnal desires in a succession of lives. This belief in reincarnation became, and remains, a major theme. Perhaps its most important implication is that the present condition of an individual is not a matter of chance, but a consequence of their good or evil actions in previous lives.

The caste system is intended to regulate this process of slow advancement through a series of lives. The whole religious concept would be meaningless if individuals could be allowed to move from the station in life to which they were born, since the Hindu faith has it they were not born into that life by accident, but by the dictate of a divine plan. The caste system, then, is much more than a social order; it is deeply involved with the religious beliefs of the people – it has an inevitability that reinforces its acceptance by those who believe in it. It also has strong associations with occupation, castes often resembling the medieval trade guilds of Europe.

As the centuries passed, castes split into sub-castes, and these again into even more complicated categories. That remains the case in India today, even though caste discrimination is technically illegal. I had Indian friends in Singapore, both well educated, a doctor of medicine and a journalist, of differing castes. When this couple married they found it expedient to live outside India.

Meanwhile in the India of today, *dalits* – untouchables – continue to be sweepers, leatherworkers and rubbish collectors, and are severely disadvantaged in almost all respects, in spite of attempts by the central government to change things. Even within the small but growing educated middle class, caste still strongly influences basic matters such as marriage alliances.

Implementing national policies, especially on a matter as fundamental as caste, is all the more difficult because of an effective regionalism resulting from India's multiplicity of languages and dialects. The print media, radio and television generally operate in their own area, rather than as national networks. Political forces have the same constraints, thus perpet-uating the strong regional influences already defined by history and tradition. In the 6th century BCE the son of an affluent *kshatriya* family with the clan name of Gautama wearied of the straitjacket of Hinduism, and renounced his wife, home and family to become a wanderer. After six years of meditation and study he is believed to have achieved perfection in the spiritual sense and so has become known as 'the enlightened one' – the Buddha. The philosophy he has left is by no means the only heresy of this period, although it became the most pervasive and important.

Buddhism, originally an offshoot and an interpretation of 'Hindu' prin-ciples, has become immensely diverse and malleable. Even though its prac-tice varies widely from region to region in Asia, it is basically a guide to conduct rather than a religious belief, based largely on tolerance, gentle-ness and moderation. Indeed, what it calls 'the middle way' is its essential. It seeks the abandonment of hatred, envy and anger, and the cultivation of purity and kindness.

While these sentiments are commonplace enough now, it must be recalled that Buddhism preceded Christianity by more than 500 years, and was a tremendous step forward in a world which had, until then, generally accepted without question the principle of an eye for an eye and a tooth for a tooth; a world in which cruelty and injustice were simply to be taken for granted. This new philosophy, born in the foothills of the Himalayas, was to become a profound influence throughout Asia. Another major religion from this time, still important in India, is Jainism, which asserts non-violence as a major principle. It was probably an influence on Gandhi when he advocated non-violence during the Indian struggle for independence more than 2000 years later. Jains believe everything in nature has a soul. Jains, who are mainly concentrated in Gujarat State, have always been merchants and are relatively wealthy and influential.

For almost 200 years the Punjab was a province of the great Persian empire until, in the 4th century BCE, the Persian King Darius the Third was defeated by the Macedonian soldier-adventurer Alexander, whose elephants pushed over the high passes of the Hindu Kush mountains and crossed the Indus River in 326 BCE. Alexander's death soon afterwards brought his short-lived empire to an end, but one of his generals, Seleucus Nicator, was able to take control of the Asian part, including the Indian province. Towards the end of the century Seleucus Nicator traded the Indian province for 500 elephants to a vigorous administrator of Indian birth named Chandragupta.

This man welded much of north India into a single state for the first time. There is some information available about him from the fragments remaining from the written account of the Greek Megasthenes, sent by Seleucus Nicator as his envoy to Chandragupta's capital, on the site of the present city of Patna.

The dynasty founded by Chandragupta is called Mauryan and was based on a city which, Megasthenes tells us, sprawled along nine miles of the banks of the Ganges and as much as a mile and a half inland. He regarded it as a pleasant, well-ordered place, and his account is of a people – or rather an upper class – accustomed to grace and beauty. There were large and pleasant gardens, in which jasmine, hibiscus, the water lily and the lotus were already cultivated for their beauty and perfume; lakes and bathing pools, where the air was cooled by fountains; and contrived grottoes for relaxation.

There was an organized civil service, whose officers specialized in the collection of taxes, inspection of irrigation works, road building and similar activities run and paid for by the state, almost entirely, it must be said, for its own financial benefit. This elaborate bureaucracy even had a war office with specialist sections dealing with such matters as elephants, cavalry and naval activities.

In spite of the luxury with which he was surrounded, Chandragupta's own regime was strictly ordered; we are told he was left only four and a half hours out of twenty-four for sleep. Administering his empire kept him fully occupied and much of his time was devoted to intrigue and receiving the reports of the elaborate network of spies he maintained. He went in constant fear of his life, regularly shifted his abode to avoid assassins, and never went out in public without an armed escort. He travelled in a gold palanquin carried by elephants, accompanied by his guards, fan, pitcher and umbrella bearers, who seem invariably to have been women. The route of his progress was marked off with ropes, and Megasthenes recorded that it was instant death for anyone who set foot inside them.

The Mauryan Empire reached its zenith under Chandragupta's grandson Ashoka. Ashoka was a great builder, but where his forebears had used wood, he built in stone, so for the first time since Harappa, buildings and sculpture were constructed that have lasted into our time. Of the numerous stone columns Ashoka set up, the capital of one, with its figures of four lions, is used as the emblem of the present government of India.

However, Ashoka is remembered mostly because he turned from cruel and amoral absolutism to institute revolutionary and remarkable reforms, unique in the world of their time. Ashoka's conversion to the ways of peace is said to have resulted from an experience of the realities of war during an expedition against the neighbouring kingdom of Kalinga. In this war it is said 100,000 people died, with as many more captives taken. Ashoka was deeply influenced by this episode of violence and loss, and by Buddhism, which spread as a result of his missionary efforts as far as Burma and Sri Lanka. An embassy was even sent to Egypt.

Ashoka was much given to setting up inscriptions of moral precepts. Thirty-five of these still exist in caves and on the monoliths previously mentioned. A system of law and order hitherto unparalleled is attributed to him, aimed at the protection of the sick, the unarmed and the helpless, and the convenience of travellers. Staged rest-houses for travellers along roads – still a feature of several Asian countries – were one of the public services he instituted. He devoted a great deal of attention to the highways, planting groves of shade trees and digging wells, and built hospitals for the care of the sick and infirm, who, until then, had died unless they were succoured by a casual charity. There was even a corps of circuit magistrates who travelled the kingdom resolving disputes. At this time Buddhism developed its most significant divergence from Hinduism, its rejection of the caste system (except in Sri Lanka). Classic accounts of Ashoka's life from Buddhist publicists present him as a saintlike figure. Whatever the truth of that there seems little doubt he was a man of some personal force of character, with a sense of humanitarianism rare in his time. The Mauryan Empire declined rapidly after his death.

Five centuries of small regional states ensued, briefly illuminated by a Bactrian Greek empire in north India under a king called Menander. Coins and statuary from this Gandharan school show unmistakable Mediterranean influence and have permanently influenced Buddhist art.

From the fourth to the seventh centuries much of the distinction and order of Ashoka's empire reappeared under the Guptas. This period is notable for exquisite paintings, like those in the Ajanta caves, its sophisticated sculpture and its Sanskrit drama, especially the plays of Kalidasa, a poet and dramatist who is regarded by some as comparable with Shakespeare. Kalidasa's *Sakuntala*, based on part of the *Mahabharata*, has been translated into many other languages and has taken its place in world literature. So prolific and varied was this literary output there is strong evidence that it was the work of a school of writers, possibly three people. The *Kama Sutra*, which has remained popular around the world to this day because it explicitly expresses erotic elements of the Hindu religion, also dates from this period.

This was the heyday of Buddhism in India, the time of the great teaching monasteries and universities that became famed throughout Asia. One of these, Nalanda, is said to have had 4000 students in the 7th century. Pilgrims came from as far away as China to study in them. One of these, Faxian, who spent ten years in India in the 5th century, has described a peaceful, well-organized and prosperous society with moderate laws and taxation. Although Hinduism was again the faith of the ruling house, the powerful and influential Buddhist community coexisted peaceably with them.

Standards of education were high among the small lettered class and important developments in algebra and arithmetic (including the decimal system of nine numbers and the zero) occurred in India in the 7th century. These innovations, so long known as 'Arabic' in the West, seem, in fact, to have been learned by the Arabs from India. There is also evidence that the concept of the zero, which appeared in India at this time, might have originated even farther east, perhaps in Indo-China.

Buddhism entered something of a decline towards the end of the era – instead there was a renewal of the influence and authority of the *brahmin* Hindu caste. Invaders from the north – the same Huns who were such a cause of concern to the Chinese – successfully attacked the Gupta state, which had fragmented into a number of smaller units by the middle of the 6th century.

Meanwhile Hindu power and culture had permeated only slowly to the south of India. This area of dense tropical jungle, steamy heat, and dangerous wildlife such as tigers and giant snakes, had little appeal to the predatory invaders from the hills. However, independent societies were evolving in the south.

Early south Indian mainland communities were based on sea-coast cities and a thriving maritime trade. It seems likely that as early as 500 BCE fishing boats had evolved into small ocean-going ships, engaged in trade as far afield as Burma and Malaya. Kingdoms of consequence arose, like that of the Tamil Cholas, which dominated much of peninsular India in the 11th century, and which became a maritime power with considerable influence in south-east Asia. The Chola state appears to have been relatively enlightened and advanced, with a system of village self-government, efficient revenue-raising, major irrigation works, and a distinctive Tamil literature and architecture.

The huge pyramidal temple the Tamils built in honour of the god Shiva is still a major landmark in the city of Tanjore, and inscriptions on its walls are a major source of information – or probable information – about the Cholas. Chola certainly seems to have been the largest and most influential state in India around the end of the first millennium, especially during the long 11th-century reign of King Rajendra. Much of its extravagant wealth, a great deal of which was devoted to ornamenting and maintaining the Tanjore temple, was obtained from marauding expeditions against Chola's neighbours.

This region's exports – among them ivory, cotton cloth, pepper and other spices, diamonds, pearls, apes and peacocks – included a considerable trade with Rome, evidenced by numerous Roman coins found in south India. But the most consequential export was the Indian cultural and architectural influence still so evident in much of south-east Asia.

4 Early South-east Asia: the Ships from India

The Indian merchant-adventurers' first journeys were probably slow passages hugging the Bay of Bengal coast, always in sight of land. Their early acquaintance with south-east Asia must have been due not so much to enterprise as the facts of geography. The art of sailing was elementary indeed, and it was not until relatively recently that one of the most important of man's inventions – how to sail efficiently into the wind – evolved.

When the first Indian argosies left the coast, they were forced to go where the wind took them. On the outward passage, between the months of June and November, that wind is the south-west monsoon, which blows with remarkable steadiness, day after day, week after week. It still propels many a sailing craft across those waters. Simply by proceeding before and slightly off the wind, a ship would naturally make her landfall on the tip of Sumatra or the Malaysian peninsula. Having arrived, the earliest Indian adventurers found it difficult to get back, since the wind persists from the south-west until the months December to May, when it blows with equal steadiness from the north-east. Hence the Indian merchant-adventurers went prepared to stay wherever they made a landfall until the monsoon changed. It was probably in this way that their customs, religion and art began to spread eastward, as far as the China Sea coast of Vietnam.

It would be seriously to underrate the south-east Asian peoples to make the simple assumption that Indian ways were grafted on to primitive societies. The point probably was that rulers or would-be rulers saw advantage in a religion and culture that would advance their own interests, and which possessed an efficient, if Machiavellian, statecraft. The Indian merchants and priest-missionaries were in fact providing ambitious rajahs with a blueprint for societies in which elites could control and use the ordinary people. These, characteristically, were wet rice farmers or fishermen – and very good ones at that, who already had quite advanced systems of local self-government.

Archaeological sites in north-east Thailand give evidence of agricultural bronze-using societies as advanced as those in other parts of the world, perhaps as early as 3000 BCE. A six-acre mound rising from ricefields at Non Nok Tha has revealed evidence of rice-growing and bronze-casting – a factory making adzes in split sandstone moulds. Iron objects have been dated back to 500 BCE. Beautifully worked bronze ceremonial drums made from the 6th century BCE for almost a thousand years at Dong-son, in what is now North Vietnam, were in use in many parts of south-east Asia, and have even been found in New Guinea. The archaeology of south-east Asia is still in its early stages, so there can be little doubt that eventually more discoveries will be made there which will reveal a clearer picture of these early societies.

The wide dispersal of the Dong-son drums indicates a thriving maritime trade before the Christian era. There is evidence of Malay shipping trading as far as China as early as 300 BCE, and engaged in the cinnamon trade by 100 BCE. From this early maritime experience quite large trading vessels evolved – up to 400 tons, with two to four masts and carvel hulls built without nails or screws. I have seen new ships very much along these lines, using wooden dowels to edge-fasten each plank, under construction along the Pattaya coast of the Gulf of Thailand, as recently as 1965. Indonesian handcrafts, like the complex creation of *batik* fabrics, are also believed to have pre-dated Indian influence.

Hence in the discussion which follows of 'kings' and 'states' it is important not to overrate the importance of their total effect on the majority of society, or that of the 'cultural grafts', for that matter. Since what written sources there are almost always deal with those kings and states, and are more concerned with eulogy than fact, it is difficult indeed to trace the development and history of the ordinary people. Nevertheless, it is worth trying to do so.

This can be attempted through a study of the south-east Asian village societies as they are today – their legends, beliefs and customs, and the evidence of archaeological remains. Deduction from these is assisted by a reasonable assumption that these societies show all the signs of having been stable and largely unchanging for very long periods of time, possibly thousands of years. They are also societies in which complex and formal patterns of personal relationships seem to have existed for a long time. This in itself would have tended to make the Indian cultural influence acceptable, and even welcome. The extraordinary profusion of carved scenes on the massive Javanese temple-mountain, the Borobadur, created more than 1300 years ago, depict fishing, market, craft and agricultural scenes very similar to what can be seen in daily life today.

Prehistoric south-east Asia gives evidence of a considerable diversity of occupation by tool-using primitive societies going back at least

30,000 years. It could be assumed that these were ancestors of indigenous Australoid peoples, the remnants of whom may be the short-statured, shy, hunting peoples, classed as negritos, who are still found in remote jungle areas of Malaysia, Thailand and the Philippines. Others moved on to New Guinea and Australia.

By the time of the first contacts with India, however, the islands and coastlines had long been settled by people who are Malay in type. Basically Mongoloid, they came from southern China, through a gradual process of cultural osmosis that must have occupied many centuries. The first Indian contacts were probably with Malay villagers close to the sea on estuaries or creeks. They made beautifully finished and polished tools from very hard stone, were excellent navigators with some knowledge of astronomy and then (as now) sailed long, narrow and graceful sailing-craft with considerable skill. This maritime tradition is still very important. To today's Malaysian or Indonesian sailors, their craft is more a way of life than simply work – as one can see along the mudflats of coastal Singapore where the racing of light, very fast outrigger models called *jukongs* is a major Malay sport, and their construction an art.

In places such as Brunei and Palembang their way of life persists, in many respects unchanged. Some, like the Bugis, spend their entire life on their ships. People living in villages often build their houses on stilts on mudflats, so they are completely surrounded by water at high tide. Most are fishermen. Otherwise for food they depend very much on the coconut, which thrives along the beaches and on the many islands of this region. This estuary culture is found particularly in places where the soil is poor, like much of the Malayan peninsula and Kalimantan (Borneo).

Loosely organized principalities at the river mouths were regarded as the personal bailiwicks, and the tax revenues the personal property, of the ruler and the clique supporting him. Pre-colonial Malay history is mostly a tedious and repetitive chronicle of the feuds, wars and disputes of these petty princelings. Often these principalities resulted from pirate alliances which preyed on passing merchant shipping – something that persisted into modern times.

Rich soils, found on plain-lands, drained swamps or hillsides where water is available, have from the earliest times been devoted to the growing of 'wet' or *padi* rice. Indeed, so old is this cultivation of irrigated rice that in some parts of south-east Asia the most suitable land was devoted to it, and expanding populations seem to have been forced into hilly regions, as much as 3000 years ago. In the mountains of northern Luzon, the main island of the Philippines, is an engineered complex of terraced ricefields and irrigation canals that is intricate in design and so large it has transformed whole mountainsides. Its construction, which is thought to have commenced more than 2000 years ago, occupied many generations. It is not known why these people, the Ifugao, decided to leave the plains and commence the staggering task of terracing such huge areas of mountains. It is possible they did it to escape malaria, since the sluggish *Anopheles* mosquito which carries that fever is seldom found higher than 2000 feet above sea level. However, the cultural history of the Ifugao in recent times indicates that building the terraces and growing rice in them is central to their social structure and religion. It seems likely that building the terraces was to the Ifugao what temple or pyramid construction was to other peoples.

But whatever the reason, the Ifugao were remarkably determined and resourceful people. If these terraces were laid end to end, they would extend 12,000 miles. First, a stone wall was built as high as 50 feet and the land behind it excavated. The trench so made was lined with impervious clay so that it would hold water, then levelled with sand and soil. Another such terrace was built above and below this, until entire hillsides were covered with parallel terraces like giant flights of steps, engineered to follow the contour lines. Coupled with this skilful engineering the Ifugao showed a considerable knowledge of hydraulics. The waterfalls and torrents of the hillsides were harnessed, bamboo pipes being used to provide a water supply to the rice terraces. Forest growth was controlled on the divides to prevent flash flooding and erosion.

While these Ifugao structures are of special interest because of their age and their extent, terraced ricefields like them can be found almost everywhere in south-east Asia, and are indicative of highly skilled and co-operative societies. The culture of *padi* rice is in itself an expert and demanding business. Without doubt the art of selecting the best-producing varieties must have begun a long time ago, and the custom of growing first in seedbeds and then transplanting the young plants must be almost as old.

There is evidence that this work was in some cases carried out under the supervision of a central authority. This was the case in the great Khmer Empire of Cambodia, but mostly it appears to have been undertaken by villagers for their own benefit. This required a considerable degree of co-operation between families, especially in negotiating the allocation of water resources, and building the elaborate irrigation systems so often used. It is also how complex systems of relationships must have developed, providing a stable, continuing ethical framework necessary for law-abiding close-settled societies. There were definite social hierarchies, favouring the old and presumably wise. Decisions, when necessary, were typically made by these councils of elders on a basis of discussion until consensus was reached – not on a majority vote, which would be regarded as socially crude.

There has always been a strong tradition of joint responsibility for all members of a group. People who are ill are looked after by their neighbours. If a family's house is burned down, the whole village will help build another. Care of children extends outside nuclear families to many other people and especially to the extended family, in which the bonds are very close.

All this is of much more than academic interest, not only because it is still the way things generally are outside the cities, but also because consensus is an important part of national consciousness, and of politics. It is a major reason why Western-style democracy has not succeeded in Asia, indeed in some places it is politely condemned as being government 'by half plus one'.

How far such ideas go back is not known. It has even been postulated that the cradle of human civilization was south-east Asia, or rather Sunda, the shallow seas linking the islands to the mainland that were dry land during the ice ages. Stephen Oppenheimer, in his *Eden in the East* (1998), argues persuasively, though by no means conclusively, that when Sunda was flooded at the end of the last glacial, a civilization which grew rice, perhaps even worked bronze, was displaced in several directions to create, or influence, those regions such as Mesopotamia and the Indus valley, which are conventionally regarded as the earliest civilizations.

The methods of growing *padi* rice are closely interwoven with animist religions – that is, worship of gods corresponding to and controlling the elemental forces of nature, together with a belief that virtually everything contains a life-force, a 'soul'. Later religions, coming from India, have not generally displaced these, but have simply added a top layer. Even in Thailand, where Buddhism is virtually universal and the state religion, the old animist beliefs are widespread. One such concerns a rice mother without whose approval the crops cannot succeed. Thai children are told about Mae Phra Phosop, and warned that if they don't eat all the rice given to them she may be offended, and refuse the life-giving rains for the next planting.

And this is not only the case in remote villages. Towards the end of the Second World War the Thai Electric Corporation in Bangkok reached the stage where it could no longer get the usual firewood and rice husks to keep its generators going. So it was decided to use surplus rice grain itself. Before this could be done a Buddhist religious ceremony, attended by two cabinet ministers and other dignitaries, was held. The chief Buddhist official speaking at this function asked the permission of Mae Phra Phosop to use some of the bountiful grain for fuel. He begged her not to be angry and visit them with her wrath. 'Mae Phra Phosop has always provided us with food,' he said. 'Now may she give us further blessings by supplying heat, wherewith we may get light, and power to drive the trams.'

The *Ramayana*, originating from the 6th century BCE, makes references to what seems to be south-east Asia, but these could have been later additions, perhaps in the 2nd century BCE. The point indicates the vagueness of the evidence on which assumptions about this period have to be made.

The first detailed description of an Indianized state comes from a 3rd-century Chinese account. The state was Funan, located in the great delta of the Mekong River in what is now southern Vietnam, strategically on the trade route between India and China. Funan's capital, Vyadhapura, was a pirate base and an entrepôt port in flat, marshy country suitable for growing rice. It sprawled along the banks of mangrove-lined creeks, and here its many ships were moored. The Chinese record says the capital was a mud-walled city of considerable size, with dark, curly-haired people who were skilled artisans, exporting jewellery of wrought gold and silver, sandalwood and pearls. Funan seems to have been regarded as relatively sophisticated for its time, but to the Chinese it was a mixed blessing – often their merchant junks, which sailed as far west as Sri Lanka, were attacked by its fast pirate ships. However, its musicians, who visited China in the 3rd century, were highly regarded there. Its rulers used Sanskrit and imposed trial by ordeal, such as carrying a red-hot chain or plunging the hands into boiling water.

Funan, which was probably a loose alliance of villages near the coast south-east of the present Phnom Penh, seems to have extended its influence beyond Vietnam into parts of what are now Cambodia and Thailand. Excavations there have revealed Roman-style medallions and ornaments. From a cultural and religious point of view its most important legacy was a belief in a line of rulers called the Kings of the Mountain, which persisted into later civilizations in several parts of south-east Asia.

Following its decline by the 6th century, its commercial monopoly was usurped by another estuary town called Shrivijaya, probably on the site of the present Palembang in Sumatra. Like Funan, it was close to fertile ricefields and was thus able to provision visiting ships. Shrivijaya prospered under the patronage of China, which needed a strong 'tributary' state in this key area. A Chinese pilgrim named Yiqing who visited there in the 7th century said more than 1000 Buddhist monks lived there, and its rulers – once again, Kings of the Mountain – had links with the Buddhist university at Nalanda, in India.

Shrivijaya has prompted much speculation as a major Indonesian naval empire, but this is based on very slender evidence. However, it does seem to have been a central point for trade in nutmeg, cloves and other spices, scented wood, especially sandalwood, and pearls, and a major intermediate port in the traffic, actually quite small, between Persia, India and China. It appears to have prospered largely because it was able to unite the *orang laut*, the sea pirates of the surrounding waters, and so guarantee they would not attack trading ships. Shrivijaya was attacked in 1025 CE by the south Indian Chola Empire, possibly because it made too exorbitant demands on Chola ships. Although it recovered from this, it finally faded into obscurity in the 14th century.

Another major kingdom flourished in central Java in the 7th century, and must have been appreciable because it built the tremendous monument called the Borobadur. This huge Buddhist shrine is a series of almost three miles of terraces built over a natural hill. The galleries of these terraces are flanked with stones on which thousands of bas-reliefs are carved with wonderful skill. There are some 400 statues of the Buddha, and the structure is crowned by a temple on the flattened top of the hill.

Another temple not far away, Prambanan, shows scenes from the *Ramayana* and was Hindu rather than Buddhist. It was built in the 9th century by the central Javanese Mataram kingdom, in very productive rice-growing country. However, while inscriptions on these monuments, intricate gold artefacts, and the use of coinage indicate a varied and sophisticated society for their time, the actual history of these ancient Javanese societies is shadowy indeed, and on present available evidence is likely to remain so. They seem to have been regional alliances based on existing village structures.

In northern Cambodia, not far from the Thai border, are the ruins of vast buildings, painstakingly fashioned from intricately carved and jointed pieces of greenish sandstone, some of which weigh many tons. They are located at Angkor Thom, which was arguably the largest city in the preindustrial world. It was the capital of the Khmer kings, and is the remnant of what was south-east Asia's most impressive yet forbidding civilization.

It is relevant that when the ageing king of Cambodia, Norodom Sihanouk, returned to his country in 1997 from a stay in Beijing, he flew directly to Angkor rather than to the capital Phnom Penh, to pray for peace between the warring factions in Cambodia. He did this because Angkor was the city of his ancestors – this is also the reason for the remarkable personal influence he maintained in his country over many decades. There is a continuing presence about these ruins which still seems to have the power to stir even the most unimaginative person, although more than 500 years have passed since the builders deserted it.

Over those centuries it has been locked in a losing fight with the jungle. Season by season, after the city was abandoned, the jungle advanced across highly developed ricefields served by one of the finest irrigation systems ever built. Birds dropped seeds on the crumbling walls. Now great fig and belan trees, with broad, buttressed roots, perch fantastically over gateways, their roots grappling with carved faces. This whole fabric of slow decay is bathed in a green light of submarine aspect, filtering down through the canopy of leaves overhead. Yet the ruins convey a sense of futility. The narrow, forbidding galleries lead nowhere. Only a slave state of the grimmest kind could have forced men to shape and raise these huge blocks of stone. Teams of prisoners and slaves, impelled by the sword and the whip, built them.

A Chinese visitor to the Khmer court at the end of the 13th century, Zhou Dakuan, said that the tribesmen from the nearby hills were often caught and sold as slaves. He remarks that they were regarded as animals and that many families had more than a hundred of them. 'If they commit a fault, they are beaten,' Zhou wrote. 'They bow the head and dare not make the least movement.' His account describes the wonderfully developed rice-growing areas based on the two great artificial lakes, the East and West Baray, which flank Angkor, and an intricate system of canals using the water of the Siem Reap River.

Khmer society was based on a highly organized aristocracy and a savage law. Often trial was by ordeal, and punishment was summary and severe. The beautifully carved friezes of the Bayon and Angkor Wat are still well-preserved and present a vivid picture of Khmer society. They show cockfighting, men playing chess, slaves cutting stone, dancing girls, scenes of intimate family life, processions, and battle scenes with warships, archers and elephants.

The Khmer people became masters of much of what is now mainland south-east Asia. Their influence extended east to the China Sea, westward through what is now Thailand to the Burmese border, and as far south as the Isthmus of Kra. The names of the Khmer kings, like those of certain Hinduized monarchs in Java, all end with the suffix *varman*, which means protector. This gives an insight into their role, which was perceived as offering spiritual and physical protection to the rice-growing majority who served them.

Construction of Angkor began during the 8th-century reign of Jayavarman II, who is thought to have been educated for kingship at the court of the Shailendra in Central Java. In the Angkor culture, then, there is again evidence of the pervasive tradition of the Kings of the Mountain, enshrining the belief that the prosperity of the people is directly linked with the sacred personality of the king. Each king was required to create a temple-mountain, a building with terraces and towers in which he would be buried after death – a custom which is among the oldest known of the human race, also seen in the ancient kingdoms of Mesopotamia.

This belief resulted in the staggering assembly of huge buildings in the Cambodian jungles which are now regarded as one of the chief wonders of the world. The most famous is the vast Angkor Wat, a mile square, the largest religious building in the world. So well was it built in the 12th century that it remains virtually intact. Although the city itself was abandoned, Angkor Wat remained in use, and was a sizeable Buddhist monastery at the time the French became aware of it in 1850. The pictorial frieze along the inner sanctuary wall is carved with a remarkable artistry. Such things, of course, exist elsewhere, but the frieze at Angkor Wat, eight feet high, extends continuously for more than half a mile.

Few things here are life-size. Even the carved hands of figures are so massive they are often more than a man could lift. It is probable that this mania for building finally weakened the kingdom so much it could no longer control its enemies. Here again, it is also possible that the *Anopheles* mosquito, breeding on the great irrigation lakes, brought catastrophic plagues of malaria. Since only the stone temples survive, where the people of this city actually lived was unclear until imaging radar from NASA (the US National Aeronautics and Space Administration) revealed the remnants of a considerable network of canals and streets to the north of the temple complex, which must once have been lined with timber houses. These radar images indicated the huge size of Angkor for a city of its time – it covered more than 400 square miles, and could have had as many as a million people. In 1431 a vassal people, one of the group called the Thais, who had come down into south-east Asia from south-west China, sacked Angkor after a seven-month siege. In 1434 the capital was moved and finally established 150 miles south on the banks of the Mekong River at Phnom Penh, which is still the Cambodian capital. Military pressure from the Thais, who had built up a considerable empire based on the city of Ayudhya, and economic factors related to trade with China, seem to have influenced the decision to abandon Angkor. This was probably a considered, relatively gradual process, rather than the sudden dramatic catastrophe conjectured by some historians. There is a theory that the sheer size of Angkor so disturbed the ecology of the surrounding area that it ceased to be viable.

North Vietnam has had strong connections with China, which it borders, from at least the 2nd century BCE. Neolithic remains indicate a population of Indonesian type, but later bronze artefacts of considerable artistry are associated with a migration of Mongoloid people south from China into the Red River delta. The population grew steadily as the swamps of the delta were engineered to grow wet rice. In 111 BCE the region became a province of China called Annam, which means 'southern kingdom'. Direct Chinese influence continued to shape north Vietnamese society for a thousand years; then the Red River delta region became independent after the demise of the Chinese Tang Dynasty. Like China, north Vietnam was Confucian, with all the attendant mechanisms of tax systems, filial piety and respect for established rites.

A glance at a map shows at once the geographic features which have several times resulted in Vietnam being divided into two, or even three, countries. The narrow coastal 'waist' bordering the mountains of Laos is as little as 40 miles wide, and separates two regions with marked historic, ethnic and cultural differences.

The south, consisting substantially of the plains and great delta of the Mekong River, was part of the empire of Angkor. The coastline north, along the narrow waist, was the considerable empire of a seafaring people, racially Malay, the Chams, whose society had acquired an Indian cultural influence as early as the 2nd century CE, and which persisted for 1300 years. This was not an empire, but again a loose federation of river-mouth towns.

Champa traded in spices and ivory, but it was chiefly known and feared for its piracy directed at the passing coastal trade. This attracted considerable annoyance from the Chinese, whose ships were nearly always those attacked, and consequently mounted a number of punitive expeditions. Champa was also noted as a slave-trading centre. Records of continual Cham wars with their neighbours were probably more often than not references to raids against neighbouring communities to obtain prisoners of war for resale. The point can be noted that, as with other south-east Asian kingdoms, power was linked to the possession of large numbers of people, rather than large amounts of land.

Judging from its architecture, Champa had considerable cultural links with Angkor with which, however, it was almost constantly at war. Constant military pressure came from China, too, after the Chams renounced Chinese overlordship in the 6th century. However, it was the Vietnamese advancing from the north who finally brought Cham influence to an end. They were virtually destroyed as a political force by persistent war with the north Vietnamese from the 11th century onwards and a Mongol invasion in 1283. However, their descendants remain a distinct ethnic group in Vietnam and in Cambodia.

The Tran Dynasty in North Vietnam not only attacked Champa, but it was successful in turning back the Mongol invasion directed by Kublai Khan. Several centuries of intermittent wars with China followed, then with the 15th century came perhaps the most successful and the first genuinely Vietnamese Dynasty. This was the Le, who, after inflicting a final defeat on the Chams in 1471, began to extend slowly into the Mekong delta.

At the time of the first contacts with Europeans, however, the Le emperors had become figureheads and the natural tendency of the country to divide had again asserted itself. Two families, the Trinh in the north and the Nguyen in the south, became the real centres of power. Cambodia, meanwhile, had dwindled both in population and influence, and had become a mere dependency of Vietnam.

5 China: the Eternal Nation

China's story is among the most remarkable of humankind; her river valleys have been the location of a society that has not only shown continuity and consistency for perhaps 4000 years, but was also the inventor of paper, printing, firearms, credit banking and paper money, rudder steering and watertight compartments for ships, blast-furnace steel production and lock systems for canals, among many other foundations and tribulations of the modern world. The transfer of such things to Europe was slow but nevertheless consequential.

China's status as the most populous country in the world is nothing new. She has been so for millennia. All Chinese, including those living far from their homeland, are aware of this sense of continuity, of a culture that has withstood time and adversity as no other human institution has done, and are deeply influenced by it. China's Communist leaders are no exception. At the time of the new state's greatest financial need, when it had been deserted by the Soviet Union, an option would have been to sell the immensely valuable solid gold and gem-encrusted artefacts in the Ming tombs near Beijing. But this was not done. Instead the tombs were carefully restored and maintained, all their treasures still in place.

The durability and individuality of Chinese culture are due to a number of factors, of which geography is among the more important. China, to the east of the mountain spine of central Asia, does not have the immediate vulnerability of the north Indian plain. These great mountains, together with the deserts to their north and the Pacific Ocean to the east, were a formidable barrier between China and the rest of the world, insulating her until the relatively recent development of efficient shipping. Trade contacts with the West before the 19th century were slight and the effects of them, especially on China, are often overemphasized. Her mercantile contacts with other parts of Asia were much more important.

North of the mountains are arid, lightly populated plains and formidable deserts. These make overland travel and trade difficult. These outer regions were not, however, completely empty. Tribes of nomads moved through them, maintaining a constant pressure on China's borders and often invading her. The Great Wall was built and rebuilt or extended many times to keep them out. Yet unlike some of those who invaded India, the 'barbarians' who successfully occupied China had no great effect on her culture. Chinese civilization was able to absorb them, even when they were conquerors.

This cultural resilience was assisted by the fact that Chinese civilization has a powerful binding force – a common written language and a body of literature of great antiquity that can be read anywhere in China, regardless of the many differences of spoken dialect. Much of this literature is concerned with the way people should live and behave. It has had a remarkable influence, which has extended beyond China, notably to Japan, Korea, Vietnam and Singapore, and is the background to what have come to be called 'Asian values'.

The tenacity of Chinese civilization also has much to do with its basic religion, ancestor worship. This ancient belief stresses the duty of sons to care for parents, both before and after death, when they are considered to have the same needs as in life. The welfare of the two human souls, a lower soul existing from conception, a higher one from birth, depends on the making of sacrifices, which can only be carried out by sons. If the souls are not tended, they can exert malign or unlucky influences on the living. An effect of ancestor worship was to make Chinese families strong, united forces, capable of great mutual effort towards common objectives. This clan and family resilience remains a significant quality of modern Chinese people.

From about 10000 BCE human societies developed relatively quickly in China under the warmer climate conditions, as they did elsewhere in the world. The archaeological record has revealed traces of developed agricultural societies by 5000 BCE. Those in the Wei and Yellow River valleys in the north grew millet on the light, friable windborne soil called loess, which can be cropped for many years before it becomes exhausted. Those in the south grew rice in irrigated fields. There is evidence of early villages located on the bays and lagoons of the south coast, dependent on fish and other seafood. Hamlets gradually grew into towns, typically surrounded by fortified walls of rammed earth. In the lower Yangzi timber houses were far from crude, using skilled wooden joinery, including the mortise and tenon.

Remnants of silk going back almost 4000 years have been found, but the considerable cost and effort of producing it would have restricted it to luxury use. Hemp was used generally for everyday fabrics, since cotton was not introduced from India until perhaps 600 CE. Hemp is now being grown again in large quantities in China. The earliest weaving shuttles also date

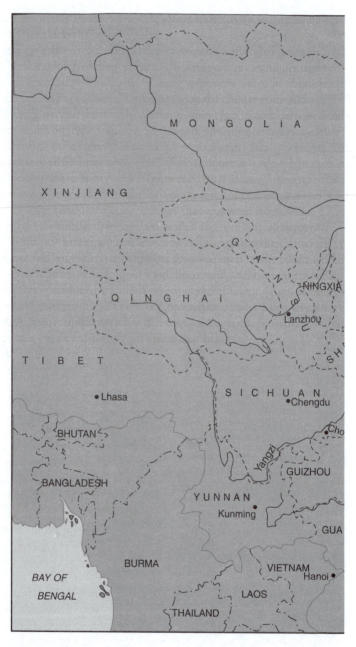

Map 2   China and Korea

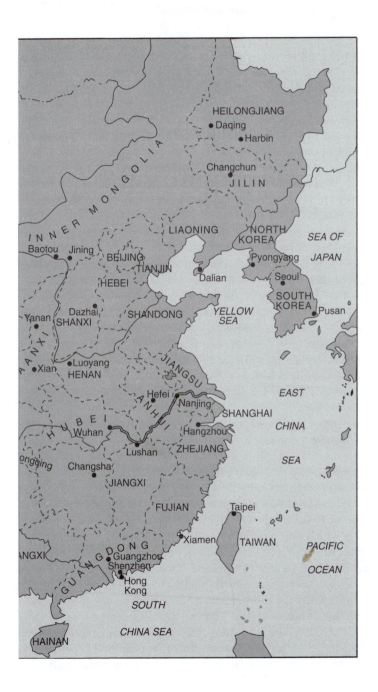

from this early time. Pottery from 2500 BCE found in north China has grace-ful proportions, with geometric decorations in several colours of consider-able artistry. At this time jade was already being worked into ornaments.

Chinese culture, then, had diverse origins, rather than developing exclu-sively in the north, as the classics suggest. In the Red Basin of the far west-ern Sichuan Province, close to the uplands of Tibet and surrounded by mountains and high plateaux, are the ruins of Baodun, an enigmatic but plainly brilliant society for its time, even by world standards, since it dates back as far as 2500 BCE. An urban area, Sanxingdui, near Chengdu, in the upper Yangzi region, has revealed burial sites and house foundations that testify to an advanced and sophisticated city covering more than a square mile – possibly the largest city in the world for that time. By 1250 BCE it was more than four times that size, with buildings suggesting specialized trades using workshops and pottery kilns.

However, it is the more than one ton of extraordinary artefacts – of bronze, gold, jade and ivory – found in two burial pits that have made Sanxingdui an archaeological site of international interest, and indicated the unique nature of its arts. The humanoid heads and masks, sometimes made of gold, are of such bizarre and unusual design that they might be from another planet. Its sophisticated bronze trees, in which small birds perch, and flowers bloom, and its ornamented ritual vessels are at technical and artistic standards as high as any known in the world of that time. This society seems not to have left any written records. It has only been studied with care since 1985.

However, other sites have been discovered near Chengdu, like that at the village of Jinsha 25 miles south, revealing artefacts showing they are clearly of the same culture. According to the Chinese annals the ancient and consequential state of Chu, dating from around 1000 BCE, had expanded to control most of south China by the 5th century BCE, and continued to do so until it was weakened by a corrupt bureaucracy and absorbed in the first unification of China by the Qin dynasty. This followed an epic military struggle, in which over a million soldiers are said to have been involved. The traditional division of Chinese history into 'dynasties' is convenient, but it needs to be regarded with caution. The fall of dynasties sometimes, but not always, caused nationwide social chaos. There were generally islands of prosperity and order in which Chinese culture progressed – even flourished. Nevertheless formal Chinese history postulates three early dynasties, the Xia, Shang, and Zhou, said to have commenced during a vague 'golden age'. Xia remains in the realm of abundant and hopeful myth, such as the reign of the Yellow Emperor, when the world was considered to be perfect. However, grey pottery found in Shaanxi Province is evidence of a pre-bronze society that could correspond with the Xia. With the Shang a somewhat clearer view is possible.

The achievements of that time suggest a brilliant and quite sudden advance in art, technology and social order. Whether these have anything to do with contact with Sanxingdui is conjectural. Early in the 20th century, inscribed bones and tortoise shells sold in Beijing for medicinal purposes were recognized as being very old. The inscriptions on them were of a strange and archaic pattern. These 'oracle bones', originally used for the prediction of future events, bore characters – and decimal numbering – so related to present Chinese writing they could be considered its antecedents. As in contemporary Chinese writing, this text did not use an alphabet representing sounds, but instead individual characters – pictures – for ideas, events, objects capable of description by words. Indeed, it was writing already highly developed. It was possible to establish the meaning of many characters, although some inscriptions are only partly decipherable. They supplied evidence of the existence of many rulers said in the traditional histories to have been of the Shang Dynasty.

Shang culture, located in the Yellow River valley, has left a number of sophisticated and beautifully worked bronzes, which indicate that northern China made a major advance in this era. When this became fully appreciated, a search for their origins began. Between 1928 and 1937 excavations at Anyang, in northern Henan Province, identified the later Shang capital of Yin, probably founded about 1300 BCE. From 1951 onwards further work in this region revealed an even earlier Shang city at Zhengzhou, probably dating to about 1500 BCE. It had massive rammed earth walls, up to 55 feet thick, surrounding an area about a mile square. In the pottery kilns inside were found clay stamps for decorating jars in patterns, like the dragon, trellis and square spiral, which would persist in future Chinese ceramics. There were also ox bones and tortoise shells with incised written characters.

There is evidence of a wealthy and powerful ruling class, with impressive tombs, probably for the kings, containing bronze weapons and ceremonial urns – also pits with the beheaded bodies of horses, dogs and humans, perhaps prisoners. Human skulls appear to have been used as drinking vessels. Shang religious beliefs were animist, with gods representing the moon, sun, wind and other natural phenomena, but the beginnings of ancestor worship were already discernible. The king's role of conducting rites to guarantee agricultural prosperity was another Shang attribute to be carried forward into the future. The Shang army used bows and arrows with bronze heads, and horse-drawn chariots. Silk was used as a fabric, the silkworms being fed on mulberry leaves, as they still are.

The historical records have it that the last Shang king ended his reign in 1122 BCE. The Shang were followed by a less distinguished line, the Zhou, who had been rulers of a border kingdom. They were feudal lords, maintaining only a formal authority over the families that had assisted the establishment of the dynasty. During the nine centuries of nominal Zhou rule, the feudal families grew more powerful and the role of the kings formal and ritualistic. Alliances and conquests led to the emergence of half a dozen major principalities, giving north China a political organization not unlike feudal Europe.

It was a time of tremendous growth, during which the Chinese states emerged from the primitive. Shang culture had been that of a small aristocracy, but now education and art became the preoccupation of a wider section of the community. A wealthy merchant class emerged in what must have been among the world's largest cities of their time, with populations of over a quarter of a million. Huge irrigation works, involving hundreds of canals, were built. The first coinage came into use. At first metal tools – hoes, knives, spades – were a means of exchange. These were soon replaced by small bronze replicas, which became China's first money. The use of iron from about 600 BCE must have given a considerable impetus to Chinese society. It was cast and forged into scythes, axes, saws, needles and weapons, much sharper and harder than the bronze in use up to that time. Craftsmen working in jade used wire saws and diamond drills.

Writing flourished, and for the first time became more than flattery of royal houses. Textbooks, poetry, and treatises on medicine, the arts, mathematics and political theory were all part of a major intellectual flowering. The scholar, able to write and read, became, as he would continue to be thereafter, an object of respect and authority. This was the time of Confucius, said to have lived between 551 and 479 BCE. His name was actually Kong Fuzi, of which Confucius is a Latinized version.

Many people know Confucius, if only because of his frequently quoted *Analects* (actually compiled after his death), of which these are typical:

> The man who makes a mistake, and doesn't correct it, makes another mistake.
> The mind of a superior man is conversant with righteousness; the mind of a mean man is conversant with gain.

As with many great figures of history, the facts of Confucius' life are unclear. However, if the scholar-teacher lived today he would probably have been considered a dangerous radical, because of his basic admonition that the welfare of the people was more important than the privileges of a ruling class. The rulers of the small state of Lu, in which he lived, disliked such ideas, nor could Confucius, during many years of wandering, persuade any other leader to accept them. He insisted on his students studying poetry, music and history to broaden their minds, a tradition continued almost into modern times in the great Chinese civil service, the mandarinate. The fact that he was a dissenter, yet was held in reverence by his students, indicates that he was probably a man of considerable personal force of character, with an innovative, revolutionary mind.

It is ironic that later Chinese Confucianism was anything but these things. Of its enormous body of writing, remarkably little came from Confucius himself. Confucianism, so long the ethical system guiding China, was developed in the work and thought of a mass of subsequent commentators.

Mengzi, who was active during the first quarter of the 4th century BCE, was such a commentator. His view was based on faith in the ultimate goodness of human nature. To him is attributed a practical Chinese political device of some importance – the 'mandate of Heaven' concept – although there are hints of its development much earlier. This idea is one of qualification of the absolute power of the ruler. It is regarded as morally justifiable, even laudable, to revolt against a cruel, unjust or even unlucky regime. In other words, a government is finally justified by its success, its ability to maintain a reasonably prosperous and equable society; an emperor by his probity, his high moral character, since only such a man would be able to intercede with the forces of Heaven to ensure prosperity.

Rather than voting at elections, this became a means of bending governments to the will of the people. The recent concessions of the Chinese Communist Party, especially its economic ones, are not inconsistent with this tradition. The habit of the Chinese Communist government of describing itself as 'correct' – that is, morally sound – may also have a connection. Contrasting with Mengzi, a second important early commentator, Xunzi, regarded human nature as fundamentally bad, in need of improvement through good government, the establishment of set rules of conduct, and the high moral example of rulers. China's formal stylized social patterns, maintained into modern times, owe much to him.

The Chinese world of this time consisted of a dozen or so large and small states grouped along the Yellow and Wei rivers, which constituted Zhongguo – the Middle Country – plus a number of others, on the western and southern fringes, which were regarded as having a lower culture. Beyond this lay the world of the 'barbarians'. Of the fringe states the most significant were Chu and Qin, in the far north-west. Qin was traditionally a bastion against the hordes farther west that were a perpetual threat to the settled Chinese countryside and wealthy cities. Not for nothing were strong walls and defence outworks the most striking feature of Chinese cities.

The ideals attributed to Confucius were suspect in his own time by those who held and influenced power, the energetic pragmatists who really decided the policy of states. Far from regarding humanity as noble and susceptible to an elevated moral example, they believed that a rigidly enforced system of law was the best means of government. This 'legalist' school reached its greatest influence in the state of Qin, which is not surprising. In Qin military effectiveness was considered of paramount importance. The entire population was subject to conscription without notice: the men to fight, and the women and old people to carry supplies and to labour at the fortifications. The army was equipped with elaborate siege machinery: tall, wooden towers on wheels, battering rams, mangonels and similar engines designed to hurl huge stones at the mud walls of beleaguered cities.

By the 3rd century BCE Qin had the 'barbarians' on its frontiers under control, and was able to use its efficient military machine against its more cultured but less martial neighbours to the east. Under the joint rule of its young king and his chief counsellor, Li Si, it eventually prevailed. Not all Qin's successes were military, for Li Si was an intriguer of ability. His negotiating was a major factor in a series of victories that led to no less than the unification of China for the first time. The king of Qin now restyled himself Shi Huangdi – the First Emperor – in 221 BCE.

His administrators had at least the virtue of energy, devoting themselves to a stream of reforms that transformed China – a name which, incidentally, derives from Qin. The width of carriage axles was standardized, a system of uniform weights and measures and coinage introduced, and – immensely important – Chinese writing reformed to make it more concise and practical and, moreover, standardized. The empire was linked by roads which must have been major engineering works even by today's standards. Qin also cut across the old feudal lines of authority, and established an efficient, if despotic, system of administration, based on division into 36 provinces, each controlled by three specialized officials responsible to the emperor.

Efficient communications and rigid discipline became the basis of unity. To further reduce the power of the great families the emperor called in all their weapons. The huge pile of bronze was melted down and cast into 12 statues, each reputed to weigh 70 tons, which were set up at the summer palace, Afang. The building of Afang is said to have involved a labour force of three-quarters of a million.

Li Si persuaded the emperor to issue an edict that books from the past, except for a few specialist texts, should be destroyed. Anyone who failed to burn his books within 30 days would be branded and sent into forced labour. The case Li Si put to the king was not, however, altogether unreasonable. Pointing out that the feudal princes were continually at war, he argued 'Why should we follow them? The empire has been pacified, law comes from a single authority, the people have work, but the scholars continue to study the past, causing doubt and trouble.' The books of the classics, compiled with great labour and almost irreplaceable, were bulky and difficult to conceal. Paper was not yet in use, and the books were mostly inscribed on ivory tablets, lengths of bamboo, and slabs of wood. When at first some scholars defied the edict more severe penalties were introduced. A huge pit is said to have been dug, and 460 scholars buried alive in it.

So Shi Huangdi earned the hatred of succeeding generations of Chinese scholars as 'he who burned the books and buried the scholars'. The story of this villainy has, no doubt, lost nothing in the telling, but the extent to which the First Emperor's reputation has been embroidered by later writers is not really known. Certainly a vast mass of stories, many fanciful, has grown up around his name. Myth has it that self-firing crossbows guard the underground passages into his tomb, and that rivers and lakes of mercury surround it.

While it is sometimes asserted that Shi Huangdi built the Great Wall, much of it already existed before his time. However, he recognized its importance as a defence against barbarians, and greatly improved the older fabric. This involved forced labour by vast hordes of people over 12 years of age, during which it is said a million workers died. Labour on the Great Wall was a common and greatly feared punishment. The existing wall is of later, Ming Dynasty, construction.

An elaborate signalling system was used by the garrisons on the wall, to bring reinforcements to any point of attack. As soon as the fast-moving horsemen appeared out of a cloud of dust to the west, signal fires were lit. During the day bundles of damp straw were used to send up columns of smoke, and at night the fires were coloured using metallic salts – the basis of the Chinese invention of fireworks.

The harshness of Qin rule and the extent of the revolution it had visited on China foredoomed it. Long before his death the emperor lived constantly in fear and told no one in which of his network of palaces he would spend the night. His fear of death led him into a deep preoccupation with immortality and a search for a potion said to procure it. He died in 210 BCE while on a tour of his empire. Such was the fear that the fact of his death would lead to a revolt, it was concealed until his body – with a load of rotting fish – could be returned to the capital.

The extraordinary scope and power of this regime was confirmed by the discovery in 1974 near the city of Xian of the Entombed Warriors – a half-buried army of almost 8000 life-sized archers, infantrymen and cavalry made from terracotta and located in several huge pits which had been roofed with pine logs subsequently destroyed by fire. Bronze chariots and many other artefacts still being unearthed here confirm that this is part of the mausoleum of Shi Huangdi, on which three-quarters of a million artisans are said to have worked. Seven human skeletons also recovered may be those of Shi Huangdi's children, murdered in the palace coup after his death, further weakening the dynasty.

Although the Chinese government has decided the substantial hill believed to house the actual burial place of the First Emperor will not yet be excavated, other archaeological work around the complex has revealed a very advanced technology for the world of its time, especially metallurgy. Bronze swords were made with a high tin content, resulting in blades of considerable sharpness and hardness. Some are uncorroded after more than 2000 years, and appear to have been coated for this purpose, probably with chrome. Blast furnaces were in use to make high-quality steel. Steel-making of this kind would not occur for another thousand years in Europe.

Here, too, appear to have been the origins of the alchemy which was to fascinate Europe a millennium later, and using much the same methods and materials. Like the alchemists, Chinese investigators of this time too often met an untimely end, either from poisoning by mercury, with which they were fascinated, or eating powdered jade, or mushrooms and fungi growing on high mountains.

Shi Huangdi's heirs and supporters were not able to maintain the empire, and in the end his family was murdered to the last child. Li Si was executed publicly by being cut in two. A period of confusion and civil war followed during which a Chu general of peasant origins, Liu Bang, founded the dynasty called the Han, which was to institute much of the pattern China would follow almost up to modern times. Liu Bang, said to be of pleasant temperament and very popular with the people, negotiated patiently to win the feudal lords to Han allegiance, but nevertheless he maintained the basic principles of the Qin state, most importantly its ability to raise immense revenues through efficient taxation. A poll tax which had to be paid in coins was imposed on every Chinese, even small children, and adults were also liable to corvée duties and military conscription. The bureaucracy with clearly defined responsibilities was maintained, but its recruitment came to recognize the values of education and ability in officials. They were often appointed in pairs to limit their power. These traditions would be a continuing thread in Chinese history.

In spite of these efforts for peace and conciliation, at first the Han state had to struggle desperately to survive. To the north and north-west, 'barbarian'

Xiong Nu armies of more than half a million men were waiting outside the Great Wall. Liu Bang met this threat with a degree of success by diplomacy and bribery rather than war. It was not until the half-century-long reign of the Emperor Wudi, which began 60 years later, that China's enemies were subdued and she became, for the first time, an empire of proportions and power significant in global terms. The Chinese call themselves the men of Han to distinguish themselves from minority groups in the outer areas. It is a dynasty particularly favoured as an historic model by the Communist government, perhaps because of the similarities between its origins and their own.

The Confucian classics reappeared and copies were made from odd fragments that had been secretly buried, concealed in chinks of walls or under roof-beams, or retained in the memories of old men. In spite of such painstaking efforts to re-create the past, much had changed. The persistent effort to centralize power had all but destroyed the old families, and the long wars during the early Han impoverished China. The early Han emperors retained the provincial system and regularly interfered in the affairs of – and supervised – the former feudal states. It was largely this genius of the Han administration to divide and rule that allowed China the centuries of peace necessary to grow into a great power.

The population grew quickly and spread farther to the south. The increased use of irrigation, and the building of canals and fleets of river boats, made possible the growth and distribution of more rice than was needed for bare subsistence. Yet most of this additional wealth went to provide a luxurious lifestyle for the scholar-officials, many of whom came from the old feudal families. Records of the time indicate that life was generally desperate and precarious for the peasants, who were frequently in debt. Interest rates were rapaciously high and they were often forced to sell their land, and even their children into slavery, to survive. As a last resort men fled into the forests, compelled to robbery, joining one of the bands of brigands greatly feared by travellers. As well as a month's labour a year required of the peasants to work on public enterprises, they were also liable to conscription for two years in the army. They were provided with the necessities of life during this service, but were otherwise unpaid.

It was within the walled cities that the arts and graces flourished, based on an overall surplus there of commodities over demand. The 1st-century historian Ban Gu claimed for the capital, Changan (the present Chinese city of Xian), that a wall a hundred miles long surrounded its offices, palaces and suburbs, with water gardens and parks featuring rhinoceroses from Kanji (south-east India), birds from Chaldea, and unicorns from Annam!

The Han empire controlled the barbarians not only at the Great Wall, but far beyond it, pushing into the Tarim Basin and Tibet almost to the boundaries of India. It used armed cavalry, with long spears, to devastating effect. Probably the world's first large-scale mass production industry equipped this army. Iron or bronze arrowheads were manufactured in millions, since individual soldiers would have at least 100 arrows for their crossbows. These weapons were highly developed instruments, and remained more deadly and effective than firearms as late as the 19th century. Of particular interest was the standardized trigger-and-string release device, mass-produced in bronze to efficient and precise specifications.

However, these military expeditions were not designed to carve out an empire but to subdue the nomad tribes, driving them far to the west so they would not be a threat to China. It became a confirmed Chinese attitude that control of neighbouring states was a prerequisite to the security of China.

As the Christian era dawned, China had its effect on the world of the West, even though both scarcely knew it. The world now had two great empires, those of the Han and of Imperial Rome, which was probably slightly the smaller. The Chinese census of CE 2 estimates 58 million people. There were trade contacts between the two empires, including an expensive and widespread fashion in Rome for Chinese silk, which at one time threatened to deplete bullion reserves. More significant was the displacement of the nomad tribes westwards, eventually to have disruptive effects in both Europe and India.

Major contributions to the Chinese tradition were developed during Han times. One of the most important was a trend towards merit and education rather than birth as a qualification for high office. This was associated with the increasing power of the central government. Unlike in Europe, feudalism would virtually disappear at this early stage. There was also a major revival of Confucianism. These two factors, organized national government, increasingly by an intelligentsia, and the use of the Confucian classics to justify – even sanctify – the system of government, led on to the development of that great public service known as the mandarinate, the longest-lived and perhaps the most successful instrument of administration mankind has seen. Its influence and traditions are still apparent in the China of today, and may well become more so in the future.

In Han times the mandarinate had already developed many of its enduring characteristics, including examinations in the classics, and adoption of the Confucian idea that the educated man was to be guided by the force of example rather than driven by the fear of punishment. It had also developed a contempt for trade and what the West calls 'private enterprise'. To the Confucian scholars this seemed opposed to true moral values. Filial piety – the respect and support of sons towards fathers, the duties of wives to their mothers-in-law – was a major Confucian idea, which was to permeate all levels of the society in time.

In spite of scholarly disapproval, there was at times almost unfettered capitalism and the accumulation of great fortunes by merchants. However, these caused such convulsions of the economy, due to 'cornering' and speculation in food, and illicit coining of currency, that the Han state eventually curbed them. Large public works and much of the significant domestic industry and distribution systems came under state control. Before controls were reimposed, capitalists in the iron and salt industries were making huge fortunes. The government nationalized these industries and ordered their former owners to run them on behalf of the state. The association of capitalism and state control that has emerged in China now is, then, a recurring theme in Chinese history, and ought not to occasion surprise. Indeed, some of the economic problems with which the Han state wrestled were not too far removed from those emerging in China today.

The invention of paper in the 2nd century was a major step forward. Writing became an almost universal occupation among educated men in Han times, and special attention was given to history. The art of paper-making spread slowly west, reaching Europe 1000 years later. Han Confucianism developed its preoccupation with systems of complex rites and relationships in almost every area of life, a desire for an ordered harmonious universe, which, once established, would go on unchanged for ever. The idea of the ruler as a civilized, virtuous example to his subjects, a sort of moral pacesetter, became firmly developed. Already Confucianism was far from Confucius. It owed much not only to the horde of commentators after his death, but even to other sources; even to the seemingly antithetic Daoism, a philosophy from Zhou times which saw men as simply part of nature, to whose mysterious forces they must adjust, changing what was about them as little as possible – forerunners of modern conservationists, among some of whom Daoism is again popular.

Music and philosophy were thought to be so closely associated that proper calculation of the degrees of pitch in the musical scale was considered essential to the proper functioning of government. Hence mathematicians and philosophers were assigned to the task of calculating them. This suggests the importance attributed to an overall harmony of the universe in human affairs. The movements of the moon, planets and constellations were also carefully studied for similar reasons. Mathematics was developed to a high degree, Zhang Heng calculating the value of pi to be 3.1622 in the 2nd century CE. He also invented the world's first-known seismograph at that time. It is not without interest that in 2000 the Chinese government announced the discovery of a Han water closet said to be 2000 years old, complete with running water, a stone seat and a comfortable armrest, thus challenging the claim of English plumber Thomas Crapper to have invented this device in the 19th century.

Han government became so closely associated with Confucianism that the decay of one involved the collapse of the other. There was a massive revulsion from the formalism of Confucianism, and from the extensive corruption at the imperial court as the corps of eunuchs ostensibly enlisted to guard the harem became a major influence on the emperors. Many people turned to the newly arrived Buddhism and even more to the anarchic Daoism. Daoism lay behind the great 2nd-century peasant revolt of the Yellow Turbans, in which millions were said to have been killed and which hastened the decline of the Han. Flood, famine and poverty increasingly weakened the Chinese nation. The 'barbarian' tribesmen took their opportunity, occupying much of north China. The Chinese fled to the alien, still lightly settled south. The so-called 'Three Kingdoms', Wei, Shu and Wu, each claimed to be legitimate successors of the Han, but the incessant warfare they pursued took millions more lives, resulting in a severe decline of China's population. They remain an important part of modern Chinese culture, due mainly to the immense popularity of a long historical novel, Romance of the Three Kingdoms, written by Luo Guanzhong in the 4th century. Meanwhile Buddhism, which reached China via the trade routes in the 1st century CE, had been rapidly gaining adherents. The form of Buddhism that came to China was the *mahayana* school, which is very different from the more orthodox *theravada* of Burma and Thailand. *Mahayana* Buddhism was a religion, already equipped with magic, gods and saints known as *bodhisattvas*, who deferred their translation to a state of divine perfection so they could intercede in Heaven on man's behalf. It postulated a paradise in which humans were given hope of a far better life. A universally revered and characteristic Chinese *bodhisattva* is Guan Yin, the goddess of mercy and exemplar of feminine virtues. Certain aspects of Confucianism, such as ancestor worship and the cult of the family, were incorporated into Chinese Buddhism, which, as it has moved eastwards, has shown itself to be one of the more flexible and malleable human philosophies. It was in this sinified form that it began its further movement eastwards across the narrow seas to the islands of Japan.

6 Early Japan and the Tang Dynasty in China

The original inhabitants of this small, sunny but cool group of mountainous islands off the coast of China were not the people now known as the Japanese. Recent archaeological evidence indicates occupancy as early as 15000 BCE by an enigmatic race who made pottery and, apparently benefiting from a brief phase of warming during the last ice age, may have been the world's first farming villagers. Then whatever social structure they had achieved appears to have been obliterated by the renewed onset of extreme cold. The broken shards of their pots reveal little else about them, except a hint that they caught and cooked fish. The record next identifies primitive hunter-gatherers who, by perhaps 5000 BCE, had established small farming settlements, and whose simple round- or pointed-bottomed pottery is radiocarbon dated back to around 10000 BCE. During the preceding ice age the Japanese islands, part of a mountain range skirting the Asian mainland coast, were joined to that mainland, allowing free passage to animals and humans.

The ancestors of today's Japanese were quite late entrants to the country. They found a people in the islands unlike themselves – short in stature, with heavy body hair, light skin colour and a language different from any other in the world. These people, the Ainu, were considered to be of Caucasian origin because of these characteristics. Recent genetic comparisons indicate links with the peoples of Russian Siberia. The Ainu, who led a primitive hunting, fishing existence, nevertheless resisted the intruders ferociously. However, the Japanese, originally settled in the southernmost island, Kyushu, eventually pushed these earlier inhabitants northward. Now only a small Ainu community of around 20,000 remains on the northernmost island, Hokkaido.

Since the early Japanese were not literate and had no historical tradition, there is little reliable information about this early period. When they arrived, and just where they came from, remain conjecture. They were, however, Mongoloid, almost certainly entering Japan from China via the Korean peninsula – although there are also intriguing signs of an ethnic connection with south-east Asia. There are links with Indonesian languages in Japanese, but the most striking resemblance is in the form of the construction of Japan's oldest and most sacred shrine, that at Ise of the sun goddess Amaterasu, the chief deity of the Shinto religion.

For a temple that attracts such veneration the Ise shrine is unassuming – no more than a small wooden hut of post and beam construction holding up a heavy, thatched, single gable, and mounted on about 50 timber piles. The shrine is believed to be an exact copy of the kind of house built by the Japanese when they first came to their islands. Every 21 years it has been pulled down and rebuilt in new, specially selected cypress, so the copy and the original are considered to be identical. It is very similar to buildings still found in parts of south-east Asia, especially in the east Indonesian island of Sulawesi and in Sumatra.

This early Japanese society is called the *yamato*, named for the region inland from the big port city of Osaka on the island of Honshu. However, it probably originated in western Kyushu and then moved gradually north-east around the shores of the Inland Sea. It built large underground tombs in a variety of shapes, in which small terracotta figures called *haniwa* have been found. These figurines indicate that *yamato* warriors used the horse and armour. Their religion, which appears to have postulated gods based on the forces of nature – in particular the sun – came to be known as Shinto, which means 'the way of the gods'.

The earliest contacts with Chinese civilization were hostile. However, trade eventually followed and a pact of friendship was concluded with two Korean states, Paekche and Silla, in the 4th century. There was also considerable migration of whole extended families, and of craftsmen and scholars from war-torn Korea. Their clan loyalties were maintained in the new country and three or four of these families became powerful enough to manipulate the imperial line. Indeed, at least one early emperor may have been Korean. Written records appear only in the 5th century, when Chinese writing came into use, hence the chronicles of earlier times cannot be taken as a reliable record. However, there is little doubt that Koreans, themselves greatly influenced by Chinese culture, were a major factor forming early Japanese society.

The briefest of summaries will serve to indicate all that is of any importance in the area of myth. The goddess Amaterasu emerges as the most important deity and her grandson, Ninigi, is said to have descended from the High Plain of Heaven to rule among men. Ninigi's great-grandson, Jimmu, is revered as the first of a supposedly continuous line of 125 Japanese emperors considered to be of the same semi-divine blood. Hence, while Chinese emperors were mortal and ruled only while they held the mandate of Heaven, Japanese emperors rule by divine right, which they pass on automatically to their descendants. To preserve this continuity, Japanese emperors must be 'above the clouds', aloof from day-to-day politics, on which they accordingly have no influence.

The issue of the divinity of the emperor is not quite as simple as it seems. He is not regarded as a god in the Western sense, so much as a human figure possessing, more than any other person or object, the quality the Japanese call *kami*, the crude meaning of which is elevation or superiority. *Kami* is a spiritual quality which persons and objects – even the islands of Japan – possess in differing amounts. This concept is important because it represents a distinctive quality of the Japanese people – a belief that the main value of the individual is as a unit in the totality of Japan. It came to be expressed in the extraordinary loyalty, often tested to the death, of Japanese retainers to their lords, the willingness of Japanese *kamikaze* pilots to die crashing their bomb-laden aircraft on the decks of American ships during the Second World War and, in more recent times, the almost feudal relationships between the huge Japanese industrial complexes and their workers.

The official Japanese religion, Shinto, is essentially animist, although it has practical characteristics which play a major part in the thought and life of Japan today. One is an insistence on personal cleanliness as the necessary companion of holiness. Worship at a Shinto shrine involves purification in both the physical and spiritual sense. The first is achieved by washing in running water and the second simply by passing under a number of large ceremonial arches called *torii*, which span the paths leading to shrines.

Another manifestation of Shinto that has become part of the Japanese character is a refreshing preference for simplicity and restraint. Its shrines are usually small structures of natural wood, deliberately left unpainted, a key to the Japanese fondness for this material. The deity is represented by a symbol, often a polished bronze mirror but sometimes a sword or the *magatama* jewel, which represent the regalia believed to have been handed to Ninigi by Amaterasu. Only the emperor, certain members of his family or his special emissary may pass the silken curtain over the entrance to the Ise shrine, for its sacred symbols must always be screened from the sight of ordinary men. Some Shinto shrines are not buildings at all. Among them are a waterfall, a rock and a mountain.

The Shinto ideal of simplicity, at the same time shunning the direct, the obvious or ostentatious, is the mainspring of all its forms of art. Where Westerners see beauty in massed displays of flowers, the Japanese purist would admire a single blossom. There are other aspects of Shinto which are not so appealing, such as a disregard for individual life and suffering, and a martial attitude involving great cruelty, much in evidence many times in Japanese history.

Japan is a mountainous country, with few large areas of flat land. Only 13 per cent is arable. Hence from the earliest times a remarkable intensity has had to be applied to cultivating the land, so that the last possible ounce of food can be grown. The traveller through Japan sees at every turn, in the elaborate cultivated terraces on so many hillsides, the results of many generations of devoted labour. Early Japan did not have to face this constraint. It was a simple clan society, still quite small in numbers, when it turned to China for its first civilized model.

Although the first millennium of the Christian era saw most of Europe submerged in the Dark Ages, these were centuries of light in Asia, and nowhere more so than in China. Under the rule of the Sui and Tang dynasties China became the strongest, most populous and advanced society the world had yet seen. However, it would be quite wrong to conclude that the centuries between the decline of the Han and the accession of the Sui were some kind of interregnum – this was a period of tremendous growth both economically and culturally, with strong and in many ways quite different societies developing in the north-west and in the Yangzi valley, and a significant spread of Chinese influence into south-east Asia.

A second major theme was the displacement of Confucianism by a complex amalgam of Buddhism and Daoism. China was to be a Buddhist society for 400 years from the 4th century. It could even be said that a dualism still apparent in China today, evidenced by the resistance of the Falung Gong movement to state suppression, is part of the millennia-long contest between the formal behaviourism of Confucianism and the desire for the mysterious, magical, individual and contemplative so distinctive of the other two great religions. Indeed, it would not be too much to describe this era as 'green' in the contemporary sense, or indeed its poets – like the Seven Sages of the Forest of Bamboo – as 'bohemian' in their aversion to rites, politics and conventions. The world's first landscape painting, more than a thousand years before it evolved in Europe, derived directly from the Daoist view of nature as remarkable, even holy, and a place of liberation of the human spirit.

The centuries of independent states gave place, in 589, to a brief preparatory dynasty, the Sui, which again united China. As with the Qin, Sui achievements were largely due to the qualities of the dynasty's founder, the Emperor Wendi. His successor, Yangdi, laid an important economic foundation for the future by building a huge network of irrigation and transport canals, among them completion of the 1100-mile Grand Canal, linking the Yangzi and Yellow rivers. This, considered by some to have been the largest engineering project in the world at that time, was nevertheless achieved at a huge human cost among the one million peasants conscripted to the work. There was nothing small about this network for waterborne transport, the southern part of which is still in use. The canals were typically over 100 feet wide, with well-constructed highways running alongside them. But Yangdi is perhaps more reasonably criticized for his despatch of huge, disastrous expeditions to fight the expanding Koguryo state in Korea. The emperor was murdered in 618 by his own courtiers, and a general of the north-west command succeeded him, commencing the Tang Dynasty.

Tang saw a pattern of administration in China which endured almost without change into the early 20th century, and in which the system of recruiting the mandarinate through very difficult public examinations became established. China had at various times during her long past experimented with codified law, and was aware of its deficiencies. The alternative was seen as entrusting decisions on legal and administrative matters to a corps of highly qualified, broadly educated men, then controlling them rigorously with a system of inspectorates and by shifting them regularly from one post to another far away. This administrative elite were the mandarins, never numerous for a country of China's size but with immense powers in their regional bailiwicks. The 'law' they administered was based on custom and precedent. Reference to any Chinese dynasty as a government invites misunderstanding. Modern governments exist mainly to make and amend laws. The Chinese dynasties and their bureaucrats maintained law and order but their main purpose otherwise was to raise revenues.

More than ever the art of graceful and elegant writing was required of the scholar-administrator. The chief examination for the *jinshi* degree, which maintained its position into the 20th century, tested administrative ability, but also literary skills – especially the composition of poetry. This tradition has not disappeared. Mao Zedong wrote poetry, as anyone who passed through Beijing airport in the 1970s would know – a translation of his poem 'The Snow' featured prominently on a wall.

Tang was the age of perhaps the best-known Chinese poets. Its two most celebrated, Li Bo and Du Fu, were contemporaries. Du Fu was a scholarly poet, well regarded by the intelligentsia of the time, but the impetuous, rebellious Li Bo has had the greater international appeal over time. A rebel against constituted authority and one who could not be bothered with study, Li Bo was a womanizer and a regular drunk, along with his companions, the Eight Immortals of the Wine-cup. Nevertheless the power and passion of his verse impressed even the emperor, although its Daoist, nature-worshipping philosophy was directly antithetic to the Confucian ideal. Li Bo is said to have drowned when, leaning from a boat, he tried to embrace the reflection of the moon in the Yangzi River.

China again became powerful militarily. All of Tibet, the Tarim River basin, and even parts of Afghanistan, came under Chinese influence. While the Tang army did use conscripted peasant foot soldiers, its cutting edge was the cavalry, very much in the tradition of the steppes, using bowmen who could effectively fire arrows at the full gallop. Even though this expansion of influence was precarious, due to long supply lines and skirmishes with growing Arab power, the overall result was to pacify Central Asia so thoroughly that traders could use the overland routes without undue fear of robberies or delays. This was the heyday of the Silk Road. A steady stream of mule and camel trains carried, among other things, paper, silk, gunpowder, spices, condiments and tea to the West. The journey was a long and perilous one, during which it was necessary to pass the dreaded 1000-mile stretch of the Taklamakan Desert. Without the bad-tempered double-humped Bactrian camel, able to survive without water for two weeks at a time, this trade would scarcely have been possible. Beautifully worked Persian gold and silver, myrrh, precious stones, Turkish carpets and glassware came from the West into China. There were also the beginnings of sea trade, particularly from the southern port of Guangzhou. It was then regarded as uncouth, dangerous and unpleasantly hot, but it was a convenient point of entry into China for Persian ships, also large vessels, as much as 200 feet long, from Sri Lanka. Silk and china were the main exports.

This was a time of major cultural transfer to the Middle East and thence to Europe, both from China and the Buddhist universities in India. This transfer was not only one-way. The capital, Changan, became the principal metropolis in the world of the 8th century, and probably also the most important repository of knowledge. It was certainly the largest, with more than a million inhabitants. There were many libraries in Changan, and there is evidence of a knowledge of, and a lively interest in, other parts of the world and their thought – the cult of Zarathustra from Persia and Nestorian Christianity among them. Neither of these took hold in China but Islam, at the height of its missionary phase, eventually attracted millions of adherents among China's border peoples, many of whom are still Muslims today.

The world's first books were printed, using wooden blocks on which all the characters for a complete page were engraved. The world's oldest known surviving printed book, a copy of the Buddhist Diamond Sutra, discovered in 2004, is dated 864 CE. The Chinese experimented with moveable type in the 11th century, but abandoned it as impractical because of the large number of Chinese characters. (In the Kangxi dictionary of 1716, there are 40,545 characters.) However, the Koreans later persisted with moveable type.

Tang China had its rebels, its eccentrics and its nonconformists, which it was well able to accommodate, but generally it was an orderly, regulated society, based on state control of the economy and good communications. In more ways than one the old China was disappearing. The emphasis was going more and more to the south where the rich ricelands of the Yangzi valley were creating a new prosperity. Although enormous efforts were devoted to building canals and roads to take this new wealth northward, Changan's days were already numbered.

The Chinese belief that it was a religious duty to have many sons provided an almost inexhaustible pool of manpower for public works. Every ten miles along the road system radiating out from Changan, post stations were built, which provided horses and other facilities for couriers of the government.

Intrigue and dissension within the imperial court itself – famously involving a courtesan, Yang Guifei – resulted in a major civil war for eight years from 755, the Rebellion of An Lushan. The Tang state was severely weakened by this conflict, from which it never really recovered. A steady deterioration, associated with an increasing shift of power to regional lords and a weakening of China's foreign policy, ended with the eclipse of the dynasty in 907. The northern 'barbarians' took over much of north China, and in the south former military governors set up their own states. There was a great deal of fighting and rebellion, the ill effects of which were compounded by regional droughts and floods.

During the Tang the very considerable influence of Buddhism on Chinese affairs was forcibly controlled. Early in the dynasty its founder, the Gaozu emperor, issued edicts asserting Confucianism and Daoism as the religions favoured by the state, castigating Buddhism as a foreign religion. Taizong, the second emperor, further regulated the Buddhist establishment, restricting its influences in secular matters. Then in the 9th century the Buddhist establishment, tax-exempt and considered far too wealthy, was systematically dismantled. Thousands of Buddhist monasteries and temples were destroyed, and their enormous assets seized by the state. Millions of acres of land were confiscated and hundreds of thousands of monks and nuns forced to return to the lay community.

Meanwhile, the influence of this large, sophisticated neighbour on Japan had been irresistible. As Chinese culture flourished, the embassies from the *yamato* people became more frequent, in spite of the perils of the journey in the crude punt-like Japanese ships of the time. Many of those who did return brought books, ranging from the Confucian classics to treatises on medicine and history. These were the main avenues through which Chinese culture was transferred to Japan. An additional major influence came from the regular stream of Chinese and Korean migrants to Japan. They were educated and cultured far beyond the Japanese, and were welcomed as associates and advisers to *yamato* chiefs. They were able to teach Japanese leaders how to read and write Chinese, in spite of its difficulty and basic incompatibility with the Japanese language.

Early in the 7th century the governing regent for the empress, Prince Shotoku, encouraged a major Buddhist missionary effort in Japan, and probably asserted the divine origins of the imperial family for the first time. In the year 646, not long after his death, reforms known as the *taika*, or great change, were instituted, on the initiative of an admirer of Tang China, Fujiwara Kamatari. The Fujiwara family was to be of major importance in Japan into modern times. The *taika* reforms were intended to strengthen the imperial government at the expense of the regional clans, through a complex bureaucracy. These reforms closely followed similar changes in China, in which all land was vested in the emperor, reallocated among the peasants, and taxed. These modifications in Japan were carried out and policed by a public service modelled on the mandarinate. The custom of making compulsory military service part of the peasants' tax burden was copied. Since the Japanese army had no external enemy to fight, the conscripts were used as labourers on public works.

Such a project was a capital city, Nara, modelled on Changan. The Empress Genmyo began this work in 694, copying Changan's layout of straight intersecting streets, its styles of architecture and landscape gardening. Tang music was also imported, and while it has disappeared in China, it has been preserved through the centuries in the Japanese Court. Nara was the first big city in Japan even though its ambitious early plans were never completed, and has given its name to the succeeding era of sinification of Japanese society.

The Emperor Shomu devoted his life and much of the energies of his people to good works inspired by Buddhism. Much of these were to the benefit of the community – almshouses, hospitals, wayside halts for travellers, improved roads and bridges. Of less practical value was the building of a 53-foot high, 560-ton statue of the Buddha, the largest bronze statue in the world and still a major tourist attraction in Nara, although it is said to be much altered from the original due to an earthquake, many fires and general neglect during its 1500-year history. A plague of smallpox came to Japan from China that was so severe it inspired the emperor to build the statue in the hope that this would ward off the disease. This work became Shomu's greatest preoccupation, at enormous economic cost to Japan.

At least seven big monasteries grew up in and around Nara. These quickly became centres of considerable influence and wealth. Abbots armed their monks as a means of protecting the monasteries against bandits, but later used these small armies aggressively, even demanding concessions from the emperor. It was probably Buddhist pressure that induced the Emperor Kammu to move to a new capital in 794. At first it was called Heian, meaning peace and prosperity, but was later simply known as the capital – *kyoto* – the name it bears to this day.

The Heian period saw something of an exhaustion of the impetus given to Japanese civilization by China. Regular contacts dwindled with the decline of the Tang Dynasty, and ceased altogether in 894. The spirit of the *taika* reforms had, in fact, vanished much earlier. The bureaucracy suffered from being a slavish copy of the Chinese one, while lacking its traditions. Japan drifted back into feudalism. One by one the provincial governors and other high officials obtained land-tax exemptions and used these to assert greater independence and power, which eventually resulted in a pattern of almost autonomous fiefdoms.

The imperial family now came increasingly under the control of the Fujiwara clan. Henceforward, Fujiwara tactics were to marry regularly into the imperial family, then force abdications in favour of heirs of tender years. This resulted in long periods of Fujiwara regency and the family became the effective rulers of Japan. This control of the nation by one of a number of powerful, competing cliques became characteristic of Japan, and is still manifest in the *ha* – factions – in modern Japan which make up so much of its political establishment.

Although Kyoto continued to be the capital until 1869, from this time on the emperors, with rare exceptions, were little more than prisoners – abstract symbols of inherited *kami* – too holy either to act on their own initiative or to be approached by ordinary men. The aristocracy grouped around the emperor drifted out of touch with the people, and, like the French Court before the revolution, devoted its time and resources almost exclusively to the pursuit of art and manners.

This society is described in clear and penetrating style in a remarkable novel called the *Tale of Genji*, written by the Lady Murasaki Shikibu, who was a resident of the Japanese Court, probably in the early 11th century. She also kept diaries, which add to its portrayal of a shallow, amoral and luxury-loving society, at times capable of considerable artistic expression, but in the main occupied with, or bored by, trifles. The courtiers feared and disliked the crude ways of the rest of the country, and for an official to be sent from the Court to the provinces was regarded as a disgrace and banishment to a virtually insupportable way of life.

However, the reality was that power now increasingly resided in the regions away from Kyoto. New areas of settlement and cultivation were opening up and the great feudal families grew more powerful. Among them were two dominating clans, both offshoots of the imperial line, who involved Japan in her equivalent of the Wars of the Roses. These two families, the Taira and the Minamoto, engaged in a struggle to replace the waning power of the Fujiwara, who had been weakened by internal dissension. At first the Taira had some success but finally their enemy, under the command of Minamoto Yoritomo, was victorious. In 1185 he established a military dictatorship which called itself the *bakufu* – meaning camp government. This regime was based far from Kyoto in the town of Kamakura, not far from the present Tokyo. So Japan was set on a path of feudal militarism that extended through to the 20th century.

The great military clans had been strengthened because of what was regarded as the disgraceful defeat of Japanese armies during a particularly stubborn revolt of the Ainu minority in the 8th century. This defeat, in 790, was the last to be imposed on the Japanese army until the tide turned in the Pacific phase of the Second World War more than 1100 years later. Widespread conscription was introduced to subdue the Ainu, who would never again be a threat to the Japanese. By the middle of the 10th century this military tradition had developed a code in many ways comparable with knighthood during the so-called age of chivalry in Europe. In Japan it was based on a hereditary caste of soldiers, the *samurai*, which was to dominate Japanese society into modern times.

Although the Kamakura period was one of military rule, it had distinguished artistic achievements, especially landscape painting and sculpture, with the first signs of an emerging style significantly different from the Chinese. Typical is a vivid statue of the *kami* of thunder, Rai-Jin, which still stands in Kyoto. It surges with a crude and even a cruel vitality: mouth open in a snarl showing savagely bared teeth; right hand raised ready to strike; staring eyes and bulbous nose.

It was at this stage that the military tradition merged with Buddhism, especially the Zen school with its stress on action and insistence on simplicity. It demands from its adherents a rigid discipline, hardship and great courage. It eschews logic – rather preferring paradoxes – 'What is the sound of one hand clapping?' It is therefore not possible to describe Zen accurately in concepts familiar to Western readers. The discipline, hardship, courage and long periods of calm meditation required of its adherents are designed eventually to create in them an inner experience which is beyond verbal description and which is the spiritual essence of Zen. This inner enlightenment is called *satori*. Nichiren Buddhism also significantly reinforced the militarist tradition, and, like the other popular form of Japanese Buddhism, the True Pure Land, obliged its adherents to little more than perfunctory observances – in the case of the former, granting salvation simply by reciting a set text, the Lotus Sutra.

Japanese architecture developed the simple, sparsely ornamented style that remains typical today. In other arts, notably flower arranging, the formal tea ceremony and garden design, equal restraint came to be practised. One classic garden consists of nothing more than 15 carefully placed stones on an area of raked, white sand.

In time, the spirit of the era seems to have inspired even the imperial family. The Kamakura government was ended in 1333 by the Emperor Go-Daigo. After some misadventures his forces were able to attack and defeat the *bakufu*. After taking, with much ceremony, the traditional small cups of Japanese rice wine, *sake*, the leaders and 1000 followers of the *bakufu* committed ceremonial suicide through the slow and painful process of disembowelling.

Go-Daigo did not, however, rule for long. His own general, Ashikaga Takauji, who had largely been responsible for the campaign against the *bakufu*, usurped power in 1338. A phase of almost constant war followed. The Ashikaga *shoguns*, or regents, were considerable patrons of the arts, but woefully inept at administration. Under their rule, Japanese society dissolved into civil war and banditry. In the 15th century Kyoto was sacked and burned. As almost all its buildings were of wood, much of the capital was destroyed.

During the confusion members of the imperial family had, at times, to beg and sell their calligraphy to stay alive. Two branches competed for the succession. Again there was something of a parallel with Chinese history, as society drifted off into anarchy. It was to wait a century for the strong men who would bring it back to order.

7 The Awakening of Europe and the Challenge of Islam

Medieval Europe still consisted largely of small villages and somewhat larger castle towns, scattered through the forests. To this comparative handful of uneducated people Asia was little more than a legend. While a few scholars were dimly aware that great civilizations flourished there, their concepts were largely of a region of queer, supernatural events, acted out by personalities either grotesque or larger than life.

Such a figure was Presbyter – or more commonly, Prester – John, a Christian monarch believed to govern, somewhere in Asia, an empire of fabulous wealth and power, administered by 72 subject kings. He was supposed to possess magical powers and devices, one of which was a mirror in which he could see events happening anywhere in his realm. It is symptomatic of the state of civilization in Europe that such stories were accepted with apparent credulity, not only by peasants but even by scholars and kings.

Through the first millennium a tenuous link with Asia had been maintained. The Venetian Empire, dominating the Adriatic, became the European terminus of three trade routes: a caravan track east from the Black Sea, an overland and sea route from Damascus, and another route through the Red Sea. Trade with the East was essentially small in bulk, because of the small size and slowness of ships, and because the land routes followed a scattered chain of oases, crossing formidable deserts and regions of predatory tribes. Only expensive luxuries like silk, fine porcelain and spices were worth carrying in these conditions, but there was a steady and lively demand for them that kept the trade alive in spite of all difficulties. Spices, especially pepper, were in high demand in a Europe which had no reliable way of preserving meat, to eliminate traces of tainting during the long winters. Other spices were highly regarded as medicines.

The efficiency of the overland routes depended a great deal on political conditions. They were quickly affected by the advent, early in the 7th century, of a new and militant religion based on one god, Allah. This

Islamic faith took a swift hold in the Middle East. It was still regional at the time of its founder, Muhammad, but grew rapidly under the control of his lifelong friend and supporter Abu Bekr, who became Muhammad's first *caliph*, or successor.

Islam drove eastward through the wandering nomad tribes, gaining adherents rapidly through its uncompromising choice of conversion to the faith or death. It absorbed and adapted the sophisticated Persian Empire and penetrated to the borders of China. To the west it occupied Spain, Portugal and half of France, presenting a ringing challenge and a brilliant civilization that helped to lift Europe from its apathy and ignorance. Trade languished on the land routes; a flourishing sea trade to southern China developed, largely in Arab and Persian ships.

Nevertheless, the new Arab religion was not spread as far as south-east Asia in its original form. It had been adapted and liberalized considerably in Persia (now Iran), before it was spread to northern India and then on to Malaysia and Indonesia by merchants operating through the entrepôt port of Cambay. This is why there are major differences in the modern world among Islamic nations, especially in regard to women. As far east as Pakistan they are discouraged, if not forbidden, to become educated, are generally restricted to their homes, and are forced to wear the *chador*, the ugly and cumbersome all-over robe, if they venture out in public. In Muslim Indonesia and Malaysia women endure no such restrictions. Indeed, the Minangkabauer people of Sumatra are matrilineal, with women substantially controlling families and responsible for their finances and property.

Muslim culture was at its height around the end of the first millennium. It was Islam's capture of Jerusalem in 1076 that drew the European states into the great, if disastrous adventure of the Crusades. However, ultimately it was Mongol hordes that eventually captured the brilliant Muslim metropolis of Baghdad in 1258. The Muslim Dynasty of the Ottoman Turks continued to present an effective block to European sea trade with the east by dominating the eastern Mediterranean and the Red Sea from the 15th century onwards. Indirect access to India and the Spice Islands was still to be had across the land routes, but this was slow and expensive. A sea route, especially one that could be travelled wholly by European ships, was much to be preferred.

In 1453 the Ottoman Turks captured and used for their capital Constantinople (now Istanbul), until that date the seat of the later, truncated Roman empire. For 50 years afterwards the Turks made concessions to one Italian state, Venice, which allowed her a virtual monopoly of the Asian trade. The merchants of Venice waxed rich, so giving the other states of Europe an even greater incentive to break this monopoly. This anti-Venetian, anti-Muslim drive, combined with a half-religious, half-commercial ambition to make contact with the empire of Prester John, induced a lifelong effort in a Portuguese prince, Henry the Navigator, to seek a sea route east via the west coast of Africa.

Henry encouraged marine studies at Sagres, in the south-west corner of Portugal, where the half-forgotten maps, sailing directions and methods of navigation of the past were carefully re-examined. Portuguese shipmasters pored over the *Guide to Geography* prepared by the Alexandrian Ptolemy in the 2nd century. Henry was assisted by the Genoese, anxious to supplant Venice.

The wooden ships, often as small as 40 tons and tragically unwieldy and top-heavy, edged their way down the stormy lee-shore of Africa. Many were lost, but the hard experience bought with the lives of ships and men led to important advances in naval architecture. A lighter, faster vessel named the caravel, and bigger designs – the armed carrack and later the galleon – were evolved and, in spite of their clumsiness, were able to survive the Atlantic storms. These larger ships also made trade in bulk commodities, rather than lightweight luxuries, feasible for the first time.

In 1487 Bartholomew Diaz reached and rounded the southern extremity of Africa – the Cape of Storms. With much rejoicing, it was renamed the Cape of Good Hope. In 1498 Vasco da Gama reached India, and the eagerly sought sea route to the east lay open. Portugal lost no time in exploiting it, despatching six expeditions between 1501 and 1505. The largest of these consisted of 20 ships manned by 2500 men, led by the first Viceroy of the East, Francisco d'Almeida. Efforts were made to drive away the interlopers, but the Portuguese won a major naval battle off the north-west Indian port of Diu in 1509. The following year the Portuguese established their base at Goa, and armed it as a fortress.

European infiltration of Asia had begun, and with it a new era. Profits on the early expeditions were so great that the share of the lowliest crew member could amount to a small fortune. A small consignment of spices brought home by Vasco da Gama in 1499 paid for the entire cost of the expedition several times over.

Other European nations were also resolved to seek adventure and fortune in the East. The dawn of the year 1520 saw the three small top-heavy ships commanded by Ferdinand Magellan four months and thousands of miles out from their home port of Seville. Sailing west, he made landfalls in the Philippines in March, and more than two years later one ship, *Vittoria*, reached home to become the first to sail around the world. By the end of the century a Spanish colony based on Manila in the Philippines was firmly established.

The Tudor monarchs of England built on the maritime tradition created by centuries of fishing in the stormy North Sea. Henry VIII brought in

Italians to advise on the design of ocean-going ships, and offered a cash bounty to subsidize the building of new merchantmen. When Francis Drake returned in 1580 from his voyage around the world he brought a package of cloves acquired at Ternate in the Malukus, then known as the Spice Islands. On the last day of 1600 the East India Company was founded, with a Royal Charter giving it the monopoly of trade with the East. Holland was next in the field. In 1602 she formed her own East India Company, with the then immense capital of more than £500,000. In 1619 the Dutch established a base at a fortified village in Java called Djakarta. They renamed it Batavia.

The geographic advantage of the Atlantic nations over those of the Mediterranean, especially Venice, was to set the pattern for the colonial era. One of the great 'might-have-beens' of history was the failure to bring to fruition the 1504 consideration by the Venetian Council of Ten for a Suez Canal. If the canal could have been built then, instead of 300 years later, Asia's major relationship with Europe would have been much earlier, and perhaps on more equal terms.

This period of exploration and trade expansion also brought the first crude enquiry into, and speculation about, economic forces. The earliest theorists, who maintained a persistent although diminishing influence for several centuries, were called the bullionists. They believed the prosperity of a nation was related to the amount of gold and silver bullion it was able to hoard. A further step was taken by the mercantilists, who held that this desirable accretion of bullion could best be achieved by having a favourable balance of trade with as many outside areas as possible – in other words, to take out more than was put in. One of the more profitable areas of commerce was the slave trade – around eight million forcibly seized and sent to America alone, plus perhaps two million more who died during transportation in appalling conditions in the slave ships. Exploitation of other races soon found philosophic rationalization, notably from the 18th-century Swedish botanist Carolus Linnaeus. Linnaeus, who was highly regarded in Europe, firmly asserted the biological superiority of the white races, and this was at times used to justify the atrocities to come.

Mercantilism was the justification for a policy followed into modern times, which assumed colonies to be chiefly valuable as places perpetually milked of their wealth to the benefit of the conquering country. Autocratic political control, backed by armed force, was used to make sure the system was maintained. This, among other things, led to the Boston Tea Party and the loss of Britain's American colonies. Its effects in Asia were, ultimately, to be no less profound.

8 Flood Tide in China: the Song, Mongol and Ming Dynasties

In 1206 a central Asian people, the Mongols, gathered in conference and elected a new leader, Genghis Khan. The choice was a prudent one, since this man already had a high reputation as a military strategist among a people notorious for their ability and ruthlessness in war. Under the leadership of Genghis Khan and his successors the Mongols built up the largest empire the world had yet seen, occupying the greater part of the Eurasian land mass. The Chinese section of this vast empire was ruled directly by the Great Khans, Genghis himself, and his successors. Regions farther west were virtually autonomous, but their rulers owed a token allegiance to the Great Khan.

The most detailed account of the Mongol Empire comes from the Venetian adventurer Marco Polo, who claimed to be in the service of the Great Khan, at that time Kublai. Marco Polo's view of the Great Khan and his empire is always favourable and often sycophantic. This is not surprising, since he was Kublai's employee. He often exaggerates, his sense of geography is vague, and most deceptive of all, he attributes to Kublai a huge and sophisticated civilization which was really the creation of the previous Chinese government.

The Mongol subjugation of China, then ruled by the cultured, refined and broad-minded Song emperors, must be recognized as one of the major events of history. Although at the time of the conquest Song China occupied only the southern half of the country, the population under its rule had already passed the hundred million mark, making it the largest nation in the world.

The simple fact of the conquest in 1279, 44 years after the initial invasion and after three years of bitter fighting was, then, a resounding event in world terms, yet it was even more so in its implications for China's future. From this time onwards China was to diverge increasingly from the ideal culture it so much admired and which the Song so closely approached. There was to be only one more native dynasty, the Ming, but powerful though it was, it became bigoted, inward-looking and conservative. In the Mongol conquest, then, was the seed of the great Chinese disasters of the 19th and 20th centuries.

A brief period of warlordism in north China followed the demise of the Tang early in the 10th century. There was a great deal of warfare and destruction, but the learning and traditions of China were preserved in the more peaceful south, especially in the Southern Tang and the Southern Han, states founded by Tang provincial governors who took control as the central authority declined. This considerable autonomy of provincial governments, something of a constant in Chinese history, is still in evidence today.

In 960 another general was acclaimed emperor, but this time the founder, Zhao Kuangyin, was so able a negotiator that he persuaded the regional military governors to become part of a united China. The Song state he founded was not only more lasting than its predecessors, but also went on to an extraordinary brilliance for the world of its time. Chinese manufacture, especially the fine porcelain that came to be known as china, was in demand throughout the world and commanded an immense export trade by the standards of the time. Guangzhou became one of the world's biggest ports.

Book printing had become commonplace and many private citizens had libraries, centuries before the production of the Gutenberg Bible, Europe's first-known printed book, in 1456. Chinese printing used engraved woodblocks – by the 11th century works employing more than 100,000 of these were printed. Seventeenth-century Western observers noted that Chinese engravers could complete a page as quickly as a European typographer could handset it with moveable type. The woodblock system also had the advantage that illustrations could be fashioned into the same page. This was done to very good effect and eventually printing in four or five colours was developed.

This ability to reproduce both words and pictures relatively quickly and cheaply gave a tremendous impetus to the arts, especially painting and letters. The works of more than 1000 Song poets are known. Printing was used extensively for pamphlets on all sorts of subjects, and to produce paper money. Iron and bronze moveable type, invented by Pi Cheng in the 11th century, was used in China to some extent in the 14th century, but eventually was recognized as impracticable because of the large number of Chinese characters.

The world's appreciation of its debt to Song China is still increasing. There is, for instance, no known European record of the supernova explosion of 1054 that resulted in the Crab Nebula, even though the star grew so bright it could easily be seen in daylight. Yet, according to the British astronomer Fred Hoyle, modern science is much indebted to the careful records the astronomers of Song China made of this event. Sunspots, studied by Europeans for the first time in 1610, had been observed and recorded in the Chinese annals

59 times during the previous 1500 years. This has made it possible for modern astronomers to calculate the solar activity cycle during that time.

Song China pioneered many features of modern economies, using paper money, cheques, promissory notes and credit banking to facilitate intercity trade. It developed inoculation against smallpox, maintained street lighting, street cleaning, sanitary and fire protection services in the cities; provided hospitals, almshouses, orphanages and homes for the aged which were financed by trusts to ensure inalienable income; and encompassed a remarkable number of inventions ranging from hand grenades and repeating crossbows to hydraulic machinery in the world's biggest ironworks.

Major textbooks covered almost all areas of science – architecture, mathematics, geography, medicine and horticulture. There was a specialist book on growing citrus fruit and in 1242 the world's first-known book on forensic medicine was published. The so-called 'arabic' system of ten-digit numbering was used in China at about the same time as it appeared among the Arabs, prompting speculation that it originated somewhere in Indo-China. There was an enthusiastic science of archaeology researching earlier Chinese coins, ceramics and bronzes. The huge library at the Imperial palace housed four celebrated works – a literary anthology going back four centuries, a thousand-chapter encyclopaedia, a vast collection of strange stories and fables, and a massive anthology of political texts and essays.

The system of recruiting the mandarinate by public examinations became fully developed, so attempting an aristocracy of intelligence rather than of family and wealth. The fact that the ability of aspiring officials to paint and write poetry was tested has often been misunderstood. The examinations were primarily for administrative ability, but the mandarins were expected to be 'complete men' – accomplished in every way.

The lightly ornamented and simply styled porcelain, such as its green celadon, the delicate painting and understated poetry of the Song have in the past been dismissed as 'primitive' by earlier Western critics, bred to the florid Victorian taste. It is only the modern West that has recognized in Song art a sophistication it has itself approached.

One of the more eminent scholar-magistrates of the period, Su Dongpo, embittered by a series of reverses in his career, wrote this upon the birth of a son:

> Families, having a child, ask that it be intelligent.
> But I, through intelligence have destroyed my whole life.
> So I only hope the baby will turn out ignorant and stupid,
> Then end a peaceful life as a Cabinet Minister.

The powerhouses of Song society were its intensive and highly organized agriculture and manufacture, producing silk, ceramics, huge quantities of iron, tea, alcohol, printed books, paper and lacquer goods, among many other things. Rice yields were greatly increased by the technique of planting out seedlings and the selective breeding of higher-yield varieties. These basics created the great cities, some of more than a million people, along the rivers, canals and seacoast, and the world's largest merchant navy. Chinese ships had up to five masts, drop-keels, balanced stern rudders and watertight compartments, and could carry up to 1000 people. The Chinese 'fore and aft' junk rig and the stern-hung rudder made these ships not only much easier to sail but also more able to sail reasonably well into the wind. Experiments in other forms of boats, especially for inland waters, were various, and included crank-operated paddle wheels. Some had up to 25 such cranks, linked by metal connecting-rods. Accurate maps and charts listed depth soundings.

The cities provided every form of pleasure and indulgence, with playhouses, shadow theatres, acrobatic and performing monkey shows, wine shops, gaming houses, and brothels open until dawn. Viewing the first plum blossoms, by the light of a spring moon, over snowfields, was a popular cult – indeed, Song poets and painters were virtually obsessed by the purity and simplicity of these flowers.

Zhang Zhi, a rich dilettante of the time, set out a list of what did and did not accord with plum blossoms. Strong wind, continuous rain, hot sun, bad poetry, gossip about current events, discussing financial matters and erecting purple screens opposite the flowers, were no-nos. The list of things that accorded with plum blossoms included gentle shade, fine mist, early-morning sun, making tea, and playing chess on a stone board (according to Maggie Bickford, in an article in *Orientations*).

The decline of Buddhism was followed by a renewed interest in Confucianism. This neo-Confucianism, which placed great stress on order in society, set rigid patterns that persisted through to the 20th century. Although it was designed to assert Confucianism as an ethic supplanting Buddhism and Daoism, in many respects it turned out to be a synthesis of all three. The new system was certainly far removed from the thought of its nominal founder. Indeed, Confucius himself was virtually deified. To him, as well as to the sun and the moon, the second-grade or 'middle' sacrifices were made.

However, Confucianism remained based on ancestor worship and the cult of the family. While having religious aspects, its main effects were ethical and conservative. This respect for established rites and definitions of conduct led eventually to the narrowness of the official mind and disinclination for change so much responsible for the Chinese disasters of the 19th century. All this applied more to the official class than the ordinary people – Buddhist influences persisted among them into Song times, and

undoubtedly contributed much towards the liberality and broadminded-
ness of the dynasty.

The Song state had a great deal of trouble with its army, in spite of spending vast sums on it. Soldiering was not highly regarded as a profession –
'Good iron is not made into nails nor good men into soldiers'. During the
period between the collapse of the Tang and the rise of the Song China had
suffered greatly from the depredations of warlords and the mandarins were
concerned to keep the military in its place. The army had become more used
to plundering than to battle. It lacked cavalry, and did not have the fine edge,
good organization and utter disregard for human life of the Mongols.

Mongol methods were total war to a degree seldom equalled before or
since. When they conquered the northern state of Jin, an event which had
already forced the Song to retreat to the south, they virtually depopulated
it. Its capital, Beijing, was almost wiped out, then burned. The Mongol
troops were under orders to exterminate the population of cities that
offered the slightest resistance and the fate of some of China's north-west
cities was a terrifying example. Some of these have never again been populated, remaining desolate to this day. It is not surprising that the southern
Song capital, Hangzhou, surrendered in 1276.

The populous and wealthy world of China presented an extreme
contrast to the Mongols. They were largely illiterate and poor, and
numbered perhaps three million. The victory brought into the conquerors'
service some shrewd and able public servants, who were able to convince
the Mongols they would be better off to maintain Chinese society as it was,
and profit from taxing it. Not only was Chinese culture largely preserved, it
was able to exert an influence on the Mongols that refined and educated at
least some of them. The great Mongol leader so admired by Marco Polo,
Kublai Khan, was sinified in this way and developed a liberality and interest
in Chinese art and culture that would have amazed his forebears.

The Mongols, who assumed the dynastic title of the Yuan, built a new,
Chinese-style capital in inner Mongolia called Shangdu – the city which
became known to the West as Xanadu. Thus the conquerors, although they
strove to retain their own identity, were largely absorbed by the conquered.
Chinese ways spread outside China itself and became fashionable in other
parts of the Mongol Empire. The military discipline initially imposed by the
conquerors even allowed China to grow physically. What is now Yunnan
Province was a separate kingdom called Nanzhao until 1253, when its Thai
people were driven south into the valleys of Laos and other parts of mainland south-east Asia.

As the Mongol empire drove deep into eastern Europe, it seems likely
that knowledge of Chinese technology carried west in this way influenced

the European Renaissance. Certainly Chinese technicians and soldiers were part of the Mongol armies – the army that besieged Baghdad in 1258 was commanded by a Chinese general. Such things as the stern-hung rudder, the wheelbarrow, the marine compass and gunpowder first appeared in Europe late in the 13th century, and the first paper was made then in Italy.

Kublai was unable to invade Japan in spite of two great expeditions he sent against those islands in 1274 and 1281. Seasonal typhoons scattered his fleet, with heavy losses. This great wind, or *kamikaze*, was regarded by the Japanese as divine intervention. In 1945, as Allied ships closed in on the Japanese islands, the same name was used for suicide aircraft that were deliberately crashed on the decks of warships.

By the early 14th century Mongol rule had already begun to weaken, its parasitic nature increasingly obvious after the death of Kublai in 1294. Mongol leaders had a curious and enthusiastic preoccupation with mystic and at times obscene aspects of Tibetan Buddhism. Tibetan lamas became influential at the Chinese court, and were able to obtain huge endowments which contributed greatly to the size and wealth of their monasteries. The Tibetans had escaped mass destruction and murder by willingly accepting Mongol suzerainty. Chinese control of Tibet continued under the Manchus from 1706 until the fall of the dynasty in 1912.

In 1333 a series of unusually severe famines began and persisted for a decade. The reserve granaries were soon exhausted. Then in 1351 the Yellow River burst its levees, bearing thousands of acres of productive farmland down to the sea and destroying hundreds of villages. By 1356 paper money had become valueless and the printing of it was discontinued. The population fell, to perhaps 80 million.

The Mongol Dynasty had by then become decadent, with frequent disputes over the imperial succession, and a warlord phase began in which district governors asserted their independence. Pressure on the peasantry became extreme, and prompted widespread rioting and rebellion. These became almost general under the leadership of a secret society called the Red Turbans from about 1350 onwards, and led to the eventual overthrow of the Mongols and their expulsion from China. Some of these mass movements, which were strongly influenced by *theravada* Buddhism, agitated for a revival of the Song Dynasty.

From early times the peasant revolt had been China's natural answer to tyrannical or inefficient government and also, grimly enough, to pressures of population. Overpopulation, combined with the failure of the central government, resulted in famine. This in turn led to insurrection. As society became further disorganized, the population was hugely reduced by starvation, massacre and sickness. When stability was resumed under a new regime the cycle recommenced.

When the Chinese peasants were pressed hard enough to revolt, they organized within mutual assistance societies, which remained dormant for many decades or even centuries, only to become active when circumstances demanded. These societies were so firmly based that even the mandarins hesitated to tamper with them. The oldest and most famous of the secret societies organizing the peasants, the White Lotus, appears to have played a consolidating role in the peasant revolts that ousted the Mongols.

The main impetus of revolt came from the south. Here Zhu Yuanzhang, who would soon drive the Mongols out of China, began his career. He was an orphan of humble origins, later to become a Buddhist monk, who rose to command a rebel group through sheer force of personality, ability in the art of intrigue, and the support of the Red Turbans. He concentrated on consolidating a significant area of power around the strategic Yangzi River city of Nanjing, which he occupied in 1356. Twelve years later, when he dominated south China, he sent a huge army north to Beijing. The Mongols fled before it without a fight. They had controlled China for barely 70 years; their successors would endure for almost three centuries.

The humble peasant-adventurer now became emperor, giving himself the reign name of Hongwu, which means 'vast military achievement'. The dynasty he commenced in 1368 he called the Ming, which could be translated as 'brilliance'. As might have been expected from the nature of his origins and career, Hongwu's authority was direct, brutal and decisive. He is said to have had a highly suspicious nature and a furious temper, imposing the death penalty more or less on whim. Although an able administrator, Hongwu refused to have a prime minister, and when fair-minded mandarins with a sense of duty ventured to remonstrate with him he had them beaten with bamboo clubs, often to death. This set a pattern of authoritarian government for the future, in contrast with the consensus politics of the Song.

Parallels can be drawn between the first decades of the Ming and those of the present Communist government in China. Both faced the need to restore a complex agricultural system almost in ruins, both used a ruthless authority to get the necessary work done, and both required the people to plant vast numbers of trees, estimated at around a billion by some authorities. With an eye to restoring the maritime tradition of the Song, Hongwu ordered the planting of at least 50 million of these trees for timber to build ships.

Hongwu remained faithful to Nanjing, which now became the capital. After his death the throne was inherited by his 16-year-old grandson, who was immediately challenged by his uncle, the Prince of Yan, a warlord based in Beijing and responsible for guarding the northern borders. He took Nanjing in 1402, becoming emperor under the reign name of Yongle. Nineteen years later he built a new capital at Beijing – the Forbidden City – which, then on the edge of China, had a vulnerability that would ultimately prove dangerous and, finally, fatal to the dynasty. The new structure was an enormous cost simply in terms of building materials and labour. Beyond that, siting the capital at Beijing not only placed it close to marauding tribesmen on the other side of the Great Wall, but also involved a huge cost in maintaining roads and canals to the south, including major repairs and extensions to the Grand Canal. Finally, it tended to encourage the persistent southern tendency towards autonomy.

In his 2002 book 1421 – *The Year China Discovered the World*, Gavin Menzies describes the sumptuous banquet for the inauguration of the new capital as indicative of

> China's position at the summit of the civilized world. In comparison Europe was backward, crude and barbaric. Henry V's marriage to Catherine of Valois took place in London just three weeks after the inauguration of the Forbidden City. Twenty-six thousand guests were entertained at Beijing, where they ate a ten-course banquet served on dishes of finest porcelain; a mere six hundred guests attended Henry's nuptials, and they were served stockfish (salted cod) on rounds of stale bread that acted as plates. ... China's army numbered one million men, armed with guns; Henry V could put five thousand men in the field, armed only with longbows, swords and pikes.

Yongle had indeed inherited vast power – the empire was now larger and more populous than the whole of Europe, and its wealth and resources far greater. Even though she had diverged from her ideal of government China was now at the pinnacle of her material power. In no way is this more forcibly indicated than by the great sea expeditions sent out during the Yongle reign, and commanded by Admiral Zheng He. Chinese records assert that the biggest ships, largely modelled on the Song fleet, were over 400 feet long and 150 feet wide – this would make them the largest wooden ships ever built in the world. They were equipped to stay at sea for many months. The Chinese already knew about the dangers of scurvy, and carried large quantities of citrus fruit in the ships to protect the crews. Otters specially trained to herd fish into nets were carried and used to provide fresh food supplies; desalination units were installed to distil seawater.

Chinese ships ranged throughout Asia – indeed as far afield as East Africa – and by the end of the first quarter of the 15th century had brought home token fealty and tribute from scores of Asian principalities. According to

Chinese records a live giraffe from Africa was brought to Beijing, and presented to the emperor.

A significant comparison can be made between Chinese sea power and the Portuguese fleet that took d'Almeida to India in 1505. With its 20 ships and 2500 men it was the largest yet to sail to Asia from Europe. Exactly a century before, in 1405, the Ming Empire sent its first fleet to India. It consisted of 62 ships and nearly 30,000 men, and was only the first of seven such expeditions. The total Ming fleet is said to have been close on 4000 ships, at least 400 of them larger warships. The next most powerful fleet in the world then, according to Menzies, was that of Venice, which could muster 300 lightly built galleys propelled by oars and quite unsuitable for other than coastal voyaging.

It is interesting to speculate on the possible shape of events had the ships of Europe, coming to Asia a century later, found it already controlled by a Chinese navy, policing a Chinese maritime empire. Looked at in this way, the cessation of China's great sea expeditions in 1433 becomes a fact of major importance in European as well as Asian history. Yongle had all the means at his disposal to dominate the world and lay the foundations of an immense empire except the will to do so. He used his great fleets casually, almost as toys. He looked, always with anxiety, to the north. The thought of permanent dominion in south and south-east Asia seems never to have crossed his mind.

The Chinese felt that in their world they had achieved perfection and came to regard all other nations with a casual arrogance and suspicion as 'barbarians'. The term *Zhongguo* – 'Middle Kingdom' – for so long used by the Chinese as the name of their country, took on new overtones as they increasingly saw it as the centre of the world, with tributary nations arrayed around it. After 1430 Chinese were forbidden to leave the country without special licences. In the 16th century the harbingers of future trouble came with a revival of Mongol unity under a strong leader, Altan Khan, who mounted devastating raids into the Beijing region in 1550. A peace treaty was agreed with China in 1570, but the northern threat remained.

In 1514 the first Portuguese ships arrived in China. Early encounters were often unfortunate, since the Portuguese almost always mixed trade with piracy, confirming Chinese suspicion of Europeans generally. When a trading post was set up at Macao in 1557 it was carefully policed by the Chinese, and Europeans were restricted to their remote base on an isolated southern peninsula. Nevertheless there were exceptions, notably Jesuit intellectuals like Matteo Ricci, who lived in China for long periods, and whose writings provided the first significant cultural and technical interchange with Europe. The development on the windswept Dutch beaches in the 17th century of land yachts – then the fastest transport vehicles in the world by far – is said to have been inspired by the Chinese custom of attaching sails to wheelbarrows.

Land contact with Europe came from the north-west, as the Muscovite Ivan IV drove east from the Volga marshes, then the border of Russia. Within one more century Russian expansionism had given China a new and troublesome neighbour and border disputes that would persist into modern times.

Whatever the shortcomings of the Ming, they presided over a vast, intensely productive state. Its major catastrophe was what is considered the world's worst earthquake in 1556, which killed an estimated 830,000 people. Much of the antiquities the tourist to China sees today are of Ming provenance, including the dynasty's subterranean tombs on the outskirts of Beijing and most of the present fabric of the Great Wall.

The Ming Dynasty did not show serious signs of weakness until the reigns of the last four emperors, entering its phase of most rapid deterioration between 1620 and 1627, when the Tianqi emperor reigned. He was only 15 when he came to the throne and was dominated by a predatory official, Wei Zhongxian, who used his power to enrich himself and strike down any honest or courageous official who sought to oppose him. The architects of the Ming demise were a formidable army of eunuchs, probably as many as 70,000 of them towards the dynasty's end. Presiding over the elaborate and ritualized life of the court, they used their position to accumulate wealth and power at any cost, including mass murder of their opponents, intimidation and at times covert assassination of emperors.

When the last Ming, the Chongzhen emperor, came to the throne in 1628 he made a final desperate effort to reorganize the government, but matters had gone too far for reform. The competent and honest men had already been destroyed and the pervading selfish and cynical factionalism had eroded the dynasty of support. The Little Ice Age, which caused recession and starvation throughout the world, also had severe effects in China, and is regarded by some scholars as a factor in the Ming decline. Very cold weather and severe droughts during the first half of the 17th century caused such severe hardship that the population may actually have declined.

Away from the intrigues of Beijing, the people suffered from a breakdown in administration, an increase in taxes, and tyranny from officials that set an ugly pattern for the future. Already the peasants were in revolt. When one of their popular leaders seized the capital in 1644 the emperor, in despair, could see no possible course except death. He hanged himself, from a branch of a tree, outside a graceful triple-tiered pavilion that still stands on Beijing's Coal Hill.

9 China: Ebb Tide

Power to replace the Ming was already waiting – to the north, as Yongle had feared. In 1583 a gifted leader called Nurhacu had persuaded a group of nomad tribes to unite in a largely military union, the Manchu confederacy. When in 1644 Beijing fell to Chinese warlord Li Zicheng, one of many who exploited and exacerbated the prevailing social disorder and poverty, the Manchus took advantage of a last desperate struggle between Li and the Ming loyalists to invade China unopposed. When they entered Beijing with the support of the Ming generals they at first insisted they were only there to support the lawful authority, but when a Ming prince was proclaimed in Nanjing they made war on him and proclaimed their own child emperor ruler of China. Seventeen years later the Ming prince was forced into exile in Burma but the Manchu agents, fully aware of the dangers of a living Ming pretender, pursued him even there and killed him by strangling with a bowstring.

Manchu rule was not easily imposed in the south, and never really accepted there. For many years, indeed, through the two and a half centuries of Manchu rule, there continued to be a persistent but small minority that affected to champion the Ming cause. Even today the slogan 'restore the Ming, supplant the Qing' (Manchu) remains in the rituals of Chinese secret societies in Singapore. It is said that one of the first actions of Dr Sun Yat-sen, after the foundation of the Chinese republic at the end of Manchu rule in 1911, was to pray at the Ming imperial tombs.

The Manchus never allowed the Chinese to forget they were a conquered people. They required all men to shave the forepart of their heads and wear their hair in a queue – perhaps better known as a pigtail – as a sign of subjection. Manchus were not allowed to work except as civil servants and soldiers and the Chinese people had to feed this large, non-productive group, located in all cities and large towns. They were forbidden to intermarry with Chinese and the original Manchu capital at Mukden was maintained.

In spite of these precautions Manchu had by the 19th century become little more than a court language and the invaders essentially sinified. The Chinese had again demonstrated their remarkable ability to assimilate a conqueror. This cultural merging was already evident at the end of the reign of the second emperor, Kangxi, in 1722. A poet and a scholar with a deep interest in all aspects of knowledge, Kangxi encouraged Christian Jesuit missionaries to live in China. Many of them stayed for years, even taking Chinese names, protected by the respect the emperor had for their knowledge and his gratitude, for the Jesuits had cured him of malaria by using cinchona bark (quinine) their order had supplied from South America. Nevertheless, when the Jesuits took exception to established Chinese rites, the emperor discouraged Christian missionary activity, which had virtually ceased by the early 19th century.

In many respects the Manchu centuries can be regarded socially and culturally as an extension of the Ming. Nevertheless China expanded to its largest territorial extent in the 18th century, with the conquest of much of Xinjiang Province and renewed suzerainty over Korea and much of Vietnam – 13 million square kilometres, compared with the 10 million of today's China. The Kangxi emperor's interest in European art and science was reciprocated in Europe, where many cultural and artistic forms went through a phase of *chinoiserie*, an interest in and copying of things Chinese.

Chinese concern about civil war in Tibet led to an invasion in 1720, the inception of a Chinese nominee as Dalai Lama and the establishment of garrisons and a residency. By that time Tibet had ceased to be the ruthless military state which, in the 7th century, had controlled an empire extending at times through much of central Asia into northern Burma and northern India. Its martial tendencies were to some extent tempered by the advent of Buddhism which, with the much older animist *Bon*, remains the basis of Tibetan religion. Nevertheless, for almost a thousand years, with brief interludes of unity, Tibet was torn by internal dissension. A particularly bitter phase of civil conflict early in the 18th century prompted the Kangxi emperor to intervene.

Although in some respects a reformer, Kangxi maintained the civil service examinations, now becoming increasingly formalized, and fully supported the Confucian ethic. To all outward appearances prosperity and order continued to be maintained during the rule of his grandson, who took the reign name of Qianlong. During his 60-year reign China showed little sign of the collapse so close ahead. The dynasty was now, for all practical purposes, Chinese. Qianlong took pride in his support for the Chinese arts, especially poetry, painting and calligraphy. He has left no fewer than 40,000 short poems of his own composition, and was a skilled horseman and archer.

Big improvements in agriculture and huge exports of ceramics, tea, textiles and lacquerware made Chinese society stable and prosperous – even affluent – during the 18th century. Only in its last decades did the processes of decay become apparent. China was undergoing tremendous changes. The most significant was the huge growth rate of the population, which had reached 320 million by 1800 – almost twice that of Europe. Populations were growing all over the world, but in the West the challenge was met by a ferment of experiment and the rapid development of new skills and technology. The Chinese government, however, was chained by an arid conservatism. Faced with the great swirl of forces for change, only dimly recognized and undoubtedly feared, it looked steadfastly to the past and resisted any attempts at innovation.

A most serious consequence was the failure to further improve agricultural methods. Overcrowding led to intensive cultivation of land until it became exhausted and would no longer bear crops. New land was often destroyed by erosion almost as soon as it was cleared. The Chinese were banned from the underpopulated grasslands of Manchuria because these had to be preserved as the Manchu homeland.

The mandarinate also deteriorated, and was now far from its ideal of broad-minded, educated men administering wisely and with moderation. Instead, arrayed in their robes of office, the mandarins travelled their domains in golden palanquins, escorted by men with whips who lashed out at any who obstructed the way or who failed promptly to grovel in obeisance. Unusual and cruel punishments became common, and were administered for trifling reasons. Death was not enough. Men were whipped on the soles of their feet until gangrene set in, or their heads confined in the cangue, a heavy wooden square which made it impossible for them to feed or care for themselves, then left to die slowly and painfully.

Manchu suspicion of the south led the government to forbid foreign trade except from Guangzhou, which was badly located in relation to the sources of the main export products, tea and silk. The administration became increasingly lazy and effete. Pirates ravaged the coast, but little was done to control them. When Qianlong died in 1799 his favourite, Heshen, was impeached on charges of amassing a huge fortune looted from the administration, and forced to commit suicide.

Yet all these abuses, all the clamouring social and economic problems, did not lead to reform and correction, but rather to an even more repressive conservatism. Poverty grew year by year as the population rose, and famines of alarming proportions developed from quite mild seasonal variations. Rural poverty gradually deteriorated to its full horrors – the exposure of newborn girl babies in the fields at night to die, the selling of children into slavery, the growing rapacity of officials and landlords, themselves struggling on the edge of the abyss. In 1795 poverty was so acute in Shanxi, Hubei and Sichuan Provinces that the White Lotus Society raised a major peasant revolt that was not to be controlled for nine years. Two desperate attempts were made on the life of the emperor, in 1812 and again in 1814, which led to harsh reprisals.

China was not to be at peace for a century and a half. Bandits and Manchu armies under the control of warlords marched through the unhappy countryside, raiding and destroying crops, burning villages, pressing conscripts into their service. So the largest country in the world, the society that had prided itself on its superiority and civilization, plunged into a trough. There had been such troughs before, but never with the same implications, for this one coincided with the reaching of the despised European 'barbarians' for the crest of the wave.

> Therefore, O king, as regards your request to send someone to remain at the capital, while it is not in harmony with the regulations of the Celestial Empire, we also feel very much that it is of no advantage to your country. Hence ... we have commanded your tribute envoys to return safely home. You, O king, should simply act in conformity with our wishes, by strengthening your loyalty and swearing perpetual obedience.

In these words Qianlong addressed the choleric George III of England when, in 1793, the British government sent its first official mission to China to establish a resident at the Manchu court. The fiction that all foreign representatives came as bearers of tribute and fealty was maintained throughout this period of early contact with the West. Moreover, China could speak from the complacency of self-sufficiency. There was nothing she wanted from the outside world. A decision was taken to cease trade with foreigners altogether.

Britain, however, was anxious to trade more extensively, especially to sell opium in China, and pressures grew rapidly after abolition of the East India Company's monopoly in 1833 brought spirited competition between a dozen companies for the lucrative return trade in tea. This inevitably brought the two nations on a collision course. The Chinese government had become concerned at the swift growth of the opium habit, especially when it began to drain silver – the effective Chinese currency at this time – out of the country. The trade had been declared illegal in 1729 and imports forbidden in 1800, but it continued to flourish nevertheless. In 1838 Beijing had sent a mandarin, Lin Zexu, as special commissioner to end the import of opium through Guangzhou, which was still the only port foreigners were allowed to use. In that year opium imports had reached the massive total of more than 2000 tons a year, and the number of habitual users has been estimated as high as ten million. The fact that many of these were soldiers and officials increased the unease of the Chinese government.

Specially built, fast ships, clippers like *Thermopylae*, *Nightingale* and *Cutty Sark*, raced from China to London at speeds as high as 18 knots. Since these ships were built for speed rather than large cargo capacity, they required a commodity they could carry economically on the outward- as well as homeward-bound passages. Opium, with its high value for its weight and ready demand in China, suited this specification and was specially grown in India for the Chinese trade.

Commissioner Lin attempted negotiation to control the trade. He even wrote to Queen Victoria, saying, 'if there were people from another country who carried opium for sale to England and seduced your people into buying and smoking it, certainly you would deeply hate it and be bitterly aroused'. There being no response, Lin demanded the surrender of all opium stocks held in Guangzhou. In June 1840, a British naval squadron silenced the Chinese batteries protecting the mouth of the Yangzi. Next, the two large ports of Xiamen (Amoy) and Ningbo were occupied. In alarm the regional authorities agreed provisionally to restore trade, but Beijing repudiated this and in January 1841, the war was resumed.

Britain's bombastic Foreign Secretary, Lord Palmerston, had sought authorization from Parliament for a punitive expedition to compel the Chinese to resume trading. 'The Chinese', he said, 'must learn and be convinced that if they attack our people and factories they will be shot.' William Gladstone, then an Opposition member, thought differently, saying, 'a war more unjust in its origin, a war more calculated in its progress to cover this country with permanent disgrace, I do not know, and I have not read of ... Our flag ... is become a pirate flag to protect an infamous traffic.' Parliament carried the motion for a punitive expedition by only nine votes.

The British warships were able to proceed up the Yangzi to the point, near Nanjing, where the Grand Canal joins the river. With the southern capital defenceless under the guns of the foreign fleet and the batteries guarding the entrance to the Grand Canal silenced, the gravity of the situation could no longer be concealed from the Court. Among the British fleet was something new and deadly – the steam-driven ironclad *Nemesis*, whose shallow draught and manoeuvrability permitted her to do enormous damage.

China was forced to sue for peace and, as a result of the consequent Treaty of Nanjing, agreed reluctantly to the resumption of trade. Britain had already seized Hong Kong (Xianggang) as a base, and it was now ceded to her. Not only Guangzhou but also four other 'treaty ports' were to be opened to British shipping. The opium trade flourished, imports doubling between 1830 and 1850. American merchants brought opium in from Turkey, and poppy plantations in China itself proliferated rapidly. These events, and the fundamental injustice of forcing narcotic drugs on the Chinese, are a very important element of history taught to Chinese school-children, and will continue to be in the future. They also featured prominently in the celebrations and media coverage in China to mark the return of Hong Kong to China in 1997. Westerners dealing with China in any way would find themselves at a disadvantage if they betrayed ignorance, or lack of a proper appreciation, of the Opium Wars and their consequences.

The Treaty of Nanjing proved unsatisfactory. The Chinese considered it to have been imposed on them by force, so they saw no reason why they should not evade its provisions if they could. The enforcement of similar treaties to the benefit of several European countries and the United States increased their anger.

This apparent Chinese intransigence resulted in a further war in 1856, designed to force her to comply. China was again defeated easily, and had to accept even more humiliating terms under the resulting Treaty of Tianjin. Now, the importing of opium was legalized, foreigners were allowed to travel anywhere in China, and Christian missionaries were given freedom to operate wherever they chose. All these provisions were accepted by the Chinese, but with a bitter underlying hatred, especially for the final one, allowing the 'pale ghosts' to preach a militant Christian ethic to compete with Confucianism. Even though there were many converts and the missionaries did a great deal of good (founding hospitals, schools and orphanages for the thousands of girl babies left out to die slowly from exposure), a solid core of opposition to them persisted, and was covertly encouraged by the mandarins.

Resistance to the treaties brought war again in 1860. A joint Anglo-French mission of 38 men had gone to Beijing under a safe-conduct agreement to discuss the deadlock over the treaty terms. They were arrested on the orders of the Court, and 20 of them died in agony. They were tightly bound in new rope, then water was thrown on them, causing their bonds to shrink slowly. A combined Anglo-French expedition marched on Beijing. Manchu cavalry, attacking at the charge, was blown to pieces from a safe distance by French artillery. Beijing capitulated and the emperor and his wife, Cixi, soon to be Dowager Empress, fled. The beautiful Summer Palace near the capital was looted and destroyed in revenge for the death of the prisoners. One of the force that carried out this work was an English officer named Charles Gordon, later to become famous for his defence of Khartoum in the Sudan, and his tragic death there. Gordon wrote to his mother: 'You can scarcely imagine the beauty and magnificence of the palaces we burned. It made one's heart sore to burn them. In fact these palaces were so large and we were so pressed for time that we could not plunder them carefully. Quantities of gold ornaments were burned, considered as brass.'

This was the last attempt by the Manchus to resist foreign domination overtly, and the Western powers now began to carve up China into 'spheres of influence'. Only jealousy between the powers, carefully cultivated by the Chinese, prevented the complete partition of the country. Nominally, it was allowed to remain independent. However, Manchu rule was now on the foreigners' terms. These included foreign control of Chinese trade and revenues – the mainstays of government. An Englishman, Sir Robert Hart, was inspector-general of the maritime customs for more than 40 years from 1863.

Having secured the compliance of the Manchu Dynasty, the powers now supported it against rival contenders, in particular the Taiping rebels. They were led by a visionary schoolteacher named Hong Xiuquan, who, in 1851, named himself emperor of a rival dynasty. The new regime, which attracted enormous support in the anti-Manchu south, was based substantially on ideas its founder had acquired from Christian tracts. The Taiping revolt was, in fact, a major civil war, similar to those which had led to the foundation of the Han and Ming dynasties. Some observers see in it the first large-scale manifestation of growing unrest and the desire for reform; a forerunner of the Communist revolution to come a century later.

Although it did advocate ideas of freedom, including the equality of the sexes and redistribution of land to the peasants, it is best not to regard the Taiping in too idealistic a light. For instance, recruits to its army had to memorize the Lord's Prayer and the Ten Commandments within three weeks on pain of execution; and the wives and children of the Manchu garrison in Nanjing were burned alive after the fall of the city.

The Taiping achieved vast initial support. Its armies swept north to the Yangzi River and may well have overthrown the Manchu but for the support the dynasty got from European gunboats, artillery and the 'Ever-Victorious Army', led by British officers. It is worth noting, however, that the Taiping were not well supported in north China, and lost much of their initiative after their capture of Nanjing. Hong from that time onwards retreated into an ever more bewildering maze of religious mysticism and religious oppression. The Taiping aroused wide opposition in the countryside because of their habit of destroying Buddhist and Daoist temples. A notable victim was the nine-storey, 250-feet-high Porcelain Pagoda at Nanjing, sheathed in white and gold tiles.

The cost of the revolt and others – there had been an independent Muslim state in Yunnan for 15 years – to China was appallingly high; it has been estimated that between 20 and 40 million people were killed over the 23 years of this huge convulsion – this represents perhaps the largest death toll from conflict in human history. Many cities were destroyed and conditions rapidly became worse in the ravaged countryside. China, which had been a substantial industrial economy, now reverted to a largely agrarian one – and an inefficient one at that – because of huge damage to complex infrastructures.

So inefficient were the Manchu armies that efforts were made at improvement – modern weapons were bought and German instructors recruited. But it was too little, too late; these measures could not prevent China's defeat by Japan in 1895 in a war over the control of Korea, which had long been a Chinese tributary state. The resulting Treaty of Shimonoseki obliged China to surrender Formosa (Taiwan), the Pescadore Islands and the strategic Liaodong Peninsula of Manchuria. Japan now had a foothold on the Chinese mainland itself.

The decisive nature of Japan's victory led many Chinese intellectuals to believe China's only chance of survival as an independent nation was an urgent process of modernization like that Japan was undergoing. One of these, Kang Youwei, was able to persuade the young Chinese emperor to issue in 1898 a series of commands that would have started such a process of reform. Instead, the dowager empress, supported by the mandarins, acted before the new measures could operate. The emperor was imprisoned until his death ten years later. Kang Youwei escaped from China in the nick of time, but six of his associates were executed. Kang was something of a socialist utopian – his writings foresee a human condition in which nation-states give way to world government; private property and the family are abolished; marriages last only a single year; children are brought up in communal nurseries.

In 1900 came the last wave of violent reaction from the old regime – the attack on foreigners and, in particular, Christians, by the so-called Boxers. The Boxers, members of a society of peasant origins called the Righteous Harmony Fists, were encouraged by the dowager empress and some of her supporters in a final effort to 'destroy the foreigners'. In fact, those to suffer most were the 'devil's disciples', the Chinese Christian converts, of whom 16,000 were killed. Armed Boxer bands, after attacking European missionaries in many parts of China, converged on Beijing, destroying the German legation and killing the minister. All Europeans withdrew into the embassy quarter, which withstood a siege for nearly two months. In August China was invaded by an international force, including Japanese,

which captured Beijing, relieved the embassies and effectively ended the
uprising. The Chinese court fled to Xian, in the north-west. Huge repara-
tions demanded by the Western powers completed the ruin of the Chinese
economy.

It was impossible that the old order should survive such events for long.
It seemed to be maintained only by the iron willpower of the dowager
empress. However, even she could see the inevitability of change. In 1901
she ordered reforms in important directions, notably in methods of education. In 1904 the old civil service examinations, based on Confucian studies
and the stilted, highly formalized 'eight-legged essay', were abandoned.
Western-style schools were introduced and accepted eagerly by the
Chinese. By 1910 there were 35,000 such schools, teaching more than a
million pupils the rudiments of a modern education. Many other Chinese
studied abroad, especially in Japan.

The younger men and women educated in this new tradition became
deeply concerned for the future of their country. The material of change
was now in place, an explosive mixture awaiting the lighting of the fuse –
nor was this long in coming. Late in 1908 the captive emperor died under
mysterious circumstances, probably poisoned by the Court mandarins. It
became obvious that the aged dowager empress was near her end – she
died the following day, having nominated the infant Puyi the tenth Manchu
emperor. Only three years later, still in early childhood, the last of the
Manchus was deposed.

The contrast between China and Japan at this stage is very significant.
Like Japan, China might have been transformed into a modern economy
and her agonies over the next half-century might have been avoided. But it
was not to be. The short-sightedness and conservatism of those who ruled
China, and the exactions of her Western predators, condemned her to the
decades of chaos and poverty which were now to ensue.

10 The Three Makers of Japan and the Tokugawa Period

Japan as a unified nation was the creation of three opportunistic and treacherous men, artful enough to outwit and confuse the multitude of regional lords who in the 16th century controlled the country, and strong enough to set an imprint that would endure for many centuries.

The Ashikaga *shoguns*, acting as regents for the Imperial family, brought political chaos to Japan but also – perhaps the one advantage of weak government – rapid advances in overall culture because of the freedom weak government gives to strong individuals and families. Although poor administrators, the Ashikaga were great patrons of the arts, which flourished, surprisingly, in conditions of almost constant war. This culminated in a bitter and largely pointless internecine conflict, the Onin wars, which in 1467 commenced a pattern of civil strife that would continue for nearly a century.

Many of the ancient families were destroyed and power became concentrated in the hands of around 150 surviving lords. Towns grew up around the fortified castles they built – the origins of many of the regional cities in today's Japan. These power figures, called *daimyo*, were to be an important factor in Japanese life from now on. Fortunes rose and fell rapidly and in this fluid environment the old feudal stratification of the community became blurred. In some cases bandit leaders rose from obscurity by sheer force of personality and came to command great influence. The relaxation of central authority made it possible for the peasants to break free of their masters for a time and revolts were frequent. Some of these led to the creation of new regions of power. However, it was the peasantry generally who bore the brunt of deteriorating economic conditions, exacerbated by locust plagues, flood and drought. Tens of thousands starved to death during the 15th century.

It was this world of distinct, almost autonomous states controlled by the *daimyo* that the Portuguese found when they reached Japan in the middle of the 16th century, in search of Japanese silver. Generally speaking, the *daimyo* were willing to trade. They were intrigued by the matchlock musket and quickly saw the significance it could have in the struggle for power. Almost at once the Japanese learned how to copy these weapons and make them for themselves. Japan's tradition of regarding weapon-making as an art is manifest in both the long and short muskets, delicately chased in silver, made at this time.

The heir to a small principality in the Nagoya region was one of the first to ponder the significance of firearms. This man, Oda Nobunaga, equipped an army with muskets almost as soon as he inherited his small estate. He used a skilful blend of force, intrigue, treachery and marriage alliances to extend his influence until in 1568 he was able to seize Kyoto. He consolidated his position by building a great castle high on the slopes of a mountain – an almost impregnable stronghold of a kind not seen in Japan before. From this secure base he launched an attack on the centuries-old Buddhist monastery complex on Mount Hiei which, by this time, amounted to several thousand buildings – almost a city. Nobunaga destroyed it completely, and massacred 2000 monks and their dependants on a single day in 1571 without a shadow of pity, so bringing a time-honoured pressure group to an end. There is no evidence that Nobunaga was a particularly religious man. His dislike of Buddhism and his interest in Christianity sprang alike from political motives.

Roman Catholic monks of the Jesuit order had arrived in Japan hard on the heels of the Portuguese traders. Christianity flourished with amazing speed, and the number of converts soon ran into hundreds of thousands, representing all classes from the *daimyo* down. Nobunaga's support undoubtedly helped. Another great persuader was the association of missionary work with trade – often the monks actually controlled trading operations.

Oda Nobunaga was at the height of his power in 1582 and in his fiftieth year when he was treacherously killed by one of his generals. He was avenged by another general, a vigorous, arrogant man named Hideyoshi. At first Hideyoshi ruled as regent for Nobunaga's infant grandson but within a year he had usurped the leadership. It was nevertheless his role to build on the foundation Nobunaga had laid down – he commanded an army of a quarter of a million men towards the end of the decade. In thus supporting the *samurai* he reduced the peasantry to an almost serf-like condition, forbidding them to leave their land and forcing them to hand in all their weapons.

Both Nobunaga and Hideyoshi were loyal to the Imperial line, and at no time tried to usurp the functions of the emperors. In fact, both men ruled in its name, probably because they understood how much the emperor

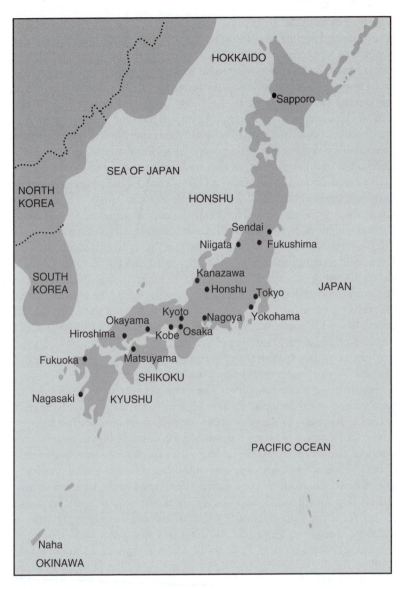

Map 3 Japan

system reinforced the rigid social structure. The *daimyo* in power at this time remained in their positions and the *samurai* – about one in ten of the population – were confirmed as a specialized military class which the unfortunate peasantry was compelled to support and obey without question. Enormous skill and effort were exerted to make the fine steel blades of the *samurai* swords, which, as the most significant possessions of the warrior class, acquired major symbolic importance and are still regarded as important works of art. Pieces of iron and pure pine charcoal were patiently hammered and folded together until after hundreds of repetitions a high-carbon steel was produced that could be sharpened to a razor edge.

Like his predecessor, Hideyoshi had been favourably disposed towards the Christians, but near the end of the century his attitude changed. The new faith was perhaps growing too fast for his liking and he suspected the Jesuits of political ambitions. In 1567 he issued an edict ordering all foreign missionaries to leave the country within 20 days. For ten years he enforced this new law only sporadically, but the problem of Christianity emerged again when the Japanese looted the wreck of a Spanish galleon blown off her course from Manila to Mexico. The Spanish captain objected vigorously, telling the Japanese about the mighty empire Spain had gained through the use of the Bible and the sword. When Hideyoshi was told of this he concluded that the missionaries might spearhead a bid for foreign political control of Japan. The following year, 1597, he crucified six Spanish Franciscan monks, three Portuguese Jesuits and 17 Japanese Christians after first torturing and mutilating them.

Hideyoshi was a swashbuckler of low birth, an adventurer, something of a *bon viveur* and an exhibitionist. He gave huge parties in the great castle he built at Osaka, delighting in showing off its utensils – even its door handles – of pure gold. He seems to have felt the need for constant action to maintain his position. This was perhaps the reason for the expedition he launched against China in 1592, without any clear idea of the vast power of the Ming empire. The advance was made through Korea, which resisted the Japanese strenuously. China took a somewhat leisurely decision to send an army. It crossed the border at the Yalu River early the next year and forced the Japanese to withdraw. However, they were back again a few years later. Hostilities continued on and off until Hideyoshi's death in 1598 ended the pointless conflict. The Koreans, who were almost completely Chinese in their culture and outlook, bitterly resented this apparently wanton attack from the people they called the *wa* (dwarves), which caused immense distress and hundreds of thousands of deaths.

Like his predecessor, Hideyoshi had left an heir, his son Hideyori, who was in the charge of two regents. These men, however, engaged in a struggle for power which ended in a great battle at Sekigahara in 1600, when the victor was a Tokugawa named Ieyasu. The Tokugawa clan was now to control Japan for two and a half centuries, into modern times.

Hideyori, who had been betrayed in this way by the man into whose charge his father had given him, retreated with his supporters into the great castle in Osaka. Its eight-storied, many-gabled central keep was defended by a series of moats and walls – the outer one two miles long – and was virtually impregnable. Ieyasu besieged it for years, and finally took it by trickery in 1615. He had promised Hideyori and his family favourable truce conditions and so persuaded them to weaken their defences. At the end of a treacherous surprise attack only one of Hideyori's family remained alive – his 8-year-old son Kunimatsu. Pitiless to the end, Ieyasu killed even this child, the last of the family of his former master.

So began the period known as the Tokugawa, during which the ruling elite imposed an iron conservatism and the rule of repression and fear throughout Japan. Of a population of 20 million about one in ten were *samurai*. The peasants, the vast majority and the mainstay of the almost totally agrarian economy, were not allowed to be educated. They were told what to grow and how, were taxed as high as 70 per cent of yield, and ordered to be frugal, diligent and submissive. In contrast to the matrilineal society in early Japan, women were now compelled to an almost slave-like state. Their property rights were removed and their husbands, who were free to be as promiscuous as they chose, could kill their wives if they were unfaithful, or even if they were considered lazy in their domestic duties. Even to look up and meet the eyes of a man other than her husband was forbidden. A husband could divorce his wife at any time, but she could not divorce him.

Thus measures were taken which froze Japanese culture along these lines so that, 250 years later, it presented a scene apparently medieval to the amazed eyes of 19th-century Europe. Japan today seems modern, Westernized even, but under the surface the Tokugawa centuries still influence it.

While in Kyoto Ieyasu lived within the moated, massive-walled Nijo Castle in a small wooden house distinguished by its beautifully decorated and painted colour panels and 'nightingale floors' – boards laid in such a way that they squeaked when trodden on, giving warning of the approach of a possible assassin. However, the later Tokugawa avoided Kyoto and instead based themselves on the little fishing village of Edo. The city which grew up there is now Tokyo, where the *shogun*'s castle walls still encircle the Imperial palace. During the Tokugawa period it became one of the biggest cities in the world, with more than a million people.

Urban life flourished under curious circumstances. The new *bakufu* – camp government – understood that its continued existence very much depended on the subjection of the great *daimyo*, especially the 'outside lords' who had opposed Ieyasu at Sekigahara. Ieyasu required them to sign regulations limiting their power and permitting a close supervision even over their personal affairs. They were forced to leave their wives and families in Edo while they were themselves absent, and were required personally to spend a certain amount of the year in the capital. Along the great high roads, such as the famed Tokaido between Kyoto and Edo, guards working at special roadblocks checked constantly on the traffic, looking for 'women coming out and weapons going into' Edo.

An elaborate spy system was introduced to check on the great families. The slightest suspicion of disloyalty could lead to part, if not all, of the estates of the *daimyo* being confiscated. They were not allowed to enter into marriage alliances, build new castles or even repair old ones without the permission of the central government. The obligation to spend regular periods in Edo led not only to the city's mushroom growth, but also helped to keep the *daimyo* too poor to cause trouble. Every great family had to maintain an establishment there. In fact, as the centuries passed, Japan was impoverished to pay for the infrastructure and amusements of the city.

The flood of money into Edo from the heavily taxed peasantry created a wealthy merchant class and a varied entertainment industry – both new departures in Japan. A family originally occupied in brewing *sake*, the Japanese rice wine, branched out into rice distribution, the general retail trade, and then banking. A *samurai* named Yataro Iwasaki set up a shipping line which rapidly expanded after Japan again became open to the world. These were the origins of Mitsui and Mitsubishi, two industrial giants of today's Japan. An entertainment complex called the *ukiyo*, 'the floating world' – teahouses, taverns, puppet shows, brothels, theatres, public baths and circuses – accumulated in Edo to serve the wealthy and leisured. There are restaurants in Tokyo that serve the same dishes – unchanged – now, as then. More specialized entertainment was also available – *sumo* wrestling and popular playhouses, the *kabuki* theatre. Because its productions were so often ribald and erotic the *bakufu* forbade the employment of actresses in *kabuki*, so female roles had to be taken by men. Brightly coloured costumes, lively music and dancing were all part of *kabuki* productions, which became enormously appealing to the ordinary people.

Then there were the bath girls and the *geisha*, a specialized female pleasure class. Particularly pretty small girls were sold to the *geisha* houses, and carefully trained in the social arts – flower arranging, the lengthy and formal Japanese tea ceremony, singing, dancing. Their occupation was then as paid companions for wealthy men.

The Tokugawa quite early considered any foreign contacts dangerous, and sealed Japan off from the outside world. A first step in this direction was to stamp out the major foreign influence – Christianity. Trade and missionary activity had earlier been closely associated. It was a time of intense commercial and religious rivalry between the Protestant and Catholic nations of Europe, and Ieyasu could not fail to be influenced by this. Both factions tried to make him suspicious of the other. Finally, he seems to have been impressed by the fact that the English and Dutch brought with them no organized religious activity like the Jesuits. The fact that many of those defending Osaka castle had been Christians increased his suspicions. In 1614 he ordered all foreign missionaries to leave Japan permanently.

However, it was the second Tokugawa, Hidetada, who began a major campaign of torturing and killing Christians extending over two decades. Many priests, and some of the congregations, accepted their cruel fate as martyrs and at least 3000 people died, in the most agonizing ways. They were immersed in caustic water, thrown on to red-hot gratings, dropped into pits of poisonous snakes, or most commonly, crucified upside-down. People suspected of being Christians were called on to trample on a picture of Christ or the Virgin Mary, and were tortured until they agreed to renounce their faith or died.

The city of Nagasaki had become a focus for Japanese Christianity, nearly all the people in the city and its surroundings having been converted. It was here that the persecution reached its terrible climax. Bad local government and ruinous taxation led the people of this region to revolt in 1637, and the uprising inevitably became associated with the Christian faith. The local *daimyo*, Matsukara, was a man of unusual cruelty and rapacity even for those times, notorious for his habit of boiling people alive in the hot springs of the region. The peasants were compared with sesame seed – the more they were squeezed, the more they would give. Almost everything was taxed – doors, shelves and candles, among other things, and the appalling torture of the Mino dance was applied to those who could not pay. They were dressed in a bulky straw coat, their hands tied behind their backs, and set alight.

Desperate from the religious persecution and the ruinous levels of taxation, 37,000 Christians and their families gathered in an old fortress called Hara on the Shimabara Peninsula, and fought to the end a force of 100,000 Tokugawa *samurai* who besieged the castle for three months. The end came in April 1638. Of those still alive in the fortress only one, a traitor imprisoned in the dungeons, was allowed to live. At Hidetada's request a Dutch ship had used her guns to breach the fortress walls. Fifteen thousand of the government's forces were killed.

This terrible civil conflict, which is still well remembered in popular arts in today's Japan, had two major effects. The first was to convince the *bakufu* that the only way to preserve Japanese society was to cut adrift as completely as possible from contacts with Europeans. Japanese were forbidden to leave the country. Those who did leave faced the death penalty if they returned. Shipbuilders were forbidden to construct anything bigger than coastal craft. After the Shimabara revolt the Portuguese traders in Japan were told to leave and warned they would be killed if they made any further attempt to make contact. At the time the traders were expelled, the Japanese still owed them considerable sums. A ship sent from Macao (on the south Chinese coast) in 1640 to try to collect the money was burned and 61 of her company beheaded. Thirteen who were spared were sent back to Macao with instructions 'to think of us no more, just as if we were no longer in the world'.

Spanish ships had already been warned away and England had abandoned its trading post in 1623 as unprofitable. Only the Dutch were permitted to remain and they were confined to a tiny, artificial island called Deshima in Nagasaki Harbour. Once a year they were allowed to leave this island to present gifts to the *shogun* in Edo. Normally they were treated with respect but sometimes they were forced to dance, jump and roll about as if drunk – these indignities apparently being designed to demonstrate the crudities of Europeans. Nowadays, thousands of Japanese a year visit a multi-million-dollar 'Dutch' theme park in Nagasaki.

The *bakufu* had made distinctions between European and Asian traders, Ieyasu encouraging trade with south-east Asia, where Japan's silver was much in demand. In the first three decades of the 17th century some 400 trading passages were made by Japanese ships, which voyaged as far afield as the Thai capital of Ayudhya. That city had its own Japanese quarter, housing more than a thousand residents.

The second major effect of the extermination of the people in Hara Castle was to cow the populace to the extent that most would accept any privation and any indignity from sheer fear. No force for reform or change was likely to persist. Japanese society, now substantially removed from any outside influence, proceeded along the lines dictated by the *shoguns*. If restrictive, this at least enforced a kind of peace, although the heavily taxed and much abused peasants revolted from time to time. Crop diversification and more intensive agriculture resulted in a modestly expanding economy, although there were severe famines causing thousands of deaths in the 18th and 19th centuries. The autocratic nature of the government encouraged extremes of authoritarianism which are almost incredible, the most celebrated example being the measures introduced by Tsunayoshi, the so-called 'dog' shogun. Worried that he had no heir, he was told by a soothsayer that his childlessness would continue until a campaign of kindness was introduced to all animals, in particular dogs, because the *shogun* had been born in the Year of the Dog. Over the next 20 years a set of regulations forbade the killing or ill-treatment of animals, canine shelters were built outside Edo to house 50,000 dogs and all Japanese, when talking to a dog, had to address it as 'Honourable Dog'.

In spite of the constraints of Tokugawa rule and their tradition of restrained and formal public behaviour, the Japanese people managed a certain wry and ribald vigour – an ambivalence still apparent today. By the late 18th century a deep respect for learning and letters had resulted in a relatively high rate of literacy. Towards the end of the Tokugawa, close on half the boys and perhaps 10 per cent of the girls were said to be attending schools, although this seems unlikely to have been the case among the peasants, only the wealthiest of whom could afford to send their children to temple schools. Book publishing was a flourishing trade, but because the modest incomes of most people made ownership of personal libraries prohibitive, lending libraries, often carried around on the backs of their proprietors, were popular. There was a rigorous book censorship of any criticism of the regime. When author Santo Kyoden published three popular satires, he was sentenced to 50 days in handcuffs and his publisher was heavily fined. Such happenings inclined most writers away from the controversial towards the fanciful, the ribald and the exotic. Erotic fiction was very popular.

The Tokugawa used the *samurai* to enforce their orders – they even had the right 'to kill and go away', not to be brought to account by the law for murder. There has been a regrettable tendency to romanticize the *samurai* and *bushido*, their so-called cult of honour, in television programmes for children, among other things, so a few balancing facts might not be out of place.

The appalling torture they meted out, often to quite innocent people, indicates a sadistic desire to kill in the most painful and prolonged way possible. For instance, pirates captured in the Straits of Korea were boiled alive in copper kettles. The terrible deaths devised for Christians were carried out by *samurai*. *Daimyo* travelling between Edo and Kyoto would be accompanied by scores, even hundreds of *samurai* hangers-on. Any commoner who did not prostrate himself abjectly enough in the dust beside the road was liable to be literally cut to pieces by the *samurai*. Hideously masked and dressed in leather and steel armour, the *samurai* were a specialized coercive force preying on their own people.

However, by the early 19th century their formidable image was much diminished. The class had not actually done any fighting since the Shimabara revolt of 1637, and had become a caricature of its former self.

While they affected to despise the growing merchant and banking class, increasingly the real power was moving to this mercantile sector. The great *daimyo* and many of the increasingly corrupt and idle *samurai* came to be deeply in the debt of the merchants. So the coming of the 19th century saw strains and tensions inside Japan which augured change in the not-too-distant future.

A small minority of scholars, who, from 1716, were licensed to import Dutch books through the Deshima post, acquired a purely theoretical knowledge of the advances Europe was making. It was noted that more ships seemed to be appearing off the coast. In 1805 a Russian ship lay for months off Nagasaki, seeking permission to land an official envoy, but finally had to sail away without achieving success. In 1824, the crew of a British whaler landed, killed cattle, and generally seem to have behaved in a lawless way. This led to a renewal, in 1825, of the decree providing that any foreigner landing should be killed. In 1837 a US ship was fired on.

The Japanese were not altogether ignorant of the outside world. They were aware of and alarmed by news of the Opium Wars and the unequal treaties that had been forced on China, and they understood that the *samurai*, with their antique weaponry and total lack of experience of war, could not defend Japan against the feared Westerners. The resulting public dissatisfaction with the regime was to be exacerbated by four years of disastrous weather and resultant famines from 1833. Even at this time there was considerable criticism of the neo-Confucian ethic of the *bakufu* as foreign and 'un-Japanese' and a resurgence among scholars of the idea that the emperors really were, as the ancient myths had it, descended from the sun goddess and virtually divine.

However much the Japanese wished the outside world would go away, it was not to be denied. The isolated isles with their Rip van Winkle atmosphere had become a source of intense curiosity. In 1846 an American mission, led by Commodore Biddle, was forced to leave without negotiating the trade treaty it sought. So the next time the Americans came they made sure it was with a suitable display of force. On 8 July 1853, Commodore Perry entered Edo's Uraga Harbour with a squadron of two steam and two sailing sloops, the largest of 2400 tons and carrying 16 guns. Under the guns of these ships Perry was able to deliver a letter from the US President requesting that some Japanese ports be opened for trade. On 16 July the 'black ships' departed, leaving Japan in a confused ferment. Commodore Perry had undertaken to return the next year for the *bakufu*'s reply. This was affirmative, although cautious, and led to the opening of two small ports remote from Edo; a token gesture only. But America followed up by sending as its first official representative Townsend Harris, a shrewd, forceful but tactful man who, after much patient negotiation, succeeded in gaining audience in 1857 with the *shogun*, Iesada. This was followed by a comprehensive treaty, not only with the United States, but with other nations. Europe became fascinated with Japan; Verdi wrote *Madama Butterfly*.

These treaties with foreigners were signed without the approval of the emperor and those who advised him in Kyoto or the majority of the *daimyo*, and because of this they occasioned widespread opposition, further eroding support for the *bakufu*, and firmly establishing two words – *sonno-joi* – 'revere the emperor, repel the barbarians' – as popular national sentiments.

The centuries of isolation had ended, and with them all pretence that Japan's society was itself static – an illusion the *bakufu* was striving to maintain. Not surprisingly, a major victim of change was the *shogunate* itself, supplanted by a restoration of the Japanese emperor to a position of symbolic national primacy. This reversion to the past was engineered not by the wealthy merchants but by disgruntled *samurai*, leading Japan into half a century of unbridled militarism and aggression.

PART II

The 'White Man's Burden'

11 The Dominators and the Dominated

The 19th and early 20th centuries saw the development of imperialism on a scale never known before. The long and traumatic Napoleonic wars were over, Europe was industrializing, and there were radical advances in the means of transport, notably shipping and railways, and naval power. A crucial factor in the conquest of empires was the development of deadlier light weapons. American farm machinery technician Richard Gordon Gatling developed a machine gun in 1862 that would fire 350 rounds a minute, a new device for mass killing which was quickly adopted by all the colonial powers. For the first time, natives inclined to fight back could be – and were – mown down in hundreds.

By this and other means it became technologically possible for a single nation to dominate much of the world. At its maximum material extent during the 1920s the British Empire occupied nearly a quarter of the land surface of the planet, inhabited by about 500 million people, then almost a quarter of world population. Wherever the eye fell on the map of the world, there were the daubs of red, marking the empire on which the sun never set.

This empire, like those of other major European powers, was substantially in Asia. The British colonies there consisted of what are now seven countries: India, Pakistan, Bangladesh, Sri Lanka, Burma, Malaysia and Singapore. There were other smaller outposts, like Hong Kong, and also spheres of influence in countries nominally independent, but prepared to accept British advice.

The imperial dissection of Asia followed a definite geographic pattern. The British Empire was westernmost, extending east from India through Burma to small, lately acquired possessions in Malaysia. Beyond Thailand, kept independent as a buffer state and twice lopped of some of its territory, was French Indo-China, now Vietnam, Cambodia and Laos. Holland controlled the western half of the archipelago of south-east Asia – what is now Indonesia. The 400 islands farther east became the Philippines, the colony first of Spain and later of the United States.

China was too big a fish for any single European state to swallow whole or, indeed, to be permitted by its rivals to do so. Instead she became divided into 'spheres of influence'. The imperialist powers exacted important concessions in major ports like Shanghai along the Chinese coast. These grew into big cities, in which a seemingly inexhaustible resource of cheap labour drove both a massive industry and a massive accumulation of human suffering, poverty and disease.

Japan maintained her independence only because she had 'Westernized' her economy and industry with remarkable speed and energy and gained the respect of the dominators by becoming a colonial power herself, annexing Korea, Taiwan and Manchuria. Thailand, under the shrewd control of her Chakri kings, escaped colonial status by bending to the wind – surrendering territory where this seemed expedient and accepting European – especially British – advice.

This geographic organization of Asia to suit the dominators, informed largely by an incessant, uneasy rivalry between them, had some strange and at times disastrous consequences. Everywhere one now looks in Asia anomalies remain – peoples divided between two or more nations, minorities cut off from the majority of their race, frontiers that defy the facts of geography. The tensions caused by these things are important, active influences in the Asia of today and will have unpredictable future effects. But for colonialism it is likely that Indonesia would have been more than one country. Sumatra might have been associated with the Malay Peninsula which its neighbours and which its terrain and people so closely resemble. Java and Madura, with their dense populations and distinctive cultures, might have made up a second. The eastern islands and the Philippines could have comprised a third.

There are hill-tribe people in north-east India who are ethnically identical with others now Burmese. The border between Afghanistan and Pakistan divides the Pashtuns. There is a substantial Malay minority in southern Thailand. The people of north-east Thailand are Laotian by language and tradition. India is showing indications of division into three regions of different interest, and throughout her history as an independent power regional influences have gained ground on those that seek to unify. Nearly all these anomalies resulted from the organization of colonial empires, which successor states have insisted on as a basis for their own boundaries.

The dominators' manipulation of the economy of the colonies to their own ends was enforced by the association of soldier and merchant so typical of the colonial era (the British East India Company maintained distinct civil and military divisions), and by a policy of actively discouraging political development in the colonial peoples. The use and enforcement of monopolies was a typical economic practice. The British *Raj* exerted severe force when Gandhi defied the Indian salt tax. By modern standards many of these monopolies would be judged criminal – those formed to sell opium are notorious examples. For instance, in 1867 the contribution made by the East Indies to the Netherlands government was almost exactly the amount raised by government monopolies in opium and salt and the management of pawnshops. While Laos was a colony, even as late as 1945, its major export was opium, and during the Japanese occupation of Korea production of the drug was legal. Throughout Indo-China opium, alcohol and salt were government monopolies so profitable they doubled colonial revenues in the first decade after their inception. Opium exports from India did not cease until 1909. While the dominators made money out of opium its production was seldom criticized and it was freely used in patent medicines and it is only since those revenues have ceased that campaigning against it as an illegal drug has become so strident.

It has been estimated that the drain of money from south-east Asia alone in the form of profits from the colonies was $3007 million in 1930. In 1925, 51 per cent of all imports into India came from Britain, although Indian exports to Britain were only 22 per cent of her total. Imports from France represented 52 per cent of all into Indo-China. The economies of the colonies were manipulated so they could be a cheap, fruitful source of raw materials, while industrial development was retarded to discourage competition with the industries of the dominators. India, before the colonial era the world's major supplier of cotton fabrics, lost this position in the 19th century to the massive textile industry that developed in the English Midlands. Effectively, Asia's share of world GDP fell from more than 60 per cent in 1800 to less than 20 per cent by 1940. This enormous decline was no accident. While the industry and economies of the dominators boomed, those of the colonies were deliberately restrained.

These economic policies contributed towards major social changes in the colonies. The most significant were a massive turnover of land to export crops, rapid population growth and underdevelopment – a lack of adequate material resources and only a tiny and limited pool of educated people. These continue today to be common problems in most of the former colonies, and are the root causes of millions of avoidable deaths, especially of children, and of disease and poverty. Unbalanced economies and a rising demand for cheap labour to work the expanding plantations drove populations into rapid growth. Java and Madura, with five million people in 1815, had twice that number a generation later, ten times as many at the time of independence, more than 20 times as many now. There were similar increases in all the 'plantation' regions of Asia.

Development of the human resource – education – varied from place to place but in none did it even begin to approach that in the dominators' home countries. At the end of the colonial era, when virtually the whole world outside the colonies was literate, the vast majority of the dominated peoples remained illiterate.

Much the same situation existed with material infrastructure. Some roads, railways, port facilities and cities were developed but these, paid for out of colonial revenues, were designed to suit the needs and interests of the dominator. Development was generally much below that achieved outside the colonies. In 1950, which could be considered the end of the colonial era, the three largest Asian nations, China, India and Indonesia, had a total of 38,000 miles of rail track, compared with 217,000 in the United States and 237,000 in Europe. Statistics on roads, factories, power-generating stations and the other resources of modern states indicate equal or more serious underdevelopment.

The fact that the colonies were regarded as the property of the master country is, then, central. The first objective of the colonial system was to make money. The colonies were businesses, run by businessmen, through most of their history, regardless of the Kiplingesque ballyhoo to the contrary. As late as 1913, J. Dautremer, the author of a standard book, *Burma Under British Rule*, wrote: 'The colonies are countries which have been conquered. They are the property of the country that administers them, governs them, and develops their riches for its own profit. Since the colony is the property of the nation, it has no right to be put on the same footing as the governing country.' These statements are broadly typical of publicly expressed attitudes at that time.

The colonial governments perpetuated a grotesquely large disparity of wealth and privilege within the Asian peoples, a situation which persists in the modern nations. Before colonialism the basic social structure was the small village community, with long-standing traditions of mutual help and consensus decision-making tempering the authority of leading families. Generally land was available to anyone who wanted to work it. But the new rulers brought with them the concepts of the European state, and a requirement for private ownership of land so it could be taxed efficiently. One man in the village became chief, who levied taxation on behalf of the central authority. That authority backed him with military force. This new system created massive financial disparity, considerable absentee ownership of land, and a bottom layer of poor, landless families. When times were bad, as during the great depression of the 1930s, this alienation of land accelerated, typically to the stage where in many places more than half the villagers lacked enough land to support them and their families. Their only recourse was to work as labourers for the wealthy.

It could be asserted that Britain made the greatest contributions of value to her colonies, especially in the 20th century. It is reasonably clear that Dutch rule in Indonesia contributed the least. They left the huge archipelago only 3000 miles of railways, compared with 16,000 in India. The Dutch refused to recognize, even at a late stage, the possibility of the East Indies becoming independent, considering only a state within the Netherlands commonwealth to be governed by the 250,000 Dutch living there.

There can be little doubt that the relatively orderly history of India and Malaysia since independence, for instance, has been due to efforts made during the later colonial era to educate some local people in business and administration, and to provide a reasonable administrative framework. That these were primarily to the benefit of the colonial business machine is beside the point. On the other hand, the chaotic problems of Indonesia during her first decades of independence were due largely to a lack of such efforts to educate. This factor is difficult to overestimate and one that those seeking to understand Indonesia should keep in mind. At the outbreak of the Second World War in 1939, the literacy rate was only 7 per cent. Such educated men as there were had in most cases been sent to schools overseas by their families. But even when these returned to Indonesia they could find only subordinate positions.

It is fair to add, however, that in Indonesia, as elsewhere, the nationalist movement came from among the tiny educated class. Also, research scholars of the colonial powers were largely responsible for bringing to the attention of these nationalists the glories of the past. French archaeologists patiently unravelled the history of the vast buildings of Angkor and began the work of restoring the ruins of the great Khmer city. Dutch scholars did as much for Indonesia. The traditions of Shrivijaya and Majapahit, which came to mean so much to the nationalists, might never have been recovered, even to the present extent, but for the work of these Dutch enthusiasts. Later pre-colonial Indonesian society, for instance, had no inkling of the meaning of the great monument of Borobadur, simply shunning it as 'a place of ghosts'.

The nationalist movements were, then, organized and perpetuated substantially by a small minority educated in Western ideas of politics. For decades the language of the Indian Congress was English. Its leader, Jawaharlal Nehru, was English-educated and the Indian constitution was drafted on Western precedents. Ho Chi Minh was educated in Communism in France. Indonesia's Sukarno was literate in several European languages and widely read in European political theory. But the future may well lie elsewhere, as some Asian statesmen recognize. I can recall many years ago hearing a speech by the architect of modern Singapore, Lee Kuan Yew, in which he predicted the arrival of new, as yet unknown, political forces and the eclipse of Western-educated leaders such as himself. The beginnings of this process are now apparent.

A second contribution of colonialism was the rule of law. Europe obtained its basic concept of an impartial codified legal system, binding equally on all citizens, from the Romans. Attitudes towards law in Asia, with few exceptions, were quite different, the law being almost invariably customary rather than codified. In south-east Asian principalities law was generally such a savage, unfair instrument that people hesitated to use it. In China there was one law for the privileged, another much harsher code for the mass of the people, and, if the popular literature, classics like the *Jin Ping Mei*, can be believed, readily and regularly influenced by bribery. In Japan one class, the *samurai*, became virtually immune from the law.

During the colonial period most of the European powers imposed their own systems of law on the subject territories for long enough to train a significant body of local people in those legal methods. Places like Japan and Thailand, even though they were not colonies, found it expedient to accept Westernized legal systems because if they had not done so, the much-hated principle called extraterritoriality, under which foreigners were immune from local law, would have continued.

12 South-east Asia: the European and Chinese Impacts

Many chapters could be devoted, without much profit, to the dynastic successions, transitory empires and constant wars which, over the centuries, make up the chronicles of south-east Asia. However, since the source material deals almost exclusively with the affairs of ruling families, and frequently shows scant regard for credibility, much less truth – for instance, we are told that a Vietnamese king, Phat Ma, straightened a sagging pillar in a ruined temple simply by looking at it – it is largely unreliable.

The real history of this region is the ebb and flow of village life; the succession of scores of generations of ordinary people, humble, unlettered but tenacious, without great possessions, patiently growing rice according to methods and rituals already so old their beginnings have been forgotten, and just as patiently devoted to traditions and art forms of considerable significance. In the 1930s Europe became fascinated with these qualities in the Indonesian island of Bali – a way of life involving personal accomplishment in one or more of the arts, a minimum of personal possessions, a disregard for any more money than is necessary, a proper regard for personal tranquillity and social harmony. There is, of course, also a downside – conservatism, strong pressure on individuals to conform, an almost complete lack of personal privacy, and, beneath an outer appearance of tranquillity, a potential for cruelty and savage mob violence.

These things are in many ways typical of village south-east Asia in most of its diverse settings. To these, the real people, the struggles and ambitions of their warring masters meant trouble from time to time, but very little more. The figures of kings appeared almost Olympian: gods, whose actions, often tyrannical and usually unpredictable, were in some vague, magic way linked to the overall prosperity of the realm and the productivity of the soil. Where great affairs of state were concerned, the people were largely powerless – and usually ignored. Little has changed. Contemporary chronicles – the modern media – when they concern themselves with Asia at all, almost invariably report on the activities of the elite classes living in capital cities that might make up, at most, 5 per cent of the Asian population.

Nevertheless, in the 16th and 17th centuries parts of south-east Asia passed through a considerable though restless phase of urbanization, with several cities exceeding populations of 100,000. Malacca was one of these prior to its occupation by the Portuguese in 1511. These merchant entrepôts, which included Aceh, Makassar (Ujung Pandang) and Ayudhya, were comparable in size to major European cities of that time. London had fewer than 200,000 people then. Significant location on the trade routes and highly productive hinterlands were the major economic reasons for this urban growth. Another was the diversion of much of the rural wealth and national manpower to the purposes of the rulers. In Thailand, for instance, the corvée could amount to as much as half the labour time of the peasants, to support a large bureaucracy and army and to carry out the physical construction of cities like Ayudhya.

Much of the population of the trading ports were transients, obliged to stay over for months at a time until the monsoons changed. They needed, and paid for, food, accommodation and other services during that time. They also provided the rulers of the city-states with a reliable source of income, with imports and exports taxed at between 5 and 10 per cent. This urban growth proved to be fragile. It depended tenuously on the authority of kings or emperors, which was frequently disputed, especially at times of succession. Bitter and protracted civil conflict at these times, and destructive wars between neighbouring realms, greatly reduced these mushroom cities, or even, as in the case of Ayudhya, led to their abandonment. Many of their population were slaves captured in war, or peasants forced into corvée labour or military service. Weakening or collapse of regimes inevitably and rapidly affected the entire urban structure. During its phase of occupation by the Portuguese, Malacca's population fell by two-thirds, and other cities later to be used as bases by the colonizers were similarly affected.

The evolution of nation-states in Europe did not, then, have its counterpart in south-east Asia until recent times, although Burma and Thailand did achieve a kind of unity. This circumstance did much to assist the colonizers. At first sight it seems strange that relatively small numbers of Europeans were able to gain a foothold in countries which were basically strong and populous, and had a considerable and sophisticated cultural and economic past. The reason was that everywhere local petty lords were at each other's throats. They were only too ready to make concessions to European adventurers to use their guns and ships against a neighbouring rival. Often enough these concessions involved the critical but mundane bread-and-butter tasks of administration, such as tax collecting. Provided some money came to the sultan or rajah, it was a matter of little concern that vastly more was extorted from the unhappy peasantry by tax 'farmers'.

Parallel with the arrival of Europeans on the scene was another virtual invasion of foreigners, the overseas Chinese, in much greater numbers and almost certainly more significant in the long term. Their descendants in south-east Asia now exceed 20 million people. It is probable that if the Chinese government had supported its people in south-east Asia to the extent that European governments supported theirs, the evolution of European colonial empires in Asia might have been greatly limited. But the Chinese government did not. The Manchus did nothing to help or support Chinese leaving for what became called the *nanyang* – the southern ocean – nor did it prevent them. Poverty, lawlessness and injustice were powerful incentives to seek a new life overseas and during the centuries of growing European influence the Chinese did so in millions. Everywhere they went they took with them their tradition of hard work and singleness of purpose, building ships, opening gold and tin mines, lending money to rulers, cornering rice markets, involving themselves in virtually every area of trade and commerce.

More than 600 junks arrived in Manila in the 30 years following its establishment as the Spanish colonial capital of the Philippines. There were 10,000 Chinese there by 1586, compared with well under a thousand Spaniards. The flood of Chinese was resented and resisted by the local people, with half a dozen massacres during the 17th century. Nevertheless the Chinese population of Manila had risen to 40,000 by 1750.

The large Chinese quarter in Ayudhya was perhaps the most solid and prosperous part of the city. The government used the Chinese as tax collectors and managers of state enterprises. Most of Thailand's trade at that time was with China, allowing little opportunity for the Dutch, French and English to gain an early foothold – an important element in Thailand's continued, although qualified, independence during the colonial era.

In Batavia (now Djakarta) Chinese control of commerce and manufacture became almost pervasive, and with the encouragement of the Dutch a large Chinese minority spread throughout Indonesia. By 1740 more than half the inhabitants of Batavia were Chinese. Many became wealthy through a system of taxation which granted the tax farmer the right to levy a range of taxes after he had offered the largest cash bid for the concession. Everything else he could wring from the populace was his – including taxes on ports, salt, opium, gambling, even duties on travel within the colony.

Opium was an important item of trade. Its use was uncommon in south-east Asia until the late 18th century, when the British growers of the poppy in Bengal and the Dutch adopted a deliberate policy of encouraging it. The Dutch administration bought the opium in Bengal to serve its monopoly in Indonesia,

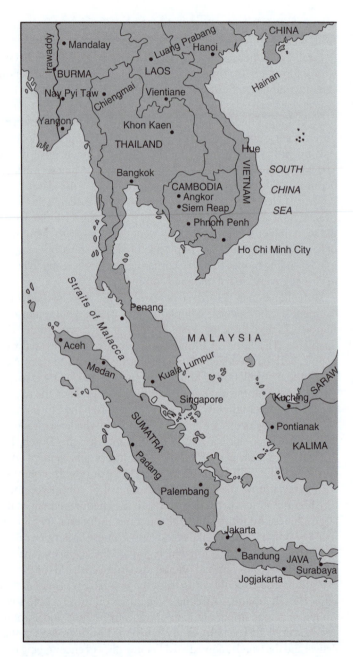

Map 4 Southeast Asia

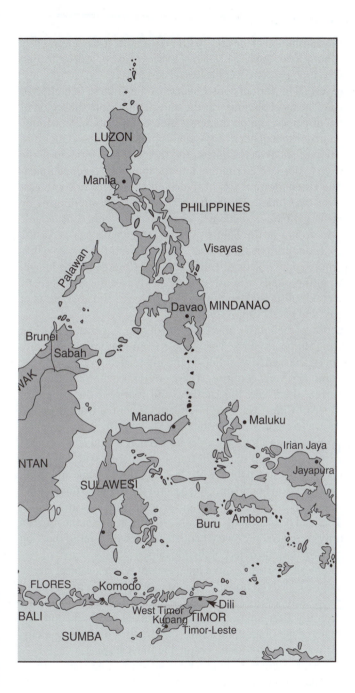

farming out the distribution of the drug to Chinese dealers. It was enormously profitable, Anthony Reid (*Cambridge History of Southeast Asia*, p. 500) estimating that profits were 3000 per cent over the Bengal cost price.

There were several important consequences of the Chinese migration to south-east Asia. The most obvious was the transplanting into the region of a large, widely dispersed and permanent Chinese population. Singapore, for instance, a major independent city-state, is mostly Chinese. One-third of the population of Malaysia is Chinese, and there are minorities in all the south-east Asian nations, often running into the millions. A second fundamental was the virtual domination of trade and commerce in south-east Asia by the overseas Chinese. While this has been resisted strenuously by the independent nations, it remains a major factor, with considerable portents for the future in the light of China's emergence as one of the world's largest economies. A third effect, deriving from the first two, has been a deep-rooted and violent resentment of the Chinese by the indigenous peoples. In thousands of south-east Asian villages the shopkeepers, moneylenders and substantial landowners are Chinese, and are objects of suspicion, envy, and barely suppressed dislike.

The destruction of the south China kingdom of Nanzhao by Kublai Khan drove increasing numbers of the Thai people from that area southward. This migration established several important and related groups, who are now split up among several countries. These groups are the Shan tribes of north-east Burma, the Thais, the Laotians and many of the people of Yunnan Province of China. National boundaries inherited from the colonizing powers are frequently unrealistic. The Mekong River, for instance, on the map appears to be a logical border between Thailand and Laos; yet because the river is the main means of transport in areas with few roads and no rail links and because people who are ethnically the same and speak the same language live on both banks, it is a factor that tends to unite rather than divide them. As late as 1964 Thai government officials in Nongkai Province of Thailand near the Mekong found villages in which the inhabitants were firmly convinced they were Laotian and had pictures of the King of Laos on their walls as the object of their loyalties.

Thailand, then called Siam, became independent when a subject city of the Khmer Empire called Sukhothai broke free in 1238 CE. So preoccupied was Angkor with wars on its other frontiers, it was forced to accept the situation. A century later Sukhothai's people moved south, far into the fertile delta plain of the Chao Phraya River, where they built a larger city. This was Ayudhya, named for Rama's capital in the *Ramayana*.

Off to the west, the Burmese gradually welded together the northern section of their old empire, called Pagan, around a city named Ava, not far

from the present Mandalay. This empire used Thai mercenaries, who ultimately set up their own kingdoms in the north under hereditary lords
called *sawbwas*. These kingdoms are the Shan states, which are still fighting
to become independent from Burma.

Burma achieved significant territorial cohesion under the rule of her
final line of kings, founded by a strenuous and ambitious soldier named
Alaungpaya, who had been a village headman. He established an entrepôt
port in the southern town of Dagon, and renamed it Yangon, which means
'the abode of peace'. Rangoon is a European rendition of this name. Next
Alaungpaya turned his armies east. In 1760, while directing an attack
against the Thais, he was killed when a cannon burst near him. However,
his army kept up the assault. It took the northern Thai city of Chiengmai in
1763, and four years later sacked and burned the capital, Ayudhya, killing its
starving people mercilessly after a 14-month siege.

Burma was so strong militarily that it was able to withstand attack even
from China when the Qianlong emperor sent an army across the border
from Yunnan State in 1766. Although the Chinese columns advanced
several times from the hill passes on to the Irrawaddy River plain, each time
they were driven back. In 1770 the Manchus were obliged to agree to peace
terms. The Burmese were aware of British expansion in India and both
knew a collision of interests must come in time, especially after the
Burmese conquest of the Kingdom of Arakan on the Bay of Bengal towards
the end of the 18th century. Early in the next century Burma occupied the
big hill state of Assam, so gaining a foothold in India itself. Matters reached
a head when the assertive General Bandula prepared to attack the large and
immensely wealthy state of Bengal.

Before he could act Britain struck the first blow. In 1824, a British fleet
made a surprise attack on Yangon and captured it easily. So began the first
Burmese war. Bandula fought well, but he had no idea of the scale of the
resources behind his enemy. Like other British campaigns of the time, the
execution of this one was criminally inefficient. Constantly plagued by
disease, the death rate was appalling; 15,000 British troops died, all but a
few hundred from disease and infected wounds. In the end the Burmese
sued for peace. They paid an indemnity of £1 million, although the war cost
Britain £13 million. Burma also lost – and Britain gained – a significant
section of the Burmese coastline, and it was agreed that a British resident
should be located at Ava, mainly to foster trade.

The Burmese were by no means anxious for closer relations, and the
peace did not last long. It was reported back to India from time to time that
British subjects in Yangon were being treated disrespectfully, and feelings
mounted on both sides. When two British sea captains were arrested on

trumped-up murder charges the British Viceroy in India, Lord Dalhousie, sent a squadron to Yangon under the command of a peppery naval officer, Commodore Lambert. When his ship, HMS *Fox*, was attacked rather ineffectually by a shore battery, Lambert, acting quite beyond his instructions, used the guns of *Fox* until he had sunk everything in sight that might conceivably have been a Burmese ship of war. So the opportunity for negotiation passed at once and war became inevitable.

Lambert's attitude – epitomizing as it does the jingoist era of British colonialism – is evident in his letter to the government of India: 'It is with deep regret that I have had to commence hostilities with the Burmese nation, but I am confident that the government of India and Lord Dalhousie will see it was unavoidable and necessary to vindicate the honour of the British flag.' In fact, the government of India and Lord Dalhousie were not at all pleased, but had to accept the second Burmese war as an accomplished fact. Constantly under fire from the British press, the dismal war dragged on, leading finally to the capture of Ava and the addition of several more Burmese provinces to the British Empire.

The resulting demoralization did nothing to improve the ethics and standing of the ruling dynasty. The court at Mandalay became notorious for its violence, injustice and squalid immorality under King Thebaw, the last of his line, who succeeded to the Lion Throne after Mindon's death in 1878. Mindon had not nominated a successor and the resulting intrigue for power led to a horrifying slaughter of princes and princesses of the royal house, both adults and children. As in other parts of mainland south-east Asia, it was forbidden to touch the person of any of the royal line, and sacrilege to spill their blood. Thus the executions ordered by Thebaw were in the macabre tradition of the past. The victims were first sewn inside red velvet sacks and then despatched by breaking their necks with blows from sandalwood clubs.

This atrocity deeply alarmed British residents in Burma, caused an outcry around the world, and brought the British government under strong pressure to put an end to Thebaw's misrule. Almost at once Thebaw began to intrigue with the French in Indo-China, with the idea of playing them off against the British. The British government now waited only for a suitable pretext for war, which Thebaw provided soon enough. A money dispute arose between the Court and a big teak monopoly company, the Bombay–Burma Trading Corporation. The British government intervened, an expeditionary force occupied Mandalay in 1885 and the following year the monarchy was deposed. The conquest of Burma was complete. Conversion of the royal palace into a British club became an ironic symbol of Burma's new status as a mere province of British India.

The burning of the Siamese capital, Ayudhya, had destroyed one of south-east Asia's most beautiful and populous cities – a source of marvel to the European traders who visited it. However, a small Thai army had been able to fight its way out of the ruins and, in spite of four more Burmese raids, regained control of the Chao Phraya River delta, the region's rice-bowl. An army officer, General Chakri, became king under the title of Rama I. So began the dynasty that still reigns, as constitutional monarchs, in Thailand today.

The destruction of their capital had taught the Thais a bitter lesson, and Rama I was guided mainly by strategic considerations in choosing a site for a new one. He decided to place the broad stream of the Chao Phraya River between him and his enemies, and found the site he needed at a village named Bangkok. Foreigners still use this name, but the Thais call their capital Krungthep, which means 'the city of angels'. Old people who had known Ayudhya in its glory were called in to advise the architects of the new city, for it was intended that it should resemble its predecessor as closely as possible. Ayudhya had been situated on low land almost completely enclosed by a great bend of the river, criss-crossed with hundreds of canals, which are called *klongs*. This was how Bangkok acquired the *klongs* which were such a distinctive feature, although most have now been filled in to provide wider roads for the city's hectic motor traffic.

The early Chakri monarchs continued to rule in the traditional barbaric and despotic fashion. The king was regarded as a god, people had to enter his presence on all fours, and as much as to touch his person meant death. His title was 'lord of life' and he held summary powers over all his subjects. When he travelled outside his palace, which gleamed with gold leaf and multi-coloured tiles, the ordinary people shut themselves away inside their houses, to avoid the risk of being seen with their heads higher than the king's, for this, even if inadvertent, was a capital offence.

In 1848 a young official, using the services of a marriage go-between, sought the release of a young woman from the king's vast harem so he could marry her. The mere intention was construed as treason. Not only were the young man and woman executed, but also eight other people, since they had known what was going on and had not informed the Court. Apart from protecting the interests of the king and aristocracy, the government took only the most casual interest in law and order. In civil cases especially, the law was so partial and illogical that few people had the temerity to resort to it.

Nevertheless, Siam became a major power early in the 19th century, determined to rival the military strength of Burma, and expanding eastward into much of Laos and Cambodia. The country was not then poor or overcrowded. Most people lived in little villages along the many waterways, vacant land was available to anyone who wanted to take it up, and the only serious burden imposed by the government was taxation. Under

Rama III this burden became greater because the government let out the right to collect taxes – the so-called 'tax farming' system. These agents, who were mainly Chinese immigrants, bid for the right to collect taxes and were allowed to keep whatever they could realize above their bid. The tax system resulted in a large slave class, perhaps as much as a third of the population. Most were persons who had voluntarily gone into slavery for non-payment of debts. They were free to transfer themselves from one owner to another and could redeem their freedom simply by repaying the debt. Few chose to do so because slaves were exempt from taxation.

Rama III agreed reluctantly to a trade agreement with Britain in 1826. The Thais did their best to ignore or circumvent it, because they had no wish to follow the Indians and Burmese into the imperial maw. Rama III saw that every skill he could muster would be needed to escape colonial domination – this became the policy of the dynasty. It was served best by Rama IV, better known to the rest of the world as King Mongkut, because the reminiscences of his children's English governess, Anna Leonowens, use this personal name. It is a pity that the Western image of this shrewd and intelligent ruler should have so much been formed by the film and musical comedy freely adapted from what were, even in their original form, rather inaccurate observations. Anna's main interest to history comes from the simple fact of her appointment. This sprang from Mongkut's awareness that his descendants might the more easily ward off the colonizing powers if they spoke English. His judgement in this matter and many others more important were major reasons for Thailand remaining at least nominally independent through the colonial era.

Mongkut was a Buddhist monk for 27 years before he became king in 1851 at the age of 47. Largely due to his reform of the Buddhist organization in Thailand it has become one of the best organized religious orders in the world. Mongkut's own character was formed by these years of monastic discipline, devotion to education and self-denial for, like other monks, he was enjoined to celibacy and could own no property other than his yellow robe, sandals and a few other necessities. He was polygamous as king because that was the custom, inspired more by the political advantage of binding many families to the throne than by the personal desires of the monarch. He permitted members of his harem to marry others in certain cases and it has been recorded that a man who abducted one of them was let off with a fine amounting to about $5.

Siam was set on the path for major reform under his rule, largely on his own initiative, for he was no reactionary forced into reforms by a national-ist movement. Indeed, he had to cajole and encourage his people into accepting liberality and change. His energies seemed to flow in every direction. He set up printing presses, encouraged Christian missionaries, promoted education, issued a modern system of currency and democratized the monarchy by making himself far more accessible to the people.

He welcomed help from the West and accepted advisers from many countries to assist in the reform of Siamese law and institutions. There was a limit to what he could do in a 17-year reign, but in that time he gave his country a decisive push from the medieval into the modern world. Mongkut was a man of considerable energy and intellectual curiosity, and even the circumstances of his death are typical. He died in 1868 as the result of a fever he caught when returning from a scientific expedition he had organized to view an eclipse of the sun. His epitaph might well have been the words of an English missionary who described his rule as 'the mildest and best heathen government on the face of the globe'.

The situation in Siam's neighbours to the east, the Indo-Chinese states which are now Vietnam, Laos and Cambodia, was quite different. A group of French Jesuit missionaries had an early and major influence. They persevered in spite of considerable persecution and the Christian community, almost entirely Roman Catholic, numbered several hundred thousand by the end of the 17th century.

In the final quarter of the 18th century a major revolt broke out in the mountains of northern Vietnam and then spread to the plains. This Tay Son rebellion was an expression of mass discontent with high taxation, official corruption and the harsh rule of the mandarins. It was the beginning of the end for the two rival dynasties in the north and the south, the Trinh and the Nguyen. The defeated Trinh fled into China; the Nguyen were driven out of Hue, their vulnerable and unstrategic capital sited according to the predictions of astrologers, and went into hiding in the far south, which was then largely unpopulated jungle.

They lived as outlaws on the islands of the Gulf of Thailand until, finally, their cause was taken up by the French Apostolic Vicar, Pignane de Behaine, who negotiated an agreement with the French government to restore the Nguyen to the throne in return for a trade monopoly and the cession of certain territories to France. At first de Behaine had difficulty persuading the French authorities in Asia to implement this agreement, but they eventually mustered a small French mercenary army which, using modern weapons, was highly effective. Not only was the southern kingdom recaptured but Hanoi in the north was also taken in 1802. The conquest of the north was relatively easy, since the Trinh leaders had already been displaced by the Tayson popular movement. Unity of

Vietnam under single rule was, then, largely the result of French exploitation of rival factions. A treaty was signed in 1862 ceding three southern provinces to France and permitting missionaries to work anywhere in the country. Six years later the French occupied three more provinces. They established a protectorate over Cambodia in 1864, and, 19 years later, over north Vietnam. Tribal areas along the Mekong River were added in 1893 and given the name of Laos. These colonies became known as French Indo-China.

13 The Malay World: Majapahit and Malacca

The Javanese empire of Majapahit, which existed for about 200 years from 1293 CE, was one of the last of the major Hinduized states of island southeast Asia, and probably the best remembered. In this lies possibly its greatest importance, for the Majapahit tradition has been adopted as part of its national heritage by modern Indonesia. Some Indonesians have seen in Majapahit a pan-Malay empire which might again be realized in the future.

There is a good deal of disagreement about how large Majapahit actually was. Tradition claims it extended beyond Java and Sumatra to most of Malaya, the Celebes (Sulawesi) and even parts of what are now the Philippines, possibly also to New Guinea. Such contentions are based substantially on what is a suspect source – an account of the empire written in 1365 by Majapahit's court historian, the Buddhist monk Mpu Prapanca, in a long panegyric poem.

Indonesia's independence leader and first President, Sukarno, referred to Prapanca's account of Majapahit during discussions, in the final years of the Japanese occupation of Indonesia during the Second World War, about the form a future independent republic might take. At these discussions the Malayan peninsula, Borneo and New Guinea were mentioned as once having been part of the Majapahit realms. While it would be extreme to regard this as evidence of Indonesian expansionist ambitions to all of these territories, the vision of a 'new Majapahit' seems to have remained in the minds of some Indonesian leaders.

Apart from its contributions to the nationalist ambition, Majapahit has had important and lasting social consequences in East Java, which is still extensively Hinduized. This is especially true of the aristocratic, or *priyayi* class. This region has only a thin layer of Islam over much earlier animist and later Hindu influences, and Bali, which can properly be associated with it in this context, remains almost entirely Hindu. It is not without interest that President Sukarno's father was from the *priyayi* class and that his mother was Balinese.

In the 14th century Majapahit became a major co-ordinator of the spice trade to Europe, based on the port city, Surabaya, and Majapahit itself, some distance up the Brantas River, on a rich, rice-growing plain. It seems to have been a loose confederation of convenience between autonomous spice-producing states owing only token allegiance. Hence, far from being an empire derived by conquest, Majapahit appears more to have been a kingdom controlling East Java, Madura and Bali, with widespread recipro-cal commercial contacts with the spice-growing Indonesian islands on one level; on another, trading relations with China and with Europe, via Egypt, which passed commodities on to Venice.

Majapahit appears to have been at its zenith during the prime-minister-ship of Gaja Mada in the latter part of the 14th century. Whatever the facts about this, Gaja Mada is regarded as a national hero. One of Indonesia's largest universities, established in Jogjakarta during the struggle for inde-pendence from the Dutch, is one of many national institutions named after him. Majapahit declined in importance after Gaja Mada died in 1364. We are told it was found necessary to appoint four ministers to do his work, but in spite of their efforts the kingdom drifted into a phase of less competent government from which it never recovered. As always, a stronger enemy was ready to take advantage of weakness. It was probably a league of Muslim princes, based on the port of Demak, that conquered Majapahit about 1520.

The Muslims who spread the faith of Allah to south-east Asia were mostly Indian. When Islam reached Indonesia and Malaysia it was substan-tially modified from the stern ascetic faith of the desert, and because of this was more readily acceptable. The mystic Sufist school of Islam has elements of magic, and a certain flexibility which allowed the incorpora-tion of ancient animist beliefs when it reached south-east Asia. And since Islam did not have professional priests, the missionaries were usually trad-ers; adoption of Islam gave a definite commercial advantage to ambitious local rajas.

These elements have important present-day implications, making neces-sary a large distinction between Islam in Indonesia and Malaysia and that in the Middle East, especially the fundamentalist branches. In the Middle East, Pakistan and Afghanistan, Muslim orthodoxy is conservative and restric-tive, whereas in Indonesia the religion is much more pliable. Women have a high degree of personal freedom and independence, play an important part in government and business, and are not limited in their movements and freedom to gain an education.

The last of the larger Malay maritime empires was the first to be located on the Malayan peninsula itself. This was Malacca, a west-coast port on the straits which bear its name. According to a 16th-century Portuguese observer, Tomé Pires, in his *Suma Oriental*, Parameswara, the founder of

Malacca, may have been of Shailendra descent, of the same blood as the dynasty that had ruled Shrivijaya. Certainly development of the two empires was similar, and they both had the same commercial motive – domination of the Malacca Straits trade. Singapore is their modern equivalent.

Nowadays Malacca's river has silted up and is useful only as a haven for a few fishing boats. The sleepy town looks out over a shallow, muddy stretch of sea over which the monsoon drives an endless succession of short, steep waves. But 600 years ago both the river and the sea approaches were readily navigable, providing a convenient port for sailing ships. The weather is seldom stormy and the two monsoons, the trade winds of this region, blow with remarkable regularity.

Because of this, Malacca was a useful stopping place for the Ming armadas. Peace, and its location on the main sea route through south-east Asia, permitted Malacca to grow rapidly. Indeed, China issued an order to Malacca's main potential enemy, Siam, not to attack the city. In the two decades from 1411, five Malaccan rulers journeyed to the Chinese court. The Gujarati Muslims from India played a major part in its brisk trade. They came to Malacca in hundreds, using all the efficiency in trade and commerce that distinguishes their descendants in India today; indeed, Indian cotton cloth and spices were the major commodities traded. Malacca's revenues came from a 6 per cent duty levied on the value of all cargoes brought in.

The first Portuguese ships to arrive in Malacca, in 1509, found the city at the height of its influence. The arrival of the Europeans caused much uneasiness among the Gujarati Muslims, who, from their experiences off the west Indian coast, knew something of Portuguese methods. They anticipated a commercial challenge in south-east Asia, and persuaded the rulers of Malacca to agree to a sudden attack on the European squadron. The Portuguese were forced to withdraw, leaving behind two burning ships, many men killed, and 19 members of a shore party held as prisoners. Revenge was not long delayed. Two years later the second Viceroy, d'Albuquerque, arrived off Malacca personally with a fleet of 18 ships, demanding, at gunpoint, the return of the Portuguese prisoners and compensation for the ships that had been destroyed.

Malacca decided to resist, and the Portuguese then took the city by storm, after several days' hard fighting. The European force was small – European forces in Asia usually were – but its discipline, superior arms and the supporting firepower of the ships allowed it to win the day. Also, resistance was far from general. Many of the merchants living in the town had no real loyalty to its rulers – they were mainly interested in ending the fighting quickly so trade could be resumed. Following their usual custom, the Portuguese consolidated their victory by building a strong, stone fortress near the river mouth. Its gateway can still be seen in Malacca, surrounded by green lawns in a park that looks over the sea.

The Portuguese had not been long in Malacca before its prosperity began to decline. Like most colonial powers, their primary objective was to make money, but the Portuguese set standards of rapacity never equalled afterwards, and so doomed their empire in Asia. Eventually they became so hated for their treachery, cruelty and greed that shipping began to avoid the port. Most of the Gujarati traders now went to ports in north Sumatra. Another European power, Holland, was to be the Portuguese nemesis. Dutch ships bombarded Malacca in 1606, and from then on blockaded the port more or less continuously. Malacca's trade became almost non-existent, and eventually the town even ran short of food, for it was dependent on rice imports from Java. The Dutch, in an alliance with Malacca's former Malay rulers, attacked it in force in 1640, and six months later the fortress capitulated.

Malacca never recovered, because the Dutch did not allow it to do so. While they held Malacca nobody else could reinstate its trading potential, and so commerce was diverted to the East Indies (now Indonesia) in which the Dutch were more interested. Dutch military government in Malacca was harsh, and much misery resulted from the hostility between the Protestant Hollanders and the Catholic Malay and Eurasian converts. Thus, the early promise of Malacca came to nothing. It became one of the first victims of the age of imperialism.

However, it was not the only one. For 200 years from 1400 south-east Asia was engaged in a busy trade with much of the world, carried in Chinese, Indian and Arab ships. This was to change as the European colonizers took over the region, usually at gunpoint. Additionally, climate change, the Little Ice Age that was to cause poverty, even starvation, in many parts of the world, resulted in a global trade recession.

Although the kingdom of Johore, at the extreme south of the Malay peninsula, achieved a certain continuity of rule it, too, was riven with dissension and strife. The rest of the peninsula reverted to small, primitive river kingdoms, passing through restless alliances and perpetual, if sporadic, warfare between neighbours. The northern states became vassals of Siam. For a time, dominance over much of the rest of Malaya was exercised by a race of sea pirates, the Bugis of Sulawesi.

British merchants began to trade in a limited way with this small, under-populated Malaya during the 18th century. One of them was a sea captain named Francis Light who, after much argument, persuaded the

British East India Company to establish a port on Penang, the small mountainous island off the north-western coast. This settlement, Georgetown, founded in 1786, was the first British foothold on Malayan soil. As usual, trade was the main consideration. The East Indiamen, as the company's ships were called, needed a base to break the long journey to and from China for tea. This trade was fast expanding. Ship design improved and tea, unknown in England before the middle of the 17th century, was fast displacing coffee and stronger beverages in popularity, its appeal to the rapidly developing British morality succinctly described in the poet William Cowper's description of 'the cups that cheer, but not inebriate'.

Thomas Stamford Raffles, who had been governor of Java during the Napoleonic wars, landed in 1819 on a small, swampy island off the Johore coast, separated from it only by a narrow, shallow channel. This island of Temasik, inhabited only by a few fishermen, seemed worthless to the Sultan of Johore, who agreed to lease it in perpetuity. The new settlement, Singapore, quickly proved its value. As early as 1824, the date of the first official census, more than 10,000 people had settled there. In 1824 Dutch and British spheres of influence were regularized by treaty. Holland withdrew her objections to Singapore and exchanged Malacca for the only British post in the East Indies, Bencoolen, on Sumatra. Two years later Singapore was united with Georgetown on Penang and Malacca as a separate colonial territory, the Straits Settlements.

14 Indonesia: the Last Independent Kingdoms and the Extension of Dutch Rule

The merchant adventurers of Holland began that country's three and a half centuries of association with the fertile islands they called the East Indies under a haze of cannon smoke. They were treacherous, cruel and rapacious, and from first acquaintance excited fear and hatred among the local people.

In these respects they differed little from their fellow European traders in this region. Journeys to and from the Indies were so hazardous that generally only criminals and others of desperate character and uncertain morality would take the risks. For many years an average loss of a quarter of the crews of ships trading to the Indies was regarded as normal. The first Dutch fleet of four ships to reach the islands in 1596 lost 145 of its complement of 249 during a voyage of 14 months. Many of these deaths were from scurvy.

Dutch exploitation might never have gone further than the casual mixture of piracy and trading typical of this earliest penetration of European influence had it not been for the ambitious vision of Jan Coen, who was appointed the first Governor-General in 1618. He foresaw a vast Dutch commercial empire in the East, with ramifications far beyond the Indies. Coen achieved control of the trading port of Djakarta in West Java and built there a strong fortress and a miniature Dutch town. Its rows of small white houses huddled close together along the banks of muddy canals, with their brown-tiled roofs, leaded-light windows and heavy shutters, were inspired by a keen homesickness for the Netherlands. In 1619 this town was given Holland's ancient name, Batavia. The small Dutch outpost did not, and could not, initially challenge the still-powerful rulers of Java. It successfully withstood some probing assaults from them, then signed agreements which technically accepted their overlordship.

Because of the remoteness of these islands from Europe, their spices had always commanded very high prices. At that time the Malukus (Moluccas) were the only place where cloves grew, and the nutmeg tree was found exclusively on Banda and Ambon. Jan Coen used a mixture of persuasion and force to secure a monopoly on this lucrative trade. He then consolidated his position by driving trade competitors, especially the English, from Indonesian waters. There were many obscure but violent incidents, of which the best remembered is the killing of a few English traders and their Chinese assistants at Ambon in 1623. In spite of an ensuing battle of words between the Dutch and English governments, the British East India Company was not interested enough to finance a lengthy war. The English disappeared from the Indies, except for a single post at Bencoolen in Sumatra.

The Dutch applied rigid controls on the economy of the islands, for they were determined not to allow the price of cloves and nutmeg to fall because of over-supply. They forced the local people to cut down and burn their trees, until spice production had fallen to a quarter of the former crop. Villagers who resisted were ruthlessly hunted down and shot, and their homes burned. Coen's expedition against Banda to secure the nutmeg monopoly is one of the horrifying incidents of colonial history. The islanders fought back bravely, but were overwhelmed by the superior weapons of the Dutch. Fifteen thousand were killed, and the survivors were forced to grow the spices for the Dutch under conditions little better than slavery. The company determined the price it would pay, and forced the growers to accept trade goods from Batavia as payment.

Since these were almost always over-valued, this barter system was very much to the disadvantage of the Indonesians. The prosperity of the islands diminished, and over the next century the population of Ambon declined by a third. So deep was the bitterness aroused by these policies that when world demand for spices increased in the 18th century even extreme measures could not induce these people to increase production of cloves and nutmeg. Finally the trees were successfully grown in India and the Dutch monopoly ended.

Meanwhile, the toehold on Java was precariously maintained. The last major Indonesian state prior to the colonial period was based on an inland capital, Mataram, in Central Java. It became large and powerful during the lifetime of an outstanding leader, Sultan Agung, who came to the throne in 1623. According to the court records of the time, he regarded himself as the successor to the great rulers of Majapahit, even though he was a Muslim. By 1625 he ruled all of Java except for small areas at the eastern and western tips of the island, which were controlled by Bali and Bantam, a vigorous state based on the West Javanese pepper trade. The society on Bali, led by Hindu-Javanese families who had fled from Majapahit, maintained a

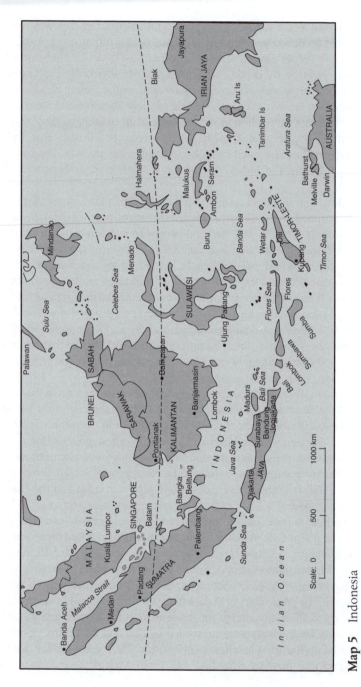

Map 5 Indonesia

well-organized opposition to both Mataram and the Dutch, keeping their own island and a small enclave on Java independent.

Between 1627 and 1630 Agung made determined efforts, both by treachery and direct assault, to destroy Batavia. The armies of Mataram placed a dam across the river that provided the fortress's water supply, and, when all else failed, instituted a siege involving thousands of soldiers. However, this massive army soon ran short of food. Dutch naval power was vastly superior – the Dutch ships destroyed a fleet of 200 boats carrying rice – and within weeks the starving army of Mataram was forced to retreat. A treaty followed guaranteeing Batavia's continued existence.

In many ways Mataram followed the traditions of Majapahit and was probably similar to even earlier Javanese kingdoms. It is consequently of interest because there are many written descriptions of it by European observers. Mataram resembled in a number of ways the Indian kingdoms of more than a thousand years before its time – the first of which we have independent accounts. The observations of the Greek Megasthenes about the Mauryan Empire in north India in the 4th century and those of Dutchmen who visited the *kraton* – the palace complex – of Mataram, bear witness to this continuity of tradition.

One similarity was the king's guard, composed of women armed with spears and lances, who were the only people allowed near the ruler when he appeared in public. Far more basic was the sacral role of the king, his place as an intermediary between the people and the feared and worshipped forces of nature, which are impressive enough in Java, with its active volcanoes and sudden, violent thunderstorms, in some places occurring on more than 300 days a year. Only the king, supported by the spirits of his ancestors, could negotiate with these forces, on which the common prosperity and safety so much depended. There are links with east Asia in the *pusakas*, or sacred objects, on which the welfare of the kingdom was believed to depend, hidden away in a secret place deep within the *kraton*.

The Sultan of Mataram's life, and that of all Javanese princes of his tradition, was surrounded by magic and mystery. He was believed to possess sacred weapons, such as swords, that could make him invulnerable; he would spend nights near the graves of his ancestors, gathering magical influence, and was believed to obtain dynamic power from the soil itself, from thunder and lightning, and other manifestations of nature. In spite of being Western-educated and well-read in European political theory, Indonesia's independence leader and first president, Sukarno, consciously followed this tradition.

The sultan was above and beyond the law. If he behaved in a peremptory, brutal and even, at times, hideously criminal fashion, this was seen by the ordinary people as a manifestation of divinity in him. The ruler was expected to live in a more extravagant, dynamic and flamboyant way than ordinary men – to be a great user of women, among other things. Because of this belief in his superhuman qualities, the rulers had absolute powers of life and death over even the highest-born, and these seem never to have been questioned.

Some Indonesian people, although apparently very gentle, have hidden capacities for violence and can be suddenly taken with a killing frenzy, described by the word *amuk* – mad. The violent murder of as many as a million people after the fall of Sukarno in 1965 is indicative. European observers were shocked when Agung's commander ordered the summary execution of 800 of his soldiers because they had failed in the attempt to take Batavia. The aristocracy, made up of princes of the royal house and of associated states, had to live in the *kraton* with the king and could be (and sometimes were), killed at a word from him at the slightest suspicion of disloyalty. Royal wrath was visited on high and low alike without mercy. The peasants suffered, as peasants did in every feudal state, and in much the same ways. They were taxed and sweated to support the *kraton* and regularly conscripted to fight the king's wars. As elsewhere in south-east Asia, such armies could number 100,000 or more, and casualties among them were often high. The relatively small population of the region before 1800 has been ascribed to this.

Nevertheless, Mataram did have a considerable prosperity and a definite system of law. Dutch observers say the region around the *kraton* was intensely cultivated, with hill after hill built up into a complex of terraced, irrigated rice fields. Several million people lived under Mataram's rule, in perhaps 3000 villages of 100 families or more, each surrounded by their fields. It was an organization of rural life still typical of much of Asia today. Although Agung was a Muslim, he did not base the law of Mataram solely on that of Islam. The religious courts existed, but the law was a mixture of the Islamic and the traditional Javanese customary code, called *adat*, which retains considerable force today.

The *kraton* itself was a rambling collection of red-brick, stone and timber buildings, gardens, pavilions and courtyards. Certain parts of it were semi-public. Much of the rest housed the king's retainers and the nobles who were kept constantly under his eye so they might have no opportunity to plot rebellion. Other parts of the *kraton* were never open to visitors or any but the highest officials. Building work for the ruler was a constant occupation for much of the community because new *kratons* were required constantly. There is an interesting echo of Angkor in the fact that every new ruler was expected to build a new *kraton*. Sometimes the residence was shifted after the passing of a certain number of years, or if the old *kraton* were defiled for ritual reasons.

Those who reflect on the difficulties of Indonesian democracy, the privileges assumed as if of right by its rulers and their families, the economic advantages they have over the ordinary people, and the ruthless decimation of whole communities, as in Aceh, Irian Jaya and Timor-Leste (East Timor), might also consider the extent to which these things are simply part of a long-standing tradition, perhaps likely to persist into Indonesia's future unless other influences can restrain them.

The rulers of Mataram did not regard the Dutch as superiors, or even as equals. Initially they were welcomed because competition between them and the Portuguese drove up spice prices. However, the sultan treated the Dutch with contempt, because they were merchants, and forced them to wait for hours in the hot sun before he received them. On the other hand, the officials of the company treated the rulers with deference, regularly offering gifts imported from Europe.

Nevertheless, during Agung's reign the Dutch had been able to consolidate. The third Governor-General, Anthony Van Diemen, took Malacca from the Portuguese. This, with the eviction of the British, left Holland as the major trading power in the Indies. Van Diemen and Agung died in the same year, 1645, and the relationship between the company and the state of Mataram began to change. Agung's successor, Amangkurat, was one of the worst of the Javanese despots, weak, autocratic and cruel. He ordered the killing of anyone he saw as opposition, even members of his own family, and is notorious for the massacre of more than two thousand Muslim 'priests' he had called into conference. In 1646 he signed a treaty that made him dependent on the Dutch for much of his personal income. Eventually his excesses alarmed the leaders of surrounding vassal states, who turned against him. The ruler of one of these led a revolt that dethroned Amangkurat. His *kraton* at Mataram was burned, his treasures looted and he died in obscurity in a village house, allegedly poisoned with toxic coconut water.

His successor, Amangkurat II – Amangkurat is a title rather than a name – who was also said to be of weak character, was restored to power by a Dutch army. The price was control of the Mataram empire by the company, which now had troops stationed permanently at the new *kraton*. With Mataram subject, Bantam's years of independence were also numbered. The Dutch took advantage of a royal quarrel there to manipulate the succession and control the state.

So the 18th century began with the Dutch empire greatly extended. Although the old kingdoms had lost their power, the Dutch did not disturb their traditions and the essential social organization. The rulers and the aristocracy remained in their traditional positions, but were not permitted to make war on one another. The Dutch, in fact, used them as agents. The nobles became 'regents', responsible for exacting a certain amount of tax from the peasants, which they had to pass on to the company. The worst features of the independent states remained – but added to them was the burden of tribute going to the Dutch. Thus the old social relationship was maintained into modern times, the privileged position of the *priyayi* still remaining a feature of Javanese society.

Batavia itself was afflicted for a hundred years with a contagious fever – probably malaria – which caused a high death rate among the Dutch settlers. The large numbers of Chinese who had settled in Indonesia now became increasingly influential. The 'regents' appointed by the Dutch were usually lazy and inefficient, and had a contempt for the details of commerce. Chinese immigrants were ready to act as intermediaries, provided they saw a good profit in it for themselves. Internal highway tolls, another burden on the ordinary people, were often 'farmed out', like other forms of taxation, to the Chinese. Because of this direct relationship with the people in what came to be an extortionist role, the Chinese came to be despised and hated. This attitude is still strong today, and lies behind regular episodes of anti-Chinese violence since independence.

Like all institutions that exist for a long time without change, the Dutch East India Company gradually deteriorated. The Chinese made money but, increasingly, the company did not. It was dissolved in 1799 because of its heavy losses and overheads and a bad record of corruption among its officials. Direct rule by the Dutch government did not mend matters significantly. Holland became embroiled in the Java War, which dragged on for five years from 1825. It was caused by Dutch interference in the succession in the important Javanese state of Jogjakarta. A prince named Diponegoro, the eldest of his family, was passed over by the Dutch, who installed a younger brother as sultan. Diponegoro led a revolt that combined many different hostilities, including those of the aristocracy against the Dutch and the ordinary people against the Chinese who were their immediate oppressors. Vague and mixed though its motives were, the war was intense and destructive. It resulted in the loss of 8000 Dutch soldiers and the death of perhaps a quarter of a million Chinese and Indonesians – mostly civilians not actually concerned with the fighting.

From 1830 Holland was involved in war at home – a nine-year revolt of her Belgian provinces that completed the exhaustion of the Netherlands Treasury, already depleted by the Napoleonic Wars. To restore her finances Holland imposed on the Indies the cultivation system, requiring the

planting of one-fifth of all agricultural land in a crop dictated by the colonial power. This crop became the property of the government. Added to
existing burdens, this resulted in such a severe 'squeeze' of the peasants that
there were major famines in Java. The cultivation system introduced new
crops to the island – sugar, coffee and indigo, and later tea, produced
entirely for export.

The vast sums pouring out of Batavia made up close to one-third of the
entire Netherlands budget over a period of 50 years. Yet barely half this
revenue came from the cultivation system. A further large sum came from
land taxes, customs duties, and monopolies in salt, opium and pawnshop
operation. Little was provided in return. No attempt was made to develop
a basic education system of any consequence, or to train Indonesians in the
professions. Introduction of universal basic schooling was considered once
or twice, late in the colonial period, but dismissed as being too expensive.

15 India under Two Masters: the Grand Moguls and the East India Company

After the decline of the Gupta Empire no unifying force comparable with it emerged for nine centuries, leaving north India at the mercy of any marauding band that chose to ride down through the passes. Revealed instead are cruel and extortionate north Indian kingdoms, like those of the Muslim sultans of Delhi, and the petty empires of scores of warlike princelings, each the predator of a tract of country dominated by a central fortress. Although incessantly preoccupied with war, these rulers, the Rajputs, contributed to their country's defencelessness by their quarrelling, lack of a common purpose, and retention of old-fashioned if romantic military methods against enemies who had cannon and had advanced the use of cavalry to an exact science. Reckless, indeed suicidal, bravery was no effective answer to these things. It was a tradition of the Rajputs, when one of their fortresses was doomed to fall, to burn all their women and children alive on a funeral pyre while the men sallied out to meet death at the hands of their enemies.

Many of the invaders who drove down from central Asia were simple destroyers, like the Huns, who were execrated in India just as they were in Europe and China. Later 'barbarians' were more cultivated, although just as cruel. They were Muslims, practising a form of Islam derived through and influenced by the civilized and artistic Persian (Iranian) culture. To these people the ornamented architecture of the Hindu temples, their many statues of gods and goddesses, elaborate rituals and use of music for worship, were evidence of an idolatry the removal of which, by fire and sword, was a religious duty. It was one that associated itself conveniently with looting. In his book *India* John Keay compares these pre-Mogul invaders with the subsequent European ones: 'Like the white *sahibs* of European colonialism, the true believers of the (Delhi) sultanate saw India simply as a source of wealth, a scene of adventure, and a subject for moral indignation spiked with prurient fantasy. They too, indeed, were colonialists. Compromise with the natives was as unthinkable as it was preposterous' (p. 308).

Buddhism in India was hastened into decline by the Muslim invaders, who slew its peaceful monks in thousands and destroyed the great teaching monasteries. Nalanda, with more than 10,000 monks and students in the 13th century, was sacked, and thousands of its occupants killed. The survivors fled north to Nepal and Tibet. One of the last to go, Vikramashila, was demolished so completely that no trace of its considerable buildings remains.

This phase of conquest and brutality is balanced somewhat by a blending of indigenous and Islamic art, notably painting and architecture. The delicate building of this time, with its shady courts, fretted walls, water gardens and tall graceful minarets, owed much to Persian influence and the dislike of the conquerors from the clean air of the hills for the hot mugginess of the Indian plain in the months before and during the monsoon rains. It is a style still very much alive, and one which spread far beyond India, as the railway station in Kuala Lumpur and the extravagant marble mosque in Brunei can testify.

It also seems likely that the spinning wheel was introduced to India from Persia about 1350, massively benefiting a cottage industry that would soon provide most of the world with its cotton fabrics.

Order and authority returned to north India with the advent of the Muslim dynasty Europe called the Grand Moguls. They added glamour, pageantry and a strange collection of legend to the world's story but, more than that, brought a unity and established methods of government that, in many respects, foreshadowed the patterns of today. At its best, it was a remarkably able administration for its time.

In 1525, with a force of only 12,000, the King of Kabul, who was to become the first Mogul emperor, Babur, marched through the Khyber gorges to conquer India. He met a defending army of 100,000 on India's traditional field of decision, the plain of Panipat, 50 miles north of Delhi, and won decisively. Babur's victory was due substantially to good discipline, highly trained cavalry, and possession of an artillery train. Fifteen thousand of the Indian army died in that battle. Judging from his own diaries, Babur was that rare combination – a visionary and a man of action with almost the skills of generalship of a Napoleon. 'I put my foot in the stirrup of resolution, set my hand on the rein of trust in God, and move

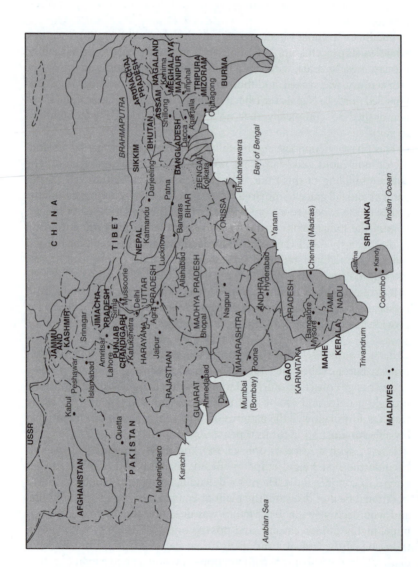

Map 6 South Asia

forward', he says, but nevertheless he maintained a close interest in the casting and transport of his field cannon.

The people of north India were accustomed to these periodic raids from the north. When Babur pushed on from Delhi to Agra, the Indians sought to placate him with the gift of an enormous diamond, thought by some to be the great stone now called the Ko-hi-noor. But Babur did not return to the mountains of the north – he laid out a garden in Agra, and made other preparations for a permanent stay, in spite of complaints in his memoirs that India lacked interesting fruits, baths and graceful buildings, and that it was steamy, hot and unattractive. Although capable enough of harsh, even cruel, actions by the standards of today, Babur was moderate and cultured for his time. He was reflective and thoughtful, with considerable powers of personality, which were fully engaged persuading his homesick followers to stay in India.

According to a chronicle of the time, when Babur's eldest son Humayun became seriously ill Babur followed a custom of his people in offering his own dearest possession, his life, in exchange for his son's restoration to health. He is said to have walked three times around Humayun's sickbed and to have pledged his own life in exchange. Humayun recovered, but Babur died at the age of 47. Humayun, heavily addicted to opium, had little of his father's powers of leadership and came close to losing the empire. He spent practically the whole of his life on the move, intriguing against, fighting with, or running away from his enemies. An enthusiastic astronomer, in 1556 Humayun missed his footing and fell down the stairs to his death when leaving his rooftop observatory. His son Akbar was several times taken hostage before his father's death made him emperor at the age of 13.

Against all expectations, all the powers of his grandfather, and more, returned to the dynasty. Akbar brought a rare genius to the task of controlling his difficult heritage. During his reign of nearly 50 years, to 1605, the Mogul Dynasty was firmly established, and even integrated with the older elements of Indian society. Although he was a Muslim for most of his life, Akbar went out of his way to win the respect and assistance of the traditional Hindu leaders and, as the decades passed, even the intolerant and wild Rajput princes came to serve him loyally. Akbar was astute enough to see that pride and self-esteem were the mainsprings of their lives, and he won them over by allowing them status symbols – the right to sound their drums in the capital, which was a privilege of royalty, or to enter the royal audience chamber fully armed.

Akbar used them in his civil service, which was organized with fixed, graded salary scales so officials did not have to depend on bribery and extortion for their incomes. This, his regularization of taxation, standardization of weights and measures and improved legal code, made India relatively peaceful and prosperous. Taxation of the peasants was limited to around a third of gross product, and the detested poll tax levied on non-Muslims remitted. Mogul India became one of the principal sources of wealth in the world, and its major port, Surat, one of the world's busiest, exporting huge quantities of cotton cloth – calico was soon to be found in large quantities in almost every European and British home. Gold and silver to pay for these cottons, silk, molasses, saltpetre and indigo – much in demand to dye military uniforms – and also huge food-crop exports, flooded into India from all parts of the world. This wealth derived from the vast resource of manpower; at this time India's population was well over a hundred million – at least three times that of the whole of Western Europe.

Unfortunately, Akbar's lively mind turned to a restless mysticism as he grew older. He established a new religion, a court cult based on the assumption of his own divinity, which sought to blend Islam and Hinduism. He even went so far as to wear the caste marks and sacred thread of the Hindu twice-born. This alarmed the orthodox among his Muslim followers, and a period of reaction set in after his death.

It was an added misfortune that his heir, Jehengir, was cruel by temperament, and reverted to such forms of punishment as flaying alive and impaling. During Jehengir's reign, in 1615, Sir Thomas Roe led a British embassy to the Mogul court. The gifts it brought were scorned as trifles, and Sir Thomas was not able to achieve as much as he had hoped. However, Jehengir formed an admiration for the quietly courageous Englishman, who stubbornly refused to knock his head three times on the floor before the Mogul, the required form of homage. Roe was able to make some trading arrangements and consolidated the first British mercantile post, which had been established by Captain Will Hawkins in Surat in 1609.

The extravagant wealth of the dynasty was at its most lavish during the reign of Jehengir's son, Shah Jahan, who is remembered chiefly because his great and lasting passion for a woman inspired one of the world's most beautiful buildings. The emperor was wholly devoted to his wife, Mumtaz Mahal. When she died in childbirth at the age of 39 after bearing him 14 children, Shah Jahan set 20,000 men to work for 22 years to build her memorial, the Taj Mahal at Agra, the most famed and lovely of all Indian monuments.

The last of the Moguls to hold more than a shadow of power was a devout and bigoted Muslim, Aurangzeb, who damaged the empire through the narrow-minded religious zeal that marked his reign from 1659 to 1707. Aurangzeb failed to control the ever-present Muslim extremist faction, which sought to persecute the Hindus. They seized the opportunity to loot and burn Hindu homes and temples, and to force Hindu officials out of office. When Hindu protesters took to the streets in large numbers they were subdued by force – on at least one occasion by sending elephants among them to trample them to death. Aurangzeb quickly lost the support of the Rajput princes, on which the empire so much depended. His most persistent enemy was the Maratha confederacy from the mountains of west India, led by a warrior chief called Shivaji. His name is important because it was later used by Hindu extremists as a symbol of their opposition to Indian Islam. In spite of his wealth and pomp, his 800 war elephants and huge army, Aurangzeb steadily lost ground against the rebels.

In 1701, six years before his death, the emperor had granted the British East India Company the right to collect revenues from land near Kolkata (Calcutta), and their influence on the trade of Bengal increased steadily from then on. During the next 40 years eight Mogul emperors, increasingly out of control of the empire, sat on the throne. Over these decades the realm split into fragments as, one by one, local officials or governors set up virtually autonomous states. So began the princely states, which were to endure into the 20th century. The largest of these states became as populous and wealthy as some of the world's leading powers of the day, the greatest of them the central Indian state of Hyderabad, whose hereditary rulers, the Nizams, became for a time the richest men in the world.

The Moguls and their administrators were, of course, a superstructure above, and supported unwillingly by, the real India, which was very different. Eighteenth-century Europe spoke in glowing terms of the treasures of Ind, but in reality the flamboyant prosperity of the Moguls was based on the exploitation and poverty of the mass of the people. After Akbar's death, the villagers suffered acutely. Mogul taxation was increased to as much as half of all produce, and even this does not take into account additional amounts extorted, less formally, by tax gatherers and local lords. Virtually all the national income that came into the hands of the governing class was spent on high living, paying retainers and the creation of private buildings, tombs and monuments. Public works like irrigation canals, roads and bridges, which would have improved the lives of the villagers, were not seen as a state responsibility. Instead local officials exacted highway tolls at strategic points, such as river fords and crossroads, for their own benefit.

Villages, then as now, stood dirty and impoverished, an untidy network set on the dusty plains. Their people were poor, vulnerable to the vagaries of the seasons and the cupidity of their rulers alike, limited in their ambitions and almost all suffering from one or more debilitating diseases. Women, worn out by bearing large families when they had scarcely left childhood themselves, were lucky indeed to survive their twenties. Those who died young were perhaps the most fortunate, since widows were traditionally burned alive on their husband's funeral pyre.

The caste system was by then fully developed. It divided Hindu society into a myriad of small groups, each of which sought to maintain its special position or privileges. In many respects the caste amounts to an exclusive society, with established rules and discipline imposed on all its members, and designed to serve their interests. Often membership of a caste group is associated with occupation, as guilds were in Europe, with work skills passing on from father to son. Closely associated is the influence and authority of the extended family, still very important in India today. India, in spite of its problems and staggering social disproportions, has evolved a remarkably diverse and vigorous culture, a reflection of a society full of subtleties and surprises. Its dance and music are distinctive, highly developed and formalized. They have also been pervasive, to the extent that the same arts throughout south-east Asia are plainly derivative from the Indian model. The elegant dances performed on the steps of Angkor Wat, and in Bali, have evolved from Indian forms. Indian art is a part of life, intimately linked with the everyday life of individuals, rather than a separate 'package' as in the West, where appreciation of the arts tends to be a spectator sport.

Perhaps because of this much Indian art is ephemeral – one gets the feeling that its great works have survived almost by accident. There is a strong sense that it is the act of creation that is important, rather than the finished work. Frequently, large amounts of time and effort are put into displays for processions, carnivals or religious occasions, using temporary materials that are destroyed or disregarded soon after they are complete. It is very much art of the moment, using colour, form, sound, light and fire to create as vivid, often as bizarre, an effect as possible.

A further dimension of Indian culture is the mysterious, even the miraculous, based on meditation and prolonged mental training. This can manifest itself in apparently impossible physical events – people who can walk on fire without being burned, who have been buried alive for long periods, withstood what would be for most people terrible injuries amounting to torture, the stopping of the heartbeat and breathing for long periods. How much of this is genuine and how much trickery is difficult to determine, and is a constant area of controversy.

During the early Mogul period the first European trading posts continued to exist in a small way, more or less on sufferance. The merchants neither exercised political power nor sought it. Their motive was trade, their ambition to amass enough capital to retire at home in comfort as soon as possible. These *nouveau-riche* 'nabobs' excited resentment and curiosity when they retired to the English countryside, not least for their acquired habit of regular bathing.

During the 17th century three major posts were established by the East India Company. These, in the order of their founding or acquisition, were: Fort St George, later to become Madras (Chennai), on the Coromandel, or south-east coast; Bombay (Mumbai) on the central-western coast; and Fort William on the Hughli River in the Ganges delta of Bengal. Fort William was later to become Calcutta (Kolkata), one of the world's biggest cities and the place from which Britain's empire in India was largely to develop.

The struggle to inherit Mogul power was intensified with the coming of the 18th century. At first circumstances seemed to favour the Hindu Maratha princes, but they were too self-seeking and disunited to take advantage of the situation. Some modern Indian historians look back on the Maratha campaigns at this time as a patriotic Hindu uprising against Islam, but the Marathas cannot really be viewed in this way after the death of their leader Shivaji in 1680. They became more interested in plunder than politics, and their power was broken in a battle with a coalition of Afghan raiders and the Muslim princes of Delhi. The Afghans emerged from this battle, at Panipat in 1761, as the strongest single force, but they had no pretensions for empire. Hence there was no Indian power left that was strong enough, and ambitious enough, to take over government of the country.

At this stage the British also had no desire to rule India; indeed, the East India Company's policy was to avoid involvement in local politics if possible. This was not necessarily the view of its officials on the spot, who understood the value of political power in promoting trade. Their influence had a far-reaching effect. One of them, Robert Clive, began the chain of events that led on to British India when he first eliminated a French foothold on the Coromandel coast, for reasons of commercial rivalry, then intervened in the succession in Bengal.

An inexperienced ruler of Bengal – he was only 19 – attacked the British settlement at Kolkata. He is said to have had more than a hundred people locked in a small room, 18 feet by 15 feet, through one tropical night. Most of them were said to have died in this 'black hole'. The apparent enormity of this event, prominently featured and coloured in almost all British histories of India written during the imperial period, depends on a single suspect source – the account of one of the survivors, one J. Z. Holwell. Now the 'facts' are disputed by several modern historians; the emotive term 'black hole' was in fact British army slang for a barracks prison; probably 64 people went into the prison, 21 survived.

Clive led a punitive expedition, regained Kolkata, and defeated a much larger Indian army at Plassey in 1757, substantially because of a secret pact with some of the Indian commanders, notably Mir Jafar, to defect. Clive, then aged 32, virtually installed Mir Jafar on the throne. The payoff was the disbursement of more than £1 million from the Bengal Treasury, of which Clive personally acquired the then huge fortune of almost £250,000. The East India Company was now in a position to control Bengal. It did so through local officials it appointed and kept in office, then consolidated its political power when in 1765 it exacted from the puppet emperor the right to collect the revenues of Bengal, Bihar and Orissa, worth as much as £3 million a year. Anarchic conditions through much of the country made further increases in British power almost inevitable. The three rapidly growing ports under British rule and British law were islands of relative peace and order amid chaos, and attracted business of all kinds.

One of the fatal weaknesses of the Mogul Empire had been its inability to foster a flourishing mercantile class with rights and influence of its own, like the sturdy British middle class even then laying the foundations of empire. The Moguls and their provincial governors dominated manufacture and trade and forced artisans and craftsmen to work for them almost as slaves. Even though merchants acquired wealth, they had no standing and no privileges. These mercantile families, who wanted only to trade fairly and lawfully, flocked to the British enclaves in thousands.

British policy from this time on was designed to subdue the entire Subcontinent. The next 50 years would be decades of regional wars to conquer Indian provinces – notably the Maratha region in the north and Mysore in the south. Two members of the Wellesley family, Lord Mornington and his brother Arthur – later to become the Duke of Wellington of Waterloo fame – were prominent in these military adventures.

Bengal, in 1769–73, suffered a famine of such intensity that, on Warren Hastings's estimate, one-third of its inhabitants died – probably as many as eight million people, generally in the most atrocious circumstances. Contemporary accounts speak of vultures, dogs and jackals eating those so weak they could no longer move, cannibalism, and the agonies of those trying to survive by eating bark and leaves. After this huge disaster a severe labour shortage disturbed the whole balance of landownership, and perhaps a third of the land of Bengal was left uncultivated for more than a decade. This was one of the blackest periods of British exploitation of India, since the forcible extraction of huge sums in tax from the peasants was maintained in spite of the extent of the famine. Tax revenues were £1.38 million for 1769/70, while famine relief offered by the company was less than £10,000.

British rule and revenues were guaranteed by taxes on land and monopolies on salt and opium, both of which were taxed. Tax exaction could be as high as 50 or even 80 per cent of a peasant's production. If the tax were not paid promptly, land and chattels were subject to seizure. However, in contrast to the agonies of the countryside the British urban enclaves prospered and grew rapidly. The Indian population of Kolkata was over a quarter of a million in 1788, in spite of a huge fire in 1780 that destroyed 15,000 homes. Mumbai and Chennai were not far behind.

The East India Company remained a commercial undertaking, based on trade and exploitation. High prices were paid for posts as company officials at the courts of Indian rulers, and large fortunes were made through 'tax-farming' the unfortunate people. The ostentation of these returning 'nabobs' continued to attract unfavourable comment at home. Clive, who became the first governor of Bengal, and his successor Warren Hastings drew widespread criticism because they had made large fortunes through the exercise of their influence. Clive was forced to defend himself on the floor of Parliament in 1772 and, after an all-night debate, was exonerated. Two years later he committed suicide in London. A similar controversy marred the reputation of Warren Hastings. Mainly as a result of these scandals, in 1773 the British government passed a regulating act which brought the operations of the East India Company under the surveillance of the Crown. While the company maintained its trading monopoly for another 40 years, political control was henceforward to be a matter for a council of directors in London, and a governor-general in India, responsible to Parliament.

The extension of British rule, while often initially resisted strenuously, was eventually accepted largely without dissension because the British, while still imposing land tax, usually kept it a little lower than had been exacted from the peasants previously. They also dealt directly with the landholders, rather than using middlemen. Collecting these revenues fairly required administration by English trained staff – this era was the real beginning of that devoted, honest, competent and unbelievably self-righteous band of Britons, the Indian Civil Service. From 1809 these young men, mostly from the public schools, were trained at the company's college at Haileybury, where they learned at least one Indian language, some Indian history and a sense of their almost divine destiny to rule and educate the 'heathen and backward natives'. Of them Rudyard Kipling wrote:

> Take up the white man's burden
> Send forth the best ye breed
> Go bind your sons to exile
> To serve your captives' need.

Unshakably convinced of their mission to govern, they were at least constructively reformist. Widow-burning was outlawed in 1829, although it continued illegally long after that. The more responsible British thinkers and statesmen began to feel the wider implications and responsibilities of their vast dominion. In 1834 the celebrated historian and essayist Thomas Macaulay, who had taken a seat on the Supreme Council for India the previous year, argued successfully for a system of education, based on the English language and European traditions, to produce 'a class, Indian in blood and colour, but English in taste, in opinions, in morals and intellect'.

This education minute has been severely criticized, especially its assertion that 'a single shelf of a good European library is worth the whole native literature of India and Arabia'. Yet English as the official language and vehicle of education, from 1835 onward, gave India, for the first time, a single language that was understood throughout the country. To some extent Persian, the court language of the Moguls, had met this requirement but it was used only by a small restricted class. A very much wider range of people learned English and India's debt to it as a unifying agency is recognized by most thoughtful Indians.

The most bitter conflicts of the expansionist phase came with the two Sikh Wars, which by 1849 resulted in the addition of the 100,000 rich square miles of the Punjab to British India – although at the cost of more than 2000 British lives. But that year also brought the 'doctrine of lapse' – a legal device requiring any Indian state where there was not an heir of natural issue to lapse to British rule. Indian princes without sons routinely adopted an heir. When they no longer had this option, seven states came under British rule over the next six years, adding several million pounds a year to the imperial revenues.

Education in the historical traditions of Europe during a phase of liberal revolutions brought to the evolving Indian intelligentsia some new and disturbing concepts – nationalism, democracy, the freedom of the individual. Up to this time no one had seriously thought of India as an entity, a possible nation. But now the tightening of the imperial grip caused serious misgivings among both Hindu and Muslim traditionalists, who could now be in no doubt of British intentions to transform Indian society.

Some historians, in particular Indian historians, regard the Indian 'mutiny' that broke out in 1857 as a consequence of this disquiet, and as the beginning of Indian nationalism. *Sepoys*, Indian soldiers in the Bengal army, turned on their officers and their families. The uprising began in Meerut after native soldiers saw 85 of their number jailed for refusing orders to bite the new Lee Enfield rifle cartridges, which had been smeared with pig and cow fat, an act forbidden to Muslims and Hindus respectively by their religions. A change of law in 1856 permitting widows to remarry – also something contrary to Hindu religious custom – may have been a contributing factor. Although the scale of the revolt was relatively small and its duration brief, the horror of it, especially that of the killing of English women and children in Cawnpore, made a tremendous impact in England. It should be recorded that British retaliation was equally brutal and a good deal more extensive, involving the destruction of whole villages, and the extermination of whole families, often completely innocent of any involvement in the rebellion.

Christopher Hibbert's *The Great Mutiny*, largely derived from carefully documented contemporary accounts, presents army officers, especially the notorious Colonel James Neil, in a very unfavourable light. When Delhi was occupied by the British, it was virtually destroyed by indiscriminate burning and looting. Thousands of people were hanged, shot or bayoneted. Another account describes how villages, many of them near Cawnpore, were surrounded by cavalry, the women and children brought out and all the men burned alive in their houses. If they tried to escape the flames they were 'cut up'. Flaying alive of mutineers was actively proposed, although there is no evidence it actually happened. In London Queen Victoria, deeply disturbed by the savagery of the reprisals, made a public appeal for moderation, and called for all Indians 'to enjoy the equal and impartial protection of the law'.

There was considerable fear that the revolt might spread throughout India, although in the event this did not happen, most *sepoy* regiments remaining 'steady'. The army at that time consisted of fewer than 50,000 British troops and more than 200,000 *sepoys* – a disproportion to be corrected after the 'mutiny'. The 'doctrine of lapse' was abolished in 1858 for fear it might prompt further revolt. More than 500 princely states would now be permitted to continue intact under British protection.

The 1857 uprising is a convenient point at which to observe the declining influence of many of the old Hindu and Muslim aristocrats. British land reforms, designed to make tax collection more efficient, disturbed the interdependent communal nature of rural communities and instead substituted definite landlord and peasant classes. In general the energetic, unscrupulous and businesslike became landlords, rather than the traditional ruling class, which was too proud to appear anxious for financial gain. When, in 1788, agricultural depression led to the forced sale of 14 per cent of Bengal lands to meet tax arrears, the buyers paid on average less than a single year's revenue. Common land, perhaps 10 per cent of all Indian land, became private property so it could be taxed, further depressing the condition of the poorest. A major survey of village India towards the end of the colonial era, in the 1930s, showed that only 39 per cent got enough to eat and that 20 per cent were virtually starving. Infant mortality was almost one in four births, life expectancy at birth about 30.

In many respects influence was going over to the mercantile middle class, the new class of British-educated, based mainly on the three big cities of British India, but especially on Kolkata. These were almost invariably from the highest castes, and were largely people who, through association with their colonial masters, had the best opportunities to improve their lot. One may perceive in them the direct ancestors of the wealthiest and middle classes of today's India.

During the final century of British rule, then, Indians on average became poorer, famines killed more people, an educated class dependent on their rulers prospered, and the colonial hold on the country tightened. In 1876 Queen Victoria was proclaimed Empress of India, leaving no doubt about how the Britons of that generation saw their imperial destiny. Back in public life after a long period of mourning for her consort Prince Albert, the queen became an enthusiastic supporter of Prime Minister Disraeli's campaign to strengthen the British Empire by any means. Imperial power was now to be vigorously advanced, especially in India, which Victoria saw as the main jewel in her crown.

Autocratic though the methods were, much of this effort was of value. An impartial and codified system of law, well-adapted to and largely based on local traditions, did much to reduce oppression and injustice. Telegraph lines and a cheap, efficient postal service were developed after 1850. Even if the devout deplored railways because they jostled all castes together in shocking proximity, Indians did not hesitate to use them after the first passenger line was opened in 1853. Also the trains were able to move food quickly, and this helped to mitigate the intensity of famines. Nevertheless rural poverty continued to increase, and in 1877 India experienced its worst famine of the century, taking perhaps five million lives. In 1883 a code was developed that placed the responsibility squarely on the government to provide adequate famine relief. After the turn of the century this proved reasonably effective, with one massive and disastrous exception – the Bengal famine of 1943.

16 Gandhi's India: the Struggle for Liberty

Universities teaching the Western humanities were founded in the three main Indian colonial cities, Kolkata, Mumbai and Chennai, in 1857, the same year as the 'Indian mutiny'. Of the two events the first was arguably the more significant, since Indian nationalism developed largely among the graduates of those universities. During the next 30 years nearly 50,000 Indians passed the entrance examinations, which themselves required literacy in English – hence the advent of a curious qualification – 'failed BA'. Nevertheless 5000 did achieve the Bachelor of Arts degree.

Christianity was an important influence on Rammohun Roy, the first Indian reformer of consequence. It was he who led a vigorous campaign that persuaded the British government to overcome its reluctance to interfere in religious customs and prohibit the custom of *suttee*, which obliged, and often forced, a widow to be burned alive on the funeral pyre of her husband. Roy had watched his own sister die in this way. In 1828 Roy founded the Brahma Samaj, which sought to reform Hindu society by introducing into it the Western ideals he so much admired, and by abolishing the caste system. His ideas interested the increasingly large middle class of officials and professional men who owed their opportunities to the British.

There was also concern for the depressed and unhappy position of surviving widows. They were condemned almost to a living death, unable to remarry and forced to live out the rest of their lives in sterile seclusion. Their hardships were the greater because for a variety of religious and social reasons girls entered into arranged marriages very young. Normally their husbands were older, and in a society which then had a life expectancy of about 30 wives frequently became widows younger than the average Western girl becomes a bride – sometimes as young as 8 or 9.

The issue was, of course, important in its own right. However, it also brought another consideration that was to cast a long shadow on India's future. This was the immediate conflict between the reformers and the forces of Hindu religious conservatism, and the revelation that the latter were easily the stronger. The educated reformers talked a great deal, but flinched from actual defiance of caste discipline. Even after remarriage became legal, religious and social pressures generally prevented it.

The second wave of nationalism was based on a political and social revival of Hinduism itself, as revealed in the ancient epics. This came with the founding of a number of regional religious organizations, one of which was the Arya Samaj, established in 1875 by Dayananda Saraswati, an Indian sage who spoke no English and had no Western education. He went back to the 'Aryan' classic text, the *Rigveda*, for his inspiration, and attempted to identify a 'pure' Hinduism free from the contamination of later influences. These religious movements were of lasting importance. They influenced many Indians to oppose social reforms introduced by Britain on the grounds that it was best for Indians first to achieve political influence and reform their society afterwards. Hence a revivalist Hinduism became a central theme of nationalism.

The dusty brick mounds of Harappa and Mohenjo Daro were still unrecognized. Half a century would pass before these ruined cities would be acknowledged as the remains of the first important Indian civilization, and no hint of their significance was available to the Hindu revivalists. Accordingly, they looked back for a tradition to the epic writings of the later Aryan-speaking invaders of India, and so attributed to the beginnings of Indian society a pastoral simplicity quite unlike the sophistication and urbanity the Harappa ruins indicate. Even after the discovery of Harappa, these early ideas tended to be rationalized, and still persist in the modern Indian's sense of national identity – belief in a Golden Age long before India came under the domination of foreigners, in which happiness and simplicity were thought to have prevailed. Gandhi was influenced by such ideas.

There were also material facts that gave impetus to nationalism. From 1837 on, a selected number of English planters were allowed to take up land and settle in India – there were almost 300 such plantations by 1870. Even though they were subject to certain conditions – for instance, planters must live on their holdings – the very fact that they were there at all was a source of uneasiness to Indians. There were many peasant revolts of one kind or another during the 19th century, but the Indigo Revolt of 1860 was among the most significant. When the European planters used at times violent and unjust methods to force peasants in Bengal to grow indigo for low financial rewards, there was a massive reaction that approached armed rebellion. Educated Indians and recently founded newspapers supported the peasants. Confronted with what became in effect a popular political movement, the colonial government finally limited the power of the planters and insisted that any further disputes must be decided in the courts.

Another influence for nationalism was the growing pressure of poverty and landlessness among the villagers. The British themselves did not usurp land to any major extent, but they did introduce a land-tenure system open to abuse. In many cases tax assessments were unfairly high – at times approaching double those during Akbar's rule. This forced hundreds of thousands of peasants from their land, which passed into the ownership of moneylenders who foreclosed on mortgages. Famines persisted, in spite of relief measures introduced by the government.

A sense of competition between the two major communities, Hindu and Muslim, induced both towards political organization. An educated Muslim, Sir Seyed Ahmad Khan, warned his people as early as 1883 about the nature of the communal problem. 'If the British were to leave India,' he said, 'who would then be the rulers? Is it possible that two nations, the Muslim and Hindu, could sit on the same throne and remain in power? To hope that both would remain equal is to desire the impossible and the inconceivable.' Sir Seyed was the leader of a movement to raise Indian Islam from the apathy and disunity into which it had fallen after the collapse of the Mogul Dynasty. Due to his efforts the Anglo-Oriental College was founded in 1875 at Aligarh, near Delhi, to provide a place at which 'Muslims may acquire an English education without prejudice to their religion'. Almost all the national leaders of what was to become Pakistan were educated at Aligarh.

The first organization with the declared objective of Indian self-government was the Indian National Congress. Its political offspring, the Congress Party, was to lead India to nationhood in 1947. However, the first Congress, in 1885, was far from being a political party in the modern sense. Of its 72 delegates only two were Muslims, and there was a solid commitment to establishing Anglo-Saxon political institutions in India. Congress members did not at this stage envisage India as a nation – rather, as 'a nation in the making'.

However, a militant anti-British nationalism was also developing. It emerged first in Mumbai and was founded not only on the Hindu revival, but more specifically on that of the Maratha people who, under their great leader Shivaji, had successfully defied the Moguls in the 17th century. The movement gained terrorist overtones. In 1896 bubonic plague spread from Mumbai south to Pune. Strong measures were needed to control it. A British official named Rand used soldiers to evacuate houses thought to be infected and to destroy property, if necessary at bayonet point. The following year an extremist murdered Rand and an associate.

The extremists found renewed opportunities during the autocratic term of office of Lord Curzon, the Viceroy from 1898. Curzon, a dedicated

Conservative, was a man of restless energy and efficiency. Almost constantly in pain, for he had to wear a leather and iron harness because of a back complaint, he was overbearing and tactless to the point of rudeness. He had no patience with 'political Indians', and stated an objective of 'assisting the Congress to a peaceful demise'. Two unpopular measures towards the end of his term led educated Bengalis to oppose him. The first restricted their influence on university administration, the second partitioned the huge state of Bengal. The partition was ostensibly to provide better government for its predominantly Muslim eastern section, the present-day Bangladesh, but was seen by Indian intellectuals as a simple 'divide and rule' situation. The protest was substantial, resulting in riots and demonstrations. These having no effect on the government, a campaign called *swadeshi* was organized to boycott British goods, especially textiles, and remained a favourite tactic of the nationalists from this time onwards.

World war in 1914 became as much the end of an era in India as in Europe. More than a million Indians were recruited into the imperial forces – thousands were killed on the Western Front in France by the first German advance on Ypres. The influence on Indians returning from the war is perhaps most graphically illustrated by a work of fiction, John Masters's *The Ravi Lancers*, which describes the profound disillusionment with European ideas caused by the senseless carnage of the war. The war effort seriously weakened British administration in India, and the loss of a considerable trade with Germany and of other export markets caused severe recession. Bubonic plague swept the country in 1917 and the following year came an even greater scourge – the world epidemic of influenza. It killed 12.5 million Indians.

The consequent unrest and rioting were aggravated by the extension of wartime laws to control revolution and sedition. The Congress in 1916 negotiated a remarkable accord in which Muslims and Hindus pledged themselves to support the common cause of home rule for India. The Congress, until now the compliant and willing partner of the imperial government, was henceforward to be its antagonist. Against this tumultuous background a new player would enter the stage, a figure of enormous significance not only in India, but throughout the world.

Mohandas Gandhi, a Gujarati who went to England in 1888 for an education in law, was admitted to the Bar at the Inner Temple in London three years later. Subsequently he went to South Africa and acquired an international reputation as leader of a movement which resisted discrimination against the Indian expatriate minority there. World attention was attracted not so much by the cause itself as by Gandhi's novel methods of mass passive resistance. Patient and non-violent acceptance of an adverse situation had long been a tradition of Hinduism, but Gandhi, who had read

Tolstoy and was impressed by him, added to it the firmness of the Russian's concept of a more militant non-co-operation with the evil and destructive. He was 45 when he returned to India in 1914 to work for the Congress, becoming its unquestioned leader in 1920.

The extension of the wartime anti-sedition laws triggered serious opposition. Gandhi rallied support against these repressive Rowlatt Acts. His intention was for a day of fasting and prayer and a business strike, but that event on 18 March 1919 led to severe rioting in Amritsar, the holy city of the Sikhs, in which five Europeans were killed and a number of buildings burned. Three weeks later a British army officer, General Reginald Dyer, issued a proclamation warning that any public assemblies in Amritsar would be fired upon.

Two factors bore on the situation. One was Dyer's order that all Indians passing through a street in which a European had been attacked should crawl, and the second, noted in the report of the later investigating commission, was that in many parts of Amritsar Dyer's proclamation had not been read. Hence a large proportion of the population was unaware of the warning.

The following day a large crowd gathered in an enclosed square called the Jallianwalla Bagh, which could be entered and left only through a few narrow gateways. Although the crowd was unarmed, and listening peacefully to a speaker, General Dyer ordered 50 Gurkha riflemen to start firing on them. They continued until they ran out of ammunition. The people inside were unable to escape the deadly, individual marksmanship, which was so effective that of 1650 rounds fired almost all found a mark, since 379 people were killed and more than a thousand injured. Many were women and children.

The brutal overkill of the Amritsar massacre and its consequences are of immense importance, for they destroyed any remaining feelings of goodwill and faith in Britain so many educated Indians had had. The world-renowned Indian author, Sir Rabindranath Tagore, renounced his knighthood. Gandhi described British rule as 'Satanic'. These reactions were due not only to the massacre but also to the fact that so many influential Englishmen approved of Dyer's actions, the House of Lords supporting a public subscription by the *Morning Post* newspaper which raised £26,000 to Dyer's benefit, some of which was spent on a sword studded with jewels. Rudyard Kipling was a subscriber. The repercussions were still considerable as late as 1997 when Queen Elizabeth, making a visit to India, was told she would not be welcome in Amritsar.

By 1920 there was open unrest in India. The Congress issued an ultimatum: complete self-rule within a year or massive civil disobedience.

When this was ignored Gandhi called for civil disobedience throughout India. Outbreaks of mob violence, notably the burning alive of 22 police in 1922 inside their station at Chauri Chaura, shocked Gandhi so much he withdrew from the campaign, retiring to a religious retreat to meditate. The rest of the decade passed without major event, although one ominous tendency was the steady deterioration of relations between Hindus and Muslims, with a growing number of deaths from communal violence.

During Gandhi's absence from active politics the nationalist cause was led by a successful lawyer, Motilal Nehru, who had given up a life of wealth and privilege to follow Gandhi. Motilal Nehru died in 1931. He was succeeded as leader of the Congress by his son Jawaharlal. Born in 1889 of blue-blood Kashmiri stock, Jawaharlal Nehru had all the advantages of a privileged birth and environment. A *brahmin* by caste, he was educated at Harrow and Cambridge and was admitted to the Bar in 1912. Like his father, he renounced his career and former way of life to work for the nationalist cause but, nevertheless, remained essentially a product of Western ways of thought and an English education. Throughout a long life of immense influence he was impatient of Indian traditionalism and caste barriers. Although he fought bitterly for Indian independence, his influence on its final form was almost entirely derived from Western political traditions.

The younger Nehru and Gandhi were close friends and associates, and with the advent of Jawaharlal to major influence, Gandhi left the spinning wheel and looms of his secluded *ashram* to return to the political battle. Within a year came a further call for independence and a civil disobedience campaign. Gandhi began this with an inspired gesture – one of protest against the much-hated government tax on salt. Making and selling salt was a government monopoly, and it was illegal for anyone else to do so. In March 1930 Gandhi, then aged 61, led a 240-mile walk to the coast, the procession growing steadily in volume during the 24 days before it reached the Arabian Sea. There he scooped illicit salt from the beach. He urged Indians to make their own salt, and thousands did so illegally.

The incident was typical of Gandhi's genius, which reached the hearts and inspired the enthusiasm of the vast mass of the Indian people. The peasantry, who had formerly not been involved in the nationalist struggle had, indeed, for centuries regarded themselves as too humble to be concerned with matters of power. Gandhi fought ferociously for the poor and downtrodden, and especially championed the cause of India's millions of untouchables. This deep concern for the underprivileged permitted Gandhi to act as a bridge between the people and the intelligentsia.

The defiance of the salt tax was vigorously repressed. By May 1930, 60,000 people were in prison, including Gandhi, Nehru and most of the other Congress leaders. Not long after Gandhi was imprisoned 2500 Indians marched on the government salt factory near Mumbai, where, according to a newspaper correspondent, Webb Miller, who witnessed the event,

> scores of native policemen rained blows on their heads with steel-shod *lathis*. Not one of the marchers even raised a hand to fend off the blows. They went down like ninepins. The waiting crowd of marchers groaned and sucked in their breath in sympathetic pain at every blow. Those struck down fell sprawling, unconscious or writhing with fractured skulls or broken shoulders. The survivors, without breaking ranks, silently and doggedly marched on until struck down.

Miller reported that two men died and 320 were injured.

Incidents like this attracted attention and sympathy throughout the world for the nationalist cause. From now on Britain was never allowed to forget it. Imports of cloth from Britain were halved, and revenues from other products, like cigarettes and liquor, considerably reduced. The Indian Communist Party, formed in 1920, grew steadily, and, due largely to Nehru's influence, socialism strongly influenced the Congress. The world depression of the 1930s affected India severely as export markets dried up. Millions of Indians abandoned their land and drifted into the cities, begging on the streets for the means of bare survival. Limited provincial self-government was introduced in 1937. It resulted in the training of a pool of experienced Indian administrators that would stand the new nation in good stead after independence.

There were also special provisions designed to encourage the princes controlling the large and small states outside British India – governing a quarter of the total population – to enter an Indian Union. Bickering, selfishness and apparent lack of wider vision made it impossible for them to avail themselves of this last chance to unite and form a significant area of power. A few years later they passed out of history largely unlamented, shorn of political power but with some even now enormously wealthy and influential within their own territories.

PART III

The Modern Nations

17 *The Second World War and the End of Empire*

Granted peace rather than war in 1939, the colonial era could have dragged on longer in Asia. But as it was, the next six years of conflict saw the empires crumble. Their demise after the end of the war in 1945 became only a matter of time.

Hitler's rapid advance – the *blitzkrieg* – across Europe brought two of the major colonial powers – France and Holland – to their knees. These countries faced four years of often brutal German occupation during which their ability to maintain the colonial machine became virtually nonexistent. Germany dictated the terms of interim government for Asian colonial regions, and these could be no more than perfunctory in the face of the continuing conflict in Europe. For the time being the colonies became a side issue.

Almost without exception they were at this time plantation economies, closely linked to those of their colonial masters. The hugely increased workforces resulting from rapid population growth depended on these plantations of export crops for their livelihood. The war in Europe caused disruption of trade and widespread unemployment, which in time led on to almost universal hardship, often extending to actual starvation. The self-sufficiency previously conferred by traditional agriculture had meanwhile been severely curtailed.

Then there was a moral effect. To a large extent, and particularly in British India, colonial rule depended more on a qualified but none the less real respect for the master country and its officials on the spot than on actual military compulsion. After Dunkirk Britain was at bay within her own islands, France and Holland occupied. The colonial masters no longer appeared all-powerful to their subject peoples, were no longer arrayed in a mystic superiority that gave them an apparent mandate to rule. It became plain that they could be defeated, they were no more than human.

Nor had the lesson of colonial affluence been lost on the Japanese, who for a decade before the Second World War had had ambitions to acquire an empire in Asia. By 1939 Japan had conquered Korea, Taiwan, Manchuria and much of the rest of China, but that was not enough. The power vacuum in southern French Indo-China, a prolific rice producer, and the Dutch East Indies, rich in oil, offered tempting opportunities. But Japan's initial attempts to expand into these areas came under strong opposition from another major Pacific power – the United States.

When in 1941 Japan occupied the southern part of what had been French Indo-China, the United States retaliated by cutting off oil supplies on which Japan was almost totally dependent, and demanded that Japan withdraw from China. The Japanese rejected this last demand. With only enough oil reserves to keep her navy active for 18 months, a rapid push as far south as the Dutch East Indies oilfields became central to Japanese war planning.

By November 1941 both sides knew that war was virtually inevitable, but the Americans had no idea how it would start and what its eventual course might be. This became obvious at dawn on 7 December, when the Japanese launched an unsuccessful attack on the American naval base in Hawaii, Pearl Harbor, with five midget submarines. Four of these were sunk by American destroyers – effectively the first action in the Pacific war. Very damaging bombing raids by more than 300 Japanese aircraft followed. Within two hours 21 warships had been sunk or severely damaged, 350 aircraft had been destroyed, mostly on the ground, and more than 4000 Americans were dead or wounded. A warning of the Japanese approach was ignored, the radar signal being attributed to friendly aircraft. The day being Sunday, most of Pearl Harbor's defences were unmanned or otherwise unready.

The Second World War had spread to the Pacific. The Japanese moved through south-east Asia with terrifying speed. Within three months they had taken the Philippines, Malaya and the Dutch East Indies, and the Pacific islands north of New Guinea. Singapore, which the British regarded as impregnable, was captured with relative ease, due mainly to a confused and inept defensive effort which culminated in the surrender of 130,000 Allied troops to a Japanese force half that size. Bad administration and inefficiency at the command level, rather than lack of courage on the part of individual units, were responsible.

The Japanese had given priority to aircraft carriers, as opposed to the battleship mentality which still dictated British and, to a considerable extent, American naval planning. Her carrier-borne force of 500 aircraft was the largest in the world. This taught another early and severe lesson when the brand-new British battleship *Prince of Wales* and the battle cruiser *Repulse*, which had sailed from Singapore without air cover, were sunk in two hours by Japanese torpedo bombers.

By 1942 the Japanese had occupied Burma, reaching Yangon in March of that year, so threatening British India. Almost half of 30,000 Allied troops were left behind dead or missing during a 600-mile retreat to the Indian border. Only the onset of torrential monsoon rains averted an invasion of India. When the Japanese again attempted to invade India in 1944 they met sharper resistance, and after 80 days of bitter fighting, were forced to withdraw. To the south-east, the occupation of most of New Guinea placed Australia at risk. The Japanese were able to exploit the invaluable resources of oil, rubber, non-ferrous minerals and food from the Dutch East Indies, and, for the time being, safely export them to the service of the Japanese war industries.

The Japanese took thousands of European prisoners of war, who were treated with the utmost brutality in camps and as forced labour on projects like the Burma–Thailand railway. One of the worst such episodes came after the fall of Bataan, in the Philippines. The American garrison were already starving and weakened, but the Japanese forced them to march 65 miles north to a prison camp. Around 30,000 Americans and Filipinos died during the last hours of the defence of Bataan or during this march. Another 22,000 died in the camp within two months. While these prisoners attracted much sympathy from the indigenous people of their former colonies, the lesson was taught again that Europeans were not superior masters, but could be reduced, even destroyed, by terrible indignities and brutality.

Initially, the Japanese positioned themselves as liberators – there was to be a new pan-Asian movement led by Japan which would eventually lead to liberation of the colonies as free peoples. At this stage the tiny Burmese independence movement was encouraged by Japan, and in the East Indies Sukarno and the other nationalist leaders were led to believe that the end of the war would bring a new independent nation, Indonesia. The Japanese organized and trained a military force that would later be the core of the army that would fight the Dutch for Indonesian independence.

However, although the Japanese had gained the empire they wanted they were not allowed to keep it. The staggering six million square miles they occupied had to be policed by only 11 army divisions – 25 others were kept in China to maintain Japanese ascendancy there. This involved supply lines of impracticable length and demands that Japan's limited industrial capacity could not meet. American submarines took a heavy toll on Japanese shipping. By 1943 ten times as many ships were being sunk than could be replaced by new construction.

Although Australia's northern city of Darwin was bombed, the country was never invaded, largely due to tenacious resistance by Australian soldiers that stopped the Japanese tide in the jungle-clad mountains of New Guinea, and a naval battle in the Coral Sea in which the Japanese were, for the first time in the war, defeated. Cut off from their supply lines, only 13,000 Japanese soldiers in New Guinea eventually survived of 140,000 who had been sent there. The huge productive capacity of the United States was now coming into play, and in August 1942 an American attack on Guadalcanal, in the Solomon Islands, raised the curtain on a series of ferocious and bloody maritime invasions that forced the Japanese north.

The Japanese fought back with almost maniacal tenacity – their soldiers had been indoctrinated with the conviction that to surrender and be taken prisoner was a disgrace and a betrayal of the emperor. Hence they almost always fought to the last man. On the insignificant eight square miles of the island of Iwo Jima, 22,000 Japanese and 7000 Americans died during a five-week battle. The Japanese took very high casualties almost everywhere – more than a million soldiers and almost half a million navy men died during the war. On Saipan a thousand survived of 32,000; on the atoll of Tarawa in the Gilberts every one of 4800 Japanese marines was killed.

In a desperate duel between aircraft carriers near the island of Midway in 1942 fortunes swayed from side to side, suggesting a Japanese victory until, almost by chance, a small American squadron – only 37 dive-bombers – found four of the six major Japanese carriers vulnerable as they refuelled and rearmed their aircraft. All four ships were destroyed. From this time onwards the United States had naval superiority in the Pacific.

One important consequence was a collapse in the colonies' almost completely agrarian economies. As more and more Japanese freighters were sunk by American submarines trade between them and Japan declined, and then virtually ceased. Burma and Thailand had too much rice, but people were starving elsewhere. Almost everywhere poverty followed unemployment, but actual food shortages worsened the situation, causing famine in many parts of island south-east Asia. Malaria, substantially under control in 1939, became epidemic almost everywhere.

As the Japanese suffered defeat after defeat their attitude towards the Asian people in the colonies they had occupied changed significantly. Now these people became subject to forced labour and the usual pattern of Japanese brutality, and as a result any sympathy they had had for the Japanese disappeared. People fled their villages into the forests to escape the general decline of law and order and mass conscription into Japanese labour gangs. Resistance movements developed almost everywhere. These guerrilla bands, which attracted the support and assistance of the Allies, generally had a Communist element, deriving from the Communist parties established during the 1920s and 1930s. One such, in French Indo-China, was the Vietminh, commanded by Ho Chi Minh, who later would lead Vietnam to independence as a Communist state. Another was the Malayan Communist movement, led by Chin Peng, who marched in the end-of-war celebrations in London, but who would later lead his guerrillas through the long Malayan insurrection known as the Emergency.

The Pacific war ended with Japan's surrender in August 1945 after the cities of Hiroshima and Nagasaki had been destroyed, at an initial cost of 170,000 lives, by the first and only use of nuclear weapons in war. But the systematic pattern of firebombing ordered by American General le May had earlier turned Tokyo and 65 other cities into deadly infernos. This carpet-bombing with incendiaries exacted an even higher cost than the nuclear attacks – 260,000 civilians were burned to death and more than two million buildings destroyed.

The occupied areas in Asia had not fared much better. Invasion and the 'scorched-earth' policies of the retreating European powers destroyed much of the already inadequate infrastructure. Burma, for instance, has still not recovered from the loss of at least three-quarters of its roads, bridges and railways. But one thing not in short supply was weapons, either left behind by retreating armies or air-dropped to resistance fighters. These were to serve, in some cases, bitter civil war, in others, the establishment of independence armies.

In most of the former colonies guerrilla movements set up interim governments as the Japanese occupation ended, and looked forward confidently to the rapid evolution of independent states. The Supreme Allied Commander in south-east Asia, Lord Mountbatten, warned the French and the Dutch they could not resume colonial government on pre-war terms. However, this advice was largely ignored, leading to major hostilities in both the former colonies. The Dutch did not persist long, but the French were more stubborn, fighting the Vietminh until they suffered a crushing defeat at a complex of mountain forts at Dien Bien Phu in 1954. Day after day, transport aircraft dropped paratroopers to reinforce the doomed forts. The Communists killed most of them before they reached the ground. Using only manpower, they moved mountain guns over what seemed to be impossible terrain until the French positions were at almost point-blank range. When Dien Bien Phu was forced to surrender, 10,000 French prisoners were taken.

This, the first defeat of a European power by an Asian resistance movement, had a tremendous impact throughout the former colonies. What could be done once might be done again. But early hopes that independence might come peacefully had been shattered in 1941. A historic meeting between British Prime Minister Churchill and American President Roosevelt produced the Atlantic Charter, which declared 'the right of all people to choose the form of government under which they will live'. But within a month, speaking in the House of Commons, Churchill declared that the charter would not apply to any of the British colonies. France and Holland continued to fight the nationalists in their former spheres of influence.

The next decade was to be one of struggle, and at the end of it virtually all of the former colonies had become independent nations.

18 South Asia: Freedom and Poverty

The south Asian nations, with more than one and a half billion people, are now the largest fraction of humans in the world. Accordingly, what happens to them must be a matter of global concern – the more so because all of the five larger countries of the region face greater and more fundamental problems than other parts of Asia. These include an uncomfortably high rate of population growth, some of the world's lowest percentages of literate people, and high incidences of poverty and fatal or disabling diseases.

About 250 million are wealthy or middle class. Most of these are in India, with perhaps ten to twenty million each in Pakistan and Bangladesh. Their lifestyles contrast forcibly with those of the billion who live in crowded, sub-standard housing, who lack clean drinking water and sanitation, who are not fed adequately and who can call on only the most minimal medical services. Some studies indicate that the wealthier are getting richer and the poor poorer – and that there seems little appetite among the better-off for measures that might improve the general good, such as higher taxes. Much of the improvements in the life of the poor are coming from non-government charities, mostly financed from donations in the West. The World Bank Group is also assisting, lending India $26 billion in the four years to 2013 – the largest amount directed to a single country. The bank will provide another $3 to $5 billion annually over four years from 2013, with particular emphasis on helping the poorer states.

Consequently there should be an eventual improvement in the conditions of life in south Asia, and the government at least in some parts of the region is making efforts in this direction. The Indian government provides work and subsidies that protect most of the poor from utter destitution, but little more than that. According to the London School of Economics roughly a quarter of the population are excluded from these programmes, due to 'rampant corruption and the state's obsession with paperwork despite widespread illiteracy amongst India's poorest citizens'. Certainly, a visitor to the region can see scant evidence of change, probably because of the sheer magnitude of the problems. The ramshackle slums that make up most of the larger cities seem to be more crowded, more broken-down, than they were 30 years ago. The industrial growth that has fostered growth of the middle class has been ecologically disastrous – heavy blanketing of smog from factory chimneys and increasing motor traffic, choked roads and streets, and a constant clangour of noise. The beautiful Taj Mahal in Agra, surrounded by slums and a whole landscape of bleak industrial buildings from which a hundred tall chimneys belch smoke, eloquently characterizes India's urban problems. In most cases industry pays its employees poorly, and they work long hours in bad conditions in often dangerous buildings. Disastrous factory accidents, due either to fire or actual collapse of buildings, occur regularly. The collapse of an eight-storey building in Bangladesh in 2013 took more than 1100 lives, mostly of young women workers and their children in crèches in the building. More than 3000 people making garments were crowded into this building, which was known to be unsafe.

The use of child labour is common, in spite of being illegal. The number of children under 14 working, many as young as 4 or 5, is estimated as high as 60 million in India, although the government admits to only 20 million. Workdays of 12 hours are common, and there is little regard for the health of these children. Damage to the eyes is only too likely for those working long hours at carpet weaving and total blindness not uncommon. In Bangladesh the number of child workers rose from 2.5 million in 1974 to 6.6 million in 1996 – this increase is attributed to the large number of people living below the poverty line – 55 million. In the capital Dhaka, over 100,000 children employed as domestic workers were under 13 and some aged only 5. According to UNICEF, many children work in places where they are exposed to hazardous chemicals, dangerous machinery and a risk of burns. The Pakistan Bureau of Statistics reported in 2012 that 3.8 million children between the ages of 5 and 14 were working in that country – roughly half in agricultural labour.

The countryside is little better than the cities, made up substantially of arid fields in which the productivity of the soil is declining alarmingly and villages which every year have to house more people in the same wretched conditions, to share food resources which become more and more limited. Five per cent of village dwellers own as much as 40 per cent of the available agricultural land – in Pakistan four per cent own 36 per cent of the land. This represents close on a doubling of the alienation of land to the rich since independence. Malnutrition oppresses about a third of the Indian population. 1.7 million children die every year before they are five – a UN report in 2012 said this was the highest incidence of child death in the world. Seven million child deaths occur in Pakistan. However, in spite of its poverty, Bangladesh set something of a record, reducing its under-5 mortality rate by two-thirds since 1990. This is claimed to be the result of better and more comprehensive health care than in neighbouring countries, and programmes educating mothers in good nutrition.

And in other ways the picture is not uniformly depressing. There are islands of hope and prosperity, like the south Indian state of Kerala, where good government and community participation have resulted in social indicators better than the rest of the region, and the tiny Himalayan kingdom of Bhutan. Neither of these are wealthy, but they are living indicators that progress is possible.

South Asia faces severe challenges from climate change. Two nations, India and Bangladesh, share the huge Ganges delta, where much of the land is barely three feet above mean tide level. This is one of the most densely populated parts of the world, accommodating around 500 people per square mile – more than 100 million people live in this flat land of innumerable interweaving streams and rivers.

This intense pressure on the available land and declining soil fertility combine to threaten a serious food supply problem in the future. Severe flooding in the north Indian state of Assam in recent years has already destroyed entire summer crops, and the Brahmaputra River there is regularly carrying dangerous amounts of floodwaters.

While rising sea levels are the immediate threat a reduction in flow of the two great south Asian rivers, the Ganges and the Indus, would threaten food supplies to tens of millions of people. Hundreds of glaciers in the Himalayas have always provided an even flow throughout the year, losing meltwater at about the same rate as replacement by snowfalls. These huge rivers of ice are now receding as the global temperature rises. As they diminish their 'balance' capacity reduces, and a pattern of alternate flooding and drought will ensue. According to some glaciologists, in a few decades river flow in the Ganges will drop as much as a 90 per cent, causing water shortages for 37 per cent of India's irrigated land, and threatening the livelihood of 500 million people.

The Indus River, which provides water to one of the largest irrigated areas in the world in Pakistan, is also highly dependent on glacial meltwater. In 2012 water flow, as low as 20 per cent of normal, failed to reach huge irrigated areas, reducing crop yields as much as 40 per cent. The Indus meets the sea in a huge low-lying delta, also threatened by sea-level rise.

Religion is one of the major causes of fatal violence in south Asia, with regular clashes between followers of two of the world's great religions, Hinduism and Islam, causing millions of deaths. The following is very much a thumbnail sketch of what is a complex problem, but may serve to illustrate the broad reasons behind this perpetual conflict.

The two religions are antithetic in many respects. Islam is strictly monotheistic, believing in one supreme deity, Allah. Its scripture, the Qur'an, is considered to be the authentic word of Allah, which all Muslims must accept without reservation. By contrast Hinduism accepts a bewildering array of gods and goddesses, and has no body of dogma that must be strictly accepted. The two religions do not accept or even mention each other in their scriptures, and philosophically share very little common ground.

Islam has it that God speaks to the world through prophets – divinely-inspired humans, of whom Mohammed is the most important. There is no Hindu equivalent. The caste system, which defines everyone's place in life, is basic to Hinduism. Muslims consider everyone to be equal before God. Islam has a strict system of religious law, called *sharia*, which is considered a strict guide to most aspects of life, Hinduism has no such thing. Muslims believe that life is a kind of test, after which individuals will be considered on their conduct, and assigned either to Paradise or Hell. Hindus believe in reincarnation, in which souls move on from one life to the next, possibly eventually achieving freedom from the human condition. Muslims are not permitted to make images of Allah or any of his prophets. Hence the statues and other representations of gods or goddesses in Hindu temples are regarded as idolatrous and blasphemous by Muslims. It is seen as a religious duty to destroy them – something that has happened many times in the past.

Muslim numbers in India are increasing. They made up 9 per cent of the total population in 1951, almost 14 per cent in 2001, close to 20 per cent in 2013. Muslims in India are highly urbanized, making up 22 per cent of the people of Mumbai and 21 per cent of those in Kolkata. Since both Pakistan and Bangladesh are mostly Muslim, it has been estimated that by 2065 Muslims will be more numerous in south Asia than Hindus and Sikhs. This is causing reactions among Hindus that range from anxiety to frenetic hatred of Islam – a Facebook page, Hindus Against Islam, expresses such unreasoning attacks on Islam as to be extremely disquieting. India's guided missiles, designed to deliver nuclear weapons, have names associated with religion: Agni, the god of fire, and Prithvi, the goddess of the earth. Pakistan has a long-range missile called Ghauri, after one of the Islamic invaders of India. Since most people in both nations are proud that they have nuclear weapons, continuing hostility between them represents a major threat to the world.

19 India

When war came to Europe in 1939, Britain had little leisure to consider the shaping of political forces in south Asia. Nehru had foreseen the war and had told the 1936 meeting of the Congress Party that 'it becomes necessary ... to declare now our opposition to India's participation in an imperialist war'. With the coming of that war, Congress demanded immediate self-government on a basis to be decided by a constituent assembly of Indians. In 1942 Britain sent a Socialist member of her War Cabinet – Sir Stafford Cripps, long known as a supporter of Indian nationalist aspirations – to Delhi. Cripps brought with him a plan for an independent India with Dominion status and the right to secede from the Commonwealth, to be established immediately after the war.

Congress turned down these proposals categorically, apparently at Gandhi's initiative. He is said to have described Cripps's proposals as 'a blank cheque on a failing bank', and wanted all Commonwealth forces out of India so a possible Japanese invasion could be opposed with a passive resistance campaign. The words 'Quit India' suddenly appeared in white paint scrawled on walls and hoardings. A major campaign of civil disobedience was to be used to force Britain's hand. However the colonial authorities reacted with force at once. The Congress was declared an illegal organization and all its leaders were arrested and jailed until the end of the war in 1945. The first riots and sabotage began in Mumbai and quickly spread to other parts of India. Public buildings were burned down, railway and telegraph lines damaged, and there was some sabotage of military installations.

So rose the sudden bitterness that was to cloud the last years of British rule – a sad blot on a record that contains so much of value. Hundreds of nationalists were killed – a Congress Party estimate put deaths as high as 25 000, with 3000 injured and 60 000 arrested before the 'Congress rebellion' was put down. But worse was to come. The year 1943 brought fresh horrors with a catastrophic famine in Bengal, the worst since 1866. The famine, little publicized at the time because of wartime censorship, is still, inexplicably, largely ignored in many histories of India and standard reference works. Estimates of the death toll range from two to four million – either figure is far higher than British empire military and civilian wartime deaths, which totalled about half a million. There was adequate food available in Bengal, but it was drained from a starving countryside to feed industrial Calcutta.

It is well documented that Bengali villages were deprived of food by speculators, offered a ready market by the demand for rice to feed the Indian army, now two million strong. Gandhi fasted for three weeks in sympathy with the Bengalis, but his gesture, a considerable one for an ageing man, was ignored. The legal requirement to declare a famine under the Famine Code was also ignored, with evidence that this was done to avoid the cost of alleviating mass distress and acknowledgment of the appalling total of deaths. Rather than sending relief stocks into rural Bengal, the British administration oversaw a huge export of grain and rice. Epidemics of cholera exploded through the weakened population, with high death rates in 1944. Lord Wavell, who became Viceroy in 1943, pleaded with British Prime Minister Winston Churchill to send a million tons of grain to Bengal, but Churchill seems to have hardened his heart. 'He hates India and everything to do with it', Wavell comments in his diaries. Eventually less than half that amount was forthcoming. Wavell's successor, the Australian R. G. Casey, organized a major programme of cholera and smallpox vaccinations.

Several of the factors mentioned above suggest a British 'scorched-earth' policy, designed to deny assets in Bengal to an anticipated Japanese invasion force, at a monstrous human cost. Those consequences severely indict British policy-makers of the time, especially Churchill, and the failure to investigate and acknowledge them is to the discredit of subsequent British governments.

So great was the output of new industries in India during the war, notably the huge Tata steelworks, that it not only cancelled out Indian indebtedness but actually gave India a credit balance in London of over £100 million. Consequently the end of the war saw the end of any economic justification for continued British rule. In July 1945 the wartime government of Churchill was defeated, and Labour, which had been critical of the India policy for some time, embarked on the task of making India free. The new Prime Minister, Clement Attlee, intended to make India independent without reservations, and was little deterred by Churchill's comment that this would involve 'the clattering down of the British Empire with all its glories'. Even so, the task proved not so simple, with strikes and demonstrations continuing in India into 1946.

Amid this confusion a dominant influence was the Muslim League, driven forward by Jinnah, its leader, who insisted on a separate Muslim nation. 'We will have either a divided India or a destroyed India', he said. 'We have forged a pistol and we are in a position to use it.' Jinnah called for a direct action day on 16 August. It was to be an ominous and tragic occasion, resulting in the death of 12,000 people, 5000 in Kolkata alone, in conditions of appalling brutality. In 1947 India was on the brink of civil war. Partition was now accepted as inevitable. New boundaries were drawn with little chance to consider local interests and loyalties with any care. Yet the line had to be drawn, and quickly. Inevitably it split village and clan groups and cut off irrigated land from its sources of water, amid a myriad of other problems. This crude surgery led to another disaster, compared with which the communal horrors of the past dwindled into insignificance. India and Pakistan became independent dominions within the British Commonwealth on 14 August 1947. At once both countries faced an explosion of communal violence on an unprecedented scale. In the border regions of the Punjab, which, together with Bengal, was partitioned, millions left their homes while Hindu, Muslim and Sikh fanatics preyed on them in a nightmare of butchery and destruction. Entire families died inside their homes as hundreds of villages were burned, and the chaos prevailing on both sides of the border cloaked every kind of atrocity – some barely imaginable. Crowded trains were found stopped on the lines without a soul still alive in them.

No accurate estimate has ever been possible of the human cost of this terrible disaster, but as many as a million people are believed to have perished. In what was probably the largest single shift of population the world has ever seen, at least six million people crossed from India into Pakistan, and slightly more migrated the other way.

Consideration of these events leads to a ready understanding of the bitterness and distrust between the neighbouring south Asian states that has led to war on a number of occasions, a host of minor military clashes, a confrontation along one of the world's most heavily militarized frontiers and an immoderate spending on weapons, including nuclear arms, by both nations that might be better devoted to easing the poverty and deprivation of so many of their people.

Following the communal tragedy in 1947, Gandhi, at the age of 78, began a fast to exact a promise from the Congress leaders that the lives and property of the 40 million Muslims still living in India should be respected. Five days later Nehru and his colleagues gave this undertaking. It was the last triumph of the man who, though he himself disliked the title, had become universally known as the *mahatma* – the 'great soul'. On 30 January 1948, as he walked out of a house in Delhi, an assassin fired three shots at Gandhi. The killer was not some Muslim fanatic, but a *brahmin* member of a Hindu extremist party, the Mahasabha. Hindu orthodoxy thus at last exacted its penalty from the man who fought so hard to rid India of its ancient hatreds, superstitions and prejudices.

India's history since independence can best be summarized – and perhaps better understood – by looking at broad trends rather than a huge mass of political detail. The early decades were difficult, with India able to feed its people only by dint of massive food imports and gifts from other countries. Gandhi's influence lived on in the person of his chief disciple, Vinoba Bhave, who walked through India for years persuading wealthy landowners to give more than a million acres of land to the poor. Much of this land was, however, stony or not otherwise of much value, so Bhave's mission had little effect on the vast mass of Indian poverty.

It can be argued that the initial policies of the Nehru era, the effects of which linger even now, were wrong because they favoured capital, rather than labour-intensive industry – steel and cement works, rather than the urgent measures needed to improve the lives of what now amounts to well over half a billion rural poor. Nehru was, of course, not alone in this – a similar situation resulted in major tragedy in China. However, years of firm control by the Congress Party and a doubling of food-grain crops due to the use of new, high-producing varieties in the two decades from 1965, brought improved conditions in which India actually became a food exporter after two decades of food imports. Nevertheless, more recently 'green-revolution' plant varieties have proved less useful and this, combined with losses of soil fertility from overcropping and the relentless growth of the population, has increased problems of poverty and disease, both in the villages and the fast-growing slum areas of the big cities.

Politically, the broad trends in India during the decades since independence have been greater regionalism, fragmentation into a multitude of small parties largely determined by caste and locality, a dwindling of strong national leadership and a gradual but definite growth of Hindu nationalism. Especially after the decline of the Nehru dynasty – two prime ministers of that family, Indira Gandhi (not related to the *mahatma*) and her son Rajiv were assassinated – the tide began to run against the Congress. This was associated with a state of emergency declared by Indira Gandhi in 1975, during which more than 30,000 people were imprisoned without trial. This severe repression had been preceded by a year of strikes, some of which involved as many as a million workers. A campaign against the union movement was widely seen as government support for the big industrial conglomerates, like Tata and Birla, that dominate Indian business. A Congress defeat at elections in 1977 handed India over to the uncertain leadership of a loose alliance, the Janata Party. By 1980 Janata had fragmented into irreconcilable factions, and Congress regained power in elections that year.

Mrs Gandhi was to survive only four more years. Late in 1984, following a bitter and bloody religious dispute with the Sikh community, she was shot down by machine-guns in the hands of two of her guards, who were Sikhs. This led on to an orgy of communal killings, in which around 10,000 Sikhs lost their lives, while 50,000 more retreated into secure camps around Delhi.

Indira's son Rajiv, an airline pilot, succeeded her. The first year of his prime-ministership brought to India an appalling tragedy, the world's worst industrial accident. Forty tons of a poisonous gas, methyl isocyanate, were released from a factory owned by a subsidiary of the multinational Union Carbide. As this gas drifted through the densely populated residential areas around the factory at least 10,000 people were killed. However, almost 30 years later Bhopal remains hideously contaminated, with as much as 12,000 tons of toxic material still in the soil. Nobody has been able to estimate the continuing effects, although there are high rates of cancer, skin ailments and children deformed at birth in the region. Protesters at a rally in Bhopal in 2011 claimed that more than half a million people had been poisoned, but this figure has been contested.

Rajiv Gandhi took India in new directions, into an era of technocrats rather than socialists, inspired by the new world order of economic rationalism. Business did well, but once again scant attention was given to the poor. However, his administration eventually was seen as too close to big business, too tolerant of tax evasions and kickbacks, especially in defence contracts. The most blatant was payments totalling almost $12 million to defence officials and politicians by the Swedish arms manufacturer Bofors to push the sale of their 155mm howitzers as major Indian field artillery. Congress was defeated in elections in 1989, and Rajiv was assassinated in 1991 by a bomb carried by a female Tamil extremist – a result of India's intervention in the bitter civil war in Sri Lanka.

The three years from 1996 brought political uncertainty that necessitated three elections. In 1996 a coalition led by the Hindu nationalist Bharatiya Janata Party – the BJP – took power. Although it fell 19 seats short of the 272 needed for an absolute majority, this result confirmed the downturn for the Congress, which won only 140 seats, apparently ending its dominance in Indian politics. Instead the people preferred a party based on the Hindu traditions and ideas of the past, with strong organization and support at grass-roots levels, and with a major commitment to local industry rather than multinationals. Many BJP members also belong to the Rashtriya

Swamansevak Sangh (RSS), a fundamentalist youth organization founded in 1925, which has been described as a cross between the Scouts and Hitler Youth, and which has been implicated in past violence against the Muslim community.

The two subsequent elections, in 1998 and 1999, brought even worse results for the Congress, then led by Rajiv's widow, Sonia Gandhi, who is Italian-born and a Christian. The BJP also failed to win a majority, depending on an alliance of smaller regional parties. In a 1998 book, *The Idea of India*, Sunil Khilnani says: 'The presumption that a single shared sense of India – a unified idea and concept – exists, has lost all credibility. . . . The new politics of India are formed on regional, race and caste lines.'

These results might encourage hopes that the diminishing influence of the British *Raj* can in time make way for government closer to the most enduring element of Indian society – the village. However, the reality is that India is run by an educated elite, the Indian Administrative Service – the *babu raj* – which functions very much as the colonial civil service did. Its conservatism and inefficiency have contributed to the failure of all governments since independence to significantly improve the lives of the poor. Perhaps only when those hundreds of millions can effectively influence events will the much-needed improvements come. This could well be the *sarvodaya* that Gandhi pleaded for at the time of independence – an abandonment of the confrontational trappings and terminology of Western-style democracy, and the disbanding of the Congress Party to make room for a political system of consensus based on the villages. There was a substantial move in this direction in 1992 when village councils – *gram panchayat* – were established. There are more than a quarter of a million of these, made up of 10 to 14 elected members. They are responsible for municipal services like public health, street lighting, water supply and schools.

Nearly 20,000 people were killed and half a million displaced in 2004 when a tsunami resulting from an earthquake off Sumatra struck the Indian coast. Elections in that year took an unexpected turn when the BJP lost power to an alliance dominated by the Congress Party, even though the incumbent government had been reformist, had brokered a peace deal with Pakistan and had created conditions for economic growth. However, since 'boom' conditions over the previous years had favoured the wealthier and done little for the vast mass of the poor, rural and lower-caste voters returned decisively to the Congress. Although the Congress election campaign had been led by Sonia Gandhi, she declined to become prime minister because there had been some controversy about her foreign birth. Instead the new prime minister was economist Manmohan Singh, a

Sikh former finance minister widely credited with economic reforms during the 1990s.

His United Progressive Alliance retained power comfortably in elections in 2009, which nevertheless again failed to give any one party a clear majority, the UPA winning 262 seats of the 543 in the Lok Sabha – the national parliament – while the BJP's total fell to 159. The UPA also increased its vote in 16 of 28 states. The National Rural Employment Act, which guarantees 100 days of work a year to all rural casual workers, is considered a major factor in this increased support for the UPA. However, support for regional parties increased – between them they took a record 52 per cent of the total vote. Post-election polling found that 70 per cent of those interviewed considered they had a greater loyalty to their region than to the nation, with only 14 per cent thinking otherwise. This was the world's biggest general election, with almost 60 per cent of an eligible three-quarters of a billion people voting. Rajiv's son Rahul campaigned significantly, taking particular issue with Hindu extremism. A member of parliament since 2004, Rahul, who was born in 1970, is expected to play a major part in future Indian politics. He was elected vice-president of the Congress in 2013.

While India has 50 cities with over a million people, two-thirds of the population live in 640,000 villages. These are the people who will dictate political directions in the future. Their view is regional rather than national, and they want jobs, a measured increase in prosperity for all levels of society, improved energy supply and better education for their children. While children get a free midday meal to encourage them to stay in school, half drop out before they finish secondary school. Teaching standards are often low, and in some places teachers don't turn up at all. The literacy rate is about 70 per cent. Skilled tradespeople and professionals like engineers and architects are in short supply. Almost half of India's schools are private, and anxious parents scrimp and save to pay their fees because they believe a good education will give their children the best chances in life.

India's environmental problems are appalling. 'Dirty' industries like tanneries dump their chemicals and other waste directly into rivers and in most places untreated sewerage also goes into waterways. According to a 2012 WHO report, around a quarter of Indian homes have no toilet and about half the population defecate in the open. India has a thriving pharmaceutical industry, which supplies antibiotics largely without any control. Because of this drug-resistant bacteria are proliferating in drains and drinking water – breeding grounds for 'superbugs'. Delhi is one of the worst cities in the world for air pollution, rivalling Beijing. Traffic is chaotic, and gridlocked in most of the cities. There is a very high road-accident rate, resulting in 134,000 deaths in 2012.

In May 1998 India heightened regional tensions with five nuclear bomb tests, including that of a fission-triggered hydrogen bomb. Pakistan quickly followed suit, both nations also claiming they had delivery systems for these weapons. India's AgniV, tested in 2012, is claimed to have a range of more than 3000 miles, and Pakistan's ShaheenIA about 2000. India and Pakistan are each believed to have about 100 operational nuclear weapons. According to the Stockholm-based International Peace Research Institute's 2012 yearbook, 'India and Pakistan are increasing the size and sophistication of their nuclear arsenals ... and both are increasing their military fissile material production capabilities.' In 2012 the Pulitzer Center expressed concerns about lax security and muddled military doctrines in the region, saying 'the real danger to the world may be the full-throttled nuclear race between India and Pakistan ... a game of nuclear chicken'. According to the same source a nuclear war between the south Asian countries would kill 20 million people immediately, and would put at least 5 million tons of smoke into the upper atmosphere, threatening a global 'nuclear winter'. In 2012 Pakistan insisted it was bringing down the threshold of nuclear use by adding small tactical 'battlefield' weapons to its arsenal. This prompted a response from India in 2013 that she would react just as massively to a 'smaller' attack as a large one – 'retaliation designed to inflict unacceptable damage on its adversary ... a limited nuclear war is a contradiction in terms'.

And India is not without its internal problems. Armed gangs are fuelling insurgencies in five of the seven states that make up the north-east region – there are said to be 26 operational armed groups whose insurgencies are causing more than a thousand deaths a year.

While most of India is not handling rural poverty well, there are some exceptions. One is the southern state of Kerala which, although very poor in terms of GDP, has better social indicators than apparently wealthier states, like the Punjab, mainly due to a more even spread of available economic assets, especially land. In 1975 Kerala was the first state in the world to elect a Communist government, and a strong left-wing influence has persisted since. It was certified by the UN as completely literate by 1991 – a rate more than double the Indian national average – has a lower population growth rate than the United States and a child mortality rate less than half than half the Indian average. Life expectancy, 71 for men and 76 for women, is more than ten years better than the Indian average. Kerala's advantages seem to be due to an extraordinary rate of community activism, a strong tradition of matrilineal hierarchies and a realistic programme of land reform. Ninety per cent of the state's 34 million people own the land on which they live – rural holdings are limited to 25 acres a family. This ensures enough food cropping to maintain a better nutrition rate than the rest of rural India, where average caloric input dropped an ominous 8 per cent between 1983 and 2004, probably due to declining output from smallholdings. The Indian Planning Commission's Human Development Report for 2011 described this as 'a serious to extremely alarming situation of hunger'. Kerala's governments seem to have concentrated on improving its peoples' quality of life rather than 'development'. Politics in Kerala have followed a pattern of alternation between left- and right-wing coalitions. In general elections in 2011 for the 140-seat Parliament the Congress-led UDF coalition won by a narrow majority of four seats. Coalitions formed by cobbling together numerous 'splinter' parties are the norm, as elsewhere in India.

After decades of severe poverty and corruption, better governance is now transforming life for the 100 million people of Bihar State, where chief minister Nitish Kumar, elected in 2005, has negotiated with the state's Maoist insurgents rather than fighting them, built hospitals, roads and schools, and got more girls to stay at school by giving them bicycles. Bihar's economy is now one of the fastest-growing in India, and it is rated as the nation's least corrupt state. In the six years to 2011 average incomes rose almost ten per cent a year. This 'Bihar miracle' (*Times of India* editorial, 28 July 2012), however, has some way to go – per capita income is still below the national average, and while the poverty level has dropped slightly. Bihar remains India's poorest state.

As anyone who has watched some Bollywood movies will have observed, Indian men are depicted as superior beings to whom women are expected to defer. The male characters often emerge as 'naughty boys' who must be indulged or forgiven even for crimes against women. Apart from poverty, the darkest side of Indian life is the appalling treatment of women as a result of these attitudes, often euphemized as 'patriarchal' – as a UN statement put it, India is the most dangerous place to be born a girl. Because most of it is covert, it is impossible to estimate the number of girl babies who are killed in their first year, simply because they are girls, but it has been estimated to be at least a million a year. This 'infanticide' is usually carried out by senior women in the family, who poison, smother or starve the child. Perhaps as many more never get to be born. Abortion is legal in India – many more girls than boys are aborted.

According to the Indian National Crime Records Bureau, 244,000 crimes against women were reported in 2012. Many of these were rape, frequently gang rape. The majority of victims were under 14; around 10 per cent were under 10. However, the International Dalit Security Network says these numbers are grossly under-reported and that 90 per cent of lower-caste victims conceal the crime because of fear of retaliation and perceived police indifference. It is customary for a woman being married to bring a dowry with her, often large enough to put her family in debt for years. Disputes over dowries lead to a high rate of 'bride burning' – the young women is doused with petrol or kerosene and set alight as a form of retaliation for what the husband's family see as defaults in dowry payments. More than 8000 cases were reported in 2012, with 91,000 in the decade to that year, but these figures are said to be much lower than the real number of such murders, which are often concealed as 'kitchen fires'. In some cases women have been killed, with their newborn child, because that child was a girl. Conviction rates of perpetrators are under 20 per cent.

The death of millions of girls from one or other of the above causes has resulted in a serious and growing disproportion in the number of men and women in India. A ratio of 947 women per thousand males in 1991 had fallen to 914 per thousand in 2012, the UN estimating that 15 million girls were not born over the last decade. With the rate of female foeticide increasing sharply, this situation will inevitably worsen. The declining number of women in the community is believed to be a factor in India's high rape rate. However, it is interesting to note that Kerala, with its enlightened policies, has the highest female sex ratio at 1058 women per thousand men.

India had high rates of growth in GDP earlier in the century – as much as 9 per cent a year – but in 2011 and 2012 this fell to less than 6 per cent – 4.5 per cent in the last quarter of 2012. Indian economists estimate a growth rate of at least 8 per cent is necessary to provide enough jobs to balance population growth. As elsewhere, the decline in prosperity has been attributed to weak global demand, but not only that. 'Farewell to Incredible India', the *Economist* remarked (June 2012), saying: 'graft, confusion and red tape have infuriated domestic businesses and harmed investment. The state is borrowing too much, crowding out private firms and keeping inflation high … the dreary conclusion is that India's feeble politics are now ushering in several years of feebler economic growth.' However, Prime Minister Singh said in 2013 he believed the current downturn was temporary, and that the economy would bounce back, although there were problems of 'corruption, bureaucratic inertia and managing a coalition government'.

Nevertheless, the Indian rupee lost 15 per cent in the year to August – this means essential commodities like coal, oil and iron ore cost more. Staple foods like flour, onions and tomatoes became more expensive, with a severe impact on the poor. Growth seemed static at 4.5 per cent, inflation was a high 10 per cent and the current account deficit stood at almost $90 billion. In an effort to stem the 'flight of capital' the government limited capital outflow and raised the duty on gold to 10 per cent. India is the world's largest importer of gold – the 860 tons imported in 2012 made up 11 per cent of all imports. It is estimated there are 31,000 tons of it in the country, worth $1.4 trillion, but this is largely in the form of jewellery or held in religious institutions. Gold worth as much as $80 billion is said to be held in one place, the Tirupati Balaji Temple in Andra Pradesh.

India's future will be very much a race with time – a struggle to defeat poverty, ignorance and ill-health in the face of the severe challenges presented by climate change, population growth and a capricious world economy.

20 Pakistan

Of all the south Asian states Pakistan seems at the greatest risk of social and political collapse. Government has been weak, veering between incompetent and corrupt 'democratic' regimes and self-serving military dictatorships. The leading figures in both have been and still are members of a small wealthy elite closely connected with the military, governing a vast mass of desperately poor and disadvantaged people. Around two-thirds of Pakistanis work on the land, often on small subsistence plots that can barely provide them with enough food, and frequently, as the tenants of wealthy absentee landlords, are trapped in a cycle of poverty and debt. More than 60 years as an independent state have done little to change this. The population, 40 million in 1947, had grown to 190 million in 2012.

A high proportion of Pakistan's population is made up of young people, but close on half of them never get a reasonable education – UNICEF estimates that 30 per cent of Pakistani children have less than two years' schooling. More than half of its women have never attended school. It is widely thought that since girls will go straight from virtual seclusion in their parents' home to the same condition in their husband's, there is no point in educating them. Pakistan has 'ghost schools', where teachers collect their wages, but fail to turn up for work. From an early age boys and girls are segregated, and there is strict observance of the Muslim instruction that women must avoid being seen by men outside their own family. UNICEF estimates that almost half of all children are suffering from chronic malnutrition and 15 per cent are 'acutely malnourished'. According to the Asian Development Bank more than half of all Pakistanis survive on less than $2 a day, and the poorest 20 per cent are worse off than they were ten years ago. Climate change is already hitting hard, causing heavier than usual monsoon rains and alternating droughts and severe flooding almost every year.

Most of the country, including its largest city, Karachi, with 13 million people, is violent and dangerous, substantially due to inadequate and discriminatory law enforcement. In his 2011 book *Pakistan* test cricketer and political activist Imran Khan concluded that 'a lack of the rule of law lies at the heart of our troubled nation's problems'. He quotes the deputy inspector of prisons, Salimullah Khan, as saying 'sixty per cent of people in Pakistani gaols were innocent. Their crime was their poverty.' Over 30,000 people were killed in terrorist-related violence in the four years to 2012, 7000 in Karachi, a city preyed on by criminal gangs which have close associations with local business. According to the nation's Human Rights Commission, at least 675 women were murdered in the first nine months of 2011, some after having been raped or gang-raped. Most of these were so-called 'honour killings', which occur when women enter into associations of which their families disapprove. The nation is racked with dissension, and suicide bombings that kill as many as 100 people occur regularly.

This unstable and corrupt state, which is still heavily dependent on foreign aid, possesses 90 to 100 nuclear weapons, about the same number as its neighbour, India, both of whom also have sophisticated weapon-delivery systems. Hostility between these two large south Asian states has persisted for decades, leading to several wars over the disputed state of Kashmir, where more than a million soldiers on both sides face each other. This nuclear stand-off presents a major threat to the world, a demonstrably greater immediate one than, for instance, Iran or North Korea's nuclear ambitions.

While Pakistan is generally considered part of south Asia, geographically and culturally it is a borderland between the Middle East and Asia. It shares a frontier with Iran and the official language, Urdu, is closely related to Arabic and Persian. However, most people in the tribal areas speak local dialects. Pakistan has close ties with the oil-rich Middle East states, especially Iran, and with China, both of whom provide economic assistance. The large majority of Pakistanis are Muslims, and the country is an Islamic state. This means that the teachings of the Koran, including *sharia*, religious law, deeply influence all aspects of life.

When partition of British India occurred in 1947 the new nation of Pakistan consisted of two areas of territory separated by almost a thousand miles of India: the present-day Pakistan and the preponderantly Muslim section of Bengal that is now Bangladesh. This curiously divided country faced many immediate problems. Because all administrative decisions had previously been made in Delhi, there were no organized transport or communications services. Relations with India were tense and frequently hostile. The first sporadic war with India over the state of Kashmir began in1947 and dragged on for two years. Kashmir became part of India because it had a Hindu raja, although most of the people are Muslim. Kashmir, eventually divided into two zones occupied by Indian and Pakistani forces, remains an intractable problem. In 1951 the nation's first prime minister, Liaquat Ali Khan, was assassinated by a Pashtun extremist, for reasons even now not clear, although the motive may have been the Kashmir situation. Growing political instability over the next six years resulted in more than a decade of martial law and dictatorship imposed by the army commander, Ayub Khan.

A supporter of the free market and private enterprise, Ayub Khan firmly believed it was the army's role to control politicians, an idea still current among Pakistan's military. He built some necessary infrastructure, including hydroelectric dams and generators, and the beginnings of industries which, with foreign investment, resulted in a growing economy, although from a very small base. However, his win in a presidential election in 1965 was clouded by allegations of vote-rigging, mainly arising from a system of 'basic democracies' – regional councils – he had introduced in 1960. His reputation suffered when a bid to seize Kashmir in 1965 failed, the war ending in 17 days without any clear conclusion. With both his popularity and his health declining, he resigned in 1969, handing over power to another general, Yahya Khan.

Yahya Khan was president for only two years. His sacking of many public servants, their replacement by army officers and relentless pursuit of his political opponents made him unpopular. Demonstrations for independence in East Pakistan were put down forcibly, but this only hardened the resolve of the freedom fighters. The crisis deepened when a huge natural disaster, a major cyclone and storm surge, hit East Pakistan in 1969. More than half a million people were killed in one of the worst natural catastrophes the world has seen. Yahya Khan was much criticized for Pakistan's failure to help with the suffering and devastation that followed. Instead the Pakistani army began an organized campaign of repression of the independence movement. This involved a degree of violence and massacre of innocent civilians almost unparalleled in history for its brutality. Probably around half a million were killed, although some estimates run as high as three million. Hundreds of villages were burned and thousands of women raped, tortured and killed. In one incident in the eastern capital, Dhaka, more than 500 women taken from the university and private homes were forced into military brothels. There is evidence of a deliberate policy to kill as many as possible of the intellectual and political elite, and to murder Hindus indiscriminately. Professors at the university were targeted in the first few days, and, with hundreds of teachers, journalists, engineers and artists, systematically tortured and killed.

India, alarmed at these excesses and the flight of 10 million people across its border, intervened. When its army entered East Pakistan it was able to defeat the Pakistani forces decisively in a fortnight. Ninety thousand Pakistani soldiers surrendered and were taken prisoner. East Pakistan became an independent nation, as Bangladesh.

Yahya Khan and the army were so discredited by the atrocities in the east and their poor showing against Indian forces that their influence declined sharply, democracy advocate Zulfika Ali Bhutto becoming prime minister after fresh elections. His first task was to recover the soldiers held in Indian prisoner-of-war camps – this involved acceptance of a peace that acknowledged the independence of Bangladesh. He also rewrote the constitution, making the president's role ceremonial only, and restoring parliamentary democracy. Bhutto nevertheless made some mistakes that proved dangerous in the Pakistani environment. A socialist, he nationalized too many industries and services too quickly – a policy that resulted in nationwide economic stagnation – and used the army to put down unrest in Baluchistan Province, causing thousands of civilian deaths. A secession movement has existed in Baluchistan, Pakistan's largest but most thinly populated state, since 1948. Bhutto's dismissal of the provincial government there in 1973 led to a major flare-up of violence. By 2012 thousands of Baluchis are alleged to have been kidnapped by Pakistani security forces, with persistent reports of 'killing and dumping', the killing of people without trial and subsequent dumping of their bodies on roadsides.

Bhutto's People's Party (PPP) won comfortably at general elections in 1977, but persistent allegations of vote-rigging led to his deposition by another general, Zia ul-Haq, later that year. Bhutto was arrested on charges of conniving at the murder of a political opponent, and ultimately convicted after a controversial five-month trial. He was sentenced to death and hanged at Rawalpindi Prison in 1979. Bhutto's family, including his daughter Benazir, were also arrested and forced into exile. There are strong suspicions that the CIA, and, indeed, the US government, were complicit because they feared Bhutto's socialist policies and close association with the Soviet Union.

Whatever the truth of this, Zia emerged as a strong ally of the United States. He imposed a severe regime of martial law and threw his weight behind US and Saudi Arabian assistance to the *mujahideen* fighting the Soviet occupiers of Afghanistan. Although there was a considerable international outcry at the execution of Bhutto this was the era of the Cold War, during which the zonal competitors sought every advantage. The United States saw the war in Afghanistan as a means to weaken the Soviet Union, which it indeed ultimately did. Hence Zia became respectable as a leading Asian anti-Communist, attracting support and money from the United States which did much to keep him in power until his death in an air crash in 1988. American President Ronald Reagan described Zia's regime as 'the front-line' ally of the United States in the fight against Communism. Zia was a devout Muslim, using the army to enforce strict Islamic principles which still influence Pakistan today.

In the last years of his life Zia faced increasing international pressure to return Pakistan to democracy, and as a result elections were held in 1988 in which Bhutto's daughter Benazir, who had been permitted to return to Pakistan, stood as a candidate for the People's Party, which had survived in exile in India. Immensely popular, she was elected and became prime minister, a post she held for two terms, 1988–90 and 1993–96.Oxford educated, Benazir was nevertheless a member of Pakistan's small privileged class and a woman, in a country traditionally opposed to any exercise of power by women. Imran Khan remarks: 'we were disappointed by Benazir; she began to behave more like an empress than a democratically elected prime minister'. Marriage to Asif Ali Zardari, who became widely known as 'Mr Ten per Cent' because he allegedly took commissions on government contracts, did not help. She faced an almost impossible task to reform Pakistan's laws and society. Indeed it proved to be impossible, and the country drifted into a renewed phase of political and economic anarchy presided over by influential groups of 'businessmen' who did not hesitate to intimidate and murder opponents.

One of Pakistan's wealthiest men, industrialist Nawaz Sharif, was prime minister after 1996 and leader of the conservative Muslim League, which held alternate terms of government with the People's Party. He provoked international protests when he ordered Pakistan's first nuclear tests in response to those carried out in India, because of fears of nuclear proliferation. The nation dropped to a low ebb on his watch, with rising unemployment and foreign debt and increasing lawlessness, facing financial default with debts of more than $30 billion against reserves of around $1 billion. Sharif interfered persistently with the judiciary and the army's top echelons, and began to lose popularity, especially after Pakistan started the pointless undeclared Kargil war with India in the high country of Kashmir – a war in which Pakistani forces were defeated and driven back by the Indian army. In the words of a senior Pakistani general, Abdul Majeed Malik, Kargil was 'a total disaster'. After a final power struggle with the army chief, General Musharraf, in 1999 Sharif was deposed, arrested and sentenced to 14 years' imprisonment. However, after the United States and Saudi Arabia intervened on his behalf, he was permitted to go into exile in Saudi Arabia, eventually returning to Pakistan in 2007.

Musharraf became the new strongman and, after an initial phase of international disapproval, like Zia before him, became respectable for much the same reasons. He became an ally in the US 'war against terrorism', although a Gallup poll in 2002 indicated that only 5 per cent of Pakistanis approved of the US campaign against the Taliban in Afghanistan. America provided massive economic and military aid to Pakistan, allowing Musharraf and the army to retain control of the country. Between 2002 and 2010 the United States gave Pakistan more than $20 billion in aid, most of which has subsidized the military. This has given rise to assertions that the US 'owns' the Pakistani army.

Nevertheless, Musharraf's record reads better than those of previous Pakistani military strongmen. He took at least initial steps to reform the economy, reduce corruption and moderate religious extremism. In 2002 a referendum to extend his term as president for a further five years attracted a 97 per cent 'yes' vote, but in elections later that year his party failed to win a majority of seats.

Benazir Bhutto, who said she was well aware of the risks to her of another return to Pakistan after living in England, nevertheless came back in 2007 to prepare for elections due to be held the following year. After two unsuccessful attempts on her life she was assassinated early in 2008. As she stood up through the sunroof of an armoured car shots were fired at her and a bomb detonated near the vehicle. The circumstances remain a mystery, and the Pakistan authorities have not been able to identify, much less find and charge, the perpetrators. However, there was speculation that an important political figure may have been involved when a prosecutor investigating the Bhutto murder was shot dead outside his home in the capital, Islamabad, in 2013.

Meanwhile, from 2004 to 2008 the immensely popular leader of Pakistan's nuclear weapons programme, Abdul Qadeer Khan, came under scrutiny for passing on nuclear secrets to nations the United States regarded as potential enemies – Iran, Libya and North Korea. Qadeer was held under house arrest for some time, but eventually pardoned – probably because the government was influenced by his standing as almost a hero in Pakistan.

Musharraf, who had to deal with this issue as well as huge public outrage over the Bhutto killing, was becoming increasingly unpopular. He became involved in a personal feud with the Supreme Court, sacking the Chief Justice, and arresting other judges. Lawyers, dressed in black suits, demonstrated against him and boycotted the courts. The People's Party, which became the government after the 2008 election, and the opposition Muslim League combined to commence impeachment proceedings against the president. After some days of stand-off, Musharraf resigned, leaving Pakistan immediately on a pilgrimage to Mecca. He subsequently undertook a lecture tour in the United States, where he is said to have been paid $150,000 per appearance. While in voluntary exile in London, Musharraf also started his own political party, the All-Pakistan Muslim League. However, when he returned to Pakistan in 2013 he was arrested on terrorist charges relating to his vendetta against the judges, and declared ineligible to stand as a candidate in the election.

Although the 2008 government was the first in Pakistan's history to serve a full five-year term, those years were chaotic, with little apparently done to solve the country's pressing problems, and characterized by the infighting and disputes with the judiciary and the army so much evident in the past. Benazir's widower Asif Ali Zardari served as president, while the first prime minister Yousaf Raza Gillani was stood down in 2012 after a contempt of court conviction. His successor, Raja Pervais Ashraf, was indicted early in 2013 on bribery charges. Nawaz Sharif was leader of the opposition during this parliamentary term and a prime mover in the deposition of Musharraf.

Former *mujihadeen* fighter against the Russians and later head of al Qaeda Osama bin Laden was shot dead by US Navy Seals – special forces – in his house in the Pakistani army town of Abbottabad in 2011, near the nation's military academy. Bin Laden formed al Qaeda – the words mean 'the base' – in 1990 as an organization to support the 35,000 Arabs who had fought the Russians in Afghanistan, but it was subsequently considered an international terrorist group. The United States strongly questioned why bin Laden had been able to live for so long with impunity in the garrison town; the Pakistan government protested at the US action taking place on their soil, and without their being consulted, and also at civilian deaths from strikes by unmanned American drone aircraft, estimated in 2013 at between 2500 and 3500 by the Bureau of Investigative Journalism. Much of the debate on these issues has involved the secretive but powerful Inter-services Intelligence (ISI), the equivalent of the US CIA, which, with a reputed 10,000 employees, is said to be the world's largest intelligence unit in terms of staff. It was strongly involved in support of the Afghan *mujihadeen* in the 1980s and almost certainly had contacts with bin Laden then. In 2010 a London School of Economics report claimed concrete evidence that the ISI was funding, supplying and supporting the Taliban insurgency in Afghanistan.

As the 2013 elections approached the Pakistani Taliban made regular attacks on political gatherings, stating that they intended to sabotage the democratic process because they wanted Islamic *sharia* law introduced through the country. More than 120 people were killed in such bomb attacks and many more injured. The Muslim League, led by Nawaz Sharif, won decisively with 125 seats, the incumbent Democrat government gained 33 and Imran Khan's PTI 28. While 86 million people were registered to vote, millions in Baluchistan boycotted the poll, and in some religiously conservative regions women abstained from voting after party leaders agreed they should not exercise their votes. Thousands more could not vote because polling places were unstaffed, and no ballot papers were available.

Sharif, who lives on a big estate south of Lahore, is a strong supporter of Islam, and is said to be close to Jamaat-e-Islami, the Pakistani version of the Muslim Brotherhood. He has links with Saudi Arabia, where he has business interests.

21 Bangladesh

Bangladesh has had a short and tumultuous history, including one very destructive war, at least five severe cyclones accompanied by catastrophic flooding and regular alternation between parliamentary democracy and military dictatorships. Of all the Asian countries, she faces perhaps the most serious threat from climate change – a 2012 World Bank report assessed her as 'highly vulnerable'. One of the most crowded countries on earth, she has 160 million people on 150,000 hectares of fertile but mostly low-lying land on the delta of the Ganges and Brahmaputra rivers. Because 10 per cent of Bangladesh is barely three feet above mean high tide level, the country is already suffering from large areas of inundation and the destruction of productive land by salt-water incursions. On some estimates the number of climate refugees from there will be above 20 million over the next half-century.

Bangladesh was born of war. As a result of partition in 1947 the former Indian state of Bengal was divided along religious lines – its eastern predominantly Muslim regions attached to the main body of Pakistan more than a thousand miles away across Indian territory. This curious anomaly led to trouble almost at once. While East Pakistan, as it was then called, shared its religion with its larger partner, the two regions differed widely in culture and language. Its people quickly felt exploited by the government far away in Karachi, and a protest movement developed almost immediately. Barely a year after the new nation was formed it gained strength when the Pakistan government tried to impose the Urdu language of the west on the largely Bengali-speaking people of the east. Major protests formed around an organization, the Bengali Language Movement, which sought to have Bengali retained as an official language. The Pakistan government reacted by using force. In 1952 four protesting students from the University of Dhaka were shot dead by police, provoking major public anger. Conflict and demonstrations continued for another four years, when Bengali was reinstated as an official language.

In 1970 the country was afflicted with one of the worst natural disasters in modern history in terms of loss of life. An estimated half a million people died when a massive cyclone, followed by storm surges, drove in over the coast. The inadequate government response to this disaster increased public exasperation. A movement for independence had been born from the years of struggle, culminating in an informal declaration of independence by a group of students in 1971. The independence leader, Sheik Mujid Rahman, was arrested in a Pakistani military crackdown, although most of his colleagues escaped into India, where they formed a provisional government. India, which in common with much of the international community, sympathized with the independence movement, supported the guerrilla movement inside East Pakistan, and late in 1971, entered the war. This armed struggle caused huge disruptions in the east, millions of people fleeing from the fighting into India. Although the war ended in less than two weeks, when the Pakistan force – almost 100,000 men – surrendered, it was marked with an appalling degree of savagery. Pakistan soldiers killed and raped people in the villages, many of which were burned down with napalm. The Bangladesh government estimated that three million people were killed, but other estimates are between 300,000 and 500,000.

The new nation of Bangladesh was then established as a parliamentary democracy, but it had sustained so much damage recovery proved difficult. A major famine in 1973/4, and another vast flood, which inundated half the country, completed the social disruption. Thousands of deaths occurred among the millions of homeless and hungry people confined in camps outside the capital, Dhaka. A virtual civil war broke out between these starving people and the police. Sections of the army turned against Sheik Mujib Rahman, who only three years earlier had been fêted as a national hero. In August 1975 he and several members of his family were murdered by elements of the army. Ensuing martial law was followed by a succession of military coups, relieved only by a return to at least the forms of democracy under President Zia, whose National Party won 207 seats of 300 in the 1979 elections. His assassination in 1981, again by dissident members of the military, led on to a decade of further military dictatorship.

However, two political parties, the Awami League and the Nationalist Party, gathered support during this period. This, with a lengthy general strike in Dhaka, forced the resignation of the dictator General Ershad in 1990 and the restoration of at least the semblance of democracy at elections the following year. An autocrat, Ershad nevertheless had a certain popularity for many years. He instituted death sentences for two unattractive classes of crime in Bangladesh, acid-throwing at women and the deliberate crippling of children to act as beggars. National elections in 1996 that resulted in an Awami League government, were, however, marred by a low voter turnout and allegations of vote-rigging. Amid widespread public disillusionment with the political process, government returned to the Nationalist Party in 2001. After six further years of unrest and disturbances, a caretaker government was appointed in 2007 to oversee fresh elections. These, held in 2009, resulted in a landslide victory for the Awami League, led by Sheikh Hasina, a daughter of Sheikh Mujib who had survived the massacre of her family. The Awami League won 230 seats in a parliament of 299.

Bangladesh's past came back to haunt it early in 2013, when 35 people were killed in violent clashes in Dhaka between Islamic extremists and police. The riots followed imposition by a war-crimes tribunal of a death sentence on Delwar Hossain Sayedee for crimes committed when he collaborated with the Pakistani army during the atrocities of 1971. The incident revealed continuing deep divisions in the community along religious lines. However, the prime minister firmly rejected demands from a rally of tens of thousands in Dhaka calling for the death penalty for blasphemy.

Bangladesh has a close association with China, but the United States is the largest market for her exports and American firms are major investors. In 2012 per capita income was $848. Villagers benefit from a micro-credit scheme run by the Grameen Bank, which has over two million members, many of them women who have obtained finance for small businesses in their village. Clothing manufacture is a major area of industry, accounting for almost three-quarters of Bangladeshi export earnings, but the workers, who are mostly women, generally have very poor working conditions. Hundreds have died in fires in death-trap factories, and when an eight-storey building in Dhaka collapsed in 2013 more than 1100 garment workers making cheap clothing for Western retailers were killed. Around 60 per cent of men are literate, and a little over 50 per cent of women. Most still work on small subsistence farms, which barely provide the means of life. Around two-thirds of children are malnourished.

Village life – that of 80 per cent of the people – is primitive and hard, with as many as a dozen people living in single-roomed mud houses with walls and a roof, but lacking other amenities. Life is a desperate battle to grow enough food and gain small amounts of money by labouring in export industries growing jute, sugar and tea. Most children must work at least five hours a day from the age of 6 or 7. There is little time to spare for schooling. As in other south Asian countries, girls are especially disadvantaged.

As sea levels rise and cyclones increase in intensity, much of the country floods regularly. A cyclone that struck in 1991 killed 140,000 people. Another in 1998 had a much smaller death-toll – around 1000 people – but caused the worst flooding in the country's history following unusually heavy monsoon rains. Damage to housing and other infrastructure was very severe. According to a Bangladesh government statement an 18-inch rise in sea level would submerge 11 per cent of coastal land. Dr Atiq Rahman , Bangladeshi lead author for the Intergovernmental Panel on Climate Change (IPCC), confirmed a rise of this order in a submission to the British government in 2008, predicting that a sea-level rise would dislocate 25 million people in coastal districts by 2060. Dhaka, with 18million people, is already one of the most crowded places on earth, but every day thousands more arrive, mostly to live in the slum suburb of Korail, where the houses are crowded so close together it is barely possible to move between them. However Dhaka, much of which is scarcely above high-tide level, is one of the most threatened cities in the world by sea-level rise. While the population will continue to increase, this will be less than it might have been, due to a successful family planning programme which has reduced the fertility rate from 6.6.children per women in 1977 to 2.3 now.

Then there is BRAC, a massive public support organization which originated in Bangladesh in 1972, and now operates in 10 other countries. It employs 97,000 community health and field workers advising people on everything from better agriculture to family planning, centred around a basic purpose to alleviate poverty. 'Barefoot lawyers' deliver legal services to the poor and fieldworkers give economic advice to women in particular, helping them with 'microloans' to start businesses. BRAC produces, distributes and markets seed at a fair price, advises villagers on health issues, and runs schools. BRAC claims its 22,000 primary schools represent the largest secular private education system in the world. They are free, using one teacher in one room for four years with the same group of students, usually children who have been deprived of education by poverty or disability, and are attended by two-thirds of a million children, the majority of whom are girls.

Yet in spite of everything that can be done, inundation of much of the land is inevitable, and the world will need to deal with millions of refugees from Bangladesh. This has plainly worried neighbouring India, which is building a security fence along the 2500 mile border with armed guards to stop people crossing.

A relatively small island, Bhola, lies between two channels of the Ganges River where it runs into the Bay of Bengal. Bhola is around 70 miles long by eight wide, and is home to two million people. Most of it is barely three feet above mean sea level. As the glaciers in the river headwaters melt faster more water rushes down the river, cutting into the muddy fringe of the island. There are houses and fields right up to the river bank, and these are disappearing rapidly into the water – a Dhaka organization known as

Coastal Watch says 11 Bangladeshis are losing their homes every hour. If the rising sea has indeed destroyed much of the country by 2050 Bhola and scores of other islands in the Bay of Bengal are likely to have disappeared completely. Meanwhile what people dread most here is the full moon, which every month raises the huge tides that sweep away arable land, roads and businesses.

Bangladesh shares with India a huge coastal archipelago, a tangle of marshy flats threaded with tidal creeks and rivers known as the Sundarman Islands. This region, where 50 million people live, is also severely threatened by sea level rise. Of the 108 islands of the Sundarmans 58 are inhabited. The rest make up a reserve of swamp forest and waterways people enter only with caution because they are the last natural refuge of the endangered Bengal tiger.

The people and government of Bangladesh are very aware of the risks associated with climate change and are doing what they can to protect themselves, building dikes to keep seawater out, and developing salt resistant strains of rice that will grow in brackish water. The countryside is dotted with thousands of elevated concrete cyclone refuges, which are also used as community centres. There are even floating schools, libraries and hospitals designed to keep working during monsoonal floods. Huge bundles of water hyacinth are being used to create floating islands on which food can be grown.

Not all of Bangladesh is flat. The Chittagong Hills Tract south-east of the delta is indeed a range of hills, in which around a million and a half people live. About half are tribal people. Relocation of 400,000 destitute Bengalis there between 1979 and 1985 met with stubborn resistance from the tribes. Although these were eventually awarded limited autonomy and a peace accord was signed in 1997 a degree of insurgency has continued, with increasing tensions over land ownership. The region's capital, Chittagong, is Bangladesh's second largest city, the largest port and the location of most of its industry, including the nation's only steel mill and oil refinery.

After Bangladesh became independent massive aid programmes were provided to deal with the almost universal problem of waterborne disease. More than three million deep tube-wells were sunk. For some years the water from these was considered safe, but now it is known the water in over 60 per cent of the wells serving 1000 villages contains enough arsenic to cause skin keratosis, cancer, and eventually, death. This is a catastrophe of epic proportions, described by Prof AH Smith, of the University of California as 'the largest mass poisoning in history ... among the greatest of any disease facing the world today. My own estimate is that one person is dying every 15 minutes and millions are suffering an illness.' There are at least 100,000 cases of skin lesions, and it is considered that one in every ten future cancer cases in Bangladesh will be caused by arsenic. Both UNICEF and the World Bank are attempting arsenic mitigation, using more than $500 million annually from foreign donors, but the problem is far from solved—high levels of iron in the groundwater are severely clogging filters.

Severe and regular flooding has drawn international attention to Bangladesh's plight—the fact that these disasters are happening regularly, and even becoming worse as the decades pass, is a reproach to the world. The problem has been studied, and it is known that the floodwaters could be controlled by reafforestation in the upper reaches of the major rivers and by a series of dams and hydro-electric generators that could also provide cheap power to the entire sub-continent. Electricity is currently available to only a minority of Bangladeshis living in urban areas, and even in these severe power shortages are common. Due to the flatness of the land, there is a little scope for major hydro-electric schemes in Bangladesh, but some of its neighbours, including Burma, Nepal and Bhutan, may in the future be able to sell power to Bangladesh. Negotiations to this end had started in 2012.

22 *Afghanistan*

Any who contemplate a military adventure in Afghanistan might first consider the British retreat from its capital, Kabul, in 1842. Of 700 British soldiers, 3800 *sepoys* – native troops – and 14,000 civilians who fled from Kabul in the winter of that year, only one survivor, a man riding an exhausted horse, made it to the British fort at Jalalabad to bring the dreadful news. Britain occupied Kabul in 1839 (300 camels were needed to carry in the wine), but as time passed the occupying force became less and less welcome until they were destroyed in retreat by the full fury of *jihad* – a new word to the world at that time. The war, which cost £50 billion in today's money, achieved nothing – the king it had aimed to supplant, Dost Mohammad, returned to his throne.

This episode was one consequence of a persistent misunderstanding of Afghanistan by foreigners. This is still evident to this day – even to refer to Afghanistan as a nation and Afghanis as a people is substantially illusory, since this is a region of many different tribal loyalties, many different languages and little common ground other than religion. Even this last is influenced by the division of the population between the major sects of Islam, there being a large Sunni majority and a significant Shia minority, which includes the Persian-speaking Hazara. For thousands of years this territory on the roof of the world has been a crossroads through which a motley and diverse series of invaders has passed. Each has left its own distinctive imprint. Geography created this situation. Afghanistan is the natural invasion route to the rich north Indian plain, and it has been used this way for at least 3000 years. Persians, Greeks, Parthians and Turks, among others, have from time to time occupied parts of the present Afghanistan, usually only for relatively short periods of time. With them came their religions.

Afghanistan is essentially divided by the foothills of the Himalaya known as the Hindu Kush, which rise to 20,000 feet. South of this range the land is mainly forbidding mountains and desert; to the north lies the great central Asian plain. Wheat and barley are the main crops supporting a subsistence agriculture, and are grown on the scarce areas of fertile land in the river valleys – barely 12 per cent of the country is arable. One of these is the beautiful Bamiyan Valley in the central mountains, home of the minority – and persecuted – Hazara people. Afghanistan is Islamic now, but the huge statues of Buddha on the cliffs overlooking the valley, destroyed in 2001 when they were blown up by the Taliban, were carved in the 3rd and 4th centuries during the expansion of Buddhism that reached as far east as Japan. Greek, Roman and Indian influences have all contributed to the culture of the Peshawar Valley in the south. In 1978, near the oasis town of Sheberghan in the northern region, Soviet archaeologists found, catalogued and put into safe storage more than 20,000 gold coins, ornaments and other valuables. This region was once famous as Bactria, where a Greek society existed for many centuries after the death of Alexander in 323 BCE. It was an important crossroads on the Silk Road. The discovery, known as 'the Bactrian gold', shows a remarkable diversity of influences ranging from Greek and Roman to Siberian Altai. In spite of Afghanistan's turbulent recent history, it survived intact in a Kabul bank vault, and was displayed in France, Italy, Holland and the United States between 2006 and 2008 before being returned to Kabul.

A huge archaeological effort is currently being mustered to retrieve the treasures of another major civilization of the Buddhist era near the village of Mes Aynak, 25 miles south-east of Kabul. This is very much a race with time, since the ruins of what must have been a large and cosmopolitan Silk Road centre from the 3rd to the 8th century sit on top of the world's second largest deposit of copper, potentially worth $100 billion – four to five times as much as the rest of the Afghan economy. A Chinese consortium has paid $3 billion for a 30-year lease on this site. Exploitation, due to commence in about five years, is likely to involve the complete destruction of the ancient ruins. In 2013, 67 archaeologists of four nationalities and 650 labourers were working to remove and preserve as many artefacts as possible. Evidence is emerging that the copper lode was first worked 5000 years ago, and that the prosperity of the Buddhist city of Mes Aynak was based on copper mining.

Persia – modern Iran – has left its mark on Afghanistan more than any other place. Persian is still the language of culture, and to an extent a unifying influence among at least 30 dialects and languages used by tribal groups. There are about 20 distinct ethnic groups, who claim origins from such disparate sources as Alexander's Greek soldiers, Arabia, Mongolia and Turkey. To add to this confusion, Afghanistan's borders do not include all the people of these diverse tribal groups. Many of them live on both sides of the borders with the former Soviet states to the north. Then there is the Durand Line, a disputed border arbitrarily drawn by the British *Raj* between India and Afghanistan that divides around 50 million Pashtuns almost equally between what is now Pakistan and Afghanistan. The Pashtuns are a very ancient people with strong tribal loyalties and traditions that provide automatic hospitality and asylum to anyone seeking help, but they are quick to take revenge for what they see as injustice. At the time of Indian partition there were calls for an independent Pashtunistan, which led to friction with Pakistan after a declaration by the Afghan government that it 'recognized neither the imaginary Durand line nor any similar line'. Allegations that Taliban fighters 'cross the border' into Pakistan miss a significant point, which is that Pashtuns on both sides see themselves as a single people, for whom the border does not exist. Pakistani cricketer and politician Imran Khan, himself of Pashtun origins, puts it this way in his 2011 book *Pakistan*:

> Anyone with even a basic knowledge of the history of the region knows that for reasons of religious, cultural and social affinity, the Pashtuns feel a deep-rooted duty to help their brethren on either side of the Durand Line. For them, the international frontier is irrelevant. So no government, Pakistani or foreign will ever be entirely successful in stopping them crossing over the 1500-mile border to support their people or feeling obliged to offer them shelter if they venture into their territory.

As Britain tightened its hold on India in the 19th century Afghanistan became a pawn in what Kipling called 'the great game' – intense rivalry between Russia and Britain. The Pashtuns, then known in England as Pathans, fiercely resisted the British during several Afghan wars. These battles and the dangers of the Khyber Pass became standard themes in British fiction – especially books for boys. This was the place where the stiff upper lip was eulogized, and death in the service of the Empire depicted as 'the greatest adventure'. However, little was achieved in these north-west frontier wars, and Afghanistan retained a precarious independence.

During the first half of the 20th century a very small Western-educated elite in the capital, Kabul, provided some appearance of modernity. However, little changed in the tribal areas, other than the evolution of a ferocious opposition to Western ways and values which were, and still are, seen as decadent and anti-Islam. These tensions resulted in a series of mini-coups as the Pashtun majority struggled to maintain a hold on what passed for government – basically a military autocracy with little authority outside Kabul. This lasted until after the Second World War, when rivalry between the Soviet Union and the United States brought outright civil war to Afghanistan. From 1955 onwards Russia made large monetary grants to Kabul, and by 1978 there were 2000 Soviet advisers in the country.

In the last days of 1979 Russia invaded Afghanistan, ostensibly to support an unpopular left-wing government. However, the real reasons were probably general Cold War paranoia and a desire to hedge a very consider-able Soviet investment. Russia lost the war, which dragged on for ten years. As other invaders had done, it found the tribes difficult adversaries. This opposition came to be known as the *mujahideen* – the word means 'fighters for God'. However this guerrilla movement was far from monolithic – indeed, its main problem was lack of unity. While attempts were made to organize it into seven factions, even these had splinter groups within them. A major point of interest was the recruitment of fighters from other Islamic countries, as far away as the Philippines and Indonesia, and insistence that the war against Russia was a holy war – a *jihad*.

The *mujahideen* was substantially but covertly provided with more than $1 billion-worth of arms by the US CIA, pipelined via Egypt and Pakistan, in the Cold War interest of weakening the Soviet Union. Saudi Arabia contributed almost as much, including the services of a young man called Osama bin Laden, who entered the ranks of the *mujahideen*. Much of this weaponry was sold off in village markets, creating a situation in which almost every man possessed – and still possesses – an assault rifle. This war cost at least 200,000 Afghan lives. Five million people fled into exile, mostly in neighbouring Pakistan. The Russians, who had almost 100,000 soldiers engaged, lost 25,000.

The apparent victors – the *mujahideen* – reverted to banditry and fighting among themselves as soon as the Russians left. The 'moderate' Islamic regime in Kabul, itself riven by factionalism, proved inadequate. Conflict between warlords from 1992 on led to widespread destruction of houses and public buildings in Kabul, and another 50,000 deaths. Conditions in the shattered country – in which thousands were dying from starvation and cold in savage winters – and continued fighting between tribal groups doomed the government from the start.

Out of this chaos came the Taliban, by processes that are far from clear. The Taliban, an extremist Islamic organization, appears to have emerged from the fundamentalist schools – the *madrassas* – in the refugee camps in northern Pakistan. Small in numbers at first, it gained recruits quickly, finally coalescing as a major political and military force under the leader-ship of Mullah Mohammed Omar, a shadowy and mysterious figure whose title is Leader of the Faithful. When by 1996 it controlled the majority of the country, including Kabul, the Taliban attracted international disapproval, not the least because of its rigid Islamic view that women should not be educated. It also commenced an intense campaign against Western values and ideas. However, the Taliban government was able to bring a measure of peace and order to the areas it controlled, and for a time enforced a ban on the opium industry, which was and is again the major supplier to the drug addicts of the West.

When, on 11 September 2001 the towers of the World Trade Center in New York were destroyed, the Taliban became the first target in the US 'war on terror', although those who perpetrated the outrage were mostly Saudi Arabian. The United States pursued the war by bombing from the air on a major scale. Incendiary weapons and cluster bombs killed perhaps 5000 people – some estimates are as high as 10,000. The Taliban fought some battles on the ground, but the majority simply melted away to regroup across the border in the quasi-independent Pashtun regions of Pakistan.

An American-sponsored and supported government in Kabul gained little influence outside the capital, the rest of the country being controlled by warlords, 'bandits' and regrouped Taliban. The war dragged on in much the same way for more than a decade, at a huge cost – more than $600 billion – with 130,000 troops from 46 countries eventually engaged, and, from 2006, NATO involvement. In 2011 US President Obama announced a staged withdrawal of American troops from Afghanistan, to be complete by 2014, and most other nations either withdrew their forces or announced that they planned to do so.

In 2012 the Northern Alliance, a long-time enemy of the Taliban, had regrouped, announcing their intention to oppose a Taliban return to power. With the Taliban entrenched in most of the country, this would seem to indicate that the war will drag on indefinitely. While it was planned to transfer security to the 180,000-strong Afghan army, many of its soldiers were not well trained, and it was plainly 'white-anted' by the Taliban. Vehicles, weapons and fuel provided by the Americans went missing regularly and morale was generally low. In 2011 and 2012 there were 67 'insider' attacks, in which infiltrators into the Afghan police and army killed 98 NATO soldiers. By 2012 the war was unpopular in Western countries, with most opinion polls indicating the majority of their people wanted a withdrawal from it.

By 2005 Afghanistan was the world's leading producer of opium, supplying at least 70 per cent of world demand, and accounting for more than half of gross national product. An estimate in 2009 put the value of the opium markets at $65 billion a year, supplying 15 million addicts. The 'warlords', many of whom are provincial governors or members of the national parliament, control and tax opium in their regions, as many as three million small farmers cultivate the poppy because it is by far the most profitable crop, and the national government in Kabul is obliged to tolerate it. Growers were getting as much as $300 a kilogram for dry opium, making it almost 50 times more profitable than growing wheat. The highly profitable processing of opium into heroin is now located within Afghanistan. According to a UN report in 2013 poppy production had increased each year since 2010.

The war has virtually destroyed Afghanistan and caused enormous hardship and privation, indicated by some of the worst social indicators in the world. According to UN figures, life expectancy for both men and women in 2013 was only 45, infant mortality per thousand births stood at 167, and around half the children were stunted from severe malnutrition. Only 12 per cent of women were literate, and only 13 per cent of households had access to adequate sanitation and safe drinking water. Infectious diseases were endemic, diarrhoea, parasitic diseases and pneumonia being the main factors, killing around one in four children before the age of 5.

23 The Mountain States: Nepal and Bhutan

Nepal and Bhutan are classic 'buffer states', extending along almost a thousand miles of the Himalayan border between China and India – this close proximity to the world's two largest nations has profoundly influenced their history, and is likely to go on doing so. Nepal is changing rapidly, and can no longer be regarded as a romanticized 'Shangri La', or as a 'small' state, for that matter. Around 9 million in 1960, its population of almost 30 million people now easily exceeds the total of the three Scandinavian nations, or of Australia and New Zealand combined. As with other South Asian states, its high birth rate can largely be set down to a failure to educate girls, most of whom marry early, and begin to bear children almost at once. Bhutan, with 700,000 people, is much smaller, wealthier and better governed.

Most Nepalese live in the Kathmandu Valley and other fertile areas in the south – about a fifth of the country – where population pressures are driving an alarmingly high poverty rate. Nepal was ranked 54th of 81 poorest countries on the World Poverty Index in 2012. The rocky, ice-bound north is hardly people-friendly – it consists of the formidable south slope of the Himalayas, including that of the world's highest mountain, Chomolungma, which means 'Mother Goddess of the Earth' – a name arguably preferable to Everest, that of a British surveyor working long ago in imperial India. Because of its wild and dramatic scenery, Nepal is a major tourist destination – 602,000 people entered the country in 2010 from almost every nation in the world. While this is a considerable source of income, the influx of so many walkers and climbers has severely stressed the country's limited facilities for travel and accommodation and has created unwelcome levels of pollution. Most places are approached only by walking tracks, and 'tea houses' along the way generally offer only rudimentary facilities. Handcrafts, garments and carpets are the main saleable commodities in what otherwise is still principally a subsistence agricultural economy. Although Nepal has historically been linked with Buddhism, 80 per cent of its people are now Hindu. Nepal was almost completely undeveloped until 1951, lacking schools, hospitals, electric power, industry and reliable communications. Even now it is heavily dependent on foreign aid to develop these things. About 80 per cent of the people still work as subsistence farmers.

Early Palaeolithic stone axe-heads found in Nepal are said to date back more than half a million years, indicating that *Homo erectus* had reached the Himalayan foothills, and was making stone tools there as early as that. Soil erosion in many places has revealed thousands of artefacts – stone axes, choppers and knives – dating to the late Pleistocene and early Holocene. From 2500 BCE onwards there were village cultures in the Kathmandu Valley and other lowlands that indicate a connection with the Ganges Plain in India. Subsequent Nepalese history is obscure, depending on the epic *Yamsavli*, which claims to describe events thousands of years back in time when the Kathmandu Valley was still a lake. Geological evidence indicates that the lake drained slowly, and probably disappeared around 18,000 years ago. Concerning itself mainly with the affairs of kings and rajas, the *Yamsavli* offers very little reliable history. However, there do seem to have been as many as 50 tiny states struggling for power against one another. In one of these, the Shakya, around 500 BCE, a prince called Siddhartha Gautama renounced his position and became the Buddha – the enlightened one – and founder of one of the world's major religions.

Nepal became a nation when the splinter states were unified by a Gurkha king, Prithvi Narayan Shah, in a series of conquests culminating in his capture of Kathmandu in 1768. A British force dispatched to support the former ruler of Kathmandu was decisively beaten. Prithvi was well aware of British expansionism in India and concerned that the small principalities that had previously made up Nepal could easily be swallowed – his policy for the future of the country is best expressed by his own wry view of it as 'a yam between two rocks' – British India and China. His policy was to keep Nepal strong, united and isolated – he refused to trade with the British, but was able to maintain a relationship of uneasy peace with them. He died at the age of 52 only seven years after his capture of Kathmandu, but the policies he established continued under his successors with varying success. The country's almost complete inaccessibility kept it isolated. The reigns of the later kings were otherwise unremarkable other than early deaths, sometimes due to assassination, infighting within the royal family, and often accession to the throne in infancy. China extended its influence at this stage, Nepal becoming technically a vassal state until 1912. Nepal was defeated in a war with the British East India Company in 1816, after which it effectively became a British protectorate, with almost a third of the country ceded to Britain in return for guarantees of nominal autonomy.

By this time a clan of hereditary prime ministers had taken control of government from the largely inept and sometimes brutally cruel monarchs. One of the few relatively enlightened such Nepalese rulers, Jung Bahadur, visited England in 1850 and on his return abolished the torture, mutilation and trial by ordeal of fire and water that were still in the legal code up to that time. While he did much otherwise to modernize what had been a backward medieval society he insisted on taking absolute power, massacring his opponents, isolating the king and finally cementing his family's position by marrying his 8-year-old son to a 6-year-old princess.

Prithvi Bir Bikram Shah (1875–1911), a grandfather of the Mahatma Gandhi, was more notable than most of his predecessors – he established modern water supplies and sanitation in parts of the country and imported its first cars. However, Nepal remained substantially primitive, under the firm control of the leading clans and an aristocracy of landlords. Its borders remained closed, and it had almost no connection with the outside world. Slavery was not abolished until 1925.

China's occupation of Tibet in the 1950s alarmed the Indian government, which sought greater influence in Nepal as a counterbalance. A treaty of peace and friendship signed in 1950 permitted free movement of people and goods between the two countries and provided for close collaboration in defence and foreign affairs. It was strengthened following an abortive Communist Party attempt to seize power in Nepal in 1952. Meanwhile Nepal had opened its borders in 1949, making possible the first ascent of Chomolungma by Edmund Hillary and Tensing Norgay in 1953. Subsequently Hillary spent a great deal of time in Nepal, building health clinics, schools and hospitals, and at other times raising funds for these projects.

At that time Nepal was struggling with its first experiment in parliamentary democracy. The Nepal National Congress, formed in exile in India in 1946, dominated a new parliament following the country's first elections in 1959. However, its promises of land reform, a free and independent judiciary, health care and free compulsory education alarmed the Establishment. In 1962 King Mahendra, backed by the army, pronounced the experiment in Western-style democracy a failure, dissolving the parliament and introducing a *panchayat* system, in which political parties were abolished in favour of government by traditional village councils. The king's absolute authority was reasserted. Hundreds of arrests of democratic activists, corruption, violence and economic stagnation characterized this period until a mass popular movement ended it in 1989. After two years of agitation an election was held in 1991, in which the Nepali Congress won a narrow victory, taking 114 of the 205 seats in the parliament. However, the new government's inexperience and attempts to carry out too many reforms at once played havoc with the economy, with the price of staple commodities rising alarmingly.

In 1992 a general strike was called. There were violent clashes in many areas, often aimed at extortionate landlords. However, when a people's movement to organize land reform the government had promised was suppressed violently, many people joined the Communist Party (Maoist) which would from now on become a major political force. It spearheaded a sporadic civil war that would convulse the country for a decade from 1996, take more than 12,000 lives and disrupt an agriculture that was already in many cases marginal. While the royal government was maintained in Kathmandu and other cities, the Communists eventually dominated the countryside. A UN report in 2012 has described acts of indiscriminate violence and torture from both sides. The report says that while both sides agreed when the war ended to resolve human rights issues, 'perpetrators of serious violations on both sides have not been accountable, in some cases have been promoted, and may now even be offered an amnesty'. Although the report recorded as many as 9000 violations, 'no one had been prosecuted in a civilian court for a serious conflict-related crime'.

In an extraordinary and tragic event in 2001 the Crown Prince, Dipendra, allegedly angered by his family's refusal to sanction his marriage to the woman he loved, shot nine members of his family dead, including his father, the king. He then apparently shot himself in the head. After three days in a coma he died. Although this disaster is said to have followed a drunken binge at a family dinner the actual circumstances remain a mystery, and have resulted in a number of conspiracy theories, some alleging the next king, Gyanendra, was involved. Gyanendra, saying he wanted to bring the civil war to an end, reimposed autocratic rule in 2005, an act which made him so deeply unpopular that he became the last Nepalese king. An alliance between the Maoists and the Congress forced his abdication in 2008, when a constitutional assembly declared a republic, ending 240 years of the monarchy. The Maoists won the most seats in the new Constituent Assembly, but failed to achieve a majority.

The drafting of a new constitution has dragged on for years, deadlocked by opposing ethnic and regional interests represented by at least 30 splinter parties. At the time of writing there was no agreement even on the timing and machinery for future elections. The time permitted to agree on the terms of the constitution has been extended three times. Because there is no constitutional provision for new elections, the Maoist-led government stayed in power in spite of mounting opposition, until in 2013 an interim government was sworn in headed by the nation's chief justice. The political instability has not helped the process of development, with unemployment at more than 40 per cent, and national income around $3 a day in 2012.

Foreigners visit Nepal mainly because of its arresting physical beauty. Sir Edmund Hillary, generally laconic of utterance, describes the remote Barun Valley in his *View from the Summit* as

> covered with some square miles of flowering crimson azaleas – a truly magnificent sight. The monsoon rain had transformed the landscape, and myriads of tiny blossoms of every colour were bursting through the arid soil. The air was thick and strong, and we breathed it deeply into our starved lungs. But we were now in a world of rain, hundreds of waterfalls drifted gracefully down the mighty rock bluffs and the heavy clouds would split for a moment to reveal some startling summit before closing in again with torrential rain. I felt it was the most beautiful valley I had ever seen.

In spite of this splendid beauty life is hard for most people. Tradition demands that menstruating women are segregated in a shed away from the house, even in harsh winter conditions, and in terms of an ancient ritual young girls are given to Hindu temples, where they receive scant care and no education. Sixty to seventy per cent of Nepalese women suffer domestic violence, this figure rising to 81 per cent in rural areas. This includes physical abuse by husbands, murders related to dowry issues and harassment from other family members. Such violence is traditional; according to a local saying, 'a daughter is born with a doomed fate'. According to former National Women's Commission chairwoman Bandana Rana, 'often police and local people try to settle domestic disputes by pressing women into accepting their "fate"'.

Daily conditions of life described on many blogs by expatriates living in Nepal mention no running water in most places; hot water almost nonexistent; no toilets more advanced than a hole in the ground; polluted air in Kathmandu because rubbish is burned on every street corner; no quiet areas or parks – everything is stressed and noisy; electricity is off for 12 or more hours a day – there is virtually none outside the cities; a general lack of heating and building insulation in a climate that is often very cold; very little clean water; not much public transport; no comfortable beds; and monotonous food, mostly rice with a bean soup and some vegetables. Most people would eat meat perhaps once a year, and around half of all Nepali children are stunted from malnutrition. The lack of clean water means diarrhoea, malaria and tuberculosis are endemic.

Life in country areas is described as stone-age. There are no roads into most villages, so everything has to be carried in on people's heads or backs.

There is no electric power in these rural areas, where thousands of water-wheels on local streams, used mainly to mill flour, are the only source of power. Design and construction of the stone and mud-brick houses are described as medieval. While there are some schools now, fewer than one in ten children get past three or four years at school. Most girls never go to school – they are regarded as domestic helpers and are expected to marry as soon as possible. Literacy rates among women are among the lowest in the world, and mortality rates among the highest. The average landholding is less than two acres, making feeding a family a constant struggle.

Bhutan is a landlocked country between China and India, at the eastern end of the Himalayas. Its remote, almost inaccessible location kept it isolated from the rest of the world until relatively recently, and its official policy still restricts the entry of tourists except under strict conditions, designed to resist foreign cultural influences. With fewer than a million people, it is one of the world's smallest nations, but the beauty of its high country and extraordinary national philosophy have given it an international image of some consequence.

Most of the people live in isolated valleys carved out by the many rivers that eventually flow into the Brahmaputra. Above these valleys are some of the highest and most majestic mountains in the world, with peaks that are perpetually snow-clad. Ten per cent of Bhutan is covered by glaciers, but these are retreating as much as a hundred feet a year because of the warming climate. The prime minister, Jigme Thinley, has expressed fears they may disappear by 2035, if not sooner. Below the snowline are forests of conifers, with large-leaved trees further south. About two-thirds of the country is forest, giving some credence to the claim that Bhutan is the world's only nation that reduces carbon dioxide in the air rather than increasing it. The south is hot and subtropical, with high rainfall.

In April 2012 a UN meeting discussing happiness was sponsored by Bhutan – perhaps more properly Druk Yul, the land of the Thunder Dragon, which is what the people of this tiny kingdom call it. This meeting was informed by a report from the Earth Institute of Columbia University in the United States which maintains that happiness doesn't necessarily come from wealth, but from health, strong social networks, political freedom, deep concern for the environment and the native culture, and an absence of corruption.

These are the principles on which modern Bhutan is being built – it is unusual, even unique, because its index of overall prosperity is not gross national product but gross national happiness, and because its state objectives are shaped around this idea. The term was first expressed in 1972 by

Bhutan's Dragon King, Jimne Singye Wangchuck, who had pledged to build an economy that would preserve the country's ancient culture and Buddhist values. These ideas, developed by the Centre for Bhutan Studies, are now being actively studied by other nations, and have been the subject of several international conferences. The centre has produced a *Short Guide to Gross National Happiness*, which stresses the importance of practical measures 'to orient the people and the nation towards happiness, primarily by improving the conditions of not-so-happy people'. According to this study, slightly over 10 per cent of people are unhappy, almost 50 per cent are 'narrowly happy' and barely 8 per cent 'deeply happy'. The centre's happiness index lists nine key attributes, ranging from psychological well-being, health and education to good governance and living standards. According to the prime minister, 'We have now clearly distinguished "happiness" from the fleeting, pleasurable "feel-good" moods so often associated with that term. True abiding happiness cannot exist while others suffer, and comes only from serving others, living in harmony with nature and realising our innate wisdom.'

Bhutan's early history is obscure, because most of the records were destroyed by a fire in the old capital of Punakha in 1827. However, legend has it that a Buddhist dignitary, Guru Rinpoche, flew over Bhutan from east to west on a flying tigress in the 8th century to subdue the evil spirits that had been hindering the establishment of Buddhism in the country. From the 10th century until the Chinese Yuan Dynasty ended 400 years later, Chinese emperors were fascinated by Buddhist ideas, and financed the building of monasteries in Bhutan. Shabdrung Ngawana, a Buddhist lama and military leader fleeing persecution in Tibet, is credited with uniting the country in the 17th century, imposing a code of law on the warlords. It was at this time that the strong regional influence imposed by Bhutan's topography was reinforced by the building of a series of *dzongs*, large, almost impregnable forts around which villages and towns cluster, and from which local warlords governed. So well were these built that many remain in use as administrative centres, a distinctive feature of the landscape. The capital, Thimphu, developed around a 13th-century *dzong*.

However, this phase of unity did not last long. During two centuries of nominal Chinese suzerainty punctuated by episodes of civil war power gradually reverted to the local governors, the *penlops*. Then in 1907 a 'popular' assembly elected the most powerful of these, Ugyen Wangchuck, as Bhutan's first king. In spite of protests from a weakened China, Bhutan became a British protectorate in 1910. The country remained almost medieval well into the 20th century, the single road connecting it with India so bad that access from outside was almost impossible. Visitors were actively discouraged. It is claimed that at that stage most Bhutanese had never seen a wheel. The Wangchuck family have ruled from 1907 onwards, traditionally regarded by the people as almost godlike figures, automatically attracting universal respect. Consequently there was consternation when in 1998 the fourth king stepped down to become head of state, assigning power to a prime minister and a cabinet of ministers – one of the rare cases when democracy has been imposed from above, rather than evolving from populist movements. A democratic draft constitution was completed in 2005, and copies sent to every citizen. It was then inaugurated in 2008, when the first elections for the National Assembly of 150 members were held. A hundred and five of these are elected by the 20 provinces for 3 years, 35 are nominated by the government – of these, 20 are the regional governors – and 10 represent the Buddhist clergy. Ministers are elected by the assembly for five-year terms – they generally come from the wealthiest families. In 2008 Jigme Khesar Wangchuck became king following his father's abdication.

Bhutan is about the size of Switzerland, and had 700,000 people in 2005, according to a census taken then. Barely 90,000 live in the capital, Thimphu. Almost all the rest are small farmers. Per capita income is $1320, literacy 60 per cent and unemployment a low 2.5 per cent. The population is mostly Tibetan, with a large minority of Nepalese. In 1975, in the neighbouring principality of Sikkim, the monarchy was deposed and the country became a part of India as a result of a plebiscite influenced by the majority Nepalese population there. This caused considerable unease in Bhutan, and led the government to expel Nepalese amounting to almost a fifth of Bhutan's population, and to ban further entry from Nepal. Thousands spent years in refugee camps in Nepal, but many have now been resettled in Europe and America.

The fragmentation of Bhutan's society is dictated largely by its geography. Three mountain ranges with peaks as high as 24,000 feet divide the country from north to south, and present an effective barrier to movement from east to west. Gangkhar Puensum, at almost 25,000 feet, is the largest unclimbed mountain in the world – since 2003 mountaineering has been banned in Bhutan. Snow-fed rivers running between these mountains have created fertile valleys in which most of the people live. In the lower altitudes of the south, near the border with India, the climate is subtropical, clad with forest, grasslands and bamboo thickets. More than 40 per cent of the country has been designated as national parks, and government policy is to restrict the forestry industry by maintaining 60 per cent of the land under tree cover.

Bhutan has very little industry and few exports, but it is already benefiting from a huge potential for hydroelectricity. The Tala Project, completed in 2007, not only provides for all of Bhutan's needs, but exports three-quarters of its 1020-megawatt capacity to India, providing almost half of national revenue. The country's hydroelectric potential has been estimated at 30,000 megawatts. Bangladesh, which has acute power shortages, is planning a 500-megawatt power station in Bhutan. Tourism is expanding, with 65,000 foreign visitors in 2011, although there are strict controls on people entering the country. Visitors must book through accredited travel agencies and pay for travel packages. While thousands of backpackers visit Nepal, they are not encouraged in Bhutan.

24 Sri Lanka

Sri Lanka, a tropical island off the south Indian coast about the size of Scotland and with a population of 22 million, has been occupied by humans – and pre-humans – for a very long time. *Homo erectus* lived there as much as half a million years ago, and modern humans making advanced stone tools, keeping domestic dogs and possibly herding livestock were in evidence 30,000 years ago. These Balangoda people, who were hunter-gatherers, were probably the ancestors of the Vedda tribes still to be found in small numbers in the centre and north-east of the island.

Two distinct migrations of people from the Indian mainland more than 2000 years ago have influenced Sri Lankan history ever since and will continue to do so into the future. The first were the Sinhalese – the People of the Lion – around 600 BCE; the second, some 300 years later, were Tamils, from south India. The Sinhalese appear to have come originally not from neighbouring south India, but from the north-west, and there has been some speculation that they might have been Mohenjodaro people displaced when the Aryans invaded the north. Certainly they were very advanced for their time. They not only knew about and worked iron, but were probably the first people in the world to smelt high-quality steel. There is evidence of thousands of sites dating back to 300 BCE, in which iron and carbon were heated together in crucibles, channelling the monsoon wind to create efficient furnace conditions. The early Sinhalese also used advanced irrigation techniques to grow rice, and quickly developed a sophisticated urban society based on their first capital, Anuradhapura, which is one of the oldest continuously occupied cities in the world.

It was important as early as the 3rd century BCE when, according to legend Prince Mahinda, either a brother or son of the Indian king Ashoka, visited Sri Lanka and converted its king to Buddhism. Certain sacred relics are said to have been transported to Sri Lanka, including the Buddha's alms-bowl, part of his collarbone and, most celebrated of all, one of his eye-teeth. Possession of this tooth became important to establish the legitimacy of kings. Now it is kept in the pink Temple of the Tooth in Kandy, where a replica of the tooth is ceremonially carried about on elephant-back each August. This procession, the Perahera, takes place every night for two weeks.

Much of Anuradhapura was destroyed during a Chola invasion in AD 993 and it never returned to its former glory. However, most of its ancient buildings, like the huge Brazen Palace, once said to have had a roof of pure copper, remain, and are major tourist attractions. These antiquities are grouped around a *peepal* tree said to be a sapling from the tree under which Buddha sat at the time of his enlightenment. Cared for by hereditary attendants throughout its 2250 years of existence, it is claimed to be the oldest historically authenticated tree in the world.

A line of kings over the 1350 years of the city's primacy at times resembled Ashoka in their attitudes and achievements – an indication of the power of Buddhism to influence societies at that time. This was the era of Sri Lanka's glory – moderate well-governed societies with their own art, notably sculpture and painting, with individual characteristics even though it derives from India. Taxation, set at 10 per cent of production, was moderate by later standards in south Asia, although the peasants were also subject to a corvée, which provided labour for the irrigation works, canals and roads. There was a strong emphasis on efficient agriculture and huge irrigation works, among the largest and most technically advanced in the world. These were based on stone-walled dams and artificial lakes, which made two and sometimes three rice crops a year possible. Twelve thousand of these 'tanks' still exist, many still providing crop irrigation, but others are overgrown or filled with sand. However, as droughts become more severe in Sri Lanka the Colombo-based Water Management Institute has proposed a $20-million project to restore them to use.

Meanwhile the Tamils in the north became stronger as a steady trickle of migrants from the mainland arrived over the centuries. By the 12th century they had evolved a separate northern state on the dry, flat Jaffna Peninsula. The Tamils, who have significant racial and language differences from the Sinhalese, are traditionally enterprising and energetic, qualities bred into them by centuries of farming the arid north of the island. In the 10th century the south Indian Chola empire invaded Sri Lanka, occupying much of the north and central plains. Thousands of Tamil migrants came in at that time, and as many more in the 14th century when a disastrous and extended civil war developed between rival generals and claimants for the Sinhalese throne. These factions recruited large numbers of Tamil mercenaries.

The Tamils gained control of more territory in the north, including the valuable and world-renowned pearl fishery. The decaying Sinhalese state was pushed south to a new capital at Kotte, near Colombo. The great irrigation works in the centre of the island were destroyed by rival armies or fell into disrepair, leaving an arid zone between the Tamil and Sinhalese kingdoms. Huge tracts of previously cultivated land reverted to jungle. Lavish pagoda building, at huge public cost, impoverished the Sinhalese kingdom, forcing it further into decline. A separate kingdom evolved at Kandy, so three rival authorities, some with warring factions, made any unity of government impossible.

Such was the situation when the Portuguese arrived in 1505, attracted by the trade in cinnamon and pepper, which were Sinhalese royal monopolies. Using a mixture of force and diplomacy, they gradually took over more and more of the fragmented society. By the end of the century they controlled virtually all the island, except for the isolated kingdom of Kandy deep in the jungle-clad hills of central Sri Lanka. During that century they became a major influence, converting millions to Christianity, and freely intermarrying with local women – as a result many families still have Portuguese surnames. Siding with one faction or another in the perpetual regional wars and succession disputes, they were able to install client kings in most places. As in other parts of Asia, Portuguese exploitation was brutal and destructive. When they successfully attacked Kandy in 1611 they burned down much of the city, a degree of destruction that invited retaliation. A Portuguese army was decisively beaten by Kandy forces in a major battle in 1638.

This time the Dutch were waiting in the background. The uneasy alliance they had formed with Kandy did not last, but they were able to destroy the weakened Portuguese presence over the ensuing decades. Thereafter Kandy fought the Dutch vigorously, but was unable to gain control of the wealthy, populous coastal regions. Finally, by 1765, after a century of conflict, Kandy accepted its landlocked situation and the necessity to trade peacefully through the Dutch. However, the Dutch Protestants were never popular, persecuting the Catholics and imposing very heavy taxes. Like the Portuguese they intermarried freely with the local people – the resultant Dutch Burghers are still a significant and influential minority in Sri Lanka.

However, the days of Dutch control of the island were numbered. Holland had sided with France in the Napoleonic Wars, and using her superior naval presence, Britain took over Sri Lanka in 1796. It became a British Crown Colony, and a profitable one, in 1802. Although the price of cinnamon had fallen, the pearl fisheries in the north yielded almost £400,000 – a huge amount at that time – in the first three years. However, an attempt to conquer Kandy in 1803 ended badly, with the British driven back and defeated after two years of savage hostilities in which no prisoners were taken. Kandyan gunsmiths manufactured efficient flintlock muskets and artillery which tended to equalize the conflict, but eventually the greater force prevailed. While an agreement in 1815 guaranteed Kandy's integrity, *de facto* control was exercised by the British from now on.

Common lands were taken from the people to grow coffee. When the Sinhalese refused the menial and badly paid work offered to them the white planters imported Tamil labourers. Later in the 19th century tea and rubber were also planted. The British favoured Burghers and high-caste Sinhalese as civil servants, creating an elite that persists today. The establishment of state schools and a university college did not extend education to most Sinhalese, rather confirming the primacy of this elite. However, in spite of its objections to the lower classes having any power, universal suffrage was introduced in 1931.The country suffered severe hardship when the 1934 monsoon failed, leading to a protracted drought and a catastrophic plague of malaria that killed more than a quarter of a million people. Out of the resultant turmoil the Marxist LSSP party was founded in 1935. Its demand for complete independence was supported by other political parties at elections for the State Council in 1936.

Sri Lanka was a major British base during the Second World War, mainly because of the island's strategic position and excellent harbours. There was considerable agitation for independence during the war years, but when it was granted in 1948 the first parliament was dominated by Sinhalese and 'Ceylon' Tamils, who saw themselves as superior to almost a million 'Indian' Tamils, the plantation workers, whom they disenfranchized in 1949. This single stroke confirmed the ascendancy of the Sinhalese in the Parliament, at the cost of marginalizing the poorer Tamils – this became an early forerunner of the disastrous ethnic war to come. Nevertheless Sri Lanka continued to function as a parliamentary democracy, with government alternating between the socialist Freedom Party, which nationalized major industries like the tea and rubber plantations and the banks, and the National Party, which favours foreign investment and close relations with the United States. The constitution was extensively rewritten in 1978, introducing a presidential system that has shifted power even more significantly to the governing elite. By that time a major Tamil revolt had commenced, spearheaded by a paramilitary force, the Tamil Tigers.

In 1956 the government had established Sinhalese as the preferred language for education and commerce, an action that would provoke rioting in the capital, Colombo, and later a major war with the Tamils. A draconic Prevention of Terrorism Act was passed as a temporary measure in 1979, and has never been repealed. It did nothing to restore peace. Tamil guerrillas began to target police stations, airports and post offices. Year by year this conflict escalated, exploding into full-scale war after communal rioting took thousands of lives. In the midst of it, in 2004, the great Asian tsunami devastated the east coast, killing 30,000 people and destroying hundreds of villages and other infrastructure. More than 150,000 Tamils left the country for Canada, Australia and the UK because of the war. More and more civilians were killed until the Tamil forces were finally defeated in 2009. The struggle had gone on for 26 years, resulted in almost 100,000 deaths, and left behind a lasting bitterness between the two communities that the next few years did little to dispel. Almost 300,000 Tamils were confined in badly run and overcrowded internment camps.

Most had been released by 2010, but conditions of life remain almost impossible for them, since their homes and businesses were almost all destroyed during the savage final months of the conflict – the UN estimates that more than 160,000 houses in Jaffna and other parts of the north were destroyed or damaged. Very few have been repaired or replaced. Once again desperate Tamils paid large sums to people-smugglers for places on small, dangerously unseaworthy boats in efforts to reach Australia. An unknown number of these have foundered, causing hundreds of deaths. In 2013 it was claimed that elements of the Sri Lankan navy were involved, taking bribes to allow some boats to leave. In 2012 the navy arrested 3000 people trying to leave, but more than 6000 others left Sri Lankan waters in small boats.

President Mahinda Rajapaksa, re-elected in 2010, again amended the constitution, lengthening the presidential term and giving himself and his family almost absolute power – two of his brothers are cabinet members. In 2013 a bill giving greater powers to his youngest brother, the minister for economic development, was obstructed in the courts, following which impeachment proceedings were commenced against the chief justice, Shirani Bandaranaike. This, and her subsequent dismissal, were widely criticized outside Sri Lanka, Canada deciding to boycott a Commonwealth Heads of Government meeting to be held in Colombo in November of that year. A pro-Tamil group burned Rajapaksa's effigy on a New Delhi street when he visited India in 2013. The state of emergency remained in that year, and human rights abuses were widely reported – Human Rights Watch claimed that several thousand people were detained without charge, often suffering torture and sexual assault.

Sri Lanka is a relatively poor country, still dependent on foreign aid, but the economy has improved modestly in the new millennium with a considerable growth in service industries, which account for more than half of gross domestic product. There is a significant export of plantation products – rice, tea, rubber and spices – garments and leather goods, and a growing income from tourism. Over a million tourists visited Sri Lanka in 2012, mainly to enjoy its world-renowned beaches. Almost two million Sri Lankans are expatriate workers, mainly in the Middle East, and their annual remittances, more than $4 billion, are a significant fraction of national income.

25 China: Two Revolutions

In 1896 there was a curious happening in England. A 30-year-old Chinese doctor, who had graduated only two years before from the medical school in Hong Kong, was kidnapped from a London street and secretly imprisoned inside the Chinese Legation. He was held there for 13 days, but before he could be spirited away to China for execution a warning note was smuggled to an English friend, and he was released by the British police.

The prisoner, on whose head the Manchu officials of the Chinese court had placed a price of £100,000, was Sun Zhongshan (Sun Yat-sen). An exile, a Christian, Western-educated, he was typical of the new class of Chinese looking for reform. The kidnapping episode did not deter him. In Tokyo in 1905 Sun formed a half-secret society, half-political party, which would develop in 1912 into the Kuomintang (Nationalist) Party, generally identified as the KMT.

In 1911 a plot against the government by officers of the military garrison at Wuchang, on the Yangzi River in Central China, was prematurely discovered. But the revolt was nevertheless successful and as the news of it spread more and more cities, especially in the south, declared against the Manchus. Sun, who was fund-raising in the United States, returned to China as quickly as possible and in the first days of 1912 took the oath as president of a provisional republic. The following month an imperial edict announced the abdication of the emperor following pressure from the army commander, Yuan Shikai.

Sun held his office for only 44 days. In order to maintain the republic, he was obliged to hand over the presidency to Yuan Shikai, who had the confidence of the foreign powers and the substantial backing of the army. However, in 1914 Yuan, a man very much in the warlord tradition, disbanded the provisional government and declared the KMT illegal. His assumption of personal rule followed the classic pattern in which new Chinese dynasties have begun – even more so when Yuan announced he proposed to declare himself the new emperor. However, his imperial ambitions were forestalled by his death, apparently from natural causes, in 1916.

Virtual anarchy followed as the warlords – many of whom had been Yuan's officers – and the KMT struggled for power. The infant Manchu emperor Puyi was suddenly restored, and as quickly deposed again. Sun renewed the declaration of the republic in 1917, but it controlled only a small part of south China when he died of liver cancer in 1925. The warlords who governed the rest were generally cruel and rapacious. Their depredations were especially damaging to the Chinese peasantry, who were taxed into almost universal poverty and starvation. One important consequence was a meeting of 12 Marxists who, inspired by the Russian revolution, formed the Chinese Communist Party in 1921. They included a young man called Mao Zedong.

Jiang Jieshi (Chiang Kai-shek) became the next leader of the KMT with the support of the army, and, for the time being, the Communists. In 1926 he led the KMT army out of Guangzhou on the Northern Expedition, which was to unify China within two years and make the republic a reality. Jiang's task was to coerce or persuade the regional warlords into accepting KMT government. Some of these men controlled whole provinces, others little more than circles of ricefield bounded by the horizon as seen from the drum tower of a central walled city.

Jiang's Northern Expedition succeeded largely because the KMT army had a sense of discipline unusual in China at that time. But a breach with the Communists was not far off. Jiang was suspicious of them, and strong pressures were brought to bear on him – including a reputed payment of £3 million by Chinese and foreign interests – to break with those he came to be persuaded were dangerous revolutionaries. Jiang, after making a triumphant entry into Shanghai in 1927, suddenly attacked the Communists, who had assisted the capture of the city, by paralysing it with a strike. Hundreds of Communists were killed in Shanghai, and the purge was extended to other areas. From Shanghai the Nationalists moved on from success to success, establishing their capital in Nanjing.

However, the Communist Party had not been destroyed. The more important leaders escaped, including Mao Zedong, a quiet, tall man of peasant antecedents from Henan Province. Mao had been trying to convince the other leaders that although classic Marxism, the revolt of an urban group, had succeeded in Russia, it was not appropriate in China. Mao's position in history depends considerably on his realization that China's essential problem was a rural one, that only a revolt based on the peasants could succeed. It is a curious irony that Jiang's purge of the Communists in 1927 brought Mao's ideas to the forefront. By eliminating so many orthodox Marxists, it diverted the Communist Party to a more realistic course that would deliver it government of China only two decades later.

Jiang was to find that he had no sooner resolved matters in the north than his old enemies, the Communists, had regrouped in the south. Mao and his ragged army killed landlords and redistributed their holdings to the peasants. Because of the extreme poverty of the peasants such methods quickly gained support and recruits. Mao, a military planner of ability and imagination, established a fundamental principle of Asian Communism with his insistence on guerrilla warfare, defined in his maxim: 'When the enemy advances, we retreat; when he retreats, we pursue; when he is tired, we attack.' However, in 1934 the Red Army allowed itself to be trapped into a disastrous 'set-piece' battle in an 'encirclement campaign' by three-quarters of a million Nationalist troops. Towards the end of the year, when it had been reduced to half its former strength, the survivors slipped through the surrounding Nationalist blockade under cover of night.

So began the legendary Long March. The Communists' objective – more than 1000 miles away – was Yanan in a remote part of Shaanxi Province in the north-west. Here there was already a substantial Communist presence, and Mao planned to join forces with it. But since strong Nationalist forces stood between them and this possible refuge the Communists were forced to march around the borders of China for almost 6000 miles. The Long March took an appalling toll – of more than 100,000 people who set out, barely 15,000 reached Shaanxi. Almost every family, including Mao's, lost some members, for wives and children accompanied the men. The journey took 368 days, during which the Communists fought 15 major battles and 300 skirmishes. This epic of suffering and endurance has become Communist China's most important body of legend, well known to every schoolchild.

The years in Yanan saw a phase of experiment that set most of the patterns the new Communist government would use later throughout China. Membership of the Communist Party grew from 40,000 in 1937 to 1.2 million in 1945. The problem of land reform was tackled seriously, if, in the end, brutally. The party was carefully organized into a pervasive network of authority, leading and guiding even at the village level. Under Mao's control the Communist Party became a consistent, carefully woven thread in the fabric of Chinese society. It owes much of its present authority to the fact that it remains so today.

By the late 1920s China was in a parlous economic state, so much so that the 300,000 Westerners running industries there based on cheap labour were beginning to lose interest. Her foreign debt by 1924 was almost $800 million – a sum she had little hope of ever repaying. Meanwhile Japan had seen colonial opportunities in the divided China. She occupied Manchuria in 1931 and set up there a puppet state named Manchukuo, over which she recalled to the throne the deposed Manchu emperor, Puyi, much later to end his life as a humble gardener in Beijing.

Open fighting began between China and Japan near Beijing in 1937. The tide of invasion swept across China, marked by a series of brutal atrocities against civilians by the Japanese. The Communists did not escape these. They attempted an offensive against the Japanese in 1940, which led to severe reprisals – Japanese orders to its troops were to 'kill all, burn all, destroy all'. This became the fate of entire villages. Some who tried to escape this fury by digging underground refuges were killed when the Japanese pumped poison gas into these tunnels. The Communist Eighth Route Army was reduced by 100,000 killed, wounded or deserted; the population under their control halved to 20 million.

The Nationalists fared little better, and the Chinese people suffered yet again, with millions of deaths from drought and flooding. When in 1938 the Nationalists breached the dykes of the Yellow River in a useless attempt to stem the Japanese advance, several hundred thousand peasants were drowned. The KMT eventually lost the entire coast and were forced back to Chongqing, west of the Yangzi gorges in the fertile and readily defended basin of Sichuan Province. Here they remained throughout the Second World War. Constantly bombed by Japanese aircraft, Chongqing's population was to inflate from 200,000 to over a million.

Jiang had done little to remedy China's poverty and despair. John Gunther's contemporary book *Inside Asia* (1936) claimed: 'About a million people die of starvation in China every year. In 1935, a normal year, 29,000 bodies were picked up off the streets of Shanghai alone, of men, women and children, dead of hunger. Many were female infants, left by their parents to starve.' Other accounts tell of seeing from the trains, running on lines elevated above the flooded surrounding country, people clinging in trees until they fell into the water, exhausted, and drowned. No attempt was made to save or help them. People trapped in flooded rivers were likewise left to drown, since it was traditionally believed to be unlucky to deprive the river gods of their prey.

Unfortunately, adversity did not improve the KMT government. It relied increasingly on terror and autocracy and its secret police came to be hated and feared. Men were conscripted to Jiang's armies who were so weak from malnutrition they could hardly walk. During the war over a million died before they could even reach the battlefields. Money and power were concentrated almost entirely in the hands of four families. One was Jiang's and another was his wife's. The ten years of Nationalist government were, on the whole, disastrous. The world depression and the huge costs of war, first with the Communists, then with the Japanese, made any general economic improvement impossible. Jiang Jieshi reinstituted Confucian values and, while some economic gains were made, albeit from a very small base, these benefited only a handful of Chinese and foreign capitalists and did little to improve the poverty and despair of the vast majority of Chinese.

More than $4 billion in US aid flooded in after Pearl Harbor, but this was largely swallowed up by corruption and the maintenance of a huge inefficient army of five million.

The Communists awaited events in the north, in rugged country too remote and poor to interest the Japanese. However, despite difficulties they were able to replace the KMT as *de facto* rulers of much of north China, regions inhabited by 95 million people. They were also eventually able to fight back against the Japanese successfully, recapturing more than two-thirds of the Japanese-occupied regions by early 1945. By this time the Communist armies had grown to almost half a million men.

When Japan was defeated in that year Jiang emerged from his battered refuge in Chongqing nominally ruler of all China. However, his plans for a major campaign against the Communists were thwarted by the battle-hardened and expanding Communist armies, and the degree of support they had among the people because they had confronted the hated Japanese. Now more confident of his authority in north China, Mao took a more extreme line, confiscating property owned by landlords and rich peasants – these two classes now became automatically proscribed, no longer 'people'. The people in hundreds of villages met to indict the wealthy, and landlords were frequently beaten, tortured or killed by angry mobs.

The Communists continued to gain popularity because of harsh and inept rule by the KMT Nationalists in Manchuria after the Japanese had left, and their membership grew rapidly. They reacted promptly to an outbreak of bubonic plague in the city of Harbin, introducing immediate vaccination and quarantine measures. This plague, which killed 30,000 people, was caused by the deliberate release by the Japanese at the end of the war of rats they had infected with plague in biological warfare experiments. The nature of these did not become fully public until a suit was filed in the Tokyo District Court in 2000 by 180 survivors of Japanese atrocities. Unit 731, the biological weapons centre in Ping Fang, near Harbin, is estimated to have killed perhaps 300,000 Chinese in experiments between 1939 and 1945, during which it mass-produced bubonic plague, cholera, typhoid and anthrax organisms.

The Western powers and Russia were anxious to see a peaceful settlement in China, but these efforts proved fruitless. In spring 1947 the war began in earnest. Jiang lost heavily in decisive battles in Manchuria in 1948 – more than half a million Nationalist troops surrendered, deserted or were killed, handing over vast quantities of US-supplied weapons to the Red Army. Barely 20,000 escaped.

Simultaneously the Communists thrust south and by February 1949 had assembled a huge army on the north bank of the Yangzi River, poised to invade China's heartland. In April nearly a million Communist soldiers crossed the river on a 300-mile front centred on Nanjing. The fall of the traditional Nationalist capital brought any organized opposition to an end. By autumn Jiang, with the remnants of his armies, had retreated to the island of Taiwan, where he was protected by US naval forces.

Mao said: 'China will no longer be a nation subject to insult and humiliation. We have stood up.' But to the Western world, especially to the United States, the advent of a Communist government in the world's most populous state seemed a disaster. One reaction was the indefinite extension of the protecting hand America held over Taiwan; another, the virtual diplomatic isolation of the People's Republic from the Western nations.

26 Modern China: the Communist State

The Communist victory saw the world's most populous nation at one of the lowest points in its long history. The currency was worthless, the great mass of the people illiterate, only a shadow of internal organization remained, the exhausted soil was eroded and treeless, and everywhere profound social, medical and economic problems clamoured for a solution.

The decades of struggle had hardened the new government to the pitch of discipline and ruthlessness necessary to attack these things – its weapon was the Party's executive arm, its elite corps of full-time executives, the cadres, the effective successors of the mandarinate. Many of them were descendants of former scholar-officials, who were substantially the only group sufficiently educated for the tasks of government.

Indeed, after a phase of 're-education', the bulk of the intelligentsia and former 'upper classes' seem to have been able to accommodate themselves to life under Communism. Not all, however, were permitted to adapt so readily. Edgar Snow, in *The Other Side of the River* (1962), says that Zhou Enlai, himself of mandarin origins, had stated that 830,000 'enemies of the people' had been destroyed up to 1954. The KMT Nationalists put the figure at nine million dead. The draconic removal of these classes from their traditional influence and landownership permitted redistribution of their property among the landless. As early as 1952 almost half of China's cultivated land had been redistributed to 300 million peasants.

Industry and business fared no better than the landlords. Banks and other major businesses were expropriated to the state, foreigners expelled and their property confiscated. Major penal sanctions, including the death penalty, were instituted to control criminal gangs and opium use. A new marriage law abolished polygamy, child marriage and the authority of families over women, and gave women the right to divorce. All this ran parallel with campaigns to raise the standards of health, education and overall prosperity and to create at least the beginnings of the industrialization the Communists saw as essential. Russian experts went to China to advise on the evolution of an industrial base that would provide the essential tools of a modern nation – good communications, cheap and plentiful hydroelectric power, and heavy industry, especially steel mills.

One of the most challenging tasks was to tame the Yellow River, long described as 'China's Sorrow' because of the flooding and drowning of millions of people when it regularly broke its levees. In 1954 the Yellow River Planning Commission began building 46 dams along the 2000-mile course of the river, a task undertaken, in a phrase popular in the Western media, by 'blue ants' – millions of blue-clad coolies using picks, shovels and wicker carrying baskets. A major afforestation scheme was started in north-west China to provide belts of trees that would hold back the sand and dust brought in by storms from the Gobi and permit the reclaiming of huge regions of semi-desert. This planting of tens of millions of trees was a remarkable achievement in world terms considering China had been almost denuded of trees for fuel only 60 years before. In 2002 China announced a $12-billion project to plant 440,000 square kilometres of forest – an area bigger than Germany – over the next ten years. In 2012 this programme was extended for a further decade, with another 26 billion trees to be planted. The objective is to have 23 per cent of China's landmass forested by 2020. The government requires every Chinese between 11 and 60 to plant three to five trees a year. It is claimed that at least a billion trees have been planted every year since 1982 by these Chinese 'volunteers'. More than 20 per cent of those in urban areas are fruit trees.

Mass immunizations were undertaken to control China's traditional scourges – smallpox, cholera, plague, typhoid and typhus. Leprosy- and malaria-control programmes were instituted where necessary. Since it was not possible to train fully qualified doctors quickly enough, a large corps of 'middle' doctors and nurses was organized into travelling teams to complete immunizing programmes as quickly as possible. These people later became known as 'barefoot doctors', although all I have seen were most correctly dressed, including shoes.

China was back at war again only five years after the successful Communist revolution. When the Second World War ended, the Soviet Union occupied the north of Korea. The Communist state established there launched a major attack on South Korea in June 1950. A UN force arrived just in time to save the south, driving the North Koreans back over the *de facto* frontier, the 38th parallel of latitude. The war was then continued into North Korean territory, although the Chinese had warned they would not accept this. A week later China launched a major offensive that drove the UN forces south of the parallel again. As more troops became involved – mostly Americans – the line was eventually stabilized at the parallel. Three million Koreans had been killed – about 10 per cent of the population – and the infrastructure seriously damaged in both zones. Negotiations to end this futile and costly stalemate began in July 1951, but Korea remains divided and the two halves of the country still face each other over one of the world's most heavily militarized frontiers.

There were other important consequences of the Korean War. One was a policy of neutralism adopted by governments representing three-quarters of the Asian peoples – the five principles of peaceful coexistence. A second was continued US policy to support and guarantee the continued existence of a separate Chinese state in Taiwan. It is an intriguing possibility that another took place thousands of miles away on China's western borders when on the same day (7 October 1950) that the UN authorized its forces to cross the 38th parallel, the Chinese despatched a small army to occupy Tibet. The population then was about one and a half million, of whom perhaps 10 per cent were Buddhist monks occupying some 3000 monasteries, the largest of which housed thousands of monks.

From the 17th century Tibet had been ruled by a line of Dalai Lamas, priest-kings perpetuated not by family succession but mysteriously 'discovered' as infants believed to be reincarnations of a previous incumbent. In fact the line was firmly established by a Chinese army which carried the seventh Dalai Lama to the capital, Lhasa, with much pomp and ceremony in 1720. The Dalai Lama governed from his remote capital with the assistance of a clique of Buddhist priests and officials, and a feudal class of nobles. Tibet, which had been virtually isolated from the world, was extremely backward by world standards, the society consisting of poor herdsmen and farmers supporting a large class of priests and nobles, who owned most of the arable land. The monasteries gained their wealth from taxes on their tenants, money-lending and trade, and law and punishment remained at a medieval level into modern times. Bands of huge 'warrior monks' – the *dob-dob* – terrorized the populace, using whips, knives and, according to some accounts, bunches of huge monastery keys as flails. When, in 1934, the respected and eminent Lungshar Dorje Tsegyal proposed a shift away from the inner circle of nobles to a national assembly, a power struggle ensued, and he was arrested. His eyes were put out by tightening a knotted rope around his head, and he died subsequently in prison.

In 1951 China signed agreements with the Dalai Lama not to disturb his authority or the Tibetan way of life. For a time the Chinese maintained this conciliatory policy, but in 1956 the Khamba tribesmen of eastern Tibet rebelled. They were supported by other elements in the community, notably the monasteries, which provided them with weapons. The Khambas had had a long tradition of hostility towards the Chinese. They had harried the

Communists at one stage during the Long March, and this, too, had not been forgotten by either side. There is considerable evidence of American CIA incitement of this revolt, the agency providing training and weapons to Tibetan militias for more than a decade before abandoning them totally in 1972.

The revolt spread throughout Tibet, reaching a climax in 1958. The Dalai Lama and his government fled into exile in India the following year. Chinese control of Tibet was now much more severely administered. The revolt was forcibly put down with a considerable loss of life, the lama (monk) class was proscribed, and the monasteries forcibly closed. The religious-feudal organization of Tibetan society was considered unacceptable by the Chinese government, who have taken all possible steps to destroy it and convert Tibet into a Chinese province like any other. To this end many thousands of ethnic Chinese have been resettled in Tibet and a major programme to 're-educate' the Tibetan people undertaken. Numerous deaths, imprisonment and incidents of torture were reported during this 'pacification' phase.

Tibetans suffered as much as Han Chinese during the 'great leap forward' in 1959 and 1960, with many thousands of deaths from starvation. However, there is now evidence that Chinese reform of agriculture and the establishment of industries and schools in Tibet have improved the lives of many people who were previously little better than slaves. Early in 2005 the Dalai Lama was quoted by the Hong Kong *South China Morning Post* as saying: 'Tibet is part of the Republic of China.' Saying Tibet was underdeveloped and materially backward, he added: 'So, for our own interest, we are willing to be part of the Republic of China, to have it govern and guarantee to preserve our Tibetan culture, spirituality, and our environment.' However, there have also been reports that China has been overexploiting Tibet's natural resources, especially its forests.

The Chinese Communist state was, then, consolidated by its redistribution of land, its establishment of a pervasive chain of authority, and its demonstration that it could improve the health and living standards of the people modestly. 'Correctness' – a severe Communist orthodoxy – became the dominant political virtue. There is abundant evidence of Chinese use of educational and psychological means to control the thought of their people; to implant hostility in their children towards outside nations regarded as enemies; and to correct 'wrong thinking' in individuals. These techniques, called 'brainwashing' by Western critics, were known by the Chinese as 'thought-cleansing'. They were designed to alter the opinions of those with critical or independent points of view, and justified by the assertion that Communism as dictated by the state must always be right, so that all citizens are bound to give it not only obedience but acceptance without reservation.

The peasants continued to live together in families, each in its own house with a small strip of land and livestock. It was nearly five years before the government began to change this rural society. Then, from 1954 onwards, a series of policy decisions attempted to organize the people into co-operatives and later into 26,000 'communes' – completely collective societies in which private ownership of land and real property was abolished. This policy was in part motivated by China's rapidly increasing population due to a falling death rate. Although heretical to Marxist theory, an intense campaign for birth control began in 1956. This 'deviation from orthodoxy' so offended many party members that it was soon discontinued, and another solution suggested. This was to be nothing less than a rapid, sudden breakthrough to complete Communism, until then seen only as an ideal to be achieved in the indefinite future. By late 1956 the government was calling for a much quicker rate of collectivization, and peasants who resisted it were punished.

In 1957 the government apparently decided to test the loyalty of intellectuals by inviting free discussion of its policies – to allow 'a hundred flowers' of opinion to blossom. There was a considerable volume of criticism; this was the time of the first Democracy Wall in Beijing University, containing posters critical of the Communist Party. When it was at its height the government countered with a sudden and severe wave of repression. An extensive purge of the public service followed. This was no small incident – more than 300,000 intellectuals, including most of China's brightest and most independent minds, were indicted as 'rightists', imprisoned, sent to labour camps, or to unaccustomed manual labour in the countryside. This unexpected blow was very significant, confirming the iron hand and severe orthodoxy of the Communist Party.

When in 1958 the central committee ordered the complete reorganization of Chinese society into 'peoples' communes', it was acting against two long-standing bases of Chinese life: respect for private property and the integrity of the family. In some places cottages were torn down and the materials used for communal barracks. Children were cared for in crèches while both parents worked at tasks assigned to them by the commune. Production quotas were fixed and the whole system dominated by an almost military discipline. In some instances the communes seem to have prospered, but in many the changes were resisted. Three successive bad seasons in many parts of China, including a serious drought in the Yellow River basin, coincided with this planned social dislocation and greatly aggravated its bad effects. Severe food rationing had to be introduced and China was forced to import large amounts of grain.

The problems were worsened by the diversion of huge amounts of labour to infrastructure development to make 'a great leap forward'. This disastrous campaign collapsed in less than two years, even though the Chinese, tough and sturdy though they are, were driven to efforts almost beyond human endurance. Fourteen-hour workdays were common, and press reports told of 'heroes' collapsing from fatigue. The huge results claimed were later shown to be false. Much effort was dissipated on badly conceived projects, such as the creation of 60,000 'backyard furnaces' to make steel. These ten-foot-high earthen structures were fed with coke and iron ore and tended by hand – very labour-intensive processes that severely depleted the agricultural land force. The product of these furnaces was often so bad it could not even be used for simple agricultural implements.

It is impossible to estimate accurately the cost of these huge mistakes, but it is generally accepted that deaths, mainly resulting from starvation, may have been as many as 30 million, with China's population actually declining by 2 per cent in 1960 and 1961. In many places the hungry and despairing populace rioted, with some reports of armed revolts against the government emerging in spite of tight censorship. The retreats from the commune system and the 'great leap forward' were simultaneous and virtually complete by 1963, although the communes have been retained as an administrative framework, with most planning and day-to-day admin-istration in the hands of much smaller production teams. Diversion of much industrial production to agricultural machinery like irrigation pumps, walk-behind tractors and fertilizer factories permitted a steady recovery in rural productivity from 1964. Nevertheless, grain production did not regain its 1955 levels until the early 1970s.

Then, in 1966, China was again plunged into chaos with a renewed strug-gle between moderate and extreme Communists – the so-called Cultural Revolution, in which the ageing Mao, crippled with Parkinson's disease, incited thousands of youthful Red Guards into a noisy and destructive campaign against traditional Chinese culture. This largely urban campaign, which was to affect China adversely for almost a decade, caused thousands of violent deaths, widespread dislocation of industry and education, and the wilful destruction of large quantities of China's art, writing and classical buildings.

In China in 1975 I saw ancient temples in which all of the images of Buddha had been smashed; saw childish and ludicrous, yet still malicious, posters reviling Confucius; heard stories of eminent scholars forced to kneel on broken glass in public recantations of their 'errors'; heard how the staff of whole universities were compelled to coach politically acceptable factory workers to academic standards in circumstances where competi-tive examinations had been abolished. Disastrous subsequent results, including attacks on the Red Guards by exasperated workers, forced the ending of these excesses; and dramatic changes in policy ensued, especially after the death of Mao and his closest associate, Zhou Enlai, from stomach cancer, in 1976. The harsh conditions during these chaotic decades may have exacted a long-term toll on those not accustomed to them. This is suggested by a 2004 report from the official Xinhua News Agency of surveys showing that intellectuals were dying ten years younger than the general community, at an average age of 53.

There were many more tragic deaths in 1976. Almost half a million people died when a major earthquake, measuring 8.7 on the Richter scale, struck the city of Tangshan. Nevertheless 400,000 people who had been trapped or injured were saved when a massive airlift from the city was organized at short notice. The earthquake destroyed 650,000 of the city's 680,000 buildings in two minutes. More than a million people were left homeless and China was forced to devote a massive effort to rehabilitation and reconstruction.

Rigid birth-control measures were introduced in 1979, penalizing families with more than one child. This in itself has created an unprecedented situation in China, a generation substantially of only children who, it must be said, have been generally spoilt, cosseted and indulged by their parents as 'little emperors'. Once, at a state dinner in China, I sat next to an aged veteran of the Long March who with every course uttered dire predictions about the risks of spoiling only children, who, he averred, could not be normal because they have not experienced the complex network of family relationships so traditional in China. In 1985 this policy was relaxed to allow rural families two children, and in 2004 in Shanghai divorced persons remarrying were permitted a second child where one partner was childless. There have been further concessions, so that by 2007 it was estimated only 36 per cent of people were subject to the one-child restriction. A second child is permitted if the first is a daughter. However the policy is still widely criticized, and in 2013 the government liberalized it further, permitting couples one of whom was an only child to have two children.

Nevertheless, even now China remains only a few steps ahead of famine, its population almost trebling from the inception of the Communist state to 2013, to 1.35 billion. That approaches a fifth of all the people in the world. To feed these China has only 6 per cent of the world's arable land – 26 per cent of its territory is desert, and much of the rest mountainous. Huge incursions of sand from the Gobi and long droughts, possibly due to climate change, have severely reduced the water supply and food production in much of the north.

While recent decades have shown a liberalization, especially in the economic sphere, there is little indication that the rigid hold the Communist Party, with more than 82 million members in 2012, has on the country will be relaxed. While there has been a considerable shift towards regional autonomy, the Communist Party and the army remain dominant in decision-making institutions at all levels of the community, and in all places. The Central Committee of the party, with several hundred members, elects a political bureau, or Politburo, of perhaps 20 people. But even this is not the ultimate leadership; that resides in a standing committee of the Politburo of seven members. The party has its own self-disciplining dynamic, regularly expelling lazy, corrupt or inefficient members, and demanding constant effort and self-criticism from its rank and file. Movements towards democracy have been decisively repressed, the most publicized example being the military suppression of student demonstrations in Beijing's Tiananmen Square and the broad boulevard that runs east from it, Changan Avenue, on 4 June 1989. Tanks and soldiers in armoured personnel carriers and trucks fired into the crowds, causing deaths variously estimated at between 200 and 2000. Thousands were subsequently arrested, with some initial executions for sedition, probably not more than 50 people. By standards of early Chinese Communist history, the reaction was moderate, with 18 people reported to have been given prison terms, some hundreds more 're-educated'. Nevertheless, the message was quite clear: 'Bourgeois liberalism', 'attempts to topple the Communist Party, overthrow socialism', were not acceptable.

While there was considerable support for the students in some major cities, especially Beijing, there is little evidence that the majority of Chinese had much sympathy for them. Most seem to have accepted the government's official line that the students were subversives, attempting to wreck the established social order. Since the incident is ignored in Chinese school history books and the media, most younger Chinese don't even know it happened. However, because the Tiananmen Square 'massacre' has been the most talked-about and written-about Chinese event in the West since the birth of the Communist state, its history is of some importance. The facts, reported by reputable Western journalists in Beijing at the time, are briefly as follows.

Demonstrations in the square began three weeks earlier, coinciding with a state visit to China by Soviet President Gorbachev, and subsequently turned violent, with hand-to-hand fighting and mobs throwing bricks, bottles and firebombs at the troops and police. On 3 June, 10,000 unarmed troops sent to the square to persuade the demonstrators to withdraw were forced to retreat. Later that day stone-throwing crowds attacked troops guarding the residences of the Chinese leaders, and seized an army bus loaded with weapons. Western reporters saw an armoured personnel carrier stopped by petrol bombs and its crew bludgeoned to death as they tried to escape. A pitched battle seemed to have occurred at Jianguomenwai, a large clover-leaf traffic interchange, where reporters noted four burned-out army vehicles and a number of dead soldiers. There are other reports of soldiers cut down, hanged, disembowelled or burned to death, and burned-out army trucks, although there is no evidence that these incidents were numerous.

Casualties on both sides were minuscule when compared with earlier events in China itself, or killings in East Timor by Indonesian soldiers, or even regular police actions by India against tribal minorities, and deaths in Afghanistan and Burma. The essential difference was that the Chinese allowed the Tiananmen events to be portrayed on world television – and they were shocking enough, including the crushing of young people under tank tracks and the shooting of young children.

However, the crackdown on 4 June plainly came after many misgivings. For instance, the 38th Army refused to move against the people and it was left to the 27th Army from Shanxi Province to make the assault. There are Western reports that they seemed frightened and on edge, and undoubtedly overreacted. Rumours, promoted by the Western media, that there might be fighting between these two armies – effectively civil war with the attendant breakdown in Chinese society that must have ensued – may well have helped to push the Chinese leadership into final action. A factor was Deng's often expressed fear of *luan* (chaos), which he associated with the Cultural Revolution and the democracy movement.

The volume of partisan criticism heaped on the Chinese government – far greater than that accompanying other recent human rights matters around the world, and repeated with monotonous regularity for more than 20 years – has had two consequences, which ought to have been foreseen by the world leaders concerned and their advisers: it has assisted the eclipse of moderate elements in the Chinese leadership and perpetuated the continuing power of the hardliners. It resulted in statements from Beijing that the Chinese government would not listen to criticisms from the rest of the world, but act only as it sees fit. Immediately after the Tiananmen conflict the Chinese media, previously achieving at least the beginnings of independence, were severely reined in, and contact with foreigners restricted. This continued until 1992, when a policy to attract more foreign investment and tourists led to a cautious and still restricted liberalization.

Meanwhile, the 11th Central Committee of the Chinese Communist Party, meeting late in 1978, had declared Mao's policies to have been mistaken and decided to 'correct the "leftist" errors committed prior to, and during the so-called cultural revolution'. The failures of the 'class-struggle' era Mao had insisted on maintaining were observed. It was decided that management of farming would revert to families, who would also be given back the right to hold private plots. The economy was now to become the most important consideration, and private enterprise and foreign investment not only tolerated but encouraged.

The driving force behind these reforms was the exasperation of the Chinese people with nearly three decades of hardship. Their architect was a tough, diminutive veteran of the Long March, Deng Xiaoping, who had been disgraced during the Cultural Revolution as a 'capitalist roader' and who spent years working in a tractor factory. Ultimately rehabilitated, his authority and iron willpower sufficed to turn China on to a new course – towards capitalism, but in the Chinese government's rhetoric, socialist capitalism. However, it was not enough to sustain his protégé and possible successor, the youthful and pro-Western Hu Yaobang, who was forced to resign as general secretary of the Communist Party in 1987 because he was seen by the party's hardliners as being 'soft' on student demonstrations for democracy. Hu's eclipse – he died of a heart attack two years later – and the repression of the student movement triggered by his state funeral in 1989 must be seen as a significant victory for hardline elements of the government. Deng retired from public life in 1994 and died in 1997.

Jiang Zemin became president, leading an upper bureaucracy largely of technocrats, 80 per cent of whom were graduates. There was a further transfer of power in 2003, but not, apparently, a change of direction. The enigmatic, little-known technocrat Hu Jintao became president and Wen Jiabao premier. Confucius, violently derided during the Cultural Revolution, was officially reinstated in 1994 as the new leaders embraced traditional Chinese culture and nationalism. The sage's 2545th birthday was marked by the opening of Confucian teaching schools and the establishment of an international association of Confucian studies in Beijing, 'representing a commitment by all the member communities of East Asia to a serious exploration of the qualities of the Confucian tradition which are producing a range of unique, non-Western approaches to cultural, social and economic organization among the growth economies of East Asia'. Its first chairman was Singapore elder statesman Lee Kuan Yew.

In July 1997, the British colony of Hong Kong, with seven million people, reverted to China on expiry of the original leases. One of the world's largest trading centres and a major tourist destination, Hong Kong appears to have settled down reasonably peaceably to incorporation within the mother country, although its prosperity has diminished somewhat and unemployment rates have increased. There have been protests at Beijing's restriction of democracy, and business has been affected by the global financial crisis. Nevertheless, Hong Kong has maintained its position as one of the world's leading business centres.

Major events in China in the new millennium were its entry into the World Trade Organization in 2001, and becoming only the third nation to put a man in space. In 2003 astronaut Yang Liwei was launched in the space vehicle *Shenzhou 5*, went around the world 14 times, and was returned safely to earth. China is planning to build a space station by 2020. As polar ice dwindles, China plans a container-ship service across the Arctic Ocean, perhaps by 2020, greatly reducing voyage times to Europe and the United States.

In 2013 Xi Jinping became China's new president, and former student activist Li Keqiang premier. Both men promised to act against the preceding 'lost decade's' increasing problems and missed opportunities for reform. This seemed to be a response to widespread public indignation at growing income disparity and 'cronyism'. In his first press conference Li Keqiang promised 'a self-imposed revolution; it will require real sacrifice, and this will be painful. We have to shake up vested interests.' It will take time to see whether these new brooms can sweep clean enough to control China's deeply entrenched financial and political pressure groups. Meanwhile, technocrats seem likely to remain in control on their watch, while China continues to be the world's largest construction job.

In his first overseas trip after his inception President Xi visited Russia, where he spoke of closer relations between that country and China, providing a stronger voice in world affairs to counterbalance the West. He raised energy co-operation as a major issue, saying: 'Oil and gas pipelines have become the veins connecting the two countries in a new century.' Speaking next in Tanzania, President Xi confirmed $20 billion in Chinese loans for African infrastructure, farming and businesses, and announced specialist training for 30,000 Africans over three years. Chinese trade with African countries reached almost $200 billion in 2012, a rise of 11 per cent from the previous year. In one of his earliest statements President Xi said that over five years China would import goods worth $10 trillion and invest $500 billion overseas, with 400 million Chinese travelling overseas as tourists.

Since Mao's death much has changed in China, new styles of life and work have evolved which he fought desperately to forestall – what he called the 'ogres' of capitalism. One of these has been the establishment of a new elite, made up substantially of the children and grandchildren of those of those who fought and suffered alongside Mao during the Long March, and who now control much of the economy and the political scene. These progeny are called 'princelings'. President Xi Jinping is one of them.

Economic liberalization has again permitted private enterprise, both small businesses and joint enterprises. It is significant that many of these are owned and managed by capitalists from Taiwan. There are once again very rich and very poor people in China, and the government, with some publicly expressed qualms, has accepted this, since the economic results have been impressive. A wide range of consumer goods is exported world-wide at highly competitive prices. Since 1978 there has been a steady growth in the gross national product of about 10 per cent per year, with impressive increases in average wages and the virtual transition of urban China to a consumer society in modest terms.

China's economy has been doubling in size every decade. She has favourable trade balances with a number of countries, including the United States, and, according to Bloomberg, in 2013 was holding a massive $3.3 trillion in foreign-exchange reserves – 30 per cent of all global reserves, and more than enough to buy all the gold in the world. In 2011 China overtook Japan to become the world's second largest economy, and in 2013 the OECD forecast it would become the largest by 2016. Nevertheless, there was some check in China's growth in 2012, when growth fell to 7.8 per cent, the slowest for 13 years, due to slackening demand both at home and abroad. This weakening trend continued in the first quarter of 2013, when growth was 7.7 per cent.

Nowhere is more typical of China's new capitalism than Shanghai. Its 630-square-kilometre high-technology cityscape has a vast new 'market economy' area at Pudong, a complex of the world's tallest buildings, and modern centres for making almost anything the world might want or need, from construction steel to computer chips. In 2004 the world's first magnetic levitation train began to operate between the city and the airport, achieving speeds of up to 250 miles an hour during its 8-minute journey. By 2013 a fast rail network of more than 1400 kilometres connected Shanghai with Beijing. China has 30 million cars, with 2.5 million more going on the roads each year. The rapidly growing urban middle class who inhabit Shanghai and other 'high-tech' cities are showing signs of adopting many aspects of Western culture – another development Mao would have hated. According to a Chinese government survey, about a third of Chinese now celebrate Christmas – but only 3 per cent do so for religious reasons.

The Chinese leadership is committed to huge infrastructure programmes – at a cost of around $750 billion – in Keynesian solutions to problems of unemployment and hesitancy in some areas of the economy. The Three Gorges Dam project on the upper Yangzi River is the world's second largest engineering project, designed to control flooding, produce billions of kilowatt hours of electric power and to make the river navigable as far inland as Chongqing, more than 1000 miles from the coast. It began producing power in 2003, against the background of severe power shortages due to China's booming industries. The dam includes massive ship-lifts, which can raise vessels of up to 10,000 tons from the lower river to the huge lake behind it. A second major works programme in global terms is a 2000-mile canal system to move water from the Yangzi to Beijing and the north of the country at a cost of $60 billion. This line of huge aqueducts is claimed to be the largest engineering work in the world. Other projects are a 2000-mile pipeline to bring natural gas from Xinjiang to Shanghai, and a nuclear-powered desalination plant in Shandong Province to produce 52 million tons of water a year.

In 2013 China faced continuing energy shortages, as well as major urban pollution. Three-quarters of the nation's electricity is produced by burning coal – its use reached 3.8 billion tons in 2012 – almost half of total world consumption. A Harvard University study estimated 100,000 premature deaths a year in China due to pollution, and the Chinese Ministry of Health said the incidence of lung cancer had doubled in the last decade. With production from its four major oilfields declining, China is now the world's largest oil importer, buying in 6.3 million barrels a day in 2013.

Nevertheless, much progress has been made in building renewable energy – China is spending $50 billion a year on this, the largest investment made by any nation and about 20 per cent of the global total. While the Three Gorges Dam is the world's largest hydroelectric generator at 22 gigawatts, China plans to install water power 20 times that capacity – 430GW – by 2020. Wind power was the nation's third largest source of power in 2011, surpassing nuclear – China plans to generate 100GW from wind by 2015, some of this from offshore installations. China produces 30 per cent of the world's solar panels, but most are exported, hence the photovoltaic solar target for 2015 is a modest 21GW. More than 100 million Chinese ride electric bicycles, which cost around $250 each; China claims its tens of millions of domestic solar water heaters are more than those installed in any other country – probably about a third of global capacity.

State-owned enterprises still dominate much of the economy, especially heavy industry, and employ at least 20 per cent of the workforce. There were 114,000 of them in 2010, including a hundred that are very large. Many are inefficient and uneconomic and are heavily subsidized, but the government has had difficulty phasing them out because this involves mass unemployment of workers who have become used to regarding their jobs as absolutely secure – the 'iron ricebowl', meaning one that could not be broken. Nevertheless, state enterprises are being closed or consolidated into vast monopolies, often at considerable social cost.

Agricultural productivity has improved since the inception of contracts with families. These mostly cover general farming, but they can be specific, allowing individual households to become specialists in such things as animal breeding and fish farming, or even the production of handcrafts.

However, the Chinese countryside retains many problems, and its peasants are generally worse off in money terms than city workers. There is a massive labour surplus in agriculture, causing tens of millions to desert the land to seek work in the cities, with varied success.

The new millennium has seen the first of the single-child generation entering on their responsibilities. This has been associated with a dramatic and significant rise in the educational standards of many young Chinese – in 2012 almost seven million graduated from university. However, a serious and persisting social problem is the increasing disproportion between the number of men and women, caused by a cultural preference for boys, cheap ultrasound, and widespread abortion of girls. In 2011 there were 51.9 per cent of male births, 48.1 female. By 2020 it is estimated that there will be 30 million more men than women, many of whom will have difficulty finding wives.

When in China on official delegations and the like it is possible at times to talk privately with the cadres who are always in attendance on 'foreign friends'. I asked perhaps a dozen Chinese the same somewhat unwelcome question. Around half angrily refused to respond. The question was: 'You are expected to obey the government in all things, give up your personal freedoms more than just about anyone else in the world would be prepared to do. How do you feel about that?'

The answer generally was something like this: 'China was poor and weak for generations. We must all agree to obey the government, if China is to catch up. Of course in many ways I don't like that, but on the whole I believe it is what we all must do, we must all pull together for China.' Impossibly idealistic? Government-dictated propaganda? Maybe. But my own impression was that many Chinese really do see it this way, a variation on 'Shut up and I'll let you get rich.' Perhaps, 'Shut up and I'll make us all great.' There is plenty of evidence of increasing middle-class affluence, according to the UN Chinese tourists spent more money travelling abroad than any other people in 2012 – $102 billion – displacing Germans as the world's biggest travel spenders. That figure was a remarkable 41 per cent more than the previous year. But as more people get rich and great, the time may not be far off when their opinions, dissenting though they may be, begin to influence Chinese policy.

Meanwhile, who are the new rich of China? Many are cadres, members of the Communist Party and the army – often enough, 'princelings' – and their families. The People's Liberation Army, which makes and sells arms, is a major player in international finance and controls at least 20,000 profit-making businesses in China. This, perhaps, is yet another way the army and the Communist party, the power monoliths of China, are seeing they remain just that in the new era of socialist capitalism.

27 Taiwan: Chinese or Not?

'The dogs have gone. The pigs are here.' Such was the wry utterance current in Taipei, the capital of Taiwan, when at the end of the Second World War the defeated Japanese left and Chinese Nationalist troops occupied the island.

In 1945, under the terms of the Yalta Agreement, Taiwan was handed back to China, then still under Jiang's governance. General Chen Yi, the Nationalist military governor sent to the island, proved so incompetent and corrupt that by 1947 the people were driven to major riots. Between 15,000 and 30,000 people were killed by the military when these were repressed, with the utmost severity. Martial law instituted then would endure for 38 years.

When the Communists took over China late in 1949, more than one and a half million Nationalist supporters, including 600,000 soldiers, fled to Taiwan, increasing the population by a quarter in a few weeks. The demands of this huge influx of people on food supplies and the economy generally were a heavy enough imposition; even worse was the use of martial law to compel the Taiwanese people to provide for an army of invaders determined to behave like conquerors.

Jiang considered his plans to use Taiwan as a base from which to attack the new mainland government sufficient justification for his harsh authoritarianism. But as time passed an invasion of China seemed increasingly less feasible. The United States recognized the legitimacy of the Communist government in Beijing, and the UN seat bestowed on Jiang's regime was transferred to China. Most nations followed the American lead and recognized Beijing. Nevertheless, the United States still considered Communism a major enemy, during the phase of uneasy peace known as the Cold War. China was warned that America would resist any attempt to invade Taiwan. However, China has continued to regard Taiwan as a Chinese province which must be incorporated into the Chinese state, and has said it will invade the island if any attempt is made to declare it an independent nation.

In spite of martial law, a modern industrial economy developed, largely through American technical and financial aid. This, together with a land-reform programme, saw Taiwan develop into one of the most prosperous states in Asia. Nationalist domination of the government survived Jiang's death in 1975, but not for long. In 1986 the Democratic Progressive Party was founded, and two years later the first native-born president, Lee Tenghui, took office. In 1991 he persuaded a 'rump' of 460 Nationalist members of a parliament of doubtful political legitimacy to retire. Taiwan's first free election brought the DPP to government, and this was confirmed in later elections for the assembly and presidency in 1995, 1996 and – by the narrowest of margins – in 2004. However, later that year it lost power in the assembly to the KMT and coalition partners, who by this stage were opposed to the idea of Taiwanese independence. This indicated more support than had been expected for the KMT attitude: 'we don't want war, or the road of provocation and tension'.

In 1995, when Lee had made a highly publicized visit to America, China began a series of intensive military exercises on the Fujian coast opposite Taiwan, together with a no less intensive verbal campaign warning that any attempt to declare independence would prompt an attack on the island. Similar warnings were issued in 2003, and during the run-up to the 2004 elections. Taiwan moved to a proportional representation system in 2005. Since then the political scene has been stable, with the KMT winning elections in 2008 and 2012.

There has been a low profile but very real rapprochement with the mainland on practical levels, including personal travel between China and the island and trade and commercial initiatives, among them a $30-billion investment in China by Taiwanese businessmen. However, Taiwan's position in the world remains an uneasy compromise, with most interested parties urging continuance of the status quo, while publicly agreeing that sooner or later there must be only one China.

Can the island's past history justify China's claim to Taiwan? The archaeological record indicates that Taiwan has been occupied by people for a long time. Its first inhabitants, arriving perhaps 6000 years ago from the mainland, were possibly the same Austronesians who spread through south-east Asia and the Pacific. Their descendants now make up rather less than 2 per cent of the present population of Taiwan.

According to the classic *History of the Three Kingdoms*, the Chinese state of Wu may have sent a military expedition to Taiwan in the 3rd century, and the Ming Admiral Zheng He noted that the island existed. However, significant migration seems not to have occurred until late in the 15th century, when Chinese from neighbouring Fujian Province began to take up land on the western plains, forcing the aboriginal tribes into the central mountains and to the rugged east coast. There was, however, considerable intermarriage between the aborigines and the Chinese, a mix still giving the Taiwanese population its distinctive nature.

Portuguese mariners established a foothold in 1517. It was they who called the island Formosa – meaning beautiful – the name by which it was known to Europeans for the next several centuries. The Dutch arrived in 1623, using the island as a base for trade with Japan, but later brought in Chinese migrants to work on sugar and rice plantations. Many of these stayed on, creating what seems to have been the first significant Han Chinese presence. The Dutch treated the aboriginal inhabitants of Taiwan abominably, destroying whole villages, and killing the inhabitants or enslaving them.

During the last years of the Ming Dynasty in China an adventurer named Zheng became a general. His son Zheng Chenggong, known in the West as Koxinga, continued the struggle against the Manchu until 1661, when he was forced to retreat to Taiwan with an army of 35,000. He campaigned successfully against the Dutch colonizers, who were forced to leave after 38 years on the island, and established what was in effect the last Ming outpost. This Chinese kingdom is regarded as a high point in Taiwanese history. However, it did not long survive Zheng's sudden death, probably from malaria, in 1683 at the age of 38. The Manchu Qing Dynasty took the island only a year later. Formerly regarded as 'a ball of mud beyond the pale of civilization', it appeared for the first time on Chinese maps and was incorporated as a prefecture, or county, of Fujian Province, which it continued to be until 1887, when it was restyled a Chinese province.

During these 200 years Chinese governments took little interest in Taiwan – a place 'the size of a pellet', and took steps to limit Chinese migration to the island. It became notorious as a haven for pirates. For a time there was a Japanese colony on the eastern side. However, continued Chinese migration, driven by a series of famines in Fujian, brought the population to perhaps two million by the end of the 19th century. A Fujian farmer is credited with having brought tea plants to Taiwan in about 1800 – the establishment of what is still a thriving industry.

When Japan defeated China in 1895, Taiwan became a Japanese possession until the end of the Second World War. The Taiwanese initially resisted Japanese occupation, establishing an independent republic which, however, endured for only a few days before Japanese troops arrived to occupy the island. Thousands of Taiwanese conscripts were killed in the Second World War, when the island was a significant naval base. Japanese control became severe, even brutal, with a major campaign to 'Japanize' the

Taiwanese people, teaching children the Japanese language and the Shinto religion. Nevertheless, there was considerable infrastructure development such as roads, railways, schools and hospitals, which provided a basis for the island's subsequent prosperity.

However, as elsewhere, the global financial crisis induced recession and relatively high unemployment, with a contraction of GDP of almost 2 per cent in 2009. The unemployment rate rose to 4.4 per cent in 2012. Taiwan's economy is very dependent on exports, and has suffered from falling world demand other than from China. Nevertheless the island is intrinsically wealthy, with gold and foreign exchange reserves of $418 billion in 2012. Taiwan's 23 million people represent less than 2 per cent of China's population, her land area less than 3 per cent. The birth rate is well below replacement, so much so that in 2010 the government offered cash prizes for 'a creative slogan that would make people want to have more babies', and announced plans to finance fertility treatment for young couples. This represents a significant generational change, since in 1964 a 3.5 per cent rate of natural increase implied population doubling in 24 years. Current trends are for an ageing population, with life expectancy rising in the last 50 years from 57 to 73 for men and 60 to 79 for women.

Whatever Taiwan's future, her small population seems almost insignificant in practical terms in the overall Chinese context. But behind the very considerable – and dangerous – level of rhetoric the island generates are three barely submerged issues of huge significance: China's insistence that what she sees as her national territory must be integrated within the nation; the large and growing dependence of the island's prosperity on China; and Taiwan's geographic position, effectively an unsinkable aircraft carrier almost within sight of the Chinese mainland, controlled by what Beijing regards as a client government of the United States.

28 Mongolia

This place of land-locked deserts and formidable mountains has seen some of the earth's oldest cultures. *Homo erectus* lived here in the crystal-lined White Cave 800,000 years ago and in a canyon in the Gobi there are rock engravings dating back to at least 3000 BCE which depict men riding horses. Other human-like forms with greatly enlarged hands and ears seem even older – so strange the local people regard these as the work of aliens. Evidence of the use of horses and wheeled vehicles dated earlier than 2000 BCE have been found at the Bronze Age Afanasevo sites. Wooden tools there have been carbon dated to 3700 BCE, and there is evidence of the early use of metals and herding of cattle and sheep by a people some anthropologists believe might have been white Caucasians. While little more than this is known of this early society – and some of it is disputed – the horse-riding nomadic lifestyle that became typical of Mongolia, and persisted for thousands of years, seemed first to appear at this time. This society evolved through several later cultures – the complex of second millennium BCE cultures loosely described as the Andronovo is typical. These people mined copper in the Altai Mountains, lived in log cabins partly underground, and buried their dead with ornamented pottery. They are widely credited with having invented the spoked-wheel chariot.

Mongolia has been the cradle of several major empires, including the largest land empire the world has seen, founded by the Mongol warlord Genghis Khan in 1206. All of these, including the first, the Xiongnu, which developed around 250 BCE, have been loose federations of nomadic tribesmen who united to attack their neighbours with large and highly organized armies. Superb horsemen, who used a tough breed of small horse in battle, they could shoot arrows from their bows while riding at a full gallop. Utterly ruthless, they frequently offered besieged cities only two choices – surrender or extermination of all their inhabitants and demolition of their city to the last stone.

The Xiongnu persisted for more than 700 years, and at their height controlled a region a good deal larger than the present Mongolia, extending into what is now south Siberia, and western Manchuria. They were a source of great concern to China, which at times fought them and at other times bribed them or contracted treaties and marriage alliances to keep the peace. The original Great Wall was built to keep them out. The Xiongnu used a pyramidal military organization, led by their emperor, the *chanyu*, and his immediate deputies, the wise kings of the right and the left, who were usually close relatives. Under the army generals were commanders responsible for units of a thousand, a hundred, and ten men. These armies could number over a 100,000. The Xiongnu were skilled metalworkers, the first to use iron in that region.

In 1206 a regional war lord called Temujin united the Mongol tribes and assumed the name of Genghis Khan. The empire he eventually conquered covered 13 million square miles, stretching west–east from Poland to Korea, and from Siberia south to Vietnam. For more than a century it included China, where Genghis's grandson Kublai became the first emperor of the Yuan, or Mongol, Dynasty. However, corruption and laziness ended that dynasty in 1368, when it was replaced by the Ming. The Ming Dynasty collapsed in tragic circumstances in 1644, allowing yet another force from the north, the Manchus, an opportunistic entry. Inner Mongolia became part of China during the Manchu-dominated Qing Dynasty, which persisted until 1911, while Outer Mongolia remained nominally autonomous. Inner Mongolia is still part of China, hence the remainder of this chapter will treat the former outer region, now independent, as Mongolia – although it is worth noting that more Mongols live in the Chinese autonomous region than in the Mongolian republic.

A first glance at the Mongolian republic might incline the reader to dismiss it as uninteresting and inconsequential – a vast emptiness. An atlas reveals pale brown and white expanses of forbidding country, the lightly inhabited tract of desert in the south called the Gobi, and range after range of rocky snow-clad mountains in the north. The climate is among the most savage in the world, ranging from 40 degrees below zero Centigrade to 37 above. Ulan Bator has the doubtful distinction of the being the coldest capital city in the world, with an annual average of 0 °C. These extremes and winters almost without rain make most of Mongolia unsuitable for cropping, and difficult even for animal farming. A need to continually move herds from place to place to find pastures is the reason for Mongolia's traditional nomadic culture.

Nevertheless, this forbidding stretch of desert and mountains played a key role in one of the most consequential events in history – the transfer of knowledge, goods and technology between China and Europe. Romantic stories about seafaring under sail overrate the importance shipping had on world affairs until relatively recently. Because ships were small the amount of cargo they could carry was limited, and prior to the evolution of steamers in the 19th century sea journeys were slow, erratic and dangerous. From the time of the Roman Empire onwards trade was essentially overland. A network of trade routes crossing central Asia – the Silk Road – carried most of the commerce between East Asia and Europe. A significant stretch of this 4000-mile journey was across the Mongolian desert, and this perilous stage had to be managed for more than a thousand years by men whose very lives depended on careful methods and expert knowledge. The sturdy Bactrian camel and teams of goats have always been the beasts of burden for this travel. Because the maximum distance camel trains can travel over shifting pebbles or soft sand is around 25 miles a day and because at the end of that day both men and beasts needed water, the routes had to be carefully planned between oases. Sometimes these were natural, but many obtained their water from *karez*, artificial underground irrigation channels. There are more than 3000 miles of these, gathering snow meltwater from the mountains, then moving it underground to reservoirs. The oldest date back almost 2000 years.

The Romans called China 'silk-weaving Ceres' – Chinese silk first appeared there in the 1st century BCE and soon became immensely popular. However for many years the Romans had no idea how silk was produced, believing it grew on trees, while the Roman Senate tried to restrict the trade because of the extent to which it was depleting Rome's reserves of gold. The Chinese inventions of paper, printing, gunpowder and the nautical compass were probably transferred to the West across the Silk Road, which became a major east–west corridor in the 13th century, when Mongol expansion through central Asia brought peace and stability to the region. The first European travellers – notably Marco Polo – travelled overland to China at this time. The decline of the land traffic after the fragmentation of the Mongol empire became a major incentive for European seafarers when they explored for a sea route to the east.

Meanwhile Mongolia itself became a diminished society during the centuries of domination by the Yuan Dynasty. Preyed on by Manchu landlords and huge numbers of Buddhist monks, it became increasingly impoverished. The revolution in neighbouring Russia and the inception of the Soviet Union resulted in almost immediate changes in Mongolia – although independence was declared in 1921, the new government was dominated by Russia from the start. The Mongolian People's Republic established in 1924, a *de facto* part of the Soviet Union, persisted for 70 years. The Stalinist purges in Russia in the late 1930s extended to Mongolia, where more than 30,000 peasants and other 'reactionaries' were killed. Among the principal victims were 18,000 Buddhist monks, who made up perhaps a quarter of the male population.

Through the years of Russian domination China continued to insist that Mongolia was part of its territory. However, at the end of the Second World War, when Russian forces seemed likely to occupy inner Mongolia, China was obliged to accept the independence of the outer republic. It was only after the collapse of the Soviets in 1989 that a bloodless revolution ended Communist rule, and resulted in real independence and the democratic political system that persists today. There are two major political groups, the People's Party, derived from the old Communist Party, and the Democrats. The June 2012 election resulted in neither party having a clear majority. However, since the Democrats won the most seats, they formed the government.

One of the last vestiges of Soviet domination disappeared early in 2013 when a giant bust of Lenin was removed from one of Ulan Bator's grandest buildings, a museum devoted to the Russian dictator built in 1980. The building subsequently housed the very considerable number of dinosaur fossils being found in Mongolia, including a 70-million-year-old *tyrannosaurus bataar*.

The loss of economic assistance from the Soviet Union, as much as a third of Mongolia's budget, resulted in a decade of financial problems, so desperate that at times basic foods had to be rationed. Poverty and unemployment increased rapidly, the global financial crisis took its toll, and the economy began to revive only in 2009 when foreign capital came in to develop the mining industry. Of the population – a little over three million – almost half live in the capital, Ulan Bator, many in decrepit shanty towns on the outskirts. The city suffers from severe air pollution, caused mainly by coal-burning power stations. Most of the rest of the people still herd livestock in ever more difficult conditions. Long droughts and usually cold and snowy winters attributed to climate change have taken a severe toll on livestock, and some farmers have lost their entire stock. During the severe winter of 2009/10 almost 10 million animals died – about 20 per cent of the national herd – leading to a doubling of meat prices. Large numbers of Mongolians have left the country to find work overseas – South Korea is a leading destination.

The barren plains and dunes of the Gobi have until recently been places to avoid, inhabited only by a few camel breeders, but over the last few decades mineral deposits have been found there with a potential value of trillions of dollars. One of these is Tavan Tolgoi, a reserve of 6.4 billion tonnes of high-grade coal, the world's largest unmined resource. A quarter of this is coking coal used to make steel, so its location close to the border with China, with the world's largest steel industry, offers a huge opportunity. International mining companies are competing to develop this resource, but the government wants majority ownership to stay with the state-owned company that holds the mining licence, and with the Mongolian people. It plans to reserve 10 per cent of the company's value to awarding 536 shares to every Mongolian, an initiative that could end poverty for many thousands.

The Oyu Tolgoi gold and copper mine is even more valuable – one of the world's treasure troves, with an estimated 21 million ounces of gold and

41 billion pounds of copper. While this mine is not yet in production, the $6 billion spent so far developing the new mines has boosted Mongolia's gross domestic product by almost 30 per cent, and has provided employment for 10,000 workers.

Tourism to Mongolia, which was almost nonexistent during the Communist era, is now expanding rapidly, with nearly half a million visitors in 2010, more than 600 hotels and tourist camps, and a growing demand for tours by *yak* caravans, offering portable accommodation in the felt-lined tents called *ger*, previously described by the Russian word *yurt*. There is considerable interest in the Gobi, and more recognition of its special qualities.

These were recorded in detail more than half a century ago by two remarkable British missionaries, Mildred Cable and Francesca French, who spent years travelling widely in Mongolia. In their 1942 book *The Gobi Desert* they say:

> We found the desert to be unlike anything we had pictured. It had its terrors, but it also showed us some unique treasures. The oasis dwellers were poor but responsive; the caravan men were rugged but full of native wit; the outstanding personalities of the oases were men of character and distinction; the towns were highly individualistic and each small water stage had some unique feature. Even the monotonous outlines of the desert, when better known, wore a subtly changing aspect, and landscapes which were similar in broad outline became highly distinctive as their detail was scrutinised.

Development of Mongolia's mineral wealth plainly has the potential to transform the nation, and is the major preoccupation of the government. By 2012 around 3000 mining licences had been issued, to exploit more copper, coal, silver and uranium mines. However, the Mongolian government is taking a hard line, insisting that the Mongolian people benefit as much as possible from mining. In 2013 Rio Tinto, which is developing the Oyu Tolgoi Mine, stopped a $5-billion programme there and announced it would lay off as many as 1700 employees and contractors because of a dispute with the government over management. The government, which owns 34 per cent of the mine, wants Rio Tinto to spend more money on the project, but the company wants to cut costs and reduce debt. Because of its remoteness, the project is very costly. A small town had to be built to house its workers, a power plant installed and water piped in from 30 miles away.

Late in 2013 a consortium of three local companies, Mongolian Miners, began to extract coal at Tavan Tolgoi. Several major overseas miners are also interested, but no decision on their participation had been made at that time.

29 Indonesia and Timor-Leste

A tropical archipelago of more than 17,000 islands of great diversity and beauty, Indonesia is the world's fourth largest country in terms of population and potentially immensely wealthy, yet slightly over half her 240 million people are poor – in the words of the *Djakarta Post*, 'hovering around the poverty line on less than US$2 a day'. According to the Asian Development Bank, Indonesia is the only south-east Asian country in which the numbers of the poor are rising – 'a situation of chronic hard-core poverty'. The World Bank reports that 55 per cent of these poor people have limited primary education, 50 per cent have no access to clean water, and a quarter of their children under 5 are malnourished. It is estimated that by 2015 almost half of this underclass will be living in city slums.

Nevertheless, like other Asian countries, Indonesia has a modestly afflu-ent middle class, defined as having a household income above $3000 a year and estimated in 2013 at about 80 million. These people buy toothpaste, ice cream, smartphones and, above all else, motor scooters. Because Djakarta, like other Asian cities, has gridlocked traffic much of the time, motor scooters are the preferred personal means of transport – Indonesia had 65million of them in 2012.

The country's extraordinary diversity – more than 350 different languages are spoken – creates huge transport and administration problems. The official language, *bahasa Indonesia*, which is basically Malay, is taught in schools as a second language, but only in recent years has it been spoken fluently by most of the population.

The first decades of independence were stormy and chaotic. The acute shortage of trained people caused grave inadequacies in administration and failures in the everyday necessities of a modern state. Telephones, elec-tric power, the railways, the ports, customs – these and many other public services came close to collapse for want of expert control.

Actual bankruptcy at this point was averted because of Indonesia's grass-roots prosperity, and continued control of the bulk of her export-earning industries by foreigners. The key industry – the oilfields – paid royalties which provided the bulk of government revenue. The Chinese, as they still do, owned most of the other industries and retail outlets, including the important rice-distribution system, and, by and large, contrived to keep these things going.

Apart from overcrowded problem regions in central and east Java, most of the villagers were protected by a bountiful natural endowment that automatically provided self-sufficiency without too much work. Much of Java looks like a well-kept garden. The small, brown houses, often set high up on stilts, are almost lost in the lush growth of fruit trees that surrounds them, and the warm, even climate demands only simple housing and clothes.

Other than the opportunity to buy such things as a bicycle, a sewing machine, a television or radio, little of the modern technical world touched most of these villages in the early years of independence. However, rapid population growth has greatly increased Indonesia's problems of poverty and disadvantage. As villages became overcrowded and arable land scarcer, millions of young people flocked to the cities to seek work, which as often as not was unavailable. A major government-sponsored birth-control programme in the last decades of the 20th century, however, did much to stabilize the population increase at about one per cent a year.

Industries in Indonesia have too often been basically uneconomic, state-subsidized to the benefit of the country's military leaders and their families, and financed by huge loans obtained overseas. Corruption continues to be endemic at all levels of government.

In 1901 a son was born to an impoverished Javanese schoolteacher of aristocratic *priyayi* origins and his wife, who was from a Balinese raja's family. This child, named Sukarno, who is said to have exhibited a lively, charming and intelligent personality very early on, became an impassioned advocate for Indonesian independence. After he was arrested in 1929 by the Dutch he was briefly released, then rearrested in 1932 and exiled to the eastern island of Flores. There he read a great deal – Abraham Lincoln, Emerson, Jefferson, Nehru, Lenin, Marx – all were absorbed during this phase of development of his political thought. As time went by he became a legend in his own time, immensely well-known and popular among the people.

When Japan surrendered in 1945, British troops, sent to the city of Surabaya to bring out British and Dutch prisoners, became involved in a major conflict with Indonesian nationalists. During three days of major street fighting 6000 Indonesians were killed, and the fledgling independence army had its first experience of real war. Before long they also encountered Dutch troops, sent to reimpose colonial rule.

In 1949 the Indonesian government published a book called *Illustrations of the Indonesian People's Revolution*, designed to capture, in words and more than 2000 drawings and photographs, the spirit of the years of struggle.

The most significant photograph in the book was taken on 17 August 1945. It is ten o'clock in the morning outside a house in a Djakarta street – 56 Pegangsaan Timur, which was then Sukarno's home. Sukarno stands before a microphone, reading from a small slip of paper held in both hands. On the same page is a close-up of the paper, half a sheet of ordinary writing paper, somewhat dog-eared and containing some 30 words of writing in Indonesian, with some deletions and crossings-out under the heading, written in a firm hand and underlined twice, *Proklamasi*: 'We, the Indonesian people, herewith proclaim the independence of Indonesia. All matters pertaining to the transfer of power, etc., will be carried out in the shortest possible time.'

The Dutch refused to accept the declaration, and as a sporadic war dragged on, international sympathy, notably from Australia and the United States, inclined towards the independence movement, especially after Sukarno was arrested and deported to the island of Bangka in 1948. In that year a major push by the Communist Party to establish itself in central Java resulted in fighting between the Communists and other elements of the army. The climax came with a battle for the town of Madiun, in which the Communists were defeated. The 'Madiun affair' does much to explain subsequent hostility between the Indonesian Communist Party and the military. On 28 January 1949, the UN called for a transfer of sovereignty 'at the earliest possible date'. Dutch rule ended in December of that year, bringing the Republic of Indonesia into effective existence.

Sukarno , who became the first president of the new nation, abolished 'The United States of Indonesia' – the federal form in which independence had been achieved – because of his mistrust of Dutch 'divide-and-rule' tactics. On 17 August 1950, Indonesia became 'a unitary state' based on central rule from Djakarta. In the same year the 1945 'revolutionary constitution', which had given such wide powers to the president, was replaced by one which made Cabinet responsible to a national parliament. So Indonesia began a disastrous experiment with Western-style parliamentary democracy.

There were already signs of disunity between Djakarta and the outer regions, which were less enthusiastic about the unitary state. The Dutch-sponsored Republic of the South Moluccas proclaimed its independence, but never gained much support. The extremist Darul Islam movement, which wanted an Islamic state, turned terrorist and fought the government from mountain strongholds in West Java and Sumatra. A major revolt began in Aceh in north Sumatra in 1953, aimed at creating an independent state, and continued sporadically until 2005, when a peace agreement giving the province limited autonomy was concluded.

Inexperience in administration began to tell increasingly as the months and years passed. To obtain revenues the government increased customs duties to a level that made smuggling really worthwhile. No resources existed to police the huge sweeps of coastline, and soon more goods were coming in over the beaches than through the ports.

In 1956, my first experience of Indonesia, it was no longer possible to get a telephone connection from one part of Djakarta to another, and the capital's streets became deeply potholed and rutted, partly due to the army's habit of running tanks over them, to the detriment of the bitumen.

There were grave difficulties in achieving coherence in the political system, divided as it was between four main influences – Sukarno, the parliament, the growing Communist Party and the armed services. Sukarno had fallen out with the army chief-of-staff, General Nasution, dismissing him in 1952. The following year Nasution published a book, *Fundamentals of Guerrilla Warfare*, which had such important implications for Indonesia's future that it deserves attention.

The Indonesian National Army, Nasution argued, 'was a guerrilla, not a professional, force, hence its members must involve themselves in politics ... . The guerrilla soldier and partisan ... is not merely a tool to be ordered about. He must be taught the country's ideology and policy. He must not be isolated from politics. He must have both feet firmly in the middle of politics.'

Nasution was back in charge of the army again only two years later, restored as chief-of-staff by the parliament while Sukarno was absent on a pilgrimage to Mecca. The Communists warned of a possible military dictatorship. When Indonesia's first democratic elections were held in 1955 six million people voted for the Communists, who had campaigned on a major 'land for the landless' theme which appealed to the poorer people.

Sukarno spent a good deal of that year out of Indonesia, refusing to listen to advice about the country's financial problems. 'Economics', he is said to have remarked, 'make my head ache.' On his return he expressed impatience with the political parties and gave notice of a new concept he had in mind called 'guided democracy'. Early in 1957 it became a reality – a kind of national consensus based on traditional village government.

An attempt to assassinate Sukarno that year shocked the Indonesian nation deeply. He survived the bombing of a school, but of ten killed, six had been children, and this had a tremendous impact in a country where children are virtually worshipped. The four men arrested turned out to be Muslim extremists of the Darul Islam movement, who reiterated their hatred of Sukarno even in the court that finally condemned them. Sukarno and those who guarded him were fully aware of the danger of a further assassination attempt. The president moved with considerable fear along the narrow ribbon of road linking Djakarta with the presidential palace at Bogor. One morning when I was driving with an Indonesian friend I heard the sound of motor horns in the distance and within minutes the leading motorcycles were in view, lights full on in the bright sunshine. There were four of them, followed by a white jeep, then a long, black car, which seemed to be empty but for the driver, and finally, more armed motorcyclists. In the front of the jeep stood an army officer, wearing dark glasses, his hand resting lightly on the windscreen. In the black car Sukarno crouched down low on the seat even though the doors were lined with sheet steel and the windows fitted with armoured glass. The white jeep became something of a legend in and around Djakarta and a host of stories, persistent, if of no verifiable authenticity, grew up around it. It was said that the officer in sunglasses used a bicycle chain, with which he lunged out to smash the windscreen of any vehicles obstructing the convoy.

In 1959 Sukarno ordered a reversion to the 1949 constitution, returning executive power to himself and weakening the other areas of government. Parliament was further debilitated by the addition of more appointed members than elected ones. But behind this apparent dominance by Sukarno a bitter and intense enmity was developing between the army and the Communists.

By 1961 Sukarno felt strong enough to demand transfer of the western part of New Guinea – West Irian – which had been a Dutch colony, to Indonesia. He entrusted a tough regular soldier, General Suharto, with the task of readying a 25,000-strong invasion force. In April the first guerrillas were dropped into the jungles of West Irian (also known as West Papua). The Indonesian military performance in this sporadic war was no better than indifferent. However, there was no stomach for the war in Holland, and this, combined with strong US opinion that Indonesia should have West Irian, carried the day.

In 1963, as Sukarno knelt in prayer at a religious meeting, a fanatic took out a pistol and fired a full magazine at him. Again he was untouched, but five people around him were wounded. Now even more elaborate measures were taken to guard him, including an elite palace guard all of the same blood grouping as the president. Its men tasted his food and drink before he touched it, and searched visitors for concealed weapons. Largely isolated from his people, Sukarno became a myth in his own time and some curious stories circulated about him. His interest in women and his marital problems were expanded to give him a reputation as a great user of women in the tradition of the rajas of the past. He was said to go out at night, embrace trees, and walk barefoot during thunderstorms. He appeared at a formal function barefoot, explaining that he wanted to pick up electricity from the ground. Such things, and the extravagance of his daily life, served only to make the common people love and revere him all the more. This adulation was not so much towards Sukarno as a person as to his position as ruler. This tradition of obedience to the ruler simply because he or she is the ruler is a continuing and significant political force in Indonesia.

When the federation of Malaysia was formed late in 1963 Sukarno opposed it – first with words and then by sending armed forces into Sarawak. In 1964 he announced 'the Year of Living Dangerously', a confrontation with what he saw as the forces of capitalism and neo-colonialism. There was increasing speculation about his health. Already an old man by Indonesian standards, he was plagued by a liver complaint that needed surgery. This he refused because he had been told by a fortune-teller that steel would cause his death. Rumours that he might die at any moment may well have been the cause of a confused military coup in September 1965.

The first action seems to have been a rebellion by left-wing elements in the army supported by armed Communist activists at Halim air base. They claimed they had acted to prevent a planned coup by the generals to depose Sukarno. Armed bands of soldiers surprised leading members of the Council of Generals in their homes during the night. Six were murdered, at least one after being subjected to torture.

General Suharto, the leader of the elite strategic reserve of the Indonesian army, became prominent at this stage, rallying loyal troops to break the 'revolt' by force of arms. There was fierce fighting with young Communist guerrillas at Halim air base and in central Java. The Communist leader, Aidit, was killed. His death was only the first of many in a massive campaign, said to be against the Communists, but actually involving a multitude of others, especially the Chinese. This huge bloodletting, the killing of as many as a million people, is perhaps the greatest stain on the Indonesian nation, and was an ominous portent for the future. Independent eyewitnesses in Indonesia during December and January reported that not only men, but also women and small children, who could not possibly have ever had a political idea, were butchered by mobs of Muslim extremists. There is evidence that the American Central Intelligence Agency and the British and Australian governments were complicit in this campaign to 'destabilize' the Sukarno government. Much of the violence involved the *marhaen*, the proletariat, landless and uneducated peasants who drifted to the cities in the hope of improving their fortunes. Often unable to find work even for a pittance, they joined one of the large aimless bands that loitered in the streets, always ready to undertake any activity, from a political demonstration to beating up a Chinese shopkeeper and looting his home.

A restless, drawn-out struggle for power between Sukarno and General Suharto continued for a year. Sukarno's policies were steadily reversed. The confrontation with Malaysia ended and Indonesia rejoined the UN. Sukarno was placed under house arrest. In February 1967, Suharto assumed all real powers of government, and a year later became Indonesia's second president, *bapak*, the father of the nation. Sukarno died in obscurity in 1970.

A stocky, slow-moving man, Suharto was born into a peasant family near Jogjakarta in 1921. During his youth he was strongly influenced by traditional Javanese beliefs, including that of the sacred persona of the leader. He was a regimental commander when the republic was formed, a colonel in 1957, and a brigadier-general and deputy-chief of the army staff three years later.

His 'new order' government continued to be anti-Communist and brought Indonesia into much closer orientation with the West and, in particular, the United States. The 350,000-strong Indonesian army became a vast administrative machine with the weapons to support its demands, controlling businesses ranging from huge corporations to village brothels, often in partnership with wealthy Chinese. By 1998, the end of the Suharto era, more than 12,000 soldiers held administrative jobs at all levels, including almost half the provincial governors and district controllers. The huge wealth accumulated by the Suharto family – estimated to be as much as $40 billion – became a major scandal. Official enquiries in 1998 estimated that a car-importing concession to Suharto's son Hutomo (Tommy) had cost the nation $1.5 billion. Hutomo was allowed to import cars from Korea without paying tax, and sell them as 'the national car' in competition with all other importers, who had to pay tax. This was only one example of a complex pattern of fraud and dishonesty, involving major political figures and their families and friends, which came to be known as 'cronyism'.

Increasing repression by the regime also caused disquiet. At least 50,000 people arrested after the events of 1965 were still held without trial, although as a result of pressure from the United States some were released by 1980 into virtual house arrest. And there were more arrests of protesters, justified, not this time on the grounds of Communist subversion, but because of alleged radical Islamic conspiracies.

On the credit side for Suharto's New Order were the birth-control programme, an impressive growth in GDP in the 30 years to the early

1990s, a doubling of the manufacturing share of GDP to 24 per cent, increases in the rice yield, and predictable responses in international affairs. However, this wealth gain was unevenly distributed, and from a small base. Much of it derived from the huge increase in the world oil price in 1974, which quadrupled Indonesia's income from this source. 'Green revolution' gains in food-crop production were mainly due to improved seed and the greater use of pesticides, but resulted in sharp disparities in wealth in rural areas between those controlling these new methods and the former small-holders, many of whom have lost their land to large agribusinesses.

While advances in industry and the raised GDP provided some general benefits, most went to the small minority of the wealthy and influential. New industry, almost always joint ventures with foreign capital, included labour-intensive manufacture like clothing and shoes, but also extended to glassware, electrical goods and motor parts. Indonesia became the world's largest exporter of plywood, although this industry eventually prompted a major scandal because of its rapid depletion of the country's timber resources and diversion of much of the proceeds to a few 'cronies'. Much of this logging is illegal, and is still continuing. Losses to revenue have been estimated at over \$1 billion, and more than two million Dyak people in Kalimantan (Borneo) alone are said to have been displaced by massive forest destruction. A further consequence has been the rapid depletion of orang-utan populations because of loss of habitat. Orang-utans – the name means 'man of the jungle' – are Asia's only great ape. Once existing in millions, the Orang-utan Conservancy estimates numbers had now been reduced to 40,000. In 2012 Indonesia was still the world's largest exporter of tropical timber – 70 per cent of the trade is illegal logging. More than 20 million acres of forest was cleared by large corporations for palm-oil plantations in the decade to 2013. The founder of the 700,000-strong Indonesian Peasants' Union, Henry Sirigih, commented: 'The presence of palm-oil plantations has spawned a new poverty and is triggering a crisis of landlessness and hunger. Human rights violations keep occurring around natural resources in the country, and intimidation, forced evictions and torture are common' (John Vidal, *The Observer*).

In the 1970s, 80 per cent of Indonesia was forested – in 2013 the figure was 49 per cent, reducing at about two per cent a year.

On 7 December 1975, Indonesia invaded East Timor, using a large naval task force, aircraft and 10,000 troops, choosing a time of political instability in both Portugal, the colonizing power, and in Australia, less than 400 miles to the south. East Timor, now called Timor-Leste, makes up roughly half of the island of that name – the western section, formerly a Dutch possession, became part of Indonesia at the time of independence. Since Indonesia had no historic, ethnic or political justification to claim the eastern half, the invasion created widespread criticism within the UN and in communities and parliaments around the world. A civil war ensued following resistance to Indonesia from FRETILIN, a political party which had declared the territory's independence not long before the invasion. The Indonesian military contended they had invaded because FRETILIN was Communist, but the organization has denied this.

In November 1975 five Australian television journalists were killed by Indonesian troops in the small town of Balibo, ten kilometres from the border of Indonesian Timor. Timorese spokesman Jose Ramos-Horta says they were simply taken prisoner by the Indonesian army and shot, and that 'the Indonesians were determined to "teach a lesson" to the Australians, as Radio Kupang (in Indonesian Timor) boasted that evening'. The Indonesian army claimed the journalists died when they were caught in crossfire. However, subsequent eyewitness accounts in 1998 indicate that they were shot and knifed by Indonesian troops in cold blood after no more than token FRETILIN resistance in Balibo had ended. Soon after the Balibo incident another Australian journalist, Roger East, was shot in particularly brutal circumstances by Indonesian soldiers on Dili wharf.

According to Ramos-Horta's book *Funu*, as many as 200,000 Timorese died between 1975 and 1981, partly due to acts of war, but substantially because of 'a deliberate strategy of starvation through destruction of food crops and continuous military operations that left the population unable to cultivate the land'. Thousands more perished later in the Indonesian occupation. East Timor was returned to world attention by major television coverage of 'the Dili massacre' – an attack by Indonesian troops in 1991 on an unarmed assembly in Santa Cruz cemetery in the capital of the territory that resulted in an estimated 300 deaths – and the award of the Nobel Peace Prize to Ramos-Horta and the Bishop of Dili, Bishop Carlos Belo.

After much negotiation the Indonesian government agreed to a vote of the East Timorese people in August 1999 to decide their future. When 78.5 per cent of the people of East Timor voted for independence, the pro-Indonesia militia and units of the Indonesian army shocked the world by visiting a terrible revenge on them, murdering, torturing, and burning down almost every town and village before they were replaced by an Australian-led peacekeeping force. However, in October the Indonesian parliament decided reluctantly to endorse the East Timor vote, making way for the evolution of a new nation in Asia – Timor-Leste. Its fortunes since have been varied. Lack of money and expertise has restricted development and repair of the country's ruined infrastructure. In 2013 around half the population of 1.2 million were living in extreme poverty, mostly surviving as subsistence farmers. However in that year $8.7 billion had been raised from initial exploitation of oil and gas reserves in the Timor Gap, the strait that separates Timor-Leste from Australia. The other main source of export income comes from coffee, grown by more than 60,000 smallholders. A training scheme for Timorese doctors in Cuba, initiated by Fidel Castro in 2002, has already provided a significant improvement of medical services, with malaria and infant mortality rates greatly reduced since 2004.

Falling oil prices in the mid-1980s severely affected Indonesia's economy, dependent as it was on this single asset. Corruption and cronyism seemed impossible to control – the more so because they were so often associated with the president's family and close associates. Banks were crippled or in some cases driven to insolvency by an increasing burden of bad debt, which by 1993 had doubled in five years to more than 15 per cent of all bank loans. The stock market index lost two-thirds of its value in the early 1990s, with an associated sharp increase in foreign debt to about $80 billion.

Suharto became increasingly unpopular, maintaining his position only because of brutal repression by the army. Following the shooting of five students by the army at a peaceful demonstration in Djakarta in May 1998, and major rioting in many parts of the country, he was obliged to resign from the presidency after 32 years in office. Under his former protégé and successor, President B. J. Habibie, came limited signs of liberalization and the promise of fair elections within a year. Habibie ordered the release of some political prisoners, reversed the ban on the formation of new political parties and restored some freedom to the public media. However, although it was evident the army remained a major source of power, continued rioting, mob murders and burning of Chinese houses and shops and Christian churches made it equally plain that they were unable, or unwilling, to maintain law and order.

These events and the economic crisis from July 1997 served to bring many problems to the surface, but not to solve them. The bare facts of that situation were alarming enough. The Indonesian rupiah plummeted wildly from July 1997, seven months later stabilizing uneasily at 9000 to the American dollar, barely a third of its pre-crash value. With the private-sector foreign debt at around $70 billion, Indonesia immediately faced its worst financial crisis for 30 years. The value of shares in Indonesian companies fell in sympathy. The situation was not improved by the effects of a long drought, which had obliged Indonesia to import large amounts of food. The cost of imported rice rose more than three times and, even after government subsidies, was twice as expensive in the shops and markets.

Meanwhile the collapse of hundreds of businesses increased unemployment by millions. Rusting steel skeletons in Djakarta's business centre were only too eloquent of the sudden cessation of work on high-rise building projects whose finance, loans coming from overseas, had dried up. Loss of income, combined with rising food prices, created a highly volatile situation, with food riots reported from many parts of the country. A disquieting aspect of these years was regular violence against the Chinese. Although barely five per cent of the population, they controlled well over half of Indonesia's wealth. More rioting, bringing thousands on to Djakarta's streets, came with a meeting of the People's Consultative Assembly in November, called by President Habibie in an effort to resolve some of the nation's problems. Hundreds more people were killed, often under the most brutal circumstances.

Habibie, increasingly revealed as verbose and inconsistent, had by late 1999 little support among the people or the army. However, elections that year were relatively peaceful. Sukarno's daughter, Megawati, achieved the highest vote, 34 per cent. An Indonesian commented: 'They voted for the father.' Even so, in a surprise decision of the parliament Megawati was defeated by 373 votes to 313 for the presidency, the frail, almost blind leader of the largest Muslim party, NU, Abdurrahman Wahid, becoming Indonesia's fourth president. Severe rioting followed the decision. Although Wahid was a widely respected religious leader, he failed to cope with Indonesia's apparently intractable problems. He seemed unable to prevent the training and arming of the extremist Islamic Laskar Jihad militia, nor its transport from Java to the Maluku Islands, where it played a major part in a campaign that killed 5000 Christians and burned down hundreds of villages and churches. Corruption among his staff and associates also diminished Wahid's influence. He was dismissed by the People's Consultative Assembly and replaced by his deputy, Megawati, in July 2001. She became Indonesia's fourth president in four years.

It cannot be said that she was a strong president, nor was she able to solve the nation's severe economic problems. If anything, she appeared to have moved closer to relying on the army. Under her presidency civil war continued to plague Indonesia, killing thousands in the Maluku Islands, West Papua and Aceh, and driving many more thousands from their homes. An ominous aspect of this was conflict between Muslim and Christian communities, which are roughly equal in numbers in the eastern islands.

A decision early in 2001 to delegate many functions, including health, education, water supply, mining and forestry to the country's 364 regencies – local areas – has tended to decentralize corruption rather than authority. This has been a considerable deterrent for foreign investment, creating even more complicated hierarchies which must be bribed by those seeking to do business in Indonesia. There was a direct outflow of \$1.7 billion in foreign investment in 2002.

On 12 October 2002, a firebomb made from the fertilizer nitrate of ammonia and fuel oil killed 200 people in the nightclub strip of the popular tourist destination of Kuta Beach, Bali. This atrocity, committed by Islamic extremists, became linked into the worldwide 'war against terror' resulting from the World Trade Center attacks in New York. The United States and Australia softened their previous hard line against the Indonesian military, resulting in a significant increase in army power. In Indonesia's first direct presidential elections in 2004 former general Susilo Bambang Yudhoyono was elected, and re-elected for a second term in 2009. A career soldier, he was Minister for Mines in the Wahid administration. Importantly, he publicly renounced the idea that the army should be involved in politics, saying 'there is no so-called social political mission in the military'. He holds a Ph.D. in agricultural economics.

In 2004 a massive earthquake and tsunami devastated northern Sumatra, including the city of Aceh, killing 240,000 people, making almost a million homeless and ruining much arable land by salt water inundation. In 2005 the peace deal between the government and the Aceh insurgents ended the long rebellion there.

Four major influences on the present and future Indonesia can be identified. One is the hold the army and the financial elite from the Suharto era still have on the community. Closely associated with this is the second – the apparent inability of that government to effectively control the country and its affairs. Increasingly administration is being exercised regionally, as often as not by local elements of the army. Third must be the continued poverty and economic inequality. Fourth is the growing strength of extremist Islamic groups in society, and the tacit support of them by both the government and sections of the military.

Will Indonesia survive as a single, united state? The risk of balkanization is real enough. Dissent in a number of regional areas, especially Aceh and Indonesian Papua, is being suppressed only by force or the threat of force from the army. While there is nominal peace in Aceh, demands for autonomy and control of the region's oil and gas revenues have not really gone away. There is a suppressed independence movement in West Papua. Credible evidence emerged in 2001 that a UN-sponsored referendum of the people there was 'just a whitewash', in which only 1022 hand-picked supporters, overseen by the army, voted unanimously for integration with Indonesia, while a million more had no choice at all. Dialogue with the Papuans effectively ended in 2003, to be replaced by harsh military rule. The army's special force, Kopassus, which has been involved in several well-documented atrocities over the years, was again operating in Papua, as also was the extremist Islamic militia Laskar Jihad.

30 Malaysia, Singapore and Brunei

Malaysia is a new nation in more ways than one – her development as an organized community has taken place almost entirely within the last century and a half. Kuala Lumpur, the capital, and now the major centre of population and industry, was settled only after tin was discovered there in 1860. In the late 19th century the total population was a small fraction of the current 30 million, probably well under a million people. They were mostly seafaring tribesmen who lived in wood and *attap*-thatched villages straggling along the muddy banks of river estuaries. Apart from the brief and limited traditions of Malacca and Johore there was little sense of nationhood.

Peninsular Malaya, the central state of today's Malaysia, was important to the British East India Company in the first half of the 19th century because of three settlements along the west and south coasts, established as staging posts on the trade route to China: George Town on the mountainous island of Penang, Malacca and the island of Singapore.

Britain was uninterested then in the jungle-clad, largely mountainous and lightly populated interior. Here were no large, fertile delta areas, significant mines of gold or precious stones, no developed societies that might provide sources of raw materials and a market for manufactures. The climate was hot, humid and enervating, most of the soil poor. There were no roads, much less railways, and except for a few miles on either side of the river estuaries, the bulk of the snake- tiger- and leech-infested country was inaccessible. It swarmed with the deadly *Anopheles* mosquito, as yet not identified as the carrier of malaria. Most of this country had never been explored, and there seemed little incentive for either Malay or European to do so. There was no land traffic between the east and west coasts, which are divided by ranges of high, steep and rugged mountains.

The opening of the Suez Canal in 1869 brought Malaya into much greater strategic and economic prominence. In 1867 the passage from London to Singapore was 116 days. Three years later a passage of 42 days was recorded. In spite of the forbidding death rate from malaria, rural poverty in their home country drove tens of thousands of Chinese to

Malaya as indentured coolies, mostly to work in tin mines in the northern states of Perak and Selangor. Up till then Malay mining had been small-scale and intermittent. Chinese labour and Chinese methods developed the industry so that by the end of the century it was the world's largest producer. The biggest migrations of Chinese were in the 1860s, when tens of thousands crowded into the shabby, lawless camps that grew up around the mines.

With scant law in up-country Malaya other than the knife and the gun, individual miners were more than willing to swear oaths of allegiance to a number of competing Chinese secret societies. These societies soon became rich and powerful, their rivalry bitter and violent. Pitched battles were frequent; members of one society boasted that their shirts were dyed with the blood of their rivals. Initiates were bound, as they still are today, to obey orders without question and to reveal absolutely no information about the society, on pain of death.

These circumstances laid the foundation for a Malayan society with a wealthy and influential Chinese minority numbering about a quarter of the population, within which secret criminal societies like the Triad prospered, exacting 'squeeze' from shopkeepers, running brothels and engaging in illegal smuggling. They beat up opponents with bicycle chains, and killed with the knife. There is still a deep underlying mistrust between the Chinese and Malay peoples.

During these formative decades struggles for power, plundering of neighbours and warfare were almost incessant among the Malay prince-lings. As new and productive tin fields came on line, so also did disputes as to who should get the royalties. Piracy off the coast became more impudent and common, with armed guards on merchant shipping regularly having to fight off attacking boats. General lawlessness in the end persuaded British authorities to intervene in 'up-country' affairs. In 1873 the authorities in Singapore were required 'to employ such influence as they possess with the native princes to rescue these countries from the ruin that must befall them if the present disorders continue unabated'. The provision, from 1874 on, of residents to advise local rulers led to an extension of British rule throughout the country. Dynastic squabbles were skilfully exploited by British diplomats to this end. The Malay rulers were obliged to accept British 'advice' in all matters except those relating to Islamic religion and custom.

By this time British interest was increased by two events that must be considered milestones. The first was the identification of *Anopheles* as the vector of malaria, and the development of measures to control it. The second was the introduction of the rubber tree from its native Brazil and recognition that here was one export crop that would thrive on Malaya's poor soils, and for whose service there was an adequate pool of cheap labour. The mass production of the car made all the difference to the infant rubber industry. It boomed from 1906 onwards, and by 1937 Malaya had more than two million acres of rubber plantations, exporting nearly three-quarters of a million tons a year.

For the first time, it became practicable for British planters to make a life for themselves and their families in the interior. Roads and railways were built, the coastal plain west of the mountains was cleared and cultivated and inland cities like Kuala Lumpur and Ipoh grew and prospered. Kuala Lumpur acquired a curious collection of public buildings, like the Jame Mosque, in the north Indian Mogul style, because in most cases the architects were Englishmen trained in India. An agreement with Thailand in 1909 resulted in four northern states, Perlis, Kedah, Kelantan and Trengannu being transferred to British Malaya. This event almost doubled the area of Malaya at the expense of its neighbour, although the Thais were happy enough to get rid of much of the troublesome Malay/Muslim minority in the south.

Although a Communist party was founded in 1930, largely among the Chinese, no independence movement evolved comparable to those in India or Indonesia. The multi-racial nature of the society was partly responsible for this. There was also by now a large minority of Tamil labourers from India, who had been imported to tap the latex sap from the rubber trees, and whose descendants now make up 8 per cent of the population. Although the world depression of the 1930s caused setbacks, life and progress continued in an orderly way – the Malaya of Somerset Maugham's novels, a placid plantation life made up of the casual social round in the Europeans' bungalows, with their wide verandas and slow-moving ceiling fans. By 1940 the population had grown to four million.

In 1941 the Pacific war burst on this peaceful scene without warning. The Japanese landed in the northern state of Kelantan only the day after the US fleet was crippled in Pearl Harbor and quickly extended their bridgehead. Early in 1942 Singapore fell. The Japanese failure to maintain preventive health services resulted in a major flare-up of malaria. The invaders treated Malaya's people with the same brutality they exhibited elsewhere in occupied south-east Asia, but reserved their especial vindictiveness for the Chinese.

A resistance movement, largely Communist, grew up among the Chinese, and continued in jungle hideaways during British reoccupation of Malaya. In 1948 the Emergency, a bitter, protracted war between the Communist independent platoons and the colonial government, began. Soon the countryside took on a wartime aspect. The villages were surrounded by 8-foot-high barbed-wire perimeter fences, closely guarded and floodlit and under curfew at night.

Working in Malaya during the last years of the Emergency, I shared the stringent conditions imposed on everyone driving a car – the order to be inside a wired perimeter by nightfall or be fired on, not to stop between villages, not to carry food, money, canvas, plastic sheeting, writing paper, typewriters, arms and a host of other things considered useful to the Communists. The Emergency dragged on largely because it was as much a Chinese as a Communist initiative. I was once a guest at a dinner of a number of wealthy Chinese in Penang, where several of the company drank so much they literally fell off their chairs, female staff of the restaurant discreetly carrying them off to bed in specially prepared rooms. One of these, a Chinese banker, after considerable brandy remarked to me: 'Ah … it is *our* army in the jungle.'

Political events were finally more effective in ending the Emergency than the very costly and often counter-productive military ones, which had included herding much of the population into concentration camps. Whole villages were forcibly depopulated, a melancholy sight as one drove through the country. The misery and poverty caused by this British army policy did much to ensure that the Communist independent platoons had so many willing recruits they were able to keep up their numbers throughout the Emergency.

All three major Asian communities formed political associations dedicated to the task of achieving independence as a parliamentary democracy. The coming of internal self-government in 1955 was unexpected. The intention of the British government was that only limited powers be given to those chosen in Malaya's first general elections in that year. However, the Alliance Party, representing all three racial groups, won 51 of the 52 elective seats, a result so eloquent that its leader, Tengku Abdul Rahman, was able to get an undertaking for full independence as soon as possible. On 31 August 1957, Malaya became an independent dominion within the British Commonwealth. It was fortunate in its first leader. A Malay prince, an educated, kindly man very aware of the risk of communal violence, one of his most eloquent acts was the adoption of Chinese orphans into his family.

Since independence deprived the Communist rebellion of any rationale, only isolated trouble spots remained and the state of emergency was officially ended in 1960. Nevertheless, the Communist leader, Chin Peng, and a small army of his most loyal and fanatical followers retreated to the jungle-clad hills at the Thai border, finally announcing the end of their armed struggle in 1989.

A major step forward was taken in 1963 with the inclusion of the British colonies of Singapore, Sarawak and Sabah with Malaya in an extended federation, called Malaysia. Oil-rich Brunei declined to become a member. Because it is mostly Chinese, the city-state of Singapore eventually, however, also elected to become an independent republic, leaving Malaysia in 1965.

Modern Singapore, a 'controlled' democracy, is nevertheless an extraordinary testament to what its architect, Lee Kuan Yew, calls 'Asian values'. Not only do five and a half million people live on this tiny island of only 250 square miles, but they do so in economic and social conditions that are almost unrivalled globally. Life expectancy at birth was 82 years in 2013 – the fourth best rate in the world, with literacy at 92.5 per cent. This is the more remarkable because the island lacks natural resources – the soil is mostly poor, and Singapore relies for most of its water on neighbouring Malaysia, to which the island is connected by a causeway. Almost all food is imported.

During the 1950s the Foreign Correspondents' Association of South-east Asia had regular lunches at the Hôtel de l'Europe (the Cockpit) in Singapore. Here I saw and occasionally exchanged a few words with a young, smartly dressed Chinese lawyer whom everyone knew as Harry Lee. You would not call him Harry now. In 1955 Lee Kuan Yew achieved the highest vote of any individual candidate in an election for an assembly in Singapore, one of three members of the left-wing People's Action Party (PAP) to be elected. The PAP, however, split into two factions, one the moderates under Lee Kuan Yew and the other a Communist 'front'. This early assembly had limited powers, but Britain extended these to full internal self-government in 1959. Lee Kuan Yew's remarkable charisma and political acumen were demonstrated then, when he attracted enormous applause by speaking to a large audience of Singaporeans in Malay after some less well-received speeches by others in English.

A general election later that year gave the PAP a landslide victory, but its internal divisions left Lee's moderates with a majority of only one. For a time the other party, the Socialist Front, seemed likely to take over the government. However, a general election in 1963 gave Lee's party 37 seats out of 51 after he undertook to provide 'performance, not promises. The millions of the dispossessed in Asia care not and know not of theory. They want a better life, a more equal and a more just society.'

The task facing the new government was far from easy. There were serious communal riots in that year – the former colony was ethnically divided, Chinese, Malay and Indian, and short of modern infrastructure and adequate housing for most of its people.

A remarkable combination of ruthlessness, efficiency and, it would seem, benevolent intent enabled Lee to continue to dominate Singapore, and to become a world figure during the next three decades. By using actions in the courts and both subtle and not-so-subtle coercion to destroy opposition in the parliament, he came close to being a one-man government. In 1968 the PAP won all 58 seats – 51 per cent of them unopposed – and has remained the government ever since. The PAP prides itself on its pragmatism. Its blend of parliamentary democracy and targeted restriction of the freedoms and political rights of the people gives it virtually unfettered power to mould the community in the ways it feels best. There would be no long-haired youth, 'decadent' music and dancing were forbidden, no one must spit in the streets, Confucian values such as respect for parents and family solidarity would apply, very severe sanctions, including the death penalty, were introduced for drug use and trafficking. Efficiency, hard work and reliability became the established virtues.

On this basis Lee Kuan Yew transformed Singapore from a ramshackle Chinese provincial city on a south-east Asian island into a modern, wealthy and influential post-industrial nation. Its former thatched shanty towns – so often the scene of horrific fires – and crowded terraces of Chinese shophouses were torn down and replaced by rows of modern high-rise apartments and a central business district skyline of tall office towers. Public transport and education facilities are among the best in the world.

A virtual obsession with hygiene transformed the city from one of many smells (it must be admitted) to a clean, aseptic metropolis, with the best educated, healthiest and most prosperous population in Asia. For instance, it is an offence not to flush a public toilet in Singapore – a small detail of strict laws controlling air and water quality and public hygiene. Singapore has a severe and harsh legal system by world standards. Its government justifies this by pointing to the island's very low crime rate.

Singapore's economic miracle derives almost entirely from the intelligence, hard work and intense competitiveness of its people, three-quarters of whom are Chinese. Something of its nature can be deduced from the fact that almost three-quarters of GDP derives from services, mostly in the fields of finance, business, trade and tourism. All but a small fraction of the remainder comes from manufacturing. Much of this, especially electronics, is in the 'smart' category, with considerable attention given to information technology, although there is a wide variety of other products from small and medium-sized enterprises. In 2012 these were suffering from competition from lower-wage countries such as Vietnam – this was considered a factor in Singapore's reduced growth – just 1.3 per cent in 2012, with a further contraction in the first quarter of 2013. In recent years there has been considerable emphasis on attracting research establishments with tax breaks and other incentives.

In spite of a check to Singapore's prosperity due to the Asian economic crisis, the PAP was elected for a further five-year term in November 2001, winning 82 of 90 elective seats. At that stage it had been the government for 39 years. Lee Kuan Yew's eldest son, Lee Hsien Loong, became prime minister in 2004 at the age of 52. Lee senior and the former prime minister for 14 years, Gho Chok Tong, remained, however, as the next most senior ministers in the Cabinet, the trio irreverently styled by some Singaporeans the Trinity – father, son and holy Gho. Lee Hsien Loong's wife, Ho Ching, is head of Temasek Holdings, a huge corporation through which the government controls much of the island's business and considerable overseas investments. Another son, Lee Hsien Yang, heads the big communications enterprise, Singtel.

One of Singapore's major problems, which it shares with other prosperous countries, is a birth rate so low that it threatens a declining and ageing population. In 2012 families averaged only 1.2 children, well below the replacement rate of 2.1. Characteristically, it was the government that took on the job of coaxing young Singaporeans into a greater interest in the 'birds and bees', with a publicity campaign including steamy love songs on the radio designed to counter a lack of interest in sex (which an official survey claimed happens only once every five days, on average). In 2013 the government introduced high cash bonuses for babies, paid paternity leave, and priority allocation of new flats as part of a $2 billion a year programme to encourage Singaporeans to have more children.

In 1841 the Sultan of Brunei gave the Borneo territory of Sarawak to an English adventurer, Captain James Brooke, in return for Brooke's help in subduing 'pirates'. The Brooke family ruled Sarawak from its *istana* (palace) in the river capital of Kuching for 105 years; over its door was the motto 'What I have I hold'. After some hesitation, the British government recognized this dynasty of 'white rajahs' in 1864 and granted British protection in 1888. After the Second World War the third rajah ceded Sarawak to the British Crown in return for a generous life pension. The Brooke rule was largely benign, concerned with preserving the traditional way of life of Sarawak – it has seven major ethnic groups – and protecting it from foreign exploitation.

The first elections were held in 1959 to establish a degree of self-rule under a legislative assembly called the Council Negri. Elections for the state government in this territory of two and a half million people have since resulted in coalitions of parties representing the major ethnic groups. Sarawak is relatively wealthy. It is one of the world's main exporters of hardwood timber while the oil and gas company, Petronas, has reserves of the equivalent of almost 30 billion barrels of oil.

Sabah, formerly North Borneo, neighbours Sarawak and, like that territory, shares a wild mountain border with Indonesian Kalimantan. Most of this has never been explored. Sabah has more than three million people, of whom 300,000 are Chinese and the rest native tribes, the Murut, Kadazan and Bajau being among the most numerous. Like Sarawak, Sabah came under British protection in 1888 and, with the small island of Labuan off its coast, became a Crown colony after the Second World War. Sabah suffered three years of Japanese occupation in that war, during which the capital, Sandakan, was virtually destroyed. It became a part of Malaysia in 1963. Like Sarawak, Sabah has an essentially agricultural economy, exporting timber, palm oil and rubber. A flourishing eco-tourist industry is supported by Sabah's six wild national parks, the best known being the world-heritage-listed Kinabalu National Park. More than two million tourists a year visit it.

Severe racial rioting in Kuala Lumpur in 1969, in which 200 people were killed, led to a suspension of the Malaysian parliament for two years and a general tightening of law and order procedures. Because of these social disturbances the government decided that Malaysia's democracy should become 'controlled'. When parliament resumed in 1971 the constitution was amended to stress Malay dominance, Malay would be the national language and Islam the official religion. The media, even parliament and the law courts, became subject to government control. A consequence of such evident racial tensions has been government preoccupation with the ethnic issue, especially the continuing situation in which most business and money is controlled by Chinese and Indians, with considerable poverty among the Malays. In 1970 over half of Malays were estimated to be below the poverty level, but as a result of government intervention to admit them into occupations formerly dominated by non-Malays, this is now said to have been reduced to under 20 per cent. There was a further outbreak of communal violence in Kuala Lumpur in 2001, in which at least 12 people were killed.

'Controlled' democracy has continued, and had hardened into outright authoritarianism by the late 1980s. The fourth prime minister, Mahathir

Mohamad, who took office in 1981, used Malaysia's draconic internal security laws – a hangover from the Emergency – to close down four newspapers and arrest 119 political opponents and independent-minded journalists in 1987. More were to follow during the next decade. People arrested under these laws could be and were imprisoned without trial. Since that time Malaysia has had a sycophantic and compliant press, and political opposition has been severely discouraged. Mahathir, the first Malaysian leader to challenge continued British economic patronage, made vigorous attempts to reduce the dominance of British companies in the rubber industry by acquiring their shares and placing them in a state-owned corporation, Permodalan. Foreign ownership of the modern sectors of the economy, more than half in 1970, is now well under a quarter.

The government has worked steadily to increase both the wealth and the status of the Malays and other indigenous peoples, who make up more than 60 cent of the population. There is now a numerous and visible Malay middle class.

The collapse of the economy in 1997 and the attendant hardships caused increasing discontent with government authoritarianism. As elsewhere in Asia, people were prepared to tolerate it as long as they were modestly prosperous – what has been succinctly described as 'Shut up and I'll let you get rich.' In 1998 this discontent coalesced around the person of the dismissed deputy prime minister, Anwar Ibrahim, leading to extensive demonstrations and pitched battles between the 'rioters' and the police. There was widespread criticism of members of the government said to be involved in 'crony capitalism'.

Anwar, who had attracted worldwide respect for his moderate and enlightened attitudes, had been expected to succeed the ageing Mahathir. Instead Mahathir dismissed Anwar, who was immediately charged with a variety of offences and imprisoned. When he appeared in court with head injuries inflicted by the arresting police, many world leaders – even those of some other Asian countries – spoke out in his support. Anwar was not alone in this predicament. Hundreds of the thousands who regularly took to the streets to support him were beaten or arrested.

Early in 1999 Anwar was sentenced to six years in prison, following a bizarre trial which raised considerable doubts about the Malaysian system of justice. However, Dr Mahathir was returned to power in an election later that year, although with a reduced majority. He stepped down late in 2003. In an election early the following year his successor, Abdullah Badawi, achieved a resounding victory. The government won 198 seats of 219 in the parliament, and the Islamic party, PAS, retained only 7 of the 27 it had won in 1999. This was widely interpreted as a vote for the status quo and an indication of public fears of Islamic fundamentalism, but the result must also have been influenced by the considerable restrictions imposed on opposition parties in conditions of 'controlled' democracy. Anwar was released from prison in 2004, but under Malaysian law could not occupy any political office again until 2008. However he resumed his political career in that year, winning a by-election and returning to Parliament as Leader of the Opposition. General elections in 2008 gave the government its worst electoral result ever, with the opposition taking one-third of the seats. Anwar faced further sodomy charges that year and two years of litigation, after which he was found not guilty.

Badawi resigned the premiership in 2009, when his deputy, Najib Razak took over. Although Razak is a strong supporter of Malay interests – he is president of the United Malay National Organisation (UMNO) – he tried to project a moderate image. Nevertheless the government made two cash handouts to almost six million poorer households in the run-up to the 2013 elections – these were widely criticized as a 'vote-buying' exercise.

Campaigning for that election, Anwar undertook to set up a strong anti-corruption commission to investigate the awarding of billions of dollars in government contracts to businesses with links to officials. Saying Malaysia called itself a democracy but 'was clearly authoritarian', he promised a return for Malaysians to the rights of free expression and religion.

Although the government won only 47 per cent of the votes cast and the opposition a clear majority at more than 50 per cent, the government secured another term in the 2013 elections, which Anwar described as 'clearly fraudulent'. Electoral boundaries in Malaysia include much smaller numbers of voters in rural electorates than urban ones – hence the vote of an uneducated *bumiputra* (son of the soil) in a remote village is effectively worth those of several research scientists or top business people in a city like Kuala Lumpur or Penang. There was plainly a racial division in this election, with Chinese and urban voters largely favouring the opposition and rural, poorer Malays the government. Bersih, an organization which campaigns for free and fair elections, commenced an enquiry to look into 'widespread ballot-tampering and the presence of "phantom" foreign voters using illegal identity cards'.

Hundreds of thousands attended a series of protest rallies, at which Anwar said there was evidence to challenge the election result in 29 seats. However, the government reacted quickly, using its draconian police powers to arrest three opposition politicians and activists and destroying hundreds of copies of opposition newspapers.

Malaysia's prosperity has revived substantially since 2000, following a temporary isolation of its economy from the international system and the injection of millions of dollars into industry in the form of low-interest loans. An advanced high-tech industry in electronics earns more than half of export income. In 2013 social and economic indicators were good, with foreign reserves at $131 billion, life expectancy in the 70s, per capita GDP above $7000, and population growth around 2 per cent. Successful offshore exploration for oil and gas after 1970 has greatly assisted the economy. Reserves are estimated at 5 billion barrels of oil and 80 billion cubic feet of gas – hydrocarbons make up nearly 10 per cent of Malaysia's export income. Palm-oil plantations began to replace the less profitable rubber estates. Manufacturing has become the most important area of export income from the mid-1990s.

Brunei, one of the world's last absolute monarchies and one of its wealthiest states, stands out in vivid contrast. The population in 2011 was 393,000, occupying some 2000 square miles of the Borneo coast. Brunei has rich oilfields, which have provided its rulers with extravagant wealth and its population an enviable array of free or very cheap social services.

Brunei's era of glory was the 16th century, when the sultanate is believed to have controlled most of Borneo and many islands in the Sulu Sea which are now part of the Philippines. It became a notorious haven for piracy until the middle of the 19th century, when the British navy destroyed the pirate fleets. Brunei's territory and influence had declined by then, and when it became a British protectorate in 1888, it was no more than a tiny, poor and obscure Muslim principality on the banks of a muddy estuary. Since oil was found near the coast at Seria in 1929, it has brought in so much money in royalties the state has had difficulty spending it. A banker in Brunei once told me that the whole population could live comfortably into the indefinite future on the income from its overseas investments.

Whether this remains the case depends on how the royal family spends the oil revenues in the future. The sultan is one of the richest men in the world, with assets at one time of about $50 billion. His current wealth is estimated to be less than half that – around $20 billion. A decline in Brunei's fortunes has been partly due to huge spending by the royal family, often to the benefit of the people, but at times on luxury items for themselves. Collecting rare and limited edition cars is the sultan's hobby. A huge 'palace of cars' accommodates more than 7000 of the world's finest, worth an estimated $5 billion. There are more than 500 Mercedes-Benz, one of which is gold-plated. His *istana* – the official residence – is said to have 1788 rooms and 257 bathrooms, the largest residential palace in the world. The town of

Brunei has a huge marble mosque, completed in 1958 to look like the Taj Mahal, modern schools, hospitals and roads. Education is free, and there is no income tax. Rice and housing are subsidized. Medical treatment is free for the military, the police and children. Small charges apply for other people.

However, with reduced output from its oilfields to increase their productive life, Brunei was suffering from its first economic problems by the turn of the millennium. In 2000 the sultan's younger brother, Prince Jefri Bolkiah, who had been finance minister, faced a lawsuit to recover $15 billion he had spent on such items as luxury hotels, jewellery, cars, aircraft and gold-plated hairbrushes. The prince settled for an allowance of $300,000 a month, and left Brunei to live in Europe. The following year an auction of his possessions was held in Brunei, raising nearly $8 million. Items on sale included a 12-foot-high bronze rocking horse, grand pianos, mirrors, antique cannon and a marble factory. However, in spite of some financial troubles, in 2010 Brunei had a gross domestic product of $17 billion, international reserves of $1.56 trillion, and a per capita GDP of $40,000. Other social indicators are high, with literacy at 91 per cent.

Brunei became an independent state in 1983 after almost a hundred years of British protection, and has close relations with Singapore, including training of defence forces. It has spent at least $2 billion on modern defensive weapons systems, such as Exocet missiles.

Earlier, in 1959, Brunei had achieved internal self-government, with three tiers of government. Of these, only the district councils were elective. The left-wing Parti Rakyat Brunei (PRB) emerged with policies for democracy and the unifying of the three north Borneo states, under the leadership of Ahman Azahari. It became a major force after achieving a large percentage of the vote in district council elections in 1962. However, when Azahari declared himself prime minister of a new state of North Borneo and announced an armed struggle, the sultan acted at once, retaining power with the help of British forces from Singapore. The PRB was proscribed and its leaders imprisoned or forced into exile. From this time onwards the sultan ruled by decree, Brunei thus becoming one of the world's few remaining absolute monarchies. Not surprisingly, it has one of the most restrictive immigration policies in the world.

31 Japan: the Iron Triangle

The opening of Japan to trade with the rest of the world after almost three centuries of isolation, and her rapid progress from a seemingly rigid feudalism to a Western-style capitalist economy, made her a major world power within a single generation. This was without doubt a revolution, although quite different from others in colonial Asia. Even so, the transformation of Japanese society after she had concluded the first trade treaties with the West in 1854 was not as sudden as it seemed. Feudalism, already far into decay, was ready to collapse at a touch.

In the decade after the 'opening of Japan' society became even more fluid. Western merchants took advantage of Japanese inexperience by exploiting the *bakufu's* unrealistic exchange rate between gold and silver, more than twice that on world markets. Foreign traders made huge profits and there was a tremendous, destabilizing drain on Japan's gold reserves. This, coupled with similar manipulation of other exportable commodities, caused disastrous rises in the cost of living (rice increasing twelvefold, raw silk trebling) in eight years.

As a result, the decision to admit foreign traders provoked widespread and increasing hostility. In 1863 the large and powerful Choshu clan fired on American, Dutch and French ships from its shore batteries dominating the narrow and strategic Straits of Shimonoseki. The following year a Western fleet retaliated by destroying the batteries. Choshu, a clan traditionally opposed to the *bakufu*, now placed themselves firmly behind the emperor. Armed with 7000 modern rifles bought from the West, in 1866 they defeated a *bakufu* army easily. The following year the *shogun*, making a realistic assessment of the facts, abdicated voluntarily.

In 1868 the 16-year-old emperor, advised by a clique largely of Choshu men and their allies the Satsuma – both clans with a higher proportion of *samurai* than the average – announced his assumption of full authority. Choshu were later to lead the development of a modern Japanese army, Satsuma a modern navy. This elevation of the emperor to lead the nation was confirmed by important changes in the state ethic. Confucianism and the various cults of Buddhism, which had been popular during the

266

Tokugawa period, were officially displaced, and Shinto, the animist religion of the ancient Japanese, restored to primacy.

However, Shinto now more than ever became not only a religion but a national cult, designed to promote belief in the virtual divinity, infallibility and invincibility of the emperor and the duty of every Japanese, if necessary, to die for him. The state machine insisted that everyone believe the myths of Japanese creation, asserting divine origin of the imperial line and the uniqueness and purity of the Japanese people. Even to question this 'emperor system' invited severe punishment. Archaeologists whose work indicated quite different conclusions about Japanese prehistory were effectively silenced until after the end of the Second World War in 1945.

The fact that the Western powers, with their modern weapons, had been able to force Japan into trade, and their own inability to resist, made a deep impression on the Japanese. Envoys sent out to study the outside world recommended that Japan adopt Western science, trade methods and industry as quickly as possible. The feudal system was officially dismantled, and the *daimyo* ceded their lands to the emperor. In 1868 the latter moved his court to Edo, which was renamed Tokyo, 'eastern capital'. The new era, called Meiji after the reign name taken by the emperor, led to the transformation and modernization of Japan at a breakneck pace. However, there was nothing democratic about the new order – Japan became effectively a police state, in which the police saw themselves as substantially occupying the position previously held by the *samurai*. Universal conscription was introduced for the armed services.

In 1871 the *samurai* lost their notorious right to 'kill and go away' and in 1877, 30,000 of their number died in a rebellion that was put down by a modern army consisting mainly of commoners. Torture as a routine legal practice was abolished in 1876. Farmers were permitted to ride horses on public roads, and to own, buy and sell land, but were required to pay a third of the yield of their crops in tax. Japan was linked to the outside world by cable telegraph, gas lit the streets of Yokohama in 1872, railways spread across the country and urban complexes, complete with steel mills, power plants and other appurtenances of the modern industrial state, grew rapidly.

All this was achieved with money wrung from the heavily taxed peasantry and young women and men who worked in textile mills and coal mines for long hours on very small wages – almost as slaves. Infanticide became common, many families killing all but the first boy and girl at birth because they could afford to feed no more. There are contemporary accounts of peasants who decapitated their starving children, unable to bear their suffering. But among the wealthier urban classes Western styles of dress, Western methods and designs and Western manners were carefully studied and emulated. The Japanese word for a Western-style business suit, *sevilo*, derives from Savile Row.

But to attribute all this to a mere passion for copying is to miss the point. The motive was astute appreciation that only by change could Japan survive as an independent nation. The Japanese did not copy the West so much because they admired it as from a desire to put themselves in a position to compete with it in material terms. The carefully restored Shinto cult was a conscious rejection of Western, indeed all foreign, cultural ideas.

Japan's new leaders were determined she should be strong. A powerful modern navy was built in British shipyards and trained by British officers, and an army was developed on the German model. A major difficulty was the position of the two million *samurai*. Eventually the class was dispersed as such, although much of its tradition was carried over into new occupations, such as police and military officers, teachers and bureaucrats. This term, rather than 'public servant', is used because the Japanese bureaucracy did not see itself as servants of the people. There is a saying, *kanson mimpi*, which means 'official exalted, people despised'.

And indeed, conditions of life and work for the ordinary people were appalling. Impoverished peasant families virtually sold their daughters into indentured labour in cotton mills and weaving sheds. Ninety per cent of workers in these 'sweated' industries were women, 13 per cent of them under the age of 14. They normally worked 12 hours a day, but workdays of up to 19 hours were not uncommon. Living in crowded and unsanitary dormitories, they fell victim to tuberculosis in millions – one 1913 statistic puts death from this disease as high as 40 per cent of factory workers, and 70 per cent among those who later retired to their villages.

The Mitsui Company's coal mines were effectively a hell on earth. Failure to meet unreasonably high work quotas in the dangerous and hot, humid conditions incurred beatings or even worse punishment, including torture. And these conditions did not just apply to men. Women and children were sent down the mines – some as young as 10. Women were defined by law as second-class citizens and exploited in every possible way, including the sale of girls from impoverished peasant families into the public brothels found in every major city. Women were educated and trained to be 'docile and modest' and to subordinate themselves completely to their husbands and their families.

Decisive land and sea victories over China and Russia established Japan as a world power – moreover, as an imperialist power, conquering and assuming control of Korea, Manchuria and Taiwan. The Koreans opposed Japanese occupation vigorously – 12,000 resistance fighters were killed in 1907 and 1908. Although the forms of parliamentary democracy had been established in Japan in 1890, they had little effect until in 1925 universal male suffrage was introduced. However, by then two major catastrophes were affecting Japan. One was the world economic depression, the other Japan's worst natural disaster until Fukushima – the 1923 earthquake and fire that destroyed most of Tokyo and Yokohama and killed more than 150,000 people. Because of a rumour that Koreans had started the fire, almost 3000 Koreans were killed by lynch mobs. These economic and natural disasters brought in a period of harsh repression of such people as labour leaders and socialists, many of whom were executed.

By the middle of the decade militarism, which had seemed to be in decline after the First World War, was again in the ascendant. From May 1925 every school of middle grade or upward had a military officer on the active list attached to it. To the new generation educated to a fanatical nationalism, moderate policies seemed only to be weakness. During the 1930s the army acted as a force above and beyond the law. A series of brutal assassinations of senior Japanese statesmen by young army officers occurred in 1932, with more such murders four years later. From then on the army, led by General Tojo, took over Japan.

Open war and invasion of China in 1937 involved atrocities that brought protests from around the world. The sacking of the Nationalist capital, Nanjing, was especially brutal. Japanese soldiers killed civilians, including women and children, mostly by the sword, and the Yangzi River, which passes through the city, was said to have literally run red with blood. The Chinese claim there were 300,000 dead. Eyewitnesses told of groups of up to 20 young people being tied together and thrown into the river to drown, people buried up to the waist in the ground then torn to pieces by Alsatians, and bizarre biological research, including injections of plague, anthrax and cholera.

In 1940 Japan placed herself on a complete war footing. The political parties were disbanded, making Japan totally subordinate to the military. A Japanese air attack on Hawaii's Pearl Harbor late in 1941 caused the loss of eight American battleships, three cruisers and at least half the effective air power of the Pacific Fleet, and brought Japan into four years of war that would ultimately prove disastrous. In spite of fanatical resistance, the Japanese were forced back from their initial Pacific conquests, which had brought them to New Guinea, the very doorstep of Australia. Damage to Tokyo was so great from aerial bombing, including probably the most severe fire bombing in human history, that its population fell from seven to three million due to casualties and evacuation. In July 1945 the Western Allies called on Japan to surrender unconditionally.

On 6 August 1945 an atomic bomb that would ultimately cause 200,000 deaths was dropped on the Japanese city of Hiroshima. Three days later a similar weapon destroyed Nagasaki. Five more days brought Japan's surrender. In the words of Emperor Hirohito, 'we have resolved to pave the way for peace for all future generations by enduring the unendurable'. Many people, including prominent national leaders and their wives, killed themselves. Thousands knelt outside the imperial palace to beg forgiveness for their insufficient efforts. Yet as a result of the war almost two million people alive in 1940 were now dead, almost nine million homeless.

Japan was ruled for seven years from 1945 by a military occupation force – virtually personal rule by the Supreme Commander for the Allied Powers, General Douglas MacArthur. Japan seemed amenable to changes in direction and its military clique became hated and despised, not so much because of the misery and damage of the war, but because Japan had been defeated.

Basically, occupation policy was to guide Japan into new and democratic ways of government, and to reshape the education system and the economy. The big industrial conglomerates, the *zaibatsu*, were dissolved because of their close association with the military. The emperor became a constitutional monarch, but his popularity grew rather than declined because of these efforts to 'democratize' his position. Many Japanese saw them as attempts to humiliate him, and this increased their feelings of loyalty. When the occupation ended in 1952 he visited the Shrine of the Imperial Ancestors at Ise and reported to them that Japan was again free.

The permanent effects of the MacArthur 'shogunate' were few indeed, since most of its reforms have been reversed. In fact the reconstitution of the *zaibatsu* and the limited restoration of the armed forces began before the Americans left, and with their concurrence. Land reform was perhaps the most valuable and lasting result of the occupation. Peasant ownership of land doubled to almost four million, the beneficiaries being former tenant farmers.

However, there was nothing temporary or illusory about the regeneration of Japan's economy, which began during the occupation and was no less impressive than that of the Meiji restoration. Japan rapidly became the world's biggest shipbuilder, a major car manufacturer, and evolved through heavy industry to become a world leader in information technology. This 'great leap forward' was based substantially on a policy of ploughing profits back into development, rather than dividends. Typical of this was the Sony Corporation, which had humble beginnings in a small Tokyo shed with an initial capital of $500. Riding on the flood tide of demand for transistor radios, it was selling over a billion dollars' worth of its products annually by the 1960s. Japan built the world's largest ship of that era, a tanker of 276,000 tons, and the world's fastest train, the Tokaido bullet train. In 1960 Japan had only 3.5 million cars and most people used an adequate public transport system. Fifty years later 57 million cars choked the roads, creating an urban nightmare of pollution and delays. This motor explosion quickly demanded more and better roads – thousands of miles of highways were built, a major element in what has become known as the concretization of Japan.

An early symptom of this was the destruction in 1967 of Frank Lloyd Wright's Imperial Hotel in Tokyo, internationally regarded as an architectural masterpiece, and so well designed that it was one of only a few buildings to survive the 1923 earthquake. A characterless 17-floor hotel replaced it. The pressure on land became enormous, leading to massive reclamation projects from the sea, such as the new Osaka airport on a wholly artificial island. Tokyo has no natural coastline left at all, and the areas adjacent to it only a few miles.

During the 1970s heavy industry began to run into trouble due to pollution and the sheer lack of suitable sites. The Tokyo–Kobe–Osaka region, the Kansai, in the words of one Japanese environmentalist, was rapidly becoming uninhabitable. Japan commenced a switch to post-industrial, high-tech industries. Strenuous efforts to decentralize these to regional technopolises – entirely new cities – have had varied success.

The massive infrastructure growth in Japan has not been driven so much by demand as by corrupt links between the government, the construction industry and the bureaucracy. This collusion, *yuchaku*, led to several public enquiries, and became so blatant that in 1994 a number of politicians and high-level businessmen were jailed. The investigations revealed that as much as $3 billion a year were being stolen from the frugal and long-suffering Japanese people – much of it going back as contributions to the Liberal-Democratic Party (LDP) government, which had authorized the expenditure in the first place and channelled it to 'suitable' contractors. These would then kick back funds to 'feed the troops', that is, to the vote-buying system of Japanese politics.

This remarkable people, the modern Japanese, had over $2 trillion stashed away in 2012 in the one financial institution they trust – and the world's largest of its kind – the Post Office Savings Bank. By the 1980s, their hard work, obedience and skills had produced an enormous river of money that spilled over from Japan into all parts of the world, but especially into Asia and Australia. Billions of dollars were used to buy land, property and golf courses; new resorts and ski-slopes burgeoned in Japan itself. Huge sums went into overseas investments, mostly in Korea and south-east Asia. When this bubble burst at the end of the decade property values in Japan fell heavily, and Japan entered a phase of financial deflation that persisted as late as 2013.The corruption scandals in the construction and finance industries contributed to loss of office by the LDP in 1993, after 38 years continuously in power. Hopes that this might presage genuine reform of Japanese politics dwindled as four uneasy coalition governments became necessary over as many years, during which Japan's financial situation caused increasing concern. Elections in 1996 brought the LDP back to government, which it retained comfortably in the 2000 elections. In both of these polls barely half of the electorate voted.

However, the *tetsu no sankakukei*, the 'iron triangle' of politician, bureaucrat and big business, appears to have survived intact, as able as ever to resist change, especially if this would threaten its common interest. Fourteen of Japan's 17 major banks stood in need of a financial bail-out because of bad debts incurred during the four recessions of the 1990s. The rescue package cost the government $50 billion. Continued heavy expenditure on often unnecessary infrastructure made Japan the second most indebted nation in the world after the United States, with a public debt of more than $10 trillion in 2013, 230 per cent of GDP. In 1995 an earthquake struck the Kobe area, killing 6000 people and destroying 20 per cent of the houses in the city. It also revealed elements of the construction industry as being more than financially corrupt. Some of the collapses of freeways and bridges were found to be due to bad building and skimping on specified material such as reinforcing steel and concrete. Assistance to the stricken city was much less than adequate, especially since offers of assistance from the outside world were refused. Kobe's experience, tragic enough in itself, also caused a further anxiety: What would happen to the Tokyo area if a similar earthquake occurred?

In 2001 a more flexible and charismatic man than was usual became prime minister. Junichiro Koizumi took over leadership of the LDP government with promises that he would end the party's faction system and revive Japan's economy. However, by the time of the next election at the end of 2003 little seemed to have changed, and the LDP lost support significantly. The main opposition, the Democratic Party, won 177 seats compared to the LDP's 237. The Democrats actually won two million votes more than the LDP, but the result was skewed by a long-standing gerrymander favouring rural voters heavily against city dwellers.

In campaigning at a 2005 election Koizumi's popularity reached its height, and the LDP got its best result for two decades. However, under LDP rules he had to stand down in 2006. His successor, Shinzo Abe, held the office for only a year – Japan had only short-term leaders for some years from this time on. They did little to revive Japan's faltering economy, instead creating income disparities that raised well-publicized fears of *kakusa shakai* –an unequal society.

In 2011 a thousand miles of the east coast of Honshu, Japan's main island, were struck by a massive earthquake and tsunami. Waves over 120 feet high smashed through sea walls to destroy scores of towns and villages. These left 19,000 people dead or missing and severely damaged a major nuclear installation, Fukushima Daiichi. As is the case elsewhere in the world, the Japanese developers of this power complex considered it economically rational to locate six reactors on the same site close to the sea. In an accident unprecedented in history the radioactive cores of three reactors suffered a meltdown, and two years later were still emitting levels of radiation that would be lethal in minutes to anyone approaching them. Because these 'China syndrome' events have never happened before scientists are uncertain about how to deal with them, but are hopeful the three rogue reactors might be cleaned up in perhaps 30 years. Meanwhile in 2013 radiation levels outside reactor 3 measured as high as 15,000 millisieverts a year. The maximum legal human exposure set by the Japanese government is 50 millisieverts a year.

Since no one has been able to find a way to store nuclear waste safely, one of the largest accumulations of high-level waste on the planet is stored in temporary holding ponds at the reactor site. This amounts to more than 1000 reactor units, each of which contain 30 to 50 fuel rods – capable in total of releasing an estimated 85 times the dangerous radioactivity emitted in the Chernobyl disaster. This storage, already damaged, is vulnerable to any future major earthquake. Since it must be flooded with water continuously to avoid a major radiation event, and because of leaks in these containment pools, storage of more than 220,000 tons of radioactive water has become an intractable problem. Unknown quantities have entered the sea, and a fish caught off the Fukushima coast in 2013 was found to have more than 2500 times the safe amount of radioactive caesium. Estimates of the time it is likely to take to make all this radioactive material safe range from 50 to 150 years, and the cost is provisionally estimated at $100 to $250 billion.

More than two years after the disaster 160,000 people were still in cramped emergency accommodation, and apart from clearing up huge amounts of radioactive debris, little had been done to replace the shattered towns from which they came, most of which will remain too dangerous to re-enter for many decades. Children are kept indoors, many families will eat only foreign-sourced food, and a severe social problem has arisen from the virtual ostracizing of refugee families considered to be 'contaminated'.

According the *Guardian Weekly*, as of February 2013 Japan had tested 133,000 children in and around Fukushima who had been exposed to iodine131, and had found abnormal thyroid cysts and nodules in 42 per cent of them. Reports of other tests of up to 57,000 children have revealed a similar result. According to a report in 2013 in the American *Open Journal of Pediatrics*, children on the US West Coast and in Hawaii, which were exposed to fallout from Fukushima, were also at increased risk of developing hyperthyroidism. Iodine 131 ultimately caused thyroid cancer in hundreds of children after the Chernobyl nuclear accident.

The government was forced to declare another nuclear incident in mid-2013 when it admitted that some of the more than 1000 temporary tanks storing radioactive water at Fukushima were leaking 300 tons of contaminated water into the Pacific Ocean every day. Radiation levels on the ground near one set of tanks rose to 2200 millisieverts – a potentially lethal dose in about four hours. Four hundred tons of radioactive water are created every day by the necessary cooling of the damaged installations, and an unknown additional amount comes from groundwater flowing down from the hills behind the plant. Fish from the sea off the plant were found to be contaminated and could not be sold. Strontium90, a bone-seeking isotope, appeared to be a major contaminant.

The Fukushima crisis proved a disaster for the Democratic Party, which had decisively won the election in 2009, and was the government when the earthquake struck. Although the future of nuclear power seemed a major issue in the election of 2012, the result was a landslide win for the LDP, which is in favour of nuclear energy, under the premiership of Shinzo Abe. This unexpected result was attributed to public anger with the government, which struggled to cope with the huge issues raised by the catastrophe, and feelings of insecurity due to the economic downturn it brought.

Shinzo Abe, an avowed conservative, took an immediate hard line over Japan's dispute with China over ownership of offshore islands, and instituted a programme of 'quantitative easing' – effectively the printing of money – designed to stimulate the moribund economy. Bank of Japan Governor Haruhiko Kurada was instructed to 'flood Japan with money' – a policy designed to end creeping deflation. He expected that increases in the monetary base of more than $100 billion a year would create inflation of up to 2 per cent within two years. The share market rose immediately, and the value of the Japanese yen depreciated sharply against other currencies. Over the next two quarters the weaker yen led to increased retail sales, in spite of higher prices, and a 70 per cent increase in the value of equities – 'a most successful application of Keynesian policies', according to Mr Abe.

The health and general welfare of the Japanese has improved vastly since the end of the Second World War. In 1920, one in eight children died as infants. That figure is now four in a thousand. Life expectancy, over 83, is the highest in the world. Like many other industrialized countries, Japan has an ageing population – the present 128 million is predicted to actually decline, to perhaps 90 million by 2060. The number of people of working age – that is, between 15 and 64 years – has been falling steadily from 87 million in 1995 to a predicted 54 million in 2050, with those over 65 rising from a fifth to 40 per cent of the population. On government estimates by 2020 there will be barely two workers to support each retiree, as against three now and four five years ago.

Will Japan revert to the worst aspects of the 'emperor system', with its overtones of military aggression, absolute obedience of the mass of the people to an oligarchy and insistence on the myths of Shinto? Probably not, if only because so many young people are well enough educated and influential enough to resist it. However, the physical means are there – Japan is one of the world's biggest spenders on weapons for its 'self-defence force', a large and modern army, navy and air force using mostly American matériel. There is some evidence of revival of Japanese nationalism, and also considerable pressure on the people and the academic community to believe in the purity and uniqueness of Japanese society. A major Japanese film, *Pride, the Fatal Moment*, was produced in 1998 which presented a picture of the Second World War idealizing the wartime prime minister, General Tojo, who was executed for war crimes in 1946. This film, which showed to capacity audiences in Japan, rewrote history in several important ways, justifying Japan's actions and derogating those of the United States, while ignoring atrocities like the carnage in Nanjing. When the Mayor of Nagasaki publicly acknowledged in 1990 that Emperor Hirohito must bear some responsibility for the war, he was shot in the back in an assassination attempt. In 2001 Japan's neighbours criticized a visit of Japanese Prime Minister Koizumi to the Yasukuni Shrine as provocative, and some Japanese politicians accused him of encouraging a dangerous nationalist trend. The shrine, which honours the war dead, was central to development of the 'emperor system' in the 1930s. In 2003 the Board of Education ordered that the Rising Sun flag be raised and the national anthem sung at all school assemblies 'without fail'. Several hundred school staff were punished for failing to comply. *Kendo* – the way of the sword, which derives from *samurai* fighting methods – is still taught to young people. However, *The New History Textbook*, compiled by a group of right-wing academics in 2000, and widely criticized because it glossed over much of the Second World War history, has been rejected by a majority of Japanese schools. An updated version was, however, again approved in 2006, resulting in another wave of protest from Japan's neighbours, including large demonstrations and attacks on the Japanese Embassy and businesses in China. 'Selective' Japanese histories appeared to be still in use in some schools in 2013, and continued to provoke controversy.

Japanese society remains hierarchic. The most important element is the group – the *dantai* – the least important, the individual person. Almost all decision making is collective – innumerable meetings and conferences are characteristic of Japanese business. Social relationships are rigid and complex, with set forms of language, especially for greetings, to be used between people of different social levels. This is the basis for the generally observed politeness and formality of Japanese people – also the absolute necessity for a *meishi*, a business or calling card, so the social position of a new acquaintance can be established on first meeting.

Something called *nakama*, the cement that holds together the groups to which all Japanese are attracted, be it a workplace, club, school or office, must be permitted to operate smoothly. *Nakama* means 'insider' and in its broadest sense, involving the whole country, includes Japanese and only Japanese. Foreigners, even though they will be treated with formal politeness, are *yosomono*, a mildly derisory term meaning 'outsider', and will remain so no matter how long they live in Japan.

Discrimination does not apply only to foreigners, of whom Koreans are the most substantial group. There is a minority of more than two million Japanese who are the equivalent of India's *dalits* – untouchables. These, the *burakumin*, are the descendants of hereditary low-caste groups who butchered animals, worked with leather, or dealt with the dead. They live in segregated communities in most larger Japanese cities, and suffer severe educational, social and economic disadvantages.

32 Thailand: Two Hats – the Struggle for Democracy

Thailand, as Siam came to be renamed, is in many respects the most advanced state in mainland south-east Asia, in spite of the fact that the succeeding authority to its absolute monarchy has been, effectively, the army. Army officers frequently wear 'two hats', meaning they have another job in the nominally civilian administration. Parliamentary democracy has been regularly punctuated by military coups, although an increasingly educated and assertive middle class has, over the last decade, become less tolerant of the pervasive influence of the military. The Thai armed forces, numbering more than 270,000, nevertheless remain a significant force in the community – even, in the last analysis, the decisive one.

King Mongkut's son, Chulalongkorn, carried on his father's policies of reform with enthusiasm when he inherited the Siamese throne in 1868. At that time there was no proper code of law, no public education system, no organization of state revenue, and no comprehensive road network. During his reign until 1910 Siam acquired these things and more. This was due in part to close relations with Britain as a result of a treaty signed in 1855. While this 'unequal treaty' regulated import and export duties at low levels, it nevertheless guaranteed Siam's status as an independent nation and was the basis of a continuing and, on the whole, progressive British influence.

Chulalongkorn sent his own children abroad to be educated and, with the help of his numerous brothers and sisters, energetically imposed on the nation a veneer, at least, of modernity. Although the nation's quasi-colonial dependence on Britain obliged him to encourage British investment and use British advisers, he was careful to recruit others from several European nations, such as the French and Belgians who helped devise the legal code. Two reforms were typical of him. He ended the custom that obliged subjects to crawl into the royal presence on hands and knees, and abolished slavery. Nevertheless he used the army to reinforce Siam's authority within what are its modern boundaries. Revolts in the Muslim south led by the raja of Pattani, in the

Chiengmai region in the north, and in the north-east, broke out when revenues were diverted from local leaders to the state. However, in 1873 a modern
revenue system was consolidated to replace 'tax farming', and the local lords
became salaried provincial governors. Chinese migration grew rapidly, reaching 10 per cent of the population at the end of Chulalongkorn's reign.

Chulalongkorn is otherwise notable for the adroitness with which he
kept his country out of the hands of any one of the great powers. Even so,
it lost more than 200,000 square miles of territory. French gunboats blockaded Bangkok, forcing Siam to return all territory east of the Mekong River
to the French colonies of Laos and Cambodia. Five years later it surrendered what are now the four northern provinces of Malaysia in return for a
British loan of £4 million to extend the Siamese railway system, ignoring a
protest from the Sultan of Kedah, one of the four, that his state 'had been
bought and sold like a buffalo'.

However, Chulalongkorn refused overtures from a group of 11 Siamese,
including four princes, who had lived abroad, to introduce cabinet government. By the 1930s the absolute monarchy was the last in the world in any
country of consequence, and was increasingly seen as an absurd and
repressive anachronism. In 1931 the king, Prajadhipok, had to go overseas
to be treated for failing eyesight and, when he returned, retired to his
seaside palace at Hua Hin to convalesce. Prince Paripatra acted as regent. It
was a time of considerable interest in the dynasty, because Rama I had
predicted it would last only 150 years. That anniversary, however, passed
without incident on 6 April 1932. Then, early in the morning of 24 June,
tanks rumbled into the grounds of the royal palace in Bangkok and Prince
Paripatra, still in his pyjamas, was taken away to join other members of the
royal family being held hostage by the leaders of a coup.

This 1932 coup, which was almost bloodless, was the work of a group of
114 mostly Western-educated people. Economic problems, compounded
by the effects of the world depression, were a major reason for the move.
Siam had insisted on staying on the gold standard when the rest of the
world had abandoned it, and as a result was pricing herself out of the world
export market for rice and timber. A National Assembly, designed to make
Thailand a modern democracy, was instituted, but it was soon to be
subverted. Although the country was introduced to the idea of representative government with apparent ease, it proved difficult to make it work. It
became necessary to invent words hitherto unknown in the language for
such concepts as revolution, politics, constitution.

The hoped-for democracy never came. One of the leaders of the coup, a
young army captain named Pibul Songgram, who was an admirer of
European fascism and Japanese militarism, took over the country in

another coup. It was he who changed the name of the country from Siam to Muang Thai, which means the land of the free people.

The Thais granted Japan free movement over their territory to invade Malaya during the Second World War, although later they had cause to regret what turned out to be permanent Japanese occupation. Pibul, briefly ousted after the war, was back in charge by 1947. Elections were held ten years later at the insistence of the United States, but were so unashamedly rigged that they led to a major public outcry. Another coup and renewed martial law brought military rule again from 1958.

I was in Bangkok at that time. Near the airport and at street junctions soldiers had dug into foxholes from which machine guns peered, belts of ammunition in the breeches. In the main streets tanks and armoured cars dominated major intersections, although the coup remained bloodless. Soldiers manning the tanks sat out on top of them, regarding the passing crowds in good-natured idleness, or reading newspapers. The public, used to this kind of demonstration, took no notice at all.

General Sarit Thanarat, who thus came to power, did do some useful things. A native of the grossly underdeveloped Isan (north-east), he diverted public funds to what had been a forgotten region, and made some attempts to curb a flourishing opium trade. He liked to walk around the streets handing out fines to people he found throwing fruit peelings on the pavement. However, like those of other Thai strongmen, Sarit's reputation did not long survive his death in 1963. It was disclosed that he had acquired a huge personal fortune, and in 1964 his estate was required to repay most of this to the national treasury.

Military rule carried on more or less continuously for more than half a century. A coup in 1971 that brought another military leader, Thanom Kittikachorn, to power led on to student demonstrations in Bangkok in 1973 and the inception of the first civilian government in 20 years. A proliferation of new political parties and trade unions seemed to promise a significant move towards democracy, but the military took over again in 1976. A short-lived civilian phase ended with yet another military coup in 1991. However, an attempt to install the army commander-in-chief, General Suchinda, as premier after elections the following year led on to ugly and tragic consequences. In what has been called 'the protest of the middle class' thousands of people took to the streets of Bangkok and other major cities. Army units opened fire on the unarmed, largely peaceful, demonstrators. At least 50 were killed, hundreds more injured and 34 declared 'missing'. The king finally intervened, and an election in 1992 led to the installation of a popular civilian leader, Chuan Leekpai, as prime minister.

Nevertheless, the power of the military effectively remained. Elections in 1996 involving the usual vote-buying and intimidation brought to the office of Prime Minister Chavalit Yungchaiyudh, a former army commander. However, public disquiet at the corruption and cronyism that contributed so much to Thailand's economic difficulties of 1997 saw Chuan Leekpai in the prime ministership again in November of that year, with a mandate for reform. The Thai constitution was rewritten to provide for a Human Rights Commission, but its ability to influence events seems doubtful, Amnesty International noting in 2002 that none of the soldiers responsible for the 1991 killings had been brought to trial.

Thailand, like much of Asia, was overwhelmed by the financial crisis. In mid-1998 the government announced the cost of the economic collapse in a single year: a recession of the economy by 9 per cent, heavy losses in the value of real property and stocks, and a million unemployed.

Thaksin Shinawatra, a former police officer, an ethnic Chinese from northern Thailand and an American-educated Ph.D., who gained control of a huge financial empire, mostly in telecommunications was reputed to be the nation's richest man when he became prime minister as a result of elections in 2001. His Thai Rak Thai (Thais love Thais) Party won 248 seats in the 438-seat House of Representatives and, with its coalition partners, had a commanding majority in both houses of parliament. Its grass-roots campaign appealed especially to rural voters, offering cheap hospital treatment, a three-year moratorium on debts, and micro-credit schemes in Thailand's 70,000 villages. By 2003 Thaksin had instructed Thai banks to lend $13 billion in a major pump-priming exercise. Much of this money was loaned to small farmers and businesses outside the capital, and resulted in steady increases in GDP – rising from 1.8 per cent in 2001 to 6.7 per cent in 2003. Farm income grew a significant 11 per cent in 2002. Thaksin, described as confident, engaging, quick-witted and amusing, became very popular with the people.

However, his government increasingly restricted the Thai media and foreign correspondents it saw as critical of the regime. Thaksin appointed his cousin commander of the army and his brother-in-law deputy police chief. By 2003 his family controlled all of Thailand's television stations and more than 10 per cent of all stocks on the Bangkok exchange. Thaksin has been quoted as saying 'democracy is a means to an end', and is an admitted admirer of former Malaysian leader Mahathir and Singapore's Lee Kuan Yew's 'controlled' democracy.

Thaksin used the army and the police in draconian exercises claimed necessary to maintain law and order and the cohesion of the nation. In February 2003 he undertook to break the illegal drug trade in three months.

By the end of April thousands of people had been shot outside any legal process as 'suspects' in this campaign. Some estimates put the number of dead at over 2500.

Thailand had rationalized its 1909 land cessions to British Malaya as a convenient way for the Buddhist kingdom to rid itself of a troublesome Muslim minority. However, the Muslim Pattani region, once a key entrepôt in Islamic maritime trade, remains a part of Thailand, and in modern times has become the centre of what the Thai government regards as a fundamentalist *jihad* army, dedicated to fighting for an independent Muslim state. Following considerable unrest in the region, in 2004 the Thai army attacked the Krue Se Mosque in Pattani, killing more than a hundred people, many of them teenage boys. Later in that year 78 young Muslim men were suffocated or crushed to death when they were 'stacked like logs', hands tied, face down, in army trucks, an incident described by Prime Minister Thaksin as 'a bit rough'.

Thailand's controlled democracy was confirmed by a landslide victory for Thaksin in general elections in 2005, in which his party won almost 400 seats in the 500-seat assembly. The Democrat Party, the main opposition and the voice of the educated middle class, came in with less than a hundred seats, *The Economist* (5 February 2005) commenting: 'Thaksin does not seem over-exercised about democratic niceties . ... Thailand is quickly becoming a one-party state.'

Nevertheless this was a personal victory for Thaksin, due to his popularity, the thriving economy, and a reduction in those below the poverty line from 21 per cent in 2001 to 11 per cent in 2006 But only a year after the election, Thaksin faced a barrage of accusations, ranging from corruption and tax evasion to a bad human rights record, and was ousted by a military coup while he was attending a UN meeting in New York. His family assets, amounting to $2.2 billion, were frozen and Thaksin moved into exile in Britain. In 2008 he was sentenced in absentia to two years' imprisonment. However, he had the funds to buy the British premier-league football club, Manchester United, for $81 million in 2007, selling it a year later for $200 million. After some time in Dubai and Cambodia, he moved to Germany in 2011.

Meanwhile Thailand's workers and farmers maintained their loyalty. This was manifest in the Red Shirt Movement, which in 2010 mustered tens of thousands of supporters who wanted Thaksin back and a return to democracy. Ninety protesters were killed by security forces, but Red Shirt support increased, if anything, over the next two years. Thaksin's younger sister Yingluck Shinawatra took office as Thailand's first woman prime minister after her Pheu Thai party won in a landslide in elections in 2011. Good-looking and personable, subsequent opinion polling has shown her even more popular than her brother.

Thailand provides free, compulsory education, and the literacy rate is a high 93 per cent. Around 300,000 students are enrolled in tertiary institutions, with as many again in open universities. The position of women is favourable by Asian standards, with equal access to men for education and work opportunities. Women are heavily represented in the professions and in business management. More than half the workforce is employed on the land, mostly growing rice, but there is a growing manufacturing industry which has absorbed about 15 per cent. Food processing, textiles and clothing, and electronics are the main industries, which are mostly centred on the capital and only large city, Bangkok.

Outside Bangkok Thailand consists mostly of a dozen or so large market towns and thousands of small villages. Almost half of these are on the immensely productive river plain of central Thailand. This fertility ceases abruptly at the sharply defined line where the lush, green rice fields, like a calm sea, meet a range of rugged, dramatic hills, full of peaks and cliffs of weathered limestone. Beyond these ranges is the north-east, comprising about a third of the nation's area.

Until the successes of Vietnamese communism made it 'strategic', this region was allowed to remain neglected, virtually medieval, approached by only a single horrific road with tottering wooden bridges. When the first medical surveys were made, it was estimated to have almost a quarter of a million lepers, but treatment in a World Health Organization programme and rehabilitation centres established by the government had virtually eliminated this disease by 1994. Other ailments, like malaria and liver fluke, remain widespread. Thai villagers' liking for raw fish kills 70 people a day from cancer caused by liver fluke. This debilitating and life-shortening parasite, which is said to affect at least a third of the population, is also endemic in most other rural areas of mainland south-east Asia.

My work in the north-east took me to hundreds of villages, many so remote they had never before been visited by Europeans. Here – other than from savage dogs, many of whom might be rabid – one meets an unfailing courtesy, a placid calmness of demeanour, and a social pattern than seems successful in spite of the absolute lack of many facilities Westerners take for granted. Life in this arid region is especially difficult during the six months of the dry season. However, one finds a bleaker picture at the fringes, the poorest most remote land to which young people have been forced because of overcrowding in their home villages. In these hamlets of the crudest shanties there is a very evident lack of hope, humanity forced back on to the ropes, existing in a narrow margin only just on the living side of death. In spite of an appalling rate of infant mortality here there are plenty of children, most with the bulging bellies that tell of acute malnutrition. There are tens of millions like this throughout village Asia. Their tragedy – and the world's – is that they don't make news, few do anything for most of them, and there is little indication that most people even know they exist.

Early in the mornings a file of barefoot, yellow-clad, shaven-headed monks would pass through the town. The mistress of every household waited smiling at the gate to put a spoonful of rice into the begging-bowl each of these men carried. But as with much else in Thailand this appearance of humble, impoverished mendicants was deceptive. The apparent poverty and the need to beg for food are chosen voluntarily by the Buddhist monkhood, many of whom are educated men and who willingly shoulder the burden of being the social cement, and running the schools, even in small villages. Almost all Thai men enter the monkhood for a period of weeks or months. There are estimated to be 140,000 Buddhist monks, occupying nearly 20,000 *wats* (monasteries), a feature of even small villages.

From time to time when I got home from work two or three would be sitting patiently on the floor of my veranda waiting for me. They spoke excellent English and were versed in the European humanities. They would have some questions for me, and after a discussion – it might be about anything from nuclear weapons to birth control – they would rise quietly and leave without a farewell. This tradition of knowledge dates back to King Mongkut, whose reforms to the Buddhist establishment stressed intellect rather than ritual, and firmly established education by the monks at village level. This extensive influence of the monks and their connections with the royal family is an important counterbalance to the power of the military in Thailand.

Thailand has a population of 70 million, growing at under 1 per cent a year. While this is a low rate of population increase, pressure on rural land, as elsewhere in Asia, is still creating problems. It has encouraged an organized trade selling young girls into prostitution, both within Thailand and overseas. As many as 30,000 are children under 18. There has been some growth in Thailand's industry, provided with cheap labour by peasants flocking to the capital in search of work. However, working conditions are often dangerous, with hundreds of deaths in recent years from factory fires. In one of these, in a toy factory in 1993, 188 workers, mostly young women from poor rural families, died, with almost 500 more injured.

Bangkok has become heavily polluted, its narrow streets unable to accommodate some of the heaviest and most congested motor traffic in the world, even though most of the city's characteristic canals – *klongs* – have been filled in to make room for cars. In 2013 it rated thirteenth worst in Asia for dangerous air pollution – polycyclic aromatic hydrocarbons – assessed at more than double the safe limit.

Thailand's exposure to climate change is almost as serious as that of Bangladesh, since most of its people, agriculture and other productive enterprises are located on the flat delta of the Chao Phraya River. Bangkok, which is home to nine million people, was hit by unprecedented floods that ravaged the country in 2011. These resulted in 815 deaths and a World Bank estimate of $45 billion in damage in the 65 of Thailand's 77 provinces which were declared disaster areas.

Like deltas all over the world, the Chao Phraya plain is sinking, mainly due to water extraction for town supplies and irrigation, and restriction of silt deposits. Bangkok is estimated to have sunk three feet in the last 50 years. This has compounded the effect of steadily rising sea levels, which are forecast to be as high as three feet this century.

New Scientist (1 December 2012) commented: 'The coastline of the Chao Phraya delta offers a glimpse of what the future is likely to hold for many people. Here land is already being lost to the sea. In places telephone poles protrude from the water more than a kilometre from the coast, marking where roads and houses have been lost.'

33 The Philippines: Trouble in Paradise

Like Indonesia, the Philippines is a chain of islands, of which Mindanao in the south, and Luzon in the north, are the largest, between them making up rather more than half the total land area of the republic. The central part consists of eight larger and thousands of smaller islands, collectively known as the Visayas. Most of the others are tiny islets – some 4000 of them so small they are not even named. Off to the west is the long, narrow Palawan, grouped around which are 200 more islets, many no more than barely visible coral reefs.

Most people live on the larger islands on coastal plains. The interiors are lightly populated, mysterious regions of smoking volcanic cones and forest-clad mountains, in which cinnamon, cloves and pepper still grow wild. The coastlines are idyllic. Atolls and islands, strands of dazzling white sand, brilliant corals, clear lagoons of placid blue-green water, are all exactly like the standard dream of a tropical paradise. There is a rich natural endowment – gold, copper, nickel, coal, uranium, and offshore natural gas fields.

Regrettably, this paradise is flawed. Population pressures are now becoming extreme, impelled by one of the highest rates of increase in the world – 2.04 per cent, representing almost two million additional people every year. Over the two decades to 2013 the population grew by almost a half to 106 million. There is also one of the world's largest gaps between the minority of the very rich and the great mass of the very poor, with almost half the population living on less than $2 a day, and more than four million unemployed. the worst jobless rate in south-east Asia. While gross domestic product is rising, on one estimate 75 per cent of this gain went directly to the 440 richest families.

With the number of malnourished children in the Philippines estimated at 16 million, legislation to provide a family planning programme has stalled for 14 years, due to opposition from the Roman Catholic Church, some of whose priests have said support for the bill would be a serious sin, punishable with excommunication. However, polling has shown that two-thirds of the nation's 75 million Catholics support government distribution of free contraceptives to those who want them.

In spite of these problems work is becoming available to hundreds of thousands in developing high-tech and service industries, which include call centres, shipbuilding and repair, and electronics, especially computer parts. These are contributing to a rising export income and growth of a largely urban middle class estimated at 18 per cent of the population.

During the ice ages land bridges connected the Philippines with Borneo and the Asian mainland. The first Filipinos whose origins can be assessed with any accuracy moved in at that time. They were small-built people of the type anthropologists call *negrito* and were closely related to the pygmies of Africa. A few thousand of them can still be found in the Visayas, where their presence gave one of its islands – Negros – its name. However, the majority of Filipinos are of Malay type, closely resembling Indonesians and Malaysians. They were seafarers who settled on the islands and established *barangays* – loosely organized autonomous states which fought one another whenever they came into contact. They had a feudal social organization based on family and clan ties – the origin of the strong family loyalties of present-day Filipinos.

One of the more common misconceptions about the Philippines – indeed, about many parts of Asia – is that Europeans 'discovered' it, and that trade and development began with their coming. In fact the major cities of the Philippines were thriving trading centres long before then. The cotton textiles for which the Ilocano people of north-west Luzon are still famed were prized by the Chinese, whose big trading junks plied regularly to Luzon with the monsoons to buy cotton. During the 14th and 15th centuries the southern part of this varied, busy world was also reached by the trader-missionaries of Islam.

· It was 40 years before Magellan's landings in the Philippines were followed up by Spain, with the establishment in 1564 of trading posts, which were eventually consolidated on Manila in 1571. The main initial importance of the Philippines to the Spanish Crown was the Manila entrepôt, for it was here that the trading of silver from the Spanish Mexican colony for Chinese goods took place. Chinese ships brought silk and a wide range of artefacts – carpets, and ornaments of jade, pearl and ivory – which became fashionable and hence valuable in Europe. Spain controlled the galleon trade between Acapulco in Mexico and Manila. These were huge ships for their time, as large as 2000 tons – virtual treasure ships, regularly carrying silk, gold and silver worth millions of dollars.

One captured by Francis Drake in 1579 carried cargo worth $35 million in today's money.

Meanwhile the missionary friars were operating in their own interests in the rest of the country. Village chiefs who agreed to become Christian became exempt from tax and their authority was deemed hereditary provided they saw to it that the rest of their village paid tribute and provided corvée labour. Large areas of what had been communal land were taken over into vast estates, the *encomienda*, owned by the Church and later by individual families.

In most cases the people of Luzon and the Visayas were receptive to Christianity, partly because they had no formal religion with which the new faith must compete. They were animists, believing in nature spirits, but there was no definite body of doctrine and no organized church with a vested interest in their religious devotion. By the middle of the 17th century there were half a million Filipino Christians, almost all Roman Catholic. The Dominican friars established what is now Asia's oldest university, Santo Tomas, in Manila in 1611. Eighty per cent of Filipinos are Catholic today, although the southern island of Mindanao is, however, almost entirely Muslim.

European trade with the Philippines increased considerably after the opening of the Suez Canal in 1869, bringing greater influence and wealth to a new and growing class of merchants. In many cases these families had Spanish blood. Possession of landed estates was such an important mark of social distinction in Spain that the Spaniards in the Philippines, both traders and priests, were anxious to acquire feudal grants of huge tracts of land and the right to administer and use the labour of the 'Indians' living on that land.

Spanish rule was cruel and oppressive. Laymen and priests alike regarded it as natural and proper that the Filipino peasants should labour for their support, and obey them implicitly. The friars of the Franciscan order were particularly grasping in their ambitions to acquire more and more land, on which they lived in idleness. The people had no part in the government of the islands, although a form of democracy was kept alive in the villages – the *barrios* – which retained the village councils they had always had. However, rapid population growth was already causing increasing poverty and restlessness. Discontent centred on the repressive policies of the government and the continued alienation of agricultural land to the religious orders.

In 1872 about 200 Filipino soldiers and workmen mutinied at the arsenal in Cavite, near Manila. They killed three Spanish soldiers and seized the port. The rebellion was planned to coincide with another uprising inside the walls of Manila itself, but its timing was premature and the revolt was easily subdued. The Spanish authorities, alarmed by the growth of nationalist feeling, executed 13 of the rebels. While most Filipinos might have accepted this, they did not tolerate so readily the further execution, by strangling on the garrotte, of three Filipino priests charged with instigating the revolt – one of them a man of 85.

Among those deeply impressed by this incident was a ten-year-old boy named José Rizal, who was to become a man of remarkable achievement and personality, and the most honoured Filipino patriot. A product of the growing middle class and educated in Europe, Rizal was a competent author, musician and painter as well as a teacher, linguist and surgeon. He was also the first serious advocate of Filipino nationalism. When he formed the Liga Filipina in 1892 he was arrested and deported to a remote part of Mindanao, even though this nationalist association was, like Rizal himself, moderate and opposed to violent methods. However, there were other nationalists who wanted direct action and, after Rizal was exiled, the cause fell into the hands of the militant Katipunan, an organization founded by Andrés Bonifacio and some associates, also in 1892.

An emissary of the Katipunan visited Rizal in exile to seek his support for an armed uprising against Spain. Rizal, however, declined. He had given his word not to try to escape from exile, and believed the people were not yet ready for independence. Without his moderating influence the nationalist movement quickly developed from an organization of talk and pamphlets into an underground resistance dedicated to violent terrorism. Rizal, who felt he was wasting his life in exile, asked to be sent to Cuba as a surgeon to the Spanish garrison there. The authorities agreed, and he was actually on his way when he was arrested, brought back to Manila and executed by a firing squad in 1896. Spain had provided the nationalist cause with its martyr. Rizal's books were read as never before and his name became a rallying cry.

Rioting and terrorism flared up in many parts of the Philippines and within a year of Rizal's death Spain was forced to commit 50,000 soldiers to the task of pacifying the colony. The Spanish eventually came to terms with the rebels, paying their leader, General Aguinaldo, to go into exile in Hong Kong. Aguinaldo complied, but used his time in Hong Kong to negotiate arms purchases for a further rebellion.

Fourteen months after Rizal's death an event far from the Philippines broke the stalemate. Relations between the United States and Spain over the then Spanish colony of Cuba reached breaking point. When Spain refused an American ultimatum to leave Cuba, a war broke out in which Spain was easily defeated. General Aguinaldo, in Singapore when he heard of the war, hurried to Hong Kong to discuss co-operation with the Americans. Shortly afterwards a US ship returned him to the Philippines. He was quickly able to raise a large revolutionary army, which mounted a siege on Manila and extended the rebellion into other parts of Luzon. The Filipinos believed the Americans were helping them to gain complete independence, since the United States was at that time regarded as a champion of oppressed colonial peoples.

The nationalists established a revolutionary civil government, with a constitution modelled on that of the United States. Although there were 13,000 Spanish troops inside Manila, the city capitulated after a two-month siege in which there had been little more than sporadic fighting. With this came the first nationalist doubts about American intentions. Manila was occupied by US forces, whose commander unexpectedly refused to allow the Filipinos to enter the city. Nevertheless, most of the nationalist army remained outside the city while Aguinaldo and other leaders withdrew to the north to establish their seat of government in the Luzon provincial city of Malolos. There they proclaimed an independent Republic of the Philippines on 15 September 1898, the first such declaration anywhere in the colonial regions of Asia.

However, the day after the republic was established US President William McKinley privately told his envoys to the Paris talks ending the war with Spain that they must press for the cession of Luzon at least to the United States. A representative was sent by the republic to Paris to plead its cause, but the other parties refused to recognize it. So matters were finalized without reference to the nationalists. Spain agreed to renounce control of the whole of the Philippines which, with Guam and Puerto Rico, became US colonies.

Responsibility for the Philippines as a colony was not welcomed by many Americans and Filipinos. The fact that the United States, an ex-colony that had had to fight for freedom, was now becoming imperial master of another people was widely opposed in America. The Filipinos found it a cause for war. In a pitched battle outside Manila in 1899 the Filipino irregulars were defeated. Two months later, Malolos was occupied by the Americans. Aguinaldo and his men retreated northwards. The bitter ensuing guerrilla war should not be underestimated, although some books dismiss it with a phrase. The civilian population, looted and oppressed by lawless elements of Aguinaldo's army, suffered most. Deaths probably exceeded 100,000. The war ended with Aguinaldo's capture in 1901 and acceptance of US rule. It cost the lives of 4200 Americans.

Thereafter matters improved rapidly. The United States granted the first elements of limited self-government with an elected lower house of parliament in 1907 and more extensive powers in 1934, although complete independence did not come until 1946. This transfer of American-style political institutions was not without its problems. Election of officials such as police chiefs has become politicized and corrupt in the Philippines. Freedom to carry arms has contributed to a high crime rate, especially a high murder rate.

However, the United States redirected many of its soldiers in the Philippines into peaceful projects. They acted as teachers in *barrio* schools, started road-building programmes, and organized such small but collectively important tasks as digging deep wells to provide the villagers with disease-free water. The importance of this work was emphasized by epidemics of cholera so severe they resulted in an actual decrease in the population. The Americans worked enthusiastically and effectively and conditions soon improved. The United States recruited and sent almost a thousand American schoolteachers to the Philippines, many of them Quakers. As none could speak the local language, Tagalog, they first had to make their pupils literate in English. A direct result is the present widespread knowledge of English, especially on Luzon. By 1921 there were a million children at school.

The United States paid the then considerable sum of $7 million to reclaim the huge estates held by the Franciscan order. The Filipinos had bitterly resented the alienation of land to the friars, and this action did much to reconcile them to US rule. Nevertheless, American land reform programmes failed to solve all the problems. Many big church estates were left untouched, and the land bought from the Franciscans was not distributed to the farmers who worked it but usually sold to wealthy Filipino families, often of Spanish blood. Most of these proved harder taskmasters than the friars had been.

American policies also resulted in the alienation of huge areas of riceland to export crops like sugar, pineapple, tobacco and coconut, to the advantage of big American corporations, but at the cost of ending Filipino self-sufficiency for food. They did little to improve the serious underprivilege of the bulk of the people; indeed, the first president of the Philippines, Manuel Quezon, commented in 1939 that 'the men and women who till the soil or work in the factories are hardly better off than they were under the Spanish regime'.

The Second World War caused terrible hardship in the Philippines. The islands' dependence on exports caused almost universal unemployment when these were cut off. In spite of the relatively small population there were not enough food crops to feed the people, and widespread starvation resulted during the years of Japanese occupation. In 1942 the Communist leader Luis Taruc launched a resistance movement in central Luzon called 'The People's Army against the Japanese'. The first word of the Tagalog translation of this is *hukbalahap*, hence the resistance fighters became known as the Huks. By 1945 the Huks had established a well-organized soviet which redistributed the holdings of absentee landlords, levied taxes, dispensed justice and even ran schools.

Post-war politics were bedevilled by the fact that three-quarters of the pre-war Congress had collaborated with the Japanese. One such, Manuel Roxas, became president as a result of a highly corrupt election in 1946. Among other things, Roxas refused to allowed Huk congressmen elected from Central Luzon to take their seats. He forced through Congress legislation pardoning all collaborators, and acts which confirmed US economic dominance of the Philippines. Under these unfortunate circumstances the Philippines became an independent republic.

The Huks returned to their strongholds to wage war on the government. After some initial successes they were controlled by a more efficient government army trained and equipped by the United States. The young Filipino Defence Secretary overseeing this campaign, Ramón Magsaysay, became president in 1953 in what were said to be the first honest elections ever held in the republic. Magsaysay introduced liberal policies, including the first genuine attempt at land reform, until, one night in March 1957 he was killed when an airliner crashed on the island of Cebu. His liberal policies were largely abandoned after his death. There was widespread rumour – although no proof – that the air crash may have been deliberate sabotage. Whatever the truth of that, the political scene again became one of barely concealed corruption and self-seeking. The economy sagged, and the national rate of growth fell far behind in its race with an explosive population increase.

Some hope for reform came with the election of a charismatic former resistance fighter, Ferdinand Marcos, in 1966, as sixth president. However, this was short-lived. During his 20-year presidency Marcos used his position to amass a huge personal fortune, exploiting and abusing the Filipino people mercilessly. Claiming that the nation was threatened again by Communism, Marcos declared martial law in 1972, and ruled thereafter as a dictator. In 1983 Marcos's military murdered his principal political rival, Benigno Aquino, shooting the popular Aquino in the head as they were escorting him from the aircraft returning him to Manila after medical treatment in the United States. More than a million people marched through Manila's streets in his funeral procession.

The government imprisoned people without trial, and there was increasing evidence of torture and murder by elements of the army to discourage opposition. Marcos's wasteful use of public money and the diversion of funds to himself and his cronies resulted in a huge foreign debt. Public unrest grew to an unprecedented extent. Two million people joined protest marches in Manila; more than a million petitioned the murdered Aquino's widow to run for president in elections in 1986. Corazón Aquino became the Philippines' first woman president, but in spite of a 60 per cent vote in her favour, Marcos refused to surrender power. Intervention by elements of the military, led by the army deputy chief of staff, Fidel Ramos, and massively supported by the people, proved necessary to dislodge him.

Again there were high hopes for significant reforms in the government and the economy. Sixteen military officers were brought to trial and convicted of the Aquino murder. However, Mrs Aquino, like most Filipino leaders since independence, came from the wealthy landowning class directly responsible for the nation's problems, and her influence proved disappointingly slight.

There was little significant improvement during the administration of President Ramos, who replaced Mrs Aquino in 1992. The rapidly growing population and the disinclination of governments to face the nation's basic and urgent problems made these beautiful islands a place of nightmare.

Widespread discontent resulted in the election as president in 1998 of 61-year-old former movie star Joseph Estrada, on declared, if vague, policies to help the poor and disadvantaged. However, by 2001 he, too, was discredited, facing allegations of corruption and criminal associations. Public indignation supported by elements of the army forced his resignation and replacement by the vice-president, Gloria Macapagal Arroyo, a former university economics academic. She was narrowly re-elected president in her own right in 2004. The presidency passed to Benigno Aquino III in 2010. He was able to negotiate a framework for new measures to end the government's long battle with Muslim separatists in Mindanao. The peace plan provides for an autonomous region to be called Bangsamoro, with its own police, internal government and legal code.

Aquino, who was popular with the voters, faced many problems, with a large public debt, dwindling tax revenues and declining foreign investment offering the government little room to effect improvements. The wealthiest 10 per cent are earning more than 20 times the income of the poorest 10 per cent, many of whom live in squatter towns on the outskirts of the major cities. When, after five days of typhoon rains, a mountain of rubbish slipped on to the shanties of people living within a garbage dump more than 200 people were killed. It was impossible to know exactly how many people were missing because nobody knows how many live in the Manila squatter colony, called Lupang Pangako – the Promised Land. However, it is thought to be the home of 80,000 slum dwellers, who live by picking over the rubbish for anything of value.

The Philippines economy, formerly essentially agricultural, is, however, making some moves into services and manufacturing, with an expanding electronics industry exporting computer parts and semiconductors. The Philippines also has the world's fourth largest shipbuilding and repair sector. The call-centre industry, now larger than India's, is a major contributor, earning $11 billion in 2011. Agriculture now makes up only 12 per cent of GDP, although it employs a third of the workforce. The economy grew 7.8 per cent in the first quarter of 2013 – much of this has been attributed to industrial growth and the $24 billion remitted home from the 10 million Filipinos who work overseas.

In late 2013 the central islands were struck by a typhoon of unprecedented ferocity, with wind gusts – in excess of 300 kpm – believed to be the most extreme ever recorded on land. More than 5000 people were killed, as many as 4 million homes damaged or destroyed, and rice crops reduced by a third. Ninety per cent of the capital city of Leyte Province, Tacloban, was destroyed.

34 Korea: Divided Nation

Although Communist North Korea and the southern Republic of Korea confront one another across one of the most heavily militarized frontiers in the world, as late as 2013 this resulted in no more than an elaborate propaganda barrage mounted by the north – rhetoric rather than war. This is almost always the case when the United States stages annual military exercises with its ally, South Korea, which it is pledged to protect. When the United States flew two nuclear-capable B2 Stealth bombers over South Korea, North Korean leader Kim Jong-un claimed he had ordered his missile batteries to prepare for nuclear strikes against the American mainland and its Pacific bases. None of this happened – in any case it is improbable that North Korea has the military hardware to carry out such a threat.

To an extent, the division of Korea is a consequence of its geography and history – the north has long had ethnic and cultural associations with China and Manchuria, while the south, although also influenced by China, has tended to look outwards, with long-standing sea-trading connections to other parts of Asia.

Korea consists of a coastal strip of Manchuria bordering China, a peninsula extending south about 600 miles, and more than 3000 islands. The north has high plateaux and mountains up to 9000 feet, a mountain chain which continues into South Korea almost the whole length of the east coast, dropping into the sea in sheer pine-clad cliffs interspersed with coves at the mouths of short east-running rivers. Westward are larger rivers, with fertile plains, and formidable mountain spurs which divide the country into definite regions. These set the boundaries of independent states early in Korea's history.

According to the mythology, in the year 2333 BCE a bear was miraculously transformed into a young woman. When Hwanung, son of the Creator, came to earth and breathed on her she gave birth to Tangun, Korea's first king. North Korea, in particular, makes much of the Tangun myth in its modern ideology, asserting a continuous culture and nationalism going back more than 4000 years, and frequently referring to Korea as 'the Tangun nation'. In 1993 North Korea announced it had found the bones of Tangun in an ancient royal tomb near Pyongyang. South Korea, anxious to promote itself as the main proponent of the ancient culture, has also made use of the myth from time to time.

The actual archaeological evidence indicates primitive Neolithic societies, hunters and shell fishermen, during the 4th millennium BCE, with agriculture evolving perhaps 2000 years later. At about that time a distinctive style of pottery ornamentation spread to Korea from China, the first evidence of a profound and enduring Chinese cultural influence. However, it was not until 109 BCE that Chinese annals record a successful invasion, after which four Han Dynasty garrison cities were established.

Wars against the Mongolian tribes during the first centuries of the Common Era forged a large and highly professional military class in the mountainous, largely infertile north of Korea. Their new state, Koguryo, became very powerful, and by the 5th century had expanded into much of Manchuria. The Sui Dynasty in China saw this large, aggressive neighbour as a threat, and despatched four huge armies – one said to have numbered over a million men – to bring Koguryo under Chinese control. The first three were defeated at great cost – it was probably the enormous drain of these Korean campaigns that weakened and brought down the Sui Dynasty. The fourth fared little better, the hostilities ending in a truce. Thousands of captured Chinese soldiers were returned home and officials of the succeeding Tang Dynasty came to Pyongyang for the rites associated with the burial of the bones of the Chinese dead.

Tang influence nevertheless came to dominate much of Korea, especially the southern state of Silla, which became a maritime trader of consequence, dominating the sea routes between Korea, China and Japan. This was the beginning of the end for Koguryo, which was defeated by combined Silla–Chinese forces in 668. Pyongyang, the capital of a state of perhaps three million people, was almost totally destroyed. Koguryo should, however, be remembered, because it unified much of Korea for the first time, and because of the resolve and toughness of its people, who after all had withstood repeated invasions from their vast neighbour for 70 years. From the 4th century on it had been an important centre for *mahayana* Buddhism, which was taken on to Japan by Koguryo monks. There is evidence for a considerable Koguryo literature, written in Chinese, most of which was destroyed at the fall of Pyongyang.

Its heir to at least partial unification of Korea was Silla, which now expanded rapidly in a close association with Tang China, subordination being guaranteed by the despatch of Silla princes to the great Chinese capital, Changan, as hostages. Thousands of Koreans studied there. Chinese medicine, astronomy, music, literature, administration and laws of land-ownership were all transferred more or less intact to Silla.

Silla's capital, Kyongju, with almost a million people, was one of the world's largest and richest cities at that time, known and admired as far away as Arabia and India. The opulence of the Silla aristocracy was based on unlimited power over the peasantry as absentee landlords, and their possession of large numbers of slaves. The numerous Buddhist monasteries were also large landowners. As the Tang Dynasty in China declined, so did Silla in Korea. Weakened by regular and bloody disputes over succession to the throne, it fell in 936 to a revived northern state, Koryo. The name Korea derives from Koryo.

The pattern, then, is one of client states of China, rising and falling in parallel with the fortunes of Chinese dynasties, nevertheless fiercely independent and following the Chinese example because they admired it rather than as a result of conquest; of a northern region of warriors and a more prosperous southern region of farmers and traders; and of efficient and ruthless oligarchies battening on a sturdy and resilient peasantry who were, however, far from compliant, rebelling regularly against their masters. Koryo was controlled by such an oligarchy, who nevertheless so admired the achievements of the Chinese Song Dynasty that they emulated, and even improved on them. Koryo celadon pottery, with its restrained ornamentation, sophistication and transparent blue-green glaze, was regarded as the finest in the world. The world's first metal movable type, cast from bronze in a sand mould, was made here in the 13th century and the oldest surviving book produced from it, the *Jikji*, was printed on paper in 1377 – almost 80 years before the Gutenberg Bible. Fragments of a work on Buddhist *Zen* teachings, in 2013 it was in the French National Library, with Korea campaigning for its return to its country of origin.

A warlord phase in the 12th century brought unrest and banditry on a major scale, followed by a succession of Mongol invasions, a small part of the huge military campaign of Kublai Khan that subjugated China. Mongol savagery was no less extreme in Korea than elsewhere. The walled cities resisted bravely, attracting praise even from Mongol generals, but in the end fell to the relentless professional assaults, which included elaborate siege machinery and fire-carts fuelled with human fat made from boiling down prisoners. Nearly a thousand Korean ships were used in Kublai's massive but unsuccessful attacks on Japan, sharing the disaster of the *kamikaze* – a divine windstorm that famously saved the day for Japan.

Mongol rule of Korea was firmly established by 1270. It was predatory to a disastrous extent, bringing fresh horrors of starvation and disruption to a society already on its knees. This occupation lasted for 130 years. By 1368 the new Chinese Ming Dynasty had driven the Mongols out of China. However, seven years before that a young Korean soldier, Yi Songgye, had been active in campaigning against the Mongols. He rose to be a general, and, after some bloody infighting among the Korean elite, became the founder of a dynasty that would endure into modern times. Its capital was Hanyang, the city now known as Seoul, and the state was called Chosen, the Land of Morning Calm.

Hanyang became virtually a new city. A conscript labour force of over 100,000 built palaces and quarters for the ever-present bureaucracy, whose tentacles now gripped the nation as never before. Every Korean was obliged to carry an identity tag bearing their name and place and date of birth for verification with an official record. The material for these virtual identity cards ranged from ivory down to plain wood according to rank. Movement outside a person's home province was forbidden, and this was closely policed. The maintenance of local law and collection of tax was led by officials called *yangban*, a hereditary ruling class whose performance was guaranteed by the despatch of their sons to the capital as hostages. Less fortunate were the next level down, basically policemen and tax-collecting clerks. They were conscripted into their duties, for which they received no payment other than what they could 'squeeze' from the peasantry.

The people actually working the land were closely supervised and controlled, five households being lumped together into a group jointly held responsible for the good behaviour and corvée responsibilities of all its individuals. Peasants paid 50 per cent of their production to the land-owner, and both were liable to a 10 per cent tax to the state. Other payments were exacted by regional government offices and a tax could be paid in lieu of compulsory military service. The state itself owned 350,000 slaves in 1484. They were often so much better off than the peasants that many free men actually sought to become slaves.

Agriculture, mainly growing *padi* rice, was carefully studied and improved wherever possible. Thousands of water-storage dams were built, and rain gauges were issued to the provinces in 1442. The land was carefully surveyed and mapped, allowing the imposition of tax to become an exact science.

Printed books, using woodblocks, were produced in thousands, often beautifully illustrated in colour. Many of these promoted the neo-Confucian ethic then current in China; family values, the authority of fathers, the obedience and humility of children – these 'virtues' became deeply incul-cated at all levels of Korean society. An alphabet of 24 letters was devised in

1443, far better suited to the Korean language than Chinese ideographs, but scholars considered it vulgar. It languished for many centuries, but is now generally used.

When the Japanese Shogun Hideyoshi conceived the unrealistic ambition of conquering China, the obvious stepping stone appeared to be Korea. Angered by Korea's natural reluctance to co-operate, he invaded the country with an army of 160,000 *samurai* in 1592, and pressed on to Seoul in spite of heavy losses. In the capital the invaders were helped by a revolt among the slaves, who set fire to buildings housing the records of their servitude. A Korean appeal to Ming China brought a less than adequate response, but did involve China in the wars, which dragged on until Hideyoshi's death in 1598.

One of the curiosities of this war was the turtle ship of Admiral Yi Sunsin, an armoured barge propelled by a square sail and 20 oars, considered to be the world's first ironclad. These fast vessels, armed with 40 cannon, caused such destruction to Japanese supply ships that Hideyoshi demanded some proof of his army's valour. The bizarre response was the despatch to Kyoto of the ears cut from almost 40,000 Chinese and Korean dead, pickled in salt. The war caused enormous destruction in Korea, including the burning of many monasteries, but the chief victim was the old social order. Much of the opposition to the Japanese had come from peasant guerrillas, and in some cases bands of slaves. The leaders of these irregulars became powerful enough to enter the ruling classes, fighting their way into positions of influence.

In the 17th century Korea was again invaded as a consequence of a power change in China. In 1637 Korea became a tributary state of the Manchus, who, although deadly enough in battle, were indolent in administration. They left Korea much to itself to recover from half a century of war. Gold, silver, cloth and especially the small Korean cavalry horses were required as tribute, but the Manchus had little permanent influence on Korean society.

Even so, restoration of the old social order was next to impossible. The slave and tax records had been destroyed, and the government found itself largely impotent from sheer lack of money. Recovery was slow and gradual, and involved important social and commercial changes. There was more private, rather than state, enterprise, and a wealthy commercial class developed. The number of slaves was greatly reduced. Their use in state enterprises ended in 1801, although private families and businesses continued to own slaves until 1894.

The centuries of Yi rule set an enduring pattern for Korean society, much of which remains today. A hereditary caste system which placed the scholar-official at the highest level made necessary accurate genealogical records spanning many generations, and quite complex rules determining who should marry whom. Of continuing importance, too, is the concept that only the 'first son' – the eldest – has *chong-che*, the mystic capacity and right to succeed his father. This, often perceived by Westerners as nepotism, extends from the control of family property and businesses through to politics. The succession in North Korea from Kim II Sung to his eldest son Kim Jong Il and grandson Kim Jong Un is indicative.

The Korean caste system, by no means as pervasive as the Indian one, nevertheless had its equivalent of untouchables, among them those who butchered animals and dealt with the dead. There remain today different ways of addressing people in different social categories. The Confucian concept of respect for elders involves the use of special honorifics whenever they are addressed, and is basic to an elaborate system of family hierarchy with a distinct ranking position for every member: the father at the top, wife obeying him, daughters (and daughters-in-law) subordinate to the mother, younger children below older ones.

However, the superficial appearance that such a system might be oppressive, even cruel, is mistaken. Korean parents tend to indulge their children, and will extend themselves financially to an extraordinary extent to educate them. Obedience and loyalty to the family structure come not so much from discipline as from the deep respect children have for their parents. Children too, take their education seriously from infancy and make every effort to learn to the limit of their capacity, to do their best in whatever they undertake. This is a significant driver of the remarkable economic growth Korea has achieved in recent decades.

By the late 18th century almost constant warring between factions of the ruling classes threatened to destabilize the monarchy. Among its difficulties was the murderous and lecherous conduct of a crazy prince, Sado. Since it would be a crime to kill royalty, by order of his father, the king, Sado was shut in a wooden box which was left out in the hot sun. Eight days later he was dead.

The ordinary people suffered appallingly from flood, famine and especially plagues. A cholera epidemic in 1821 dragged on for two years, killing a million people. The impotence of central administration led the people to resort to mutual aid societies, and villages worked together in specialist co-operative enterprises – these traditions persisted into modern times, and were the inspiration for the New Community Movement designed to improve village life in the 1970s. Banditry was widespread, as also were regional revolts against the central authority. One of these, in 1811, developed almost into civil war.

During a famine resulting from two years of drought in 1812 and 1813 over a million people starved to death. As the countryside sank into deeper and deeper despair crime and rebellion became even more prevalent. Merchants and officials were slaughtered in 18 southern cities by bands of peasants, and in 1894 followers of a religious and mystic cult, Tonghak, began a revolt so serious that China and Japan once again intervened in Korean affairs.

As in China, the 19th century brought increasing contacts with European ships, which were attacked and looted when they appeared. In 1866 an American ship, the *General Sherman*, was boarded and burned when she grounded in the Taedong River, following an incident in which American sailors fired into a crowd on the river bank. Reprisals were inevitable. In 1871 American warships fired on the batteries at Kanghwa Island, which guards the entrance to the river. When the marines landed to attack the forts the Korean defenders fought back ferociously, but ineffectively, since they lacked modern weapons.

Four years later a similar incident involved a Japanese naval vessel. These incidents prompted an official Korean policy of strict isolation from the outside world. However, gunboat diplomacy would not be denied. Following the arrival of a formidable Japanese fleet in 1876, a treaty was signed with Japan, opening three ports to international trade. Subsequent trade treaties were signed with Britain, several European states and the United States. The number of these treaties does not indicate any desire on the part of Koreans to 'open up' the country. Rather, it was hoped that by dealing with many contending interests outside influences would be kept at bay.

Such was the situation when the Tonghak rebellion brought both Chinese and Japanese expeditions to Korea. At that time Japan was modernizing itself rapidly. One of the last acts of the *shogunate* had been the establishment in 1865 of the Institution for the Study of Barbarian Literature, which two decades later became the Tokyo Imperial University. Those selected to study the ways of the outside world recommended that Japan adopt Western science, trade methods and industry.

In Korea a 'progressive' faction, sponsored by Japanese, felt Korea should take this same course. The conservatives, centred around the monarchy, maintained their allegiance to China. Two successful Japanese wars – with China in 1894/5 and Russia in 1904/5 – decided the outcome. In 1905 Korea was placed under Japanese 'protection', and in 1910 it was formally annexed to Japan. Ironically, ideas of nationalism and freedom had reached young Koreans mainly from Japanese intellectuals, only to be crushed by Japanese military imperialism. The Koreans resisted strenuously – hundreds of villages were burned and perhaps 20,000 people killed.

Japan's colonial control of Korea, which lasted until the end of the Second World War in 1945, continued to be harsh – even brutal, and still influences Korean attitudes to Japan. Resistance movements persisted throughout the occupation, during which thousands of people were killed or imprisoned. In 1919, Korean protesters were burned alive in a church in which they had taken refuge at Sunron, near Seoul. As other colonizers had done elsewhere, Japan did improve the infrastructure, creating an extensive rail network, chemical fertilizer plants, and major irrigation and land-clearing works to maximize the rice crop, needed to meet food crop shortages in the Japanese homeland, where the population was growing rapidly. Half the Korean rice crop went to fill Japanese stomachs, causing mass malnutrition and poverty in Korea.

Koreans were ordered to take Japanese surnames, and even the use of the Korean language was banned. Shinto shrines were built, at which Koreans were forced to worship. During the Second World War almost two million Koreans were conscripted as slave labour in Japan, much of it 12-hour days under appalling conditions in mines. Among these conscripts were well over 100,000 'comfort women' – young girls forced into prostitution to serve Japanese soldiers. Seven thousand Koreans were set to work in 1944 to build a retreat bunker near Mount Fuji for the Japanese Emperor, under conditions so harsh that over a thousand died. At least 10,000 Korean conscript workers died in the atomic bombing of Hiroshima and Nagasaki.

As the war ended, the Russians occupied the north of Korea, US forces the south. Two states, Communist north and American-supported South Korea, resulted. Both were harshly authoritarian and corrupt. By June 1950 they were at war – a war that was really an expression of the zonal rivalry between the United States and the Soviet Union and China.

This war caused enormous suffering and loss to the Korean people – two million military dead, three million civilians. This created a whole generation of widows and orphans and a massive loss of infrastructure from which Korea recovered only slowly. A major American aerial bombing campaign began with General MacArthur in command, ordering the destruction of every aspect of infrastructure and human society, even village houses, in North Korea. The capital, Pyongyang, was virtually destroyed. The war solved nothing, achieved little except destruction, the two rival states at the end still facing each other after a ceasefire agreement across the 38th parallel of latitude.

South Korea subsequently passed through a phase of remarkable industrial development, making it a major exporter of many commodities until this expansion was checked by the 1998 Asian economic crisis. Most families had television sets, refrigerators and washing machines. South Korea became a major shipbuilder and exporter of motor vehicles. Education was actively encouraged – now almost the whole population is literate. The massively increased industry and urbanization resulted in major changes in Korean society, including a drop in the rural population to only 18 per cent, compared with 55 per cent in 1965. Nevertheless these decades of growing prosperity were marred by a virtual state of war between the workers and the big industrial conglomerates, backed by a rigidly authoritarian government and a large and frequently brutal military, who did not hesitate to use mass killing, torture and imprisonment to put down opposition.

A military coup in 1961 brought Park Chung Hee, a former officer in the Japanese army, to power as virtual dictator. Although some of the trappings of democracy appeared in 1963, Park, by now president, continued as an autocrat. In 1972 he imposed martial law, with rigid suppression of any opposition, a situation which continued until his assassination in 1979. Little changed during the rule of several dictators who succeeded him. However, the Korean people, increasingly unhappy with the corruption and authoritarianism of the government, took to the streets in millions in 1987 in protest. This pressure and others forced slow progress towards greater freedom. In 1992 President Kim Young Sam made vigorous attempts to control corruption and redress some of the wrongs of the past. Two former dictators were indicted and sentenced to jail terms. Relations with North Korea, however, deteriorated, Pyongyang announcing in 1996 that it would no longer honour the agreements which had ended the Korean War in 1953.

In 1997 the much-persecuted democracy activist Kim Dae Jung was elected president of South Korea. During the previous two decades several attempts were made to murder him: a sentence of death on him for sedition was commuted only after American intervention in 1980; he was exiled in 1982; and on his return to Korea two years later, was placed under house arrest. However, his accession came in difficult times – the severe recession caused by the Asian financial crisis. It left Korea with debts estimated at more than $150 billion. It is typical of the Korean people that they made a gift to their government of gold jewellery and other family treasures which, when melted down, amounted to a staggering 220 tons of bullion. It is also typical that as unemployment mounted to almost 9 per cent, suicides of laid-off workers became numerous – so numerous that the government had to grease the framework of a bridge in Seoul to prevent people climbing it and jumping off.

These conditions eroded Kim's support, and in 2002 self-made lawyer and political activist Roh Moo-hyun narrowly won an election to become president. Mr Roh was anxious to improve relations with North Korea and expressed concern at US actions in Iraq and Afghanistan. He survived an attempt to impeach him on a technicality in 2004, but accusations of corruption persisted until he was succeeded by former Hyundai CEO and mayor of Seoul Lee Myung-bak in 2008. Park Geun-hye continued this swing to conservative politics when she was elected president in 2012. South Korea's first woman president, she is the eldest child of former president and military dictator Park Chung-hee. She took a tougher line with an increasingly bellicose North Korea, different from the 'sunshine' policy of previous administrations, but remained committed to the unification of the two Koreas. However the issue of most importance to Koreans in 2013 was the economy, which was showing signs of stagnation because of its reliance on exports, heavily reduced because of recession in so many international markets. There was an increasing gap between rich and poor, with around 15 per cent of the population below the poverty line. Nearly half of these were the rising number of older people, many of whom are not covered by state pensions.

Meanwhile, one of the world's few remaining Communist states persisted in North Korea, its nature and policies readily identifiable with its past. For its population – 25 million – North Korea is intensely militaristic, with its regular armed forces numbering over a million, the fourth largest in the world. However in 2013 it was estimated almost 10 million people, including reservists and paramilitaries, were involved in North Korea's military machine, one of the largest number under arms in the world. This figure is maintained by compulsory conscription of adults, men and women, for three to as long as ten years. Almost a third of the country's GDP is spent on the military.

This regime has presided over a shattered economy, with poverty so extreme it had resulted in deaths from starvation in rural areas during the late 1990s estimated by some observers to be in the millions. US Congressman Tony Hall, who visited North Korea in November 1998, put deaths at between one and three million, and quoted UN statistics indicating that 30 per cent of North Korean children under 2 were acutely malnourished. He brought out with him a bag of 'substitute food' being distributed at a government food station: 'Dried leaves and straw, so coarse even cattle would turn away from it,' Mr Hall said. 'They grind it into powder and make it into noodles. The noodles have no nutrition and are indigestible, leaving people holding their aching stomachs.'

While the worst effects of the famine were controlled from 1998 after large infusions of foreign aid, a UN report in 2013 assessed more than a quarter of North Korean children as chronically malnourished and stunted. Defectors have reported people surviving from soup made of grass and leaves because of high food prices and shortages, with as much as a third of the population dependent on international food aid. Dissent is severely discouraged, typically being punished by imprisonment in the *Kwan-li-so*, the political penal labour colonies, where conditions are so severe thousands die every year from starvation or ill-treatment. Many thousands of North Koreans attempt to escape across the border with China. It has been reported that when they are sent back to Korea they also are imprisoned in these concentration camps, in which as many as 200,000 people are said to be confined. In 2013 UN Human Rights investigators concluded people in these camps were suffering 'unspeakable atrocities', former Australian High Court Justice Michael Kirby describing 'a large-scale pattern of abuse that may constitute systematic and gross human rights violations'. North Korea, which refused the investigators entry to the country, claimed the evidence had been 'fabricated and invented by forces hostile to North Korea'.

North Korea is reclusive and secretive, shunning contact with the outside world as much as possible. Because foreign observers are discouraged and allowed little freedom of movement if they do get into the country, there is little accurate information about it. However, North Korea is developing nuclear facilities capable of producing weapons-grade fuels, and in 1998 test-fired a long-range ballistic missile into the Pacific. This Taepodong missile is said to have a range of 2000 km – enough to reach all of South Korea and much of Japan. North Korea's nuclear programme was deferred in 1994 when the US government, with Japan and South Korea, agreed to provide North Korea with two light-water nuclear reactors – a type not suited to extracting weapons-grade material – and 500,000 tons a year of fuel oil until the reactors were operational. However, the United States renounced this deal in 2002, on the grounds that North Korea had resumed its nuclear weapons programme. North Korea has reserves of about 300,000 tons of high-quality uranium ore.

North Korea does not deny its nuclear weapons programme, claiming it has enough fissile material for five or six bombs. It also exports missiles, one of the numerous trading, manufacturing and mining businesses run by the armed services. The country's president, Kim Jong Un, is so secretive and reclusive that his neighbours and the large powers find it difficult to assess whether he indeed has the weapons to start a nuclear conflict and, if so, whether he might actually do so. His own people know as little about him. A huge and pervasive public relations effort portrays him as a hero who must be adulated.

This propaganda campaign is carried to an extent and cost which seems bizarre, especially when it is set beside the country's abject poverty and hundreds of thousands of hungry children. Thousands of people dressed in colourful costumes regularly sing and dance in public performances in praise of The Dear Leader. Revering crowds file past the white marble statue and embalmed body of his grandfather, Kim Il Sung, who died in 1994, within a mausoleum complex said to have cost at least $100 million, constructed when the famine was at its height.

North Korea tested atomic weapons in 2006 and 2009, and carried out another underground test in 2013. Their yield is said to be small – less than the Hiroshima bomb – but increasing. While North Korea does not seem to have an intercontinental ballistic missile capability, her current arsenal may be capable of delivering a nuclear weapon as far as Tokyo. Most informed estimates are that North Korea could have 12 to 16 small nuclear weapons by 2016 and missiles of considerably longer range.

35 Vietnam, Laos and Cambodia

Vietnam, once a much oppressed colony of France, and then a Communist state, improved its economy and the life of its people rapidly after two decades of destructive war and the trauma of recovery. This change of values in 1986 away from doctrinaire Communism to a market economy – similar to the Chinese model – is not yet complete, and Vietnam remains a one-party state, with a Communist Party of 2 million. While the economic indicators have improved, a rash of corruption, bad debt and billion-dollar defalcations in 2012 checked investor confidence in Vietnam. There is also increasing concern about the government's human rights record.

As the world depression of the 1930s deepened, French exploitation of the Vietnamese people became extreme. Tens of thousands were herded into palm-thatched sheds in the plantations and forced to work 12 hours a day or more tapping rubber trees. Plantation owners in France insisted on such high production quotas that workers dropped with exhaustion or even died. There is evidence that some who failed to meet the quotas were punished by being beaten on the soles of their feet, after which they were forced to run.

In 1930, 8000 people set off on a protest march to the provincial capital of Vinh. The march was peaceful, and to emphasize its pacific nature the front ranks were all women and children. It has been said that the first use of military aircraft against civilians was at Guernica, during the Spanish Civil War, but six years before that, Potez biplanes from the French Armée de l'Air attacked the Vinh marchers on a narrow section of road, hemmed in on both sides by paddy-fields and trees. The first 22-lb bombs were dropped on the front of the march, among the women and children. After dropping their full load of six bombs the three aircraft strafed the marchers with Lewis machine-gun fire.

Following the discovery in 1916 of plans for a rebellion against the French, nationalist feeling was effectively subdued by police measures for two decades. However, many of the 100,000 Vietnamese conscripts who fought for France during the First World War had come back with nation-alist and some with Communist ideas. These last looked for leadership to a man then known as Nguyen Ai Quoc, which means 'Nguyen the patriot'. Later called Ho Chi Minh, he formed the Indo-Chinese Communist Party in 1930, a year of widespread unrest resulting from the unemployment and poverty caused by the world depression. Large plantings of rubber and rice had massively alienated land away from the peasants, who had no option but to become plantation labourers or coolies. By 1930, 3 per cent of land-owners held almost half of all land, while three out of four peasant families had none at all.

The Communists led uprisings and proclaimed two soviets – self-contained rebel states – in the north. French repression of these was severe to the point of brutality and again included the strafing and bombing of villages from the air and systematic torture. By early 1932 thousands of Vietnamese had been herded into prisons and concentration camps without decent facilities. As many as 1500 people were killed by French forces and 1000 more died of disease and starvation in the camps. There was some liberalization in the second part of the decade – due mainly to Leon Blum's Popular Front government in France – but the economic and political scene remained substantially unchanged at the coming of war again in 1939. France, quickly overwhelmed by the German *blitzkrieg*, was subsequently governed by the puppet Vichy regime, which permitted Japan to occupy Indo-China from late 1940 onwards.

At this stage there was already a group of North Vietnamese patriots, partly Communist, known as the Vietminh, the League of Independence. They fled across the border into China following an attack on them by the Vichy authorities in 1941. Among the Communists was 30-year-old Vo Nguyen Giap, a teacher of humble origins who had achieved a doctorate at Hanoi University. He was later a teacher. When Giap fled to China his wife and her sister were both arrested by the French and died in captivity.

In 1942 the Americans saw the value of the Vietminh as a resistance movement against the Japanese, but it was thought that the name of Nguyen Ai Quoc should not be used because of its pre-war associations. This was why the Vietminh leader assumed the name of Ho Chi Minh, which means 'he who enlightens'. When the Japanese surrendered in August 1945, the Vietminh took over control of the northern city of Hanoi – by the end of the month there was a Vietminh government claiming control of the whole of Vietnam. It was backed by a toughened partisan army of about 12,000.

The returning French at first offered independence within a French Union, but ultimately negotiations failed because they refused to accept a government that included what was then a minority of Communists. Instead a Dominion government was set up that was virtually devoid of popular support. The result, quite the opposite of that sought by the French, was a significant increase in Communist influence within the nationalist movement which, by 1949, had become Communist-dominated. Alarmed, the US government began to provide military equipment to France for use in Vietnam.

This did not happen without some misgivings. In the *New York Herald Tribune* (4 April 1950), respected commentator Walter Lippman seriously questioned French motives and wrote the following prophetic words: 'The French army can be counted to go on defending south-east Asia only if the Congress of the United States will pledge itself to subsidise heavily – in terms of several hundred million dollars a year and for many years to come – a French colonial war to subdue not only the Communists but the nationalists as well.' This identifies accurately the beginning of the great tragedy of Vietnam.

The Vietminh quickly infiltrated the Red River delta around Hanoi, proving more than a match for 180,000 French troops in almost a thousand concrete forts. Unrealistic direction of the war from Paris and a fear that the Vietminh would invade Laos led the French to attempt the defence of a mountain hollow called Dien Bien Phu, more than 200 miles from Hanoi in wild upland country, in 1954.

A ferocious Vietminh assault destroyed the steel-matting aircraft runways, cutting off Dien Bien Phu for good. In an attempt to reinforce it, day after day transport aircraft dropped paratroopers over the doomed forts. The Communists killed most of them before they reached the ground – the French surrendered after 56 days. Such was the bitterness of the struggle that the survivors who returned to France were described as being 'like Christ off the Cross'. When Dien Bien Phu surrendered it represented the first defeat of a major European power by an Asian Communist army. It cost the French 16,000 dead or captured and ended their will to go on fighting. They had lost a battle, a war and an empire.

The United States was unwilling to accept the Geneva agreements that ended the war, because they had created a new Communist state, North Vietnam, above the 17th parallel of latitude. Close on a million people, mostly Catholics, fled to the south. For several years, the northern and southern halves of the country devoted themselves to consolidation and recovery.

The first prime minister of South Vietnam, Ngo Dinh Diem, was firmly supported by the United States. The Geneva agreements had stipulated that elections be held in 1956 to determine who would govern the whole of Vietnam. When Diem, already unpopular in the south because of his autocracy and nepotism, refused to hold the elections four years after the agreed date, the Hanoi government decided to invade the south. The ensuing war was inconclusive for many years while US and Australian troops became increasingly involved.

In November 1960 Diem narrowly missed being deposed in a coup organized by paratroops of his own army. In 1963 the world was shocked by the campaign Diem – a Catholic Christian – launched against the Buddhists, especially by the protest suicides of seven monks, who soaked their robes in petrol and set fire to themselves. Soon afterwards elements of the army arrested and later murdered Diem, with other members of his family. During the phase of political instability that followed, ten prime ministers held office in 20 months. American military advisers had been assigned to Vietnam in 1962, and by 1968 half a million foreign troops were involved in a destructive and controversial war that seemed to have no ending and increasingly no point.

The death rate on both sides and the refusal of many young Americans and Australians to accept conscription to fight in Vietnam brought massive public opposition to the war, especially after the massacre by American soldiers of 400 unarmed civilians, mostly women and children, in the village of My Lai in 1968. And this was not the only such atrocity. Less well known is Operation Speedy Express, in which the 9th US Infantry Division killed thousands of civilians in the Mekong Delta to increase their 'body count', knowing these people were unlikely to be Vietcong fighters. These incidents and a worldwide outcry at the devastation of huge tracts of forest from aerial spraying of a dangerous herbicide, Agent Orange, hastened the ending of the war and the reunification of Vietnam as a Communist state. The war took over a million Vietnamese and 67,000 American lives, and cost the United States $150 billion. The 8 million tons of bombs dropped amounted to almost four times those dropped in the entire Second World War – probably the heaviest weapons assault in human history.

The extensive use during the war by the United States of Agent Orange, a defoliant containing a dangerous dioxin – both a poison and a teratogenic agent – caused widespread famine and later created what has been described as 'a genetic time bomb'. As late as 2012 Western observers were describing the continuing occurrence, in generation after generation, of birth defects, at times amounting to horrendous malformations of foetuses and infants. A Vietnamese woman doctor told me of 'many third-generation cases ... some poor families try to have a normal child, they end up with four, five, all malformed, or with mental problems or leukaemia. The worst are like beasts; they have to be kept in cages.' In 2012 the Vietnamese government estimated the number of severely deformed children at 150,000. This continuing tragedy is happening almost entirely in the south of Vietnam, where Agent Orange was used extensively, rather than in the north, where the defoliant was not used. In 2012, 50 years after the event, the US government allocated $41 million to a clean-up of Agent Orange still in the soil. Prior to that European governments and non-governmental organizations had given $23 million for site restoration, health care and reforestation.

So deep was the trauma of the war that Vietnam was not immediately assisted by the West to recover from the damage caused by the heavy aerial bombing. During this phase of recovery the economy remained stagnant, and the country was afflicted with serious humanitarian problems. Almost a million people were sent to 're-education' camps, in which at least 100,000 died from starvation and hard labour. During the late 1970s there was a huge exodus from the country when thousands put to sea in small boats. Many of these 'boat people' drowned at sea; others were preyed on by pirates – on some estimates 200,000 people were lost. Only in the late 1980s was Vietnam able to approach normality, with moves away from doctrinaire Communism towards a free-market economy and enhanced relations with the outside world. The economic reforms implemented by the Vietnamese Communist Party in 1986 legalized private ownership of farms and businesses, abolished price control, withdrew support from some loss-making state enterprises and opened the country to foreign investment. A trade embargo imposed by the United States was lifted in 1992.

With 89 million people in 2012, Vietnam has become one of the region's leading developing economies, with an annual growth rate of 7 to 8 per cent over the previous decade. High-tech industry, including information technology and a wide range of manufacturing, have spearheaded a major switch away from what had been mainly an agricultural economy. While real growth slackened during 2013, the electronics sector continued to prosper. Mobile phones and computer parts became the largest export item during the first half of the year – the current account surplus was a record in 2012 at 5.9 per cent of GDP. The Chu Lai free economic zone, which offers generous tax and land-rent concessions, has attracted a variety of foreign businesses – about a third of these are Chinese. By 2012 it accommodated 72 projects worth $1.7 billion.

Vietnam's human rights record has been criticized in recent years, especially its treatment of the Montagnard hill-tribe minority in the central highlands, many of whom have fled into neighbouring Cambodia. According to official figures 103 people were sentenced to death in 2003, mostly for drug offences and murder, and 64 were executed, often publicly before large crowds at the Thu Duc execution grounds near Ho Chi Minh City (formerly Saigon). Since 2004 statistics of death sentences have been declared a state secret; however, according to Amnesty International only 58 were executed in the five years to 2012, and none at all in that year, following new laws in 2010 reducing the number of crimes punished by death. However, these still include 'threats to national security'. Although Vietnam has been under pressure from the UN to exempt peaceful protests in 2013, laws providing the death penalty were used against bloggers and critics exposing nepotism and corruption in the government. At a trial of 14 Catholics on such charges early that year the defendants' lawyer claimed the police had used torture and concocted false evidence to implicate the accused.

There has been major financial trouble in the state-owned enterprises, which make up almost half of the economy, and which the government has said it will maintain. The shipbuilder Vinashin was almost brought to its knees by $4.5 billion of debt, defaulting on a $600-million foreign loan. Nine of its executives, some of whom are said to have connections with the prime minister, Nguyen Van Dung, were jailed. The head of Vietnam Electricity was sacked after losses of more than $1 billion.

Development of oil and gas fields has greatly assisted the economy, with exports of 191,000 barrels of oil a day in 2012 providing almost a quarter of the country's export income. Vietnam has coal reserves of 3.7 billion tons. Timber exports were limited in 1992, to preserve forests which still cover about 40 per cent of the country. A considerable recovery in the rice industry has made her the world's third largest exporter, and has resulted from redistribution of land to poor farmers. Tourism is an important industry. Almost seven million foreigners visited Vietnam in 2012, 11 per cent more than the previous year.

A population of 27 million in 1957 had risen to 89 million in 2012, although the growth rate had fallen to a little over one per cent in that year. There is now some concern over a significant ageing of the population. Most social indicators are good, with a literacy rate of 93 per cent in 2010, and a UN assessment that poverty had declined from 58 per cent of the population to 21 per cent in the two decades to 2012, lifting 30 million people out of poverty.

Like Thailand and Bangladesh, much of Vietnam is located on a large low-lying delta – that of the Mekong River – and is already being affected by sea-level rise and land subsidence. This represents a threat to Ho Chi Minh City, where 9 million people, about 10 per cent of the population, live. Almost half of the city is less than three feet above sea level – according to the Asian Development Bank, nearly 70 per cent is vulnerable to extreme flooding.

Among the great buildings of Angkor, early in the 14th century a marriage took place between a princess of the Khmer royal line and the 16-year-old son of an exiled chief from the region now called Laos. This youth,

Fa Ngum, was educated at the court of Angkor by Buddhist monks and scholars, and subsequently led a Khmer army of 10,000 back to recapture his father's lands. The kingdom thus established was based on the town of Luang Prabang in the mountainous north of Laos, and was called Lane Xang – the Land of the Million Elephants and One White Parasol.

The transference of Khmer methods and culture to this remote hill country allowed the new kingdom to develop rapidly. There was considerable territorial expansion. What is now Isan – north-east Thailand – became part of Lane Xang, hence the strong Laotian influence still evident in its language and culture. After almost four centuries of continuous existence Lane Xang was replaced by three principalities based on the main towns, Luang Prabang, the present capital, Vientiane, and Champassak in the south. All were subject to constant interference, and at times long periods of occupation, by either Vietnam or Thailand. Vientiane, the most vulnerable, was conquered by Siam (Thailand) in 1778. It was not until 1896 that French pressure forced the return of these Vientiane lands to Laos.

As with Afghanistan, it can be argued that Laos does not exist as a national entity, but is a group of tribes artificially welded into a 'nation' by the French colonial administration. This view is supported by the considerable autonomy of the provinces, which, from the establishment of the Communist government in 1975, have collected their own taxes and conducted independent trade with the outside world. These provinces are often dominated by local 'strong men' who operate almost independently. Difficult communications encourage regionalism – barely 20 per cent of the roads are sealed and many are almost impassable. Most of Laos consists of high rugged mountains that march across the country, range after range, to form an almost complete barrier to easy communication. These are clothed in dense forest, and all but the larger towns can be approached only by footpaths. Again, like Afghanistan, Laos has many different ethnic groups and dialects. Many of these minorities are in border areas, and consist of peoples also living in neighbouring countries – the Lao people are considered to make up less than half the total population. There is little industry of consequence other than the illegal export of opium, which is grown by the Meo (Hmong) hill tribes, some mining, and timber-felling, much of which is also technically illegal.

Like many south-east Asian countries, Laos has exploited its considerable timber resources to feed the increasing world hunger for wood. The extent of this logging of some of the world's largest and most beautiful rainforest has attracted considerable criticism. Three 'development' companies run by the military have been given the right to exploit the forests to an extent that is unsustainable. This appears to be largely to the benefit of Thai interests, especially the military, who dominate government and business in that country. In 2012 there were reports that the Vietnamese military were also involved in illegal logging in Laos, especially of rosewood, which is in high demand for furniture.

French colonial dominion over Laos was unprogressive, but not onerous. A few French scholars became interested in the region's past and resurrected and rationalized the history of Lane Xang, by that time almost lost in obscurity. This permitted Laos to acquire at least the theoretical basis of a national identity. Nevertheless, nationalist feeling scarcely existed until the 1930s, when a Marxist group was established in northern Laos. This, the Pathet Lao, was probably the mildest and most eclectic Communism in the world until in 1954 it was stiffened by cadres from the Vietminh, at that time locked in their final struggle with the French. A shadowy, slow-moving war ensued until, with the ending of the Vietnam War, the Communists controlled most of Laos, subsequently forming the government. In 1975 the Lao monarchy was dissolved, and replaced by the Communist People's Democratic Republic. With this the long-drawn-out war also ended.

Among its less attractive aspects was heavy American B52 bombing of many parts of Laos, including a remote and beautiful upland, the Plain of the Jars, and the narrow red laterite road in the jungle-clad east known as the Ho Chi Minh Trail, which the Vietcong used to move weapons south. Over two million tons of bombs were dropped on Laos, as much as the United States used in the Second World War, and huge numbers of these are still scattered around the countryside, unexploded and causing hundreds of deaths in the villages – many of these are children. A major feature of the war was recruitment by both the Americans and the Communists of Meo hill tribesmen, who were thus compelled to fight against each other. By 1964, 7000 Meo volunteers were being provided with rice, weapons and pay by a CIA operation based on Udorn Thani, in north-east Thailand. More than 400,000 people fled the country in 1975 – about half to the United States – and the Australian and US governments agreed to accept more in 2004.

The new government was considerably influenced in its policies and actions by Communist Vietnam, which had embraced a Leninist philosophy derived from the former USSR. It undertook a purge of its former antagonists, directed with particular ferocity against the remaining Meo hill tribesmen, who were now to be largely abandoned by the United States. As many as 30,000 people were consigned to re-education camps, under harsh conditions. The king, queen and crown prince, all of whom had tried to stand aside from the conflict, died in one of these places – the king reportedly from starvation.

Although, like Vietnam, Laos converted to a 'market' economy in 1986, it is an almost universally deprived country, largely undeveloped and frozen in a static subsistence agricultural economy. Surveys in 2010 indicated that almost three-quarters of households were poor, with 26 per cent below the poverty level. Thirty per cent of children under 5 are underweight. Three-quarters of the population of 6.5 million work in agriculture, mostly subsistence farming. Opposition political parties are not tolerated and the media are strictly controlled. The government, effectively a Politburo of nine, has a reputation for being reclusive, corrupt and at times brutal. An Australian woman, Kerry Danes, wrongly imprisoned in Laos, subsequently publicized details about the Phonthong Detention Centre, 'where prisoners, male and female, were kept in tiny sweltering cells and had to kneel in order to address their guards. Many were suffering malnutrition and severe dehydration, others had gone mad. Torture during interrogations, conducted by special police from outside the prison, was routine, including the infamous wooden leg blocks, which interrogators stood on, rolling them back and forth along prisoners' legs, causing excruciating pain.'

The opening of two bridges across the lower Mekong has made possible road traffic between Thailand and Laos for the first time. A network of roads into China, Cambodia, Vietnam and Burma, and the first railways in Laos, planned under the proposed Greater Mekong Sub-region Scheme, would further reduce the country's isolation, perhaps in time making it an entrepôt for the whole region. There is also an 18,000-megawatt hydro-electricity potential along the rapidly flowing Mekong River, which Thailand is anxious to exploit. The great natural beauty of Laos, its quietude and picturesque towns, attracted a growing tourist trade, peaking at 735,000 visitors in 1993, although numbers dropped sharply the following year. Sporadic terrorist attacks linked to the former regime reduced the number of tourists, with a consequent general depression of the economy, but by 2012 tourist arrivals were up 14 per cent over the previous year to more than three million.

However, with a steady stream of trucks taking thousands of logs along the improved Ho Chi Minh Highway into Vietnam, the beautiful forests of Laos are dwindling, although tree planting of some kind still covered 69 per cent of the country in 2010, according to the World Bank. Among the exploited areas are natural teak and rosewood forests, some of the few left in the world. Since under Lao law exports of unmilled logs are banned, almost all of this is illegal, but little seems to be done to control what is a blatantly obvious trade. The offending companies are said to have links to the military in Vietnam and senior officials in Laos.

A Lao government decision in 2012 to go ahead with a giant hydro-electric dam at Xayaburi, on the Mekong, attracted widespread protest, especially from Vietnam and Cambodia, the downstream nations. The $3.5-billion dam, financed by a consortium of Thai banks, will generate 1285 megawatts of power, most of which will go to Thailand. Ten other dams on the Mekong in Laos are planned, raising concerns that this will change the character of the earth's last untamed great river forever. There are also fears that damming the river will disrupt a fishing catch on which millions of poorer people depend for food. According to the NGO International Rivers, more than 60 million people live along and depend on the Mekong.

Although the French maintained the monarchy in Cambodia throughout the colonial period, they did little else for the country. Education and health services were minimal. Between the world wars roads and railways were built to service rubber plantations and to facilitate rice exports, to the benefit of French planters and an increasing number of Chinese business-men. The Cambodian peasant was, however, heavily taxed – around a third of his income in direct tax and indirect taxes on rice, salt, opium and alcohol.

Cambodia was at this time the epitome of the decadent Asian state. The king maintained a harem of 400, spent money at will on all kinds of extrav-agances – Filipino bands, 250 elephants, yachts, boats and carriages – with the willing concurrence of the Cambodian peasantry. The king was seen as near-divine, an indispensable link to the gods on high who condemn the crops to failure through flood or drought, or kill with lightning. The prof-ligacy of his material possessions and apparently abundant virility were considered essential to his status.

In 1941 the French selected, from some 400 possible contenders for the throne, the 18-year-old Prince Norodom Sihanouk. He led the traditional life of leisure and luxury over the next decade, but even in this he displayed the restless energy that was to become characteristic. He interested himself in jazz music, wrote his own songs, learned to play the saxophone and conducted his own band. He travelled widely, married four times and had 13 children.

France granted Cambodia a measure of self-government in 1949, but real independence did not come until after Dien Bien Phu in 1954. Sihanouk abdicated in favour of his parents, became leader of a political party that won a landslide victory in a general election and made a widely publicized transition from king to prime minister. He held this position until his father's death in 1960, when he again became head of state.

For several years Cambodia under Sihanouk became something of a model for south-east Asia. A large rice-export surplus kept the economy in a healthy state and provided funds for development – schools, health clinics and irrigation works. A descendant of the Khmer kings, Sihanouk took a particular interest in the restoration of Angkor, which became a major tourist destination. Driving through Thailand to Angkor at about that time, I can recall being impressed at the succession of tidy, prosperous and placid villages in Cambodia. After living in north-east Thailand, with its sad-eyed children showing the tell-tale pot-bellies that betray malnutrition, it was a pleasure and a relief to see well-dressed and well-fed children and contented-looking communities.

Unfortunately this Arcadian situation was not to last. Sihanouk disagreed with American policies in Vietnam, predicting that China would come to dominate the region, and basing Cambodian policies on what he saw as an inevitable need for an accommodation with her. In 1960 the two countries signed a treaty of non-aggression and friendship. Sihanouk broke off diplomatic relations with Thailand and South Vietnam, and in 1963 demanded an end to all US aid programmes, under which $65 million had been given to Cambodia during the previous eight years. He asserted that his reason was evidence of a US Central Intelligence Agency (CIA) plot to overthrow his government, in the same way, he claimed, as the CIA had engineered the downfall and murder of Ngo Dinh Diem in South Vietnam. Cambodia turned, not to the Communist world, but to France to replace the American projects.

The end to US aid, which, including funding of the army, probably amounted to a quarter of Cambodia's revenues, and declining income from the rice crop, caused considerable financial hardship. The army became particularly disgruntled and its leader, General Lon Nol, disenchanted with Sihanouk. The head of state divorced himself almost completely from national affairs, almost completely preoccupied with his newest enthusiasm, making films.

In spite of Cambodia's neutralism, she eventually became involved in the Vietnam War. The Vietnamese Communists used the wild eastern section of Cambodia, near the border, to move supplies and men, and this attracted heavy American bombing in that region. A coup in 1970 by General Lon Nol, by then prime minister, resulted in Sihanouk's downfall and exile. Lon Nol, who was strongly pro-American, committed Cambodia to a disastrous direct involvement in the war. His offensives against the Vietnamese in that and the following year were failures, in which the Cambodian army suffered severe losses. From this time on, Vietnamese and local Communists, and disaffected peasants and hill tribesmen, continued to fight the Cambodian army.

Lon Nol was defeated, deposed and fled the country in 1975, leaving Cambodia in a state of virtual anarchy. It was then subjected to four nightmare years of Communist Khmer Rouge government from 1975 under the leadership of a former schoolteacher, Saloth Sar, who took the revolutionary name of Pol Pot. Mass killings, justified as 'class struggle', destroyed 20 per cent of the Cambodian people, including nearly all of the educated and professional classes and the Vietnamese minority of about half a million, in brutal mass executions that shocked the world. People were executed on the flimsiest of pretexts – often simply because they wore glasses, this being considered the mark of an intellectual. Estimates of the dead are as high as 1.7 million. In an echo of China's 'great leap forward' Cambodians were driven to 12-hour work days in the interests of a Four Year Plan for the economy that had little hope of realization. Many more people died of overwork and malnutrition. Meanwhile relations with Vietnam became increasingly strained.

In 1979 a Vietnamese invasion was on the whole welcomed by most Cambodians. Nevertheless the occupation brought another decade of social disintegration and death, since many Cambodians resented the Vietnamese presence and the Khmer Rouge continued to fight. Although the Vietnamese withdrew their armies from Cambodia in 1989, factional fighting continued and it was not until 1991 that an uneasy peace was signed. Hun Sen, a former Khmer Rouge battalion commander and later a leading figure in the government imposed by the Vietnamese, emerged as the major focus of power, even though his People's Party ran second to the royalist Funcinpec in UN-sponsored elections in 1993. Hun Sen refused to surrender power and entered into a fragile coalition with Funcinpec, until he finally consolidated his position with a violent coup in 1997 in which many of his political opponents were killed and others arrested – more than a hundred officials and supporters of Funcinpec perished at this time. Hun Sen's People's Party won the largest part of the vote – 41 per cent – in elections in 1998 held in this climate of fear and regarded by international observers as seriously flawed. Hun Sen has been prime minister ever since. The last Khmer Rouge gave themselves up in 1998, but there was no peace, with regular reports of killings and torture by the Hun Sen government of political opponents, and savage police attacks on demonstrators. Sihanouk, restored to the throne in 1993, found himself little more than a figurehead.

His health declining after he handed the monarchy over to Prince Norodom Sihamoni in 2004, he spent most of his remaining years in China, where he died in 2012.

War, revolution and oppression have severely damaged what was previously a prosperous and peaceful country, now plagued by a major cluster of endemic diseases, continuing malnutrition and one of the highest rates of infant mortality in the world. A UN food programme statement in 2012 estimated that 40 per cent of Cambodia's children were chronically malnourished, due to shortfalls in food production from subsistence farms. Life expectancy is low, at 58 for men and 64 for women. Due to the murder of so many teachers by the Khmer Rouge, few schools can operate effectively, and the literacy rate is under 50 per cent.

Cambodia has been especially cursed with landmines, estimated at between two and six million, which will take at least a century to clear up. So much of the agricultural land is seeded with these deadly devices that they regularly kill at least 50 innocent civilians – often children – every month and injure several times that number. It is claimed that Cambodia has the world's highest number of amputees for its population because of this. Landmine contamination has also severely affected food production, making large areas too dangerous to work in.

By 2008 Cambodia's capital, Phnom Penh, showed some signs of growth, with high-rise buildings appearing for the first time and the emergence of a small middle class. Offshore oil reserves of about 500 million barrels were due for development in 2012, but late in that year the project was deferred until 2016. Cambodia is still very dependent on foreign aid, and material advances are largely due to Chinese technical and financial assistance. But on the downside, there has been little sign of 'trickle down' to the great majority of poorer people – on the contrary, many are forced from their land to the benefit of large and aggressive agribusinesses. Fourteen women were in jail in 2012, including a leading journalist, and a young girl was shot dead in the same year because she was protesting against a 'land grab'. Since the beginning of the century 300,000 people have been forced from their homes and land by government sales of land concessions.

What economic growth there is comes from 330,000 young, nimble-fingered and low-paid women on a minimum wage of $80 a month, who churn out clothing and footwear worth more than $4 billion in foreign exchange – this amounts to 80 per cent of the country's export income. One South Korean-owned garment factory in Phnom Penh employs 1300 women, who can produce 20,000 items of clothing a day. There are nearly 300 more like it, most of which are owned by investors from China and Taiwan. In 2013 there were strikes and violent demonstrations in many of these, workers complaining of low wages, bad conditions and long hours.

Long-time democracy activist Sam Rainsy returned from exile to lead the Cambodia National Rescue Party in elections in 2013. The government lost 29 seats, retaining 68 against the opposition's 55. Nevertheless Rainsy refused to accept this result, claiming that vote-rigging and other electoral irregularities had so distorted the count that his party ought to have won government. Police using smoke grenades and water cannon disrupted a protest meeting of 20,000 in Phnom Penh, leaving one person dead and hundreds injured. The opposition boycotted the first meeting of the new parliament, and undertook to hold more protest rallies.

36 Burma: Rule by the Gun

Of the countries of south-east Asia Burma (Myanmar) is perhaps the most varied and beautiful, ranging as it does from placid beaches in the south through broad and fertile river plains to snow-clad uplands in the wild border regions with China and Laos. Cherry trees, rhododendrons, magnolia and juniper grow wild in these mountains, in which bears, tigers, leopards and elephants can still be found. A timeless river life continues on and alongside the huge Irrawaddy, over a thousand miles long, that divides the country as it flows to a fertile delta, once the most prolific rice-growing region in the world. Teak from rapidly reducing forests is moved along the river, mostly into China. The Irrawaddy is the main highway of Burma, used by river steamers, fishing boats and barges on which whole families live out their lives.

The people are equally varied. As in so much of Asia, Burma's boundaries were determined by the colonial power, and they include at least seven racial groups in a country that can be divided into four distinct regions. The majority are the Burmese, making up about 70 per cent of the population. Most are Buddhist, a friendly, tolerant and cultured people, conservative and bred from early childhood to have a deep respect for established authority, politeness in social relationships, and education. They have a particular dislike of violence, both by virtue of a long-standing Buddhist influence but also due to an older animist belief which has it that those who die a violent death become evil though influential spirits called *nats*.

Burma's paradox is that for more than two decades it was ruled, absolutely against the declared intention of its people, by a violent, cruel, inept and self-seeking military government, which imprisoned, killed or tortured its own people as a matter of routine if they offered even token opposition, or refused to be driven into slave labour to the financial benefit of army officers. One of its actions was to rename the country Myanmar, but such is the disrepute in which the regime is held that this name has been extensively disregarded.

There was a much-publicized 'liberalization' in 2011, which saw some political prisoners released, some opposition members elected to parliament, and some freeing-up of press censorship and labour laws. Although this did achieve its probable objectives – to enhance Burma's international reputation and encourage greater foreign investment – the parliament has no real powers, the army is still in control and many of the abuses it has inflicted on the country continue.

Burma was governed as a province of India until 1937 – virtually the whole of the colonial period. The delta of the Irrawaddy, some 200 by 100 miles of flat plain, was largely jungle and tall grass when the British came. When they left it was a cultivated region of ten million acres, growing two-fifths of the world's rice – rice said to have been the best in the world. Largely because of this rapid expansion of agriculture, Burma's population of four million in 1825 increased fourfold over the next 100 years. But this increase in productivity did not benefit the average Burmese, and the British only indirectly. Although the larger trading ventures were British, the rice-growing industry that was so large a factor in the country's sudden social and economic revolution was substantially controlled by Indian businessmen.

The diversion of such large areas of land to a rice monoculture severely damaged a placid self-sufficient village life previously typical of Burma. The agrarian problems which had reduced so many Burmese peasants to destitution by the 1930s were exacerbated by the rapacity of the money-lending class, the Chettiars, who lent the Burmese peasants money on the security of their ricefields, then foreclosed on the mortgages. Interest at 18 per cent was common, and rates up to 100 per cent not unusual. The situation was aggravated by the volume of indentured labour brought in annually from India to help plant and harvest the rice crop – almost half a million in 1927 alone. While many of these Indians returned home, probably a million stayed.

Britain, which could have imposed controls on immigration and the alienation of land, did not do so until it was too late. Almost universal poverty and unrest afflicted the Burmese in the final decades before the Second World War. Violent anti-Indian rioting in the capital, Yangon (Rangoon), in 1930 was symptomatic: 120 Indians were killed and more than 1000 injured. Rioting continued on and off throughout the ensuing years. Often these disturbances seemed to have religious origins, but their intensity and duration were really due to increasing rural poverty as the world depression deepened. As yet the rebellions were regional and lacked specific direction. The factor common to most of them was a demand to separate Burma from the Indian administration.

During the stormy years of the 1930s a group of students at the university, founded in Yangon in 1920, banded together under the name of *thakins*, and it is in the activities of this group that a revolutionary nationalism can first be seen. The word *thakin* means 'master', and was customarily required of Burmese when addressing a European. The Burmese *thakins* adopted it as an assertion of their racial equality. They were to become very important to Burma, for among them were most of the leaders who would bring the country to independence.

As in India, internal self-government was granted in 1937, although Britain retained control of foreign policy, defence and finance, and the power to overrule the legislature in an emergency. However, this new constitution did separate Burma from India. In the light of later events, it is important to note that the new government had jurisdiction over little more than half the country. Large areas in the northern, eastern and western border regions, occupied by non-Burmese racial groups, were outside its authority. The most important minority are the Shans, who are akin to the Thai and Lao peoples, and the warlike hill tribes called Karens, from among whom the British recruited most of the colonial police and militia.

The first years of internal self-government were stormy, as communal problems worsened. In 1938, 200 Indians were killed and hundreds of their houses and shops looted and burned. Civil disobedience campaigns became common, with persistent strikes and demonstrations. At times the transport system of Yangon was disrupted by scores of women lying down across the tram lines. British goods, and the shops that sold them, were picketed and boycotted.

Matters did not improve with the coming of the Second World War. An opportunistic lawyer named U Saw, who became prime minister, arrested most of the *thakin* nationalists on the grounds of subversion. However, one of the more important, Aung San, escaped to Japan. U Saw was arrested and exiled when the British discovered that he too was negotiating with the Japanese.

When the Japanese occupied Burma in 1942 they brought with them a puppet government headed by Ba Maw and the *thakin* exile Aung San, at the head of a nucleus anti-British Burmese army called the Thirty, which had been organized in Bangkok. Although the Japanese were at first welcomed as liberators, their arrogance and brutality during the war years soon reversed public opinion. In August 1944 Aung San turned against them, operating a secret underground that was to become Burma's leading political party.

After the war the Labour government in Britain was willing to grant Burmese independence. Aung San did not live to see it. On a July morning in 1947 six hired gunmen assassinated him and six of his colleagues. The former prime minister, U Saw, who had been released from internment, was convicted of instigating this political massacre, and hanged early in 1948.

The astrologers, always consulted in Buddhist countries on the timing of events, decided that 4.20 a.m. on 4 January 1948 was the most auspicious moment for Burma's freedom. Accordingly, from that time she became an independent republic, outside the British Commonwealth, under the prime-ministership of one of the surviving *thakins*, a gentle, devout Buddhist named U Nu. U Nu adhered so strictly to the Buddhist principle of taking no life that it is said he made his Cabinet use a side entrance rather than step over a stream of ants crossing a corridor, and so risk killing one of them.

The country was immediately beset with problems – Communist, Shan and Karen insurrections among them. Within weeks U Nu had lost control of all of Burma outside Yangon. The rebels had no difficulty arming themselves, for both Japanese and Allied arms dumps remained open to any comer. There were many Communist cells in the army and they deserted practically en masse, leaving the Yangon government with only a few loyal battalions and provincial units. Forty-four members of the Constituent Assembly left it to become insurgents. For eight years Burma was the scene of an almost incredibly confused pattern of intrigue and violence. The main sufferers were the civilian population. The rebels blew up bridges, rail track and roads, and ambushed trains and river ferries. Passengers were held until their relatives paid ransoms.

The government moved closer to the Communist world in 1953, when it refused any further US economic aid. At the end of 1954 Burma concluded barter agreements with China and Russia that committed a million tons of rice a year – rather more than half her export surplus – until 1960. Considerable disillusionment resulted from this, due to the slow delivery and poor quality of the Communist goods offered in return.

Matters reached a crisis in 1962, when the army commander, General Ne Win, who had been one of the Thirty, took over the government. A complex ideology, known as the Burmese Way to Socialism, was evolved, owing much to traditional customary law. Patterns for the present – and probably the future – were set by Ne Win's inception of a cadre system within the army, a special corps of army cadets trained at a centre near Yangon. Recruitment was competitive and very selective – Ne Win plainly regarded them as a class of future leaders.

Burma was now to be almost completely sealed off from the world. Ne Win's regime was reluctant to allow any foreigners into the country, and had a passion for keeping foreign influences to a minimum. Much of this was directed at Indians. Their businesses were steadily nationalized and the owners deported during the 1960s. This did not result in improvements – many factories and shops were grossly mismanaged after they became government-owned.

In spite of attempts to revive and reform agricultural practice, rice production continued to decline. Community health remained among the worst in the world, with high rates of infant mortality and almost a million registered lepers. Military rule took a turn for the worse from 1988, when repression of unrest and student riots became brutal, the army using its weapons, torture and imprisonment to eliminate any opposition. At least 3000 people were killed by the army in that year, including hundreds of students cut down by machine-gun fire in Yangon. The Burmese media were heavily censored, and public assemblies of more than five people made illegal.

The military permitted elections in 1990, which were won by the National League for Democracy, led by Aung San's daughter, Aung San Suu Kyi, in a landslide victory, taking 392 seats of 485 contested. Parties supported by the army won only 2 per cent of the seats. Suu Kyi, after an education abroad, had returned to Burma in 1988 to care for her ailing mother. She became a rallying point for democratic forces almost at once, and was placed under house arrest in 1989. The State Law and Order Restoration Council (SLORC) refused to hand over power to the democratically elected party. Suu Kyi was awarded the Nobel Peace Prize in 1991, and showed outstanding courage in maintaining an international profile while coming under persistent attack from the military. Her followers also suffered sustained and vicious persecution.

Meanwhile, social and economic conditions continued to deteriorate in what is now one of the world's poorest countries. Burma's export of more than three million tons of rice a year before the Second World War had fallen below a million tons in 1967, and was 778,000 tons in 2011. Exports of teak and other hardwoods make up around half of Burma's small export income. Probably Burma's most valuable export is a theoretically illegal one. According to the UN Office on Drugs and Crime, land use for opium production increased 17 per cent in 2012, although the government has a programme to eradicate poppy-growing. Burma, the world's largest opium source after Afghanistan, produced 25 per cent of the global opium supply in that year, much of it refined locally into heroin before being exported. The United States and a number of other countries applied trade sanctions in protest at the human rights record of the Burmese military. These were strengthened in 1997 and again in 2003, restricting private investment in Burma. There was some easing of these in 2011. Burma's population, 54 million in 2012, is growing by only 1.07 per cent, not because of effective birth-control measures, but because of the almost universal poverty and ill health. HIV/AIDS is a major problem, partly due to the number of Burmese women who are driven by poverty into prostitution in neighbouring Thailand.

The sheer size of the military, over a million in 2012, has become a millstone around Burma's neck. Nearly 40 per cent of all government spending has been devoted to it, compared with about two per cent each for public education and health care, although the 2012/13 budget proposed at least doubling these. The armed forces have emerged as a separate elite, provided with subsidized housing, health care, food and transport. Thousands of ordinary citizens have been conscripted at gunpoint as slave labourers on railways, pipelines and business ventures, such as tourist hotels, often owned by army officers and their families.

Virtual slave labour was also used to build the extraordinary complex which is now the national capital, Nay Pyi Taw – this translates as the Abode of Kings – in the decade from 2002, at a cost the military refuses to disclose, but which has been estimated at several billion dollars. This place is not so much a city as a series of connected strongpoints, a cross between a pleasure garden, a strategic retreat, and a home for the Burmese military and bureaucrats. With broad, well-paved boulevards, five golf courses and a soccer stadium, it provides an extravagant lifestyle for its occupants. Beijing-based author Brook Larmer, who visited it, describes 'a zoo equipped with an air-conditioned penguin house, a safari park, even a 480-acre "landmark" garden including wooden houses inhabited, on occasion, by ethnic minorities in native garb – a sort of human zoo' (*National Geographic*, August 2011). Burma's orientation towards China, with whom she has considerable trade and cultural contacts, appeared to shift abruptly in 2011, when President Thein Sein postponed plans for the $3.6-billion Myitsone dam across the Irrawaddy River, saying it 'was being built against the will of the people'. It was designed to produce as much as 3600 megawatts of power, 90 per cent of it for export to China, and was to be the first of seven dams in the Irrawaddy headwaters.

On 30 May 2003, as Suu Kyi, briefly released from house arrest, and her supporters were travelling along a quiet road in northern Burma, their road convoy was attacked by government-recruited militia, who brutally killed between 70 and 80 unarmed people, using spears, stones and knives, and injured many others. Suu Kyi herself was fortunate to escape injury or worse. Although the government did its best to conceal the facts about this 'black Friday', it is alleged that 30 convicts were taken from Mandalay Prison to a nearby army camp, where they were ordered to make the attack in company with others similarly recruited. It is also claimed that this militia did not know who they were to attack. Adding to the bizarre nature of this violent and tragic incident, some of the attackers were reported to have been dressed as Buddhist monks.

Immediately after this Suu Kyi was returned to close house arrest, in spite of an international outcry. Japan and the United States suspended their aid programmes and the United States banned all Burmese imports.

In spite of a cosmetic, so-called 'road map to democracy' in Burma sponsored by the military, an Amnesty International delegation to the country late in 2003 were denied access to Aung San Suu Kyi, and reported that human rights abuse in Burma showed no signs of improvement. Repressive elements hardened further in 2004, with the dismissal of the prime minister, Khin Nyunt, and the foreign minister, Win Aung, both of whom had been regarded as relatively moderate. Soe Win, believed to have been involved in the 'black Friday' affair, became the new prime minister.

In 2008 the huge cyclone Nargis devastated the densely populated Irrawaddy delta. More than 130,000 people were killed or reported missing, and damage to crops and property exceeded $10 billion. According to the World Food Programme, 'vast rice-growing areas have been wiped out and whole villages totally eradicated' – around two-thirds of Burma's ricefields were affected. Although more than a million people were left homeless the regime's response was negative, among other things delaying the entry of international relief supplies.

Faced with increasing international disapproval and crippled by trade and money sanctions, the regime instituted some reforms in 2011. Aung San Suu Kyi was released from house arrest, and more than 200 political prisoners freed. New laws permitted the formation of trade unions and allowed the right to strike, and there was some relaxation of press censorship. In 2012 Suu Kyi was elected to parliament, her National League for Democracy winning 41 of the 44 seats it contested. After she had had discussions with President Thein Sein, the state media reported they had agreed to 'work together in matters of common interest that will really benefit the country and the people'.

However the military still controls the parliament, and, although the regime denies this, there are estimated to be 2200 political prisoners still confined, and there are still reports of corruption and human rights abuses, continuing battles with minority ethnic groups and allegations of vote-rigging by the regime in the 2012 elections. A Human Rights Watch report released that year says forced labour and military conscription are still imposed, there has been continued blockage of international aid, and attacks on civilians and private property, rape, torture and the use of land-mines continue. In Aug San Suu Kyi's words, 'Ultimate power still rests with the army, so until we have the army solidly behind the process of democratization we cannot say we have got the point where there will be no danger of a U-turn.'

A friend who visited Burma in 2013 as a tourist was struck by the intensity of the military and police presence on the streets, and the public fear of them. A widely travelled person, he said he had never seen so many armed soldiers and police anywhere else – 'they are everywhere'. Tourist movements were tightly controlled and visitors advised not to raise political matters with locals. However, his impression was that many people want the name Burma restored, and he remarked on the large number of timber barges on the Irrawaddy, proceeding upstream with teak logs, presumably for China.

37 The Asian Century?

Will this be the Asian century? This term, which was probably first used in conversations between Chinese and Indian leaders Deng Xiaoping and Rajiv Gandhi in 1988, has turned up in various contexts thousands of times since. Vague enough to be accepted at face value by many people, it nevertheless has connotations that need to be looked at more carefully. Will one or more of the Asian nations assume global leadership, militarily, economically and perhaps most important of all, in developing a political philosophy which might inform government of most of the world? What methods are being used to achieve that most illusory measure of prosperity, higher gross national product – is anything really changing for the mass of Asian people, billions of them, in the villages, urban slums and industrial sweatshops?

If one considers sheer weight of numbers significant, Asians are already the largest regional group. Of 7.2 billion people in the world in 2013, more than four billion were Asian. Asia's three biggest nations, China, India and Indonesia, make up almost 40 per cent of the world's population – 2.8 billion people (UN figures).

Then there is the matter of money. China's reserves of $3.3 trillion are allowing her to invest heavily in many parts of the world, not the least in the United States. China's acquisition of the world's largest pork producer and processor, Smithfield Foods, for $4.7 billion, made it the new employer of thousands of Americans in scores of rural communities. Buying AMC Entertainment, one of the largest movie-theatre chains in the United States, gives China control of more movie-ticket sales than anyone else in the world. Both China and India are investing heavily in Australian coal mines, and China has made major acquisitions of agricultural land in that country.

These events are manifestations of globalization which, viewed simplistically, is an increasing interchange of products, ideas and cultures around the world. In practice it is rather more than that – in the words of billionaire investor George Soros, 'It's not trade that makes it global, it's the movement of capital.' He was referring to the trillions of dollars of 'wandering' opportunistic money, enabled by modern technology to be shifted almost in moments from one country to another, preying on currencies and whole economies. 'Flight of capital' was a major contributor to a collapse of the economies of South Korea and almost every south-east Asian country in 1997, wiping $2 trillion from the value of their stock markets, and making millions unemployed.

Something similar began to happen in 2013. The printing of nearly $3 trillion in 'new' money – so-called 'quantitative easing' – in the United States and heavy printing of money in Japan swamped the world with cheap credit, greatly increasing the volume of 'wandering' money. Even vague hints that the printing presses might be slowed down was enough to prompt a major 'flight of capital' from many of the underdeveloped economies, creating crises of confidence they could ill afford. The worst early effects were felt in India, but the economies of Thailand, Indonesia, Taiwan and Malaysia also weakened.

Most of the world's very poor – those who are actively malnourished, in bad health, inadequately housed and denied education – live in Asia, and their numbers have already increased in this century to more than a billion. This continuing poverty and population growth seem likely to remain major world problems, especially if Asian economies continue to be disrupted by massive currency and equity trading manipulation. While the need to improve the lot of the poor is obvious on compassionate grounds alone, if remedies are delayed, the catastrophic global economic, environmental and social consequences are no less important. Virtually all resources – food, water, energy, arable soil, minerals, fisheries – will become scarcer, and ocean and air pollution will increase. Lakes and rivers everywhere are becoming polluted and depleted; and almost half of all humans lack access to safe and adequate drinking water. And while grain harvests have increased, the critical annual production per person has not – it is hovering at around 350 kg. More destructive climate change, water shortages and the chronic overuse of soils seem almost inevitable, and must almost certainly reduce food production in the future – prices had already risen dramatically by 2103. Hence it seems probable that evolution of 'the Asian century' will be checked – and soon – by the natural and demographic influences already in play: the billions of Asia will not be able to evolve into affluent consumerist societies like those of the West and Japan, because the planet's resources are finite and its tolerance for pollution is limited. Consequently, the drive to emulate the material profligacy of the West evident in several Asian countries, and its encouragement by elements in the West, are terrible and potentially disastrous mistakes. Some simple statistics make this clear. According to a UN report, in 2006 the wealthiest 10 per cent of the world's people consumed over 85 per cent of its resources, while half the world's population had to share barely one per cent. On 2012 figures from the OECD, per capita wealth ranged from $540,000 in Switzerland down to $5500 in India. Even large surrenders of Western affluence could not permit significantly larger consumerism in the developing world.

It has been fashionable to speak of the 'Asian tigers' and 'Asia's economic miracle'. While both these terms could be applied to China and Singapore, elsewhere they were inappropriate, as the financial catastrophes of 1997 and 1998 and the difficulties of recovery afterwards have shown. The reality is that the so-called 'tiger' economies brought substantial wealth to a tiny minority in India, Korea and south-east Asia, low wages by Western standards to a somewhat larger but still small fraction of industrial workers, and did little to ease the massive problems of the majority of the people, who still live in villages and work on the land. The reality behind the 'miracle' was and remains the existence of a low-paid, compliant workforce ready for exploitation by Western, Chinese, Taiwanese and Japanese capital.

Much of this industry has been based on money borrowed or invested from abroad, low wages and bad, often dangerous and unhealthy, work conditions. Thousands of workers protested in the streets of the Bangladeshi industrial suburb of Ashulia in 2012 after a factory fire killed 110 people, mostly young women, who were making clothing for fashionable Western brands. The following year over 1100 died when an eight-storey building in Dhaka, condemned as unsafe, collapsed. More than 3000 workers were crammed into the building. Many of the dead were children, who died in crèches provided so their mothers could work. Millions of young women in the poorer countries typically work 12 hours a day, 6 days a week at sewing machines in overcrowded, dimly lit and poorly ventilated factories. There are more than four million garment workers in 5000 factories in Bangladesh alone, and 300,000 in Cambodia.

Frequently industry is subsidized by governments, at the initiative of officials who are themselves the main beneficiaries. While wretched working conditions persist, too often borrowed money has been spent on infrastructure of no real service to the bulk of the people, such as urban office towers and golf courses. Burma's new and artificial capital, Nay Pyi Taw, is perhaps the most flagrant example of lavish lifestyles provided to an elite at the expense of the poor. This illusory prosperity does create, for a time, work for peasants who leave the villages and the fields to become labourers and factory workers, and who later often become unemployed. In most places pressure on rural land makes it difficult for these displaced workers to go back to where they came from.

Discontented, desperately poor, with little hope for the future, they have become a dangerous, idle class, forced into crime, driven to become social and political malcontents. Such people, most of them young, now number in the scores of millions.

None of this is to say that development in Asia over the last three decades has been uniformly bad. There have been innumerable innovative and useful projects, as the many examples in Japan and China and the advanced position of India in information technology demonstrate. It becomes a question of what form development should take in Asia as a whole. Plainly, if the two and a half billion people in China and India follow the consumerist models of the West, as Japan has already done, the consequences for the world will be disastrous.

Innovative forms of industry that conserve resources and use energy minimally could contribute significantly to a happy, fulfilling and healthy lifestyle for the millions now disadvantaged. Appropriate infrastructure built on the existing societies and economic structure – safe water supplies, fuel-conserving cooking stoves, better health services, cheap solar-powered or spring-wound computers with internet capability, village access roads and bridges, rubber tyres for buffalo wagons, simple value-added industries – these are the kind of things that are really needed. Such objectives are consistent with the tradition of co-operation, the almost universal respect for education and the ambition, frugality and will to work typical of much of Asia. The 1997 financial crash destroyed many productive and basically sound enterprises because depreciated local currencies made it impossible for them to meet their loan obligations. Achievement of an innovative and conservational industry may well require a considerable diversity of ownership and direction, and a versatile workforce. Unfortunately the tendencies in many parts of Asia are in the opposite direction. These obstacles to free enterprise are therefore worth considering.

The cartel or monopoly system, during the 1930s characterized by the Japanese *zaibatsu*, is again prominent in several Asian countries. The modern name in Japan is *keiretsu*, but the system is much the same, and is dominated by much the same interests. *Keiretsu* are agglomerates which control whole areas of commerce, from manufacturing through wholesaling to retail shops. Among other things, they provide an effective method of eliminating competing products, especially foreign ones, and tend to discourage innovation. In South Korea the equivalent is the *chaebol*, large conglomerates like Samsung, Hyundai and Daewoo, which generally were fostered by government patronage during the Korean War from the billions of aid dollars poured in by the United States. Almost without exception they are owned or controlled by families from the country's traditional aristocracy.

In India, most of the capital and industry is controlled by a few families; in China the military and the Communist Party have huge business involvements. In Pakistan Bhutto campaigned against the 22 families he said dominated the national economy. Big business, the army and politics have been closely associated in Indonesia, where most large enterprises have been controlled by the generals and their immediate families. In both these countries, as well as in Thailand, Burma and North Korea, the army has come to dominate most lucrative business. Huge fortunes were accumulated by Filipino President Ferdinand Marcos from funds that should have been used for public welfare. This money, deviously transferred to foreign banks, is still being pursued by the present government.

The question that might well be asked is why the Asian peoples concerned tolerate their oppressors. Sometimes, of course, they do not, but where the usurping authority happens to be the armed forces, dissent becomes debatable when you are likely to be shot for it. Much of the blame for this situation must attach to the nations who make and supply arms, not for the purposes of defence, but to equip minorities to murder, oppress and terrorize their own people. Perhaps the most despicable are those who have made the millions of landmines which now litter several Asian countries, regularly killing or maiming thousands of the innocent, in many cases small children, and likely to go on doing so for many decades to come.

Part of the reason for acceptance of tyranny lies in the way children are educated and brought up, taught from their earliest years to be respectful to their elders and to established authority – a tradition of conservatism, a learned reluctance to question or interfere with established institutions. As a Cambodian proverb has it: 'Choose the path your ancestors have trod.' In many parts of Asia at least a minority are better educated and less likely to accept such ideas and constraints. But when this 'middle class' publicly seeks reforms, they encounter a powerful disincentive when they are shot down in the streets, as they have been in Burma, Thailand and Indonesia, by their own army or police.

The growth of industry in Asia has been associated with rapid and large rises in population, and the advent of mega-cities – or perhaps more accurately, mega-regions. Greater Tokyo and Yokohama has 37 million people and Djakarta 26 million, while Seoul, Delhi, Shanghai, Manila and Karachi all have over 20 million. Such large concentrations of humanity are a problem in themselves, but they are the worse because of the nature of these cities. Most have huge overpopulated fringe areas of slums and shanty towns, in which people lead seriously deprived and difficult lives. Disease and shortened life spans are the norm.

They, and their environs, are also heavily polluting. According to a World Bank estimate in 2007, 16 of the world's 20 worst polluted cities are in China. This is due to massive use of coal, which produces more than two-thirds of China's energy. According to an Indian Council of Agricultural Research report in 2010, 'sustainable agricultural development and food security will be one of the key challenges for India this century. ... The quality of the land is deteriorating due to heightened nutrient mining, soil erosion, increasing water scarcity, adverse impacts of climate change and accumulation of toxic elements in soil and water.' Earlier, the independent Tata Energy Research Institute in India described as a 'quiet crisis' soil erosion and depletion now affecting 57 per cent of India's productive land. The report predicted drops in the yields of 11 major food crops in India by as much as a quarter. The researchers said the area of critically eroded land had doubled over 18 years, partly due to deforestation for fuel or to create new farmlands. Intensive farming and the high use of fertilizers were also resulting in rapid depletion of soil nutrients. According to the UN Food and Agriculture Organization, 27 per cent of India's soil is badly degraded, with barely a third unaffected at all. But perhaps the most telling example of the pollutant effects of largely uncontrolled development are the huge forest fires every year in Sumatra and Kalimantan, which spread a pall of smoke over much of south-east Asia, inflicting respiratory illnesses on tens of thousands, and disrupting air and sea transport. These massive fires, which are caused by illegal forest-clearing to produce palm oil, brought the worst pollution of the year to Singapore in 2012.

This all seems a gloomy enough picture. Is the future, then, inevitably one of an increasingly urbanized and impoverished mass of oppressed people in Asia, limited only by the ancient scourges of hunger and disease, visiting increasingly large volumes of pollution on the world?

Not necessarily so. A concerted and effective world effort to end poverty and ignorance is the best and most obvious answer – a fully multilateral diversion of only 10 per cent of world spending on arms to poverty alleviation could achieve this without materially affecting the world balance of power. Beyond the merit of making people happier, wealthier and better educated is another – the well-proved axiom that when people prosper they have fewer children, so this is the most effective and humane way to keep world population down. And then there is the near-certainty that with education they will eventually become more independent-minded and able to govern themselves fairly. The modern revolution in news and information exchange must also help, because it has made it next to impossible for tyrant regimes to persecute their own people without some exposure. One example is the use of the internet to expose the excesses of the Burmese military and to encourage trade boycotts against them, and to react against the heavy censorship of news in Malaysia. Another was the massive world news coverage of the suppression of the democracy movement in China's Tiananmen Square in 1989.

The problem of pollution in the mega-cities of Asia may also provide its own solutions. The people who live in these places are becoming increasingly exasperated, and more aware of the formidable health risks to themselves. With motor traffic at gridlock levels in many Asian cities air pollution must also increase. The incentives exist for the large-scale development of economical and low-polluting fuel-cell, compressed air and hybrid vehicles in Asia, which could be exported and compete effectively in Western markets. It is not without significance that electric mini-taxis are replacing fossil-fuel vehicles and man-powered rickshaws in Dhaka, and that the first two mass-produced petrol-electric hybrids were developed and marketed in Japan.

In order to grow, such promising but often fragile twigs of progress need encouragement and assistance from the Western world. However, foreign aid budgets are dwindling and many Asian countries are crippled by vast mountains of debt, usually incurred by unscrupulous dictators and military regimes. Industry, driven by Western capital and Western ideas, mostly produces what Western consumers want, not what Asia needs. The yawning gap between rich and poor will only be bridged when there is understanding that genuine progress in the Asian nations can come most easily and naturally upwards from the village structure, and that such developments, like the proliferation of solar cookers in India, are the most likely to be sustainable. The simplest solutions, such as higher-bearing fruit trees, efficient fish-farms, safe water supplies made possible by impervious roofing on houses and rainwater tanks, local industries at least initially labour-intensive, simple farm and irrigation machinery, and reliable grain seed, are necessary to encourage a modest overall growth in prosperity. Appropriate and immediately useful small industry would grow naturally from that. There is plenty of evidence that aid funds would be better channelled by Western governments to non-governmental organizations, which are more experienced and have a far better track record in the field than governments.

None of the above is suggested on purely charitable or altruistic grounds. The world economy can expect huge opportunities if and when the average income and security of the billions of Asian people can be steadily improved, if only slowly. Conversely, with the Asian peoples becoming the greater part of world population, sheer lack of markets must increasingly cripple the world economy if a practical and major effort to remedy poverty is not made. Imagination and innovation are needed in this cause. For instance, there is potential for a vast industry in the countries with desert or semi-desert and abundant sunlight to provide the metropolitan powers with hydrogen made from dissociating water or ammonia through the use of solar power, or through the use of catalysts. Research into this technology is well advanced in Israel and elsewhere. Fuel cells run on hydrogen. This example is quoted because it is of a nature that would provide the Asian countries with a permanently renewable, non-polluting source of industrial income. Liquid hydrogen could be carried by existing tanker fleets or pipelines to the metropolitan powers.

World assistance to Asia will need to accommodate a proper understanding and acceptance of Asian traditions. Unpalatable though this conclusion may be, control of whole peoples by authoritarian regimes is likely to continue because, failing some potent new influence, the tradition favours them. If they are progressive, as the Singapore government has been, 'controlled' democracies have their values. However, world indifference to plainly bad regimes – or worse, support for them for muddled political or unscrupulous economic reasons – ought not to continue.

On the other hand, the West, having taken the trouble to understand the Asian traditions, must also accept that it would be naïve, dangerous and inappropriate to promote Asian governments and economies which are clones of Western models. New solutions, based on existing Asian social patterns, minimal pollution, the best possible use of resources and permanently renewable energy, are, then, not only desirable but essential. Given encouragement and support in the right direction, these solutions could well be devised by the Asian peoples themselves, with the potential to offer new models to the world. This presents a remarkable opportunity, a third-millennium challenge well worth meeting.

Hence the West should recognize the rejection in Asia of the Western political style in favour of new forms consciously based on past traditions. This is evident in the growth of Hindu nationalism in India, the recent adaptations of Chinese Communism, the resurgence of Shinto in Japanese political rhetoric, the persistence of autocratic governments in south-east Asia, the inability of 'progressive' politicians like Aung San Suu Kyi, Imran Khan, Anwar Ibrahim and Sam Rainsy to prevail in their countries, and a turning towards traditional Islam in Pakistan, Bangladesh and Afghanistan.

Finally, in many cases the tide is turning towards better outcomes. UN figures in 2012 revealed that 6.6 million children in the world died before they reached the age of 5, but that this figure is barely half the number in

1990. And while almost 800 women still die in childbirth every day, these deaths are far fewer than in the past, due to much better public health measures in China, Malaysia, Sri Lanka and Thailand, and a huge effort towards better maternal and child health by five major international agencies.

So will this be the Asian century? I doubt anyone could answer that question with confidence – the outcome must depend on many things impossible to predict. A return by the Asian nations to cultural and economic equality with the rest of humanity seems more likely – hopefully, in a world that can offer all its citizens lives that are fairer, more peaceful and more prosperous than they are today.

Further Reading

The following books provide a more detailed account of the countries dealt with, together with some others, outside the mainstream, which might offer the reader useful and unusual insights.

General

H. Smith, *The World's Religions* (2009)

China

E. Behr, *The Last Emperor* (1987)
I. Chang, *The Rape of Nanking* (1998)
J. Fenby, *Penguin History of Modern China* (2009)
C. P. Fitzgerald, *China: A Short Cultural History* (1980)
W. Wo-lap Lam, *Chinese Politics in the Hu Jintao Era* (2006)
C. Martin, *The Boxer Rebellion* (1968)
P. Nolan, *China at the Crossroads* (2003)
P. P. Pan, *Out of Mao's Shadow* (2008)
C. Patten, *East and West* (1998)
R. Ritter, *Modern China* (2008)
J. A. G. Roberts, *A History Of China* (2011)
J. D. Spence, *The Search for Modern China* (2000)
A. Waley, *The Opium War Through Chinese Eyes* (1958)
Yang Jisheng, *Tombstone: The Great Chinese Famine* (2008)

Taiwan

R. C. Bush, *Untying the Knot* (2005)
R. Denny, *Taiwan: A Political History* (2003)
M. Harrison, *Legitimacy, Meaning and Knowledge in the Making of Taiwanese Identity* (2006)
J. F. Keating, *Taiwan: The Struggles of a Democracy* (2006)

J. Mann, *The China Fantasy* (2007)
J. Manthorpe, *Forbidden Nation* (2005)

Tibet

P. French, *Tibet, Tibet* (2003)
C. M. G. Goldstein, *A History of Modern Tibet* (1999)
P. Levy, *Tibet* (1996)
D. Snellgrove and H. Richardson, *A Cultural History of Tibet* (1995)

Japan

P. Ayer, *The Lady and The Monk* (1992)
B. M. Bodart-Bailey, *The Dog Shogun* (2006)
J. W. Dower, *Embracing Defeat: Japan in the Wake of World War 11* (2000)
A. Gordon, *A Modern History of Japan* (2003)
M. Hane and L. G. Perez, *Modern Japan* (2009)
Mikiso Hane, *Peasants, Rebels and Outcastes* (1982)
J. Hersey, *Hiroshima* (1946 and 1989)
M. B. Jansen, *The Making of Modern Japan* (2002)
J. L. McClain, *Japan: A Modern History* (2002)
Murasaki Shibiku, *The Diary of Lady Murasaki* (1996)
R. Storry, *A History of Modern Japan* (1960)
D. T. Suzuki, *An Introduction to Zen Buddhism* (1949)

Korea

M. Breen, *Kim Jong-Il* (2004)
H. Conroy, *The Japanese Seizure of Korea* (1960)
B. Cumings, *Korea's Place in the Sun* (1997)
Djun Kil Kim, *The History of Korea* (2005)
M. J. Seth, *A Concise History of Korea* (2006)
S. Winchester, *Korea* (2005)

South Asia

S. Bose and A. Jalal, *Modern South Asia* (2003)
B. H. Farmer, *An Introduction to South Asia* (1993)
D. Ludden, *India and South Asia* (2002)
M. Yunus and A. Parmar, *South Asia* (2003)

India

S. Bose, *Kashmir* (2005)
S. Bose, *Transforming India* (2013)
B. Chandra, *A History of Modern India* (2009)
D. Faisal, *The Impossible Indian: Gandhi and the Temptation of Violence* (2012)
L. James, *Raj: The Making and Unmaking of British India* (1997)
J. Keay, *India* (2000)
S. Khilnani, *The Idea of India* (1998)
B. D. and T. Metcalf, *A Concise History of Modern India* (2006)
P. Robb, *A History of India* (2011)
S. Tharoor, *India* (2006)

Bangladesh

S. Bose, *Dead Reckoning* (2011)
D. Lewis, *Bangladesh* (2011)
S. Mahmud Ali, *Understanding Bangladesh* (2010)
S. Raghavan, *A Global History of the Creation of Bangladesh* (2013)
R. Sisson and L. E. Rose, *War and Secession* (1992)
W. van Schendel, *A History of Bangladesh* (2009)

Pakistan

O. Bennett Jones, *Pakistan: Eye of the Storm* (2012)
I. Khan, *Pakistan* (2011)
A. Lieven, *Pakistan: A Hard Country* (2012)
I. Talbot, *A Modern History of Pakistan* (2009)
J. Yusufali, *Pakistan* (1990)

Afghanistan

G. Arney, *Afghanistan* (1989)
W. Dalrymple, *The Return of a King* (2013)
M. Ewans, *Afghanistan* (2003)
A. Rasanayagam, *Afghanistan: A Modern History* (2005)
A. Rashid, *Taliban* (2010)

Sri Lanka

F. A. Boyle, *The Tamil Genocide by Sri Lanka* (2009)
K. M. de Silva, *A History of Sri Lanka* (1981)

H. Perera, *Buddhism in Sri Lanka* (2013)
J. Spencer, *Sri Lanka: History and the Roots of Conflict* (2002)
G. Weiss, *The Cage* (2012)
N. Wickramasinghe, *Sri Lanka in the Modern Age* (2005)

Nepal and Bhutan

G. Corvinas, *Prehistoric Cultures in Nepal* (2007)
E. Hillary, *View From the Summit* (1999)
M. Lawoti, *Towards a Democratic Nepal* (2005)
S. von Einsiedel, *Nepal in Transition* (2012)
J. Whelpton, *History of Nepal* (2005)

M. Aris, *Bhutan: The Early History* (1979)
L. Leaming, *Married to Bhutan* (2011)
K. Phuntsho, *The History of Bhutan* (2013)
M. Richard, *Bhutan* (2008)

Southeast Asia

P. Church, *A Short History of Southeast Asia* (2005)
I. C. Glover, *Southeast Asia from Prehistory to History* (2004)
D. G. E. Hall, *History of Southeast Asia* (1981)
M. Osborne, *Southeast Asia* (2013)
N. G. Owen, *The Emergence of Modern Southeast Asia* (2005)
D. R. SarDesai, *Southeast Asia, Past and Present* (2010)

Indonesia

T. Abdullah, *Indonesia: Towards Democracy* (2009)
A. Beatty, *A Shadow Falls: in the Heart of Java* (2009)
C. Brown, *A Short History of Indonesia* (2003)
R. B. Cribb, *Modern Indonesia* (1995)
E. Douwes Dekker, *Max Havelaar* (1868)
R. E. Elson, *The Idea of Indonesia: A History* (2008)
J. Martinkus, *A Dirty Little War* (2001)
R. L. Parry, *In the Time of Madness: Indonesia on the Edge of Chaos* (2006)
J. Ramos-Horta, *Funu: The Unfinished Saga of East Timor* (1987)
M. C. Ricklefs, *A History of Modern Indonesia* (2008)
A. Vickers, *A History of Modern Indonesia* (2005)
B. H. M. Vlekke, *Nusantara* (1959)

Philippines

J. S. Arcilla, *An Introduction to Philippine History* (1998)
J. Fenton, *The Snap Revolution* (1986)
L. H. Francis, *A History of the Philippines* (2010)
M. C. Halili, *Philippine History* (2004)
S. K. Yan, *A History of the Philippines* (2009)

Burma

J. F. Cady, *A History of Modern Burma* (1960)
M. W. Charney, *A History of Modern Burma* (2009)
Thant Myint-u, *Where China Meets India* (2011)
Aung San Su-kyi, *Freedom from Fear* (1995)

Thailand

C. Baker, *A History of Thailand* (2009)
C. Baker and P. Phongpaichit, *A History of Thailand* (2009)
R. Syamananda, *A History of Thailand* (1971)
D. K. Wyatt, *Thailand: A Short History* (2003)

Vietnam, Cambodia and Laos

M. A. Ashwill, *Vietnam Today* (2005)
O. Chapuis, *A History of Vietnam* (1995)
N. DeMarco, *Vietnam, 1939–45* (2004)
S. Karnow, *Vietnam* (1991)
Ngo Van, *In the Crossfire* (2000)
K. W. Taylor, *The Birth of Vietnam* (1983)
N. Turse, *Kill Anything that Moves: The Real American War in Vietnam* (2013)

D. P. Chandler, *A History of Cambodia* (2008)
J. Corfield, *The History of Cambodia* (2009)
M. Osborne, *Sihanouk* (1994)

G. Evans, *A Short History of Laos* (2002)
O. Meeker, *The Little World of Laos* (1995)
M. Stuart-Fox, *A History of Laos* (1997)

Malaysia and Singapore

B. W. and I. Y. Andaya, *A History of Malaysia* (2001)
Kwa Chong Guan, D. Heng and Tan Tai Tong, *Singapore* (2009)

Lee Kuan Yew, *The Singapore Story* (1998)

G. Liu, *Singapore: A Pictorial History* (2001)

V. Matheson Hooker, *A Short History of Malaysia* (2012)

M. Ravinder Frost and Yu-mei Balasingamchow, *Singapore: A Biography* (2009)

C. M. Turnbull, *A History of Modern Singapore, 1819–2005* (2009)

Index